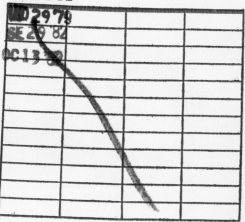

The *real* Teachers

Compiled and edited by
PHILIP STERLING

The _real_ Teachers

Vintage Books
A Division of Random House
New York

FIRST VINTAGE BOOKS EDITION, September 1973

Grateful acknowledgment is made to the following, for permission to reprint material:

Atlantic-Little, Brown: From Teacher in America by Jacques Barzun.

Doubleday & Co., Inc.: From The Sot-Weed Factor by John Barth. Copyright © 1960 by John Barth.

E. P. Dutton & Co., Inc., From Echo in My Soul by Septima Clark with LeGette Blythe. Copyright © 1962 by Septima Poinsetta Clark.

Freedomway Magazine: Poem from Freedomways, Vol. 11, No. 3, 1971.

Humanities Press Inc.: From The New York City Teachers Union 1916–1964 by Celia Lewis Zitron.

Statesman and Nation Publishing Co.: Extract from "Newstyle Nursery Rhymes" by Roger Woddis in New Statesman, October 23, 1970.

The New York Review of Books: From The Open Classroom by Herbert Kohl. Copyright © 1969 by Herbert Kohl.

Prentice-Hall, Inc.: From Up the Down Staircase by Bel Kaufman. Copyright © 1964 by Bel Kaufman.

Library of Congress Cataloging in Publication Data

Sterling, Philip.
    The real teachers.
    Interviews.
    1. Education—United States—1965–   . 2. Education, Urban—United States. 3. Teachers—United States. I. Title.
[LA271.S7 1973]   371.1'00973   73–5668
ISBN 0–394–71967–0

Manufactured in the United States of America

For Dorothy, who is relevant

*A good teacher will teach well
regardless of the pedagogical theory he suffers from.*
—*John Barth*

ACKNOWLEDGMENTS

I wanted to find and convey some *sense* of the actuality of being a socially conscious inner-city schoolteacher in a society that generates "inner-cities" and condemns people to live in them. Along the way, I needed information, insights and practical advice from many people. The understanding and painstaking quality of their responses often made the difference between finding and floundering. None of them, however, can be considered accountable for what I've written. My hearty thanks to the following—

In New York: David Emery, industrial psychologist; James Magnusson, field researcher, Center for Urban Education; Linley Stafford, manager, Editorial Information Center, NEA; Dr. Max Wolff, professor of education and sociology at Long Island University; Loretta Barrett and Marie Dutton Brown (Philadelphia), Nathan Garner (Detroit) and Richard Stiller (the Bronx), former classroom teachers in the cities indicated; Ronald Evans (principal), Maude Nelson (administrative assistant) and Samuel F. Williams (assistant principal) at the Arthur A. Schomburg Intermediate School; Babette Edwards, member of the local governing board of the Schomburg I.S.201 complex; Lloyd Hunter, public information officer, and Walter Lynch, community liaison director, of the Ocean Hill–Brownsville Demonstration District.

In Boston: Alice Ansara, remedial reading specialist; Melvin H. King, executive director, and Toye Brown Lewis, education director, of the New Urban League of Greater Boston; Jeanne McGuire, at the Education Development Center, Cambridge.

In Philadelphia: Oliver Lancaster, assistant director of the Office of Integration and Inter-Group Education of the Board of Education; Samuel Staff, principal of Stoddart-Fleisher J.H.S.; Robert A. Eaverly, principal of Sayre J.H.S.

In Washington: Philip King, George W. Jones and Rosena J. Willis at the National Education Association; Kenneth Haskins, principal of the Morgan Community School; Jeanne Walton, field representative, Washington, D.C. Teachers Union, Local 6, American Federation of Teachers.

In Cleveland: Don Freeman, director of the League Park Center; Glenn Hawkins, of the Education Task Force, Cleveland Council of Churches; Dr. Samuel Gorovitz, dean of Adelbert College, Case Western Reserve University; Roland Johnson, Foundation Associate in the Cleveland Foundation.

In Detroit: John Anderson, principal of Foch J.H.S.

I am also indebted to Charles F. Harris, executive director of Howard University Press, for his supportive interest and guidance during the early stages of this project.

And thanks to Joan Emery and Margaret Anderson for their proficiency in transforming tape-recorded speech into verbatim typescripts.

CONTENTS

CONTENTS

INTRODUCTION

How can we judge the worth of a society . . .
predict how well a nation will survive and
prosper? . . . we propose yet another criterion:
the concern of one generation for the next.
If the children and youth of a nation are
afforded opportunity to develop their capacities
to the fullest, if they are given the knowledge
to understand the world and the wisdom to change
it, the future is bright. A society which neglects
its children, however well it may function in other
respects, risks eventual disorganization and demise.
                                    —*Urie Bronfenbrenner*

I don't remember much of Jesse Beer's Physics but I remember Jesse Beer. He was the only authentic teacher I ever knew during my years in public school. His commitment and his deep respect for students turned the arcana of eleventh-grade science into a believable and interesting human activity. Though he never lectured, he somehow managed to convey to us the *feeling* that man's capability for discovering and using rational explanations of natural phenomena had compelling moral implications for the individual and for society. That was important.

I was not at all interested in Boyle's law of gases but I was intensely preoccupied with the nature of our society, which I tried to understand in terms of the relationships between its constituent categories: rich and poor, rulers and ruled, employers and workers, privileged and oppressed. As the son of a seasonally unemployed immigrant house painter, the bias from which I examined these relationships was predictable and wholesome. And I didn't keep my conclusions entirely to myself. I suggested, as explicitly as I dared, in class and out, that the status quo had to go.

More than Jesse Beer's classroom virtuosity I value the fact that he dignified my concern by understanding it and by engaging me in discussions about it. His message was, "If you want to fight the system, okay, but be prudent in choosing issues and occasions. And keep your flanks covered because the system strikes back. Your grades are barely passing. That can do you in. Cool it for now and do lots of homework." Then he offered a swatch of his own personal history to authenticate his concern for me. He was teaching school, he told me, because his opposition to American participation in World War I had cost him his job as an industrial chemist at Chase Brass and Copper.

Later I understood why so few of my teachers had come anywhere near Jesse Beer's mark and why so many had treated me with perfunctory sympathy, indifference or hostility.

Schools do not and never did make the society. Society makes the schools. It designs, operates and vests power in them for the only purpose conceivable to it: to maintain and perpetuate itself with as little change as possible. The motivation is as elemental and compelling as that of a bear catching fish. Perpetuation of the system, whether the bear's or society's, comes first. Too bad for the fish. Too bad for the kids who have no stake in keeping everything the way it is but whose lives may well depend on drastic, all-pervading change.

Since society also made the schools in which teachers were taught, teachers themselves were required on pain of dismissal to be collaborators with or passive accomplices of the system. Those who refused the role of accomplice, who presumed to function with independent minds and/or methods were suppressed, removed or encapsulated in their classrooms by self-confident principals who tolerated them only because they wished to appear innovative or liberal. Scattered and without representation, they didn't amount to much as a force capable of interdicting the closed relationship between school and society.

Nevertheless, the Jesse Beer types have persisted from his own time in the 1920s to the present. They have led a precarious but tenacious life in sequestered corners of the school system. Sometimes furtively, sometimes defiantly, they have practiced their profession at higher levels of social consciousness and personal concern for their students than have the great majority of their colleagues. There is a difference, however, between Jesse Beer and his latter-day successors which arises from the enormous difference between the social environment then and now.

In the carefully limited social warfare of the 1920s the schools were treated as a demilitarized zone. Then during the 1930s and 1940s, reality—the depression, militant trade unionism, a second world war, the atomic bomb, the Cold War—trampled down the barbed wire. The teaching profession slipped through these openings in uncertain pursuit of a living wage and improved working conditions. By the late 1950s the profession's collective-bargaining perimeter on economic and intraprofessional issues was securely established, to the accompaniment of rhetoric proclaiming a nobler objective as well—freedom to teach humanely and creatively. To most teachers this objective merely meant greater autonomy in classroom management and in lesson planning. To the atypical few, the "irregulars," it meant much more: freedom to help their students learn how to examine and understand social reality; freedom to develop in them self-confidence and the desire to change whatever needs changing. They were bent not only on imparting skills but on developing their students' intellectual abilities and aspirations.

Ironically it is not the trade union successes, to which they contributed substantially as activists, organizers and spokesmen, but the general escalation of social warfare that has given these "irregulars" new importance. The fiction of the school "as neutral zone" could not survive the stones thrown at black kids walking to desegregated schools during the years of "deliberate speed" counseled by the Supreme Court. But unequal education, for which "integrated" schools were to be the death blow, survived very handily, both in its own right and as a symbol of the generalized inequality imposed on racial minorities. Yet—nothing is ever entirely wasted. The long, still-active desegregation effort demonstrated once and for all that inequality of education is not simply a form of regional backwardness but a national characteristic.

In the 1960s another reality intruded: the transformation of the largely decorous struggle for the advancement of colored people into a militant black freedom movement toward racial and cultural self-determination. Inevitably, urban school systems and their very buildings and corridors became central battlegrounds for settlement of immediate social, political and cultural issues. The conflict has reached levels of intermittent ferocity in the big cities, where millions of Blacks and Puerto Ricans cultivate the hope of something more than nominal equality under law.

It follows that only those who can respond with their own humanity to the humanity of black, Puerto Rican, Chicano or Indian kids can be effective teachers in big-city schools. To teach responsibly, they must recognize the function and effect of racial oppression—what it's for and what it does to whom. They must want to disconnect and destroy institutional racism as a regulating mechanism— in hopes of making the whole social machine run better or at the risk of seeing it shut down for redesign or replacement. That is, they must understand the nature of our society and reveal it more realistically, and in many respects differently, than the terms of their employment require.

Though they are a small, not easily measurable minority, there are many more such teachers today than there possibly could have been in Jesse Beer's day. Their number and quality have increased in direct ratio to the disenchantment among the best-educated youth with the values to which our society pretends.

Their presence in the classroom arrested popular attention during the 1960s by such strong signals as James Herndon's *The Way It Spozed to Be*, Herbert Kohl's *Thirty-Six Children* and Jonathan's Kozol's *Death at an Early Age*. These are stirring and truthful statements of social-and-school-system reality. Their joint and several indictments of what's been happening remain cause for public anxiety. But is there in such single-handed struggles to liberate children from the oppressions of ghetto schooling any cause for hope? If so, how much and what kind? How many mute, inglorious counterparts of the Kohls and Kozols can there be among the nation's 2.1 million elementary and high school teachers? At best, can they be more than the isolated exceptions that prove the rule, in the usual way, by displaying their statistical minitude against the magnitude of the norm?

The 1968 New York teachers' strike to prevent control of school districts by black communities confirmed that the rule still prevailed. But there were teachers who, rejecting the strike, challenged the rule in greater numbers and to greater effect than it had ever been challenged before. Mostly white, these "irregulars" refused to be alienated from their black and Puerto Rican students. They withstood the pressure of their tradition-bound colleagues and defied their white trade union leadership. These were also the teachers who strive, as a matter of professional habit, to help children develop their highest capacities, to achieve knowledgeable understanding of the world and to reach for the wisdom with which to change it.

In the inner cities, "the peculiar institution" of our time, these "irregulars" now constitute a distinct pedagogic variety significant far beyond the narrow limit of their numbers. Both sides, the oppressed and the privileged, need them in the struggle to decide how and for whose benefit education shall be conducted. The children and the parents/communities welcome them as protagonists in the quest for a greater good than the American past has afforded to racial minorities. The school systems accept them (at arm's length) as a hedge against the greater evil portended by trash baskets burning in the boys' johns. Vulnerable but quite possibly extirpation-proof, they're likely to be around awhile.

"I was determined to know beans," said Henry Thoreau. In somewhat the same mood, I was determined to know these teachers—not through the authority or the opinion of others but by the authenticity of my own experience. I could not quite say, as Thoreau did of his two and a half acres, that "This was one field not in Mr. Colman's report." Every square foot of every field in our time has its own Mr. Colman and is duly reported on. But like Thoreau: "I considered that I enhanced the value of the land by squatting on it." I didn't want to sample, tabulate or analyze these teachers, nor to devise any formal model of their reality. I just wanted to ask as many questions of as many as I could meet, and listen to them for as long as they would let me. Accordingly, the mood became the method. I went to places where I thought it made sense to go; I interviewed teachers who indicated that my interest made sense to them. Whenever possible, I watched them at work in their classrooms. Or I talked to them. Either way, I ran my tape recorder and watched them while they talked about the inner-city schoolteaching experience.

They were easier to find than I had expected. I asked around among the few teachers in my own orbit in megalopolitan New York. One teacher, one school, one city, led to another. The list of individuals worth checking out snowballed into hundreds. I stopped asking. In Boston,

New York, Philadelphia, Washington, Cleveland and Detroit, I visited twenty-one schools, listened to a hundred classroom teachers, to several dozen school administrators, black-community spokesmen, a few education specialists and uncounted students.

Most of all, I wanted to meet white teachers. Why? Because there are still so many of them in entirely or partly black classrooms. I wanted to know if indeed there were white teachers who understand the passion for Big Change in the lives of black and other racial minorities and who bring this understanding to bear in the daily exercise of their profession. Even in the District of Columbia, where 80 percent of the classroom teachers are black, such white teachers have a contribution to make. In New York City, where 58 percent of the students but only 9.5 percent of the teachers are black or Puerto Rican, whites who can teach with full respect for the humanity of minority kids and without racial or class antagonism toward the parents/ communities are certainly to be valued. (In the other four cities I visited, the percentages of black classroom teachers were: Boston, 5.1; Philadelphia, 32.2; Cleveland, 38.2; Detroit, 41.4.)

I sought out black teachers, too, though nowhere near as many, because as individuals they can be, and en masse they *are*, part of the solution rather than part of the problem.

What did I ask these teachers, white and black? Anything that came into my head: Who were they? Where did they come from? What were the choices for greater good or lesser evil that confronted them in their classrooms, in the communities they served, in the school systems to which they must give some measure of subservience? Under what difficulties and to what envisioned ends did they enact "the concern of one generation for the next"? In short, how did they hack it, and why did they bother?

Their answers were honest. From the flow of their

conversation a variety of self-portraits emerged, impassioned, sternly objective, unconsciously dramatic, depending on the personalities and experiences of the individuals. All were discerning, informative, unpretentious. The thirty interviews I have managed to crowd into this collection comprise less than a third of those I recorded. Nevertheless, these thirty are characteristic of the others. Most of these teachers are young, in their twenties or early thirties. All are fresh in mind and spirit, that is, in their views of the world and in their relationships with their students. None of them saw himself as a revolutionary, social missionary or educational genius. Nor did I. I saw each just as a certain kind of teacher, the kind Jesse Beer was, only much more so.

Some are no longer in the schools they were in when I talked to them. Two, indeed, were fired by the Boston School Committee before I met them. Two others have been promoted to assistant principalships in predominantly black schools. One has become director of curriculum planning for a public school system in the Middle West. All except two, one recently retired, the other on sick leave, are still teaching or directing the work of other teachers.

The vacuum left by each of these departures is a matter of considerable importance to the school and the kids. Such classroom teachers are in short supply and are wished for less eagerly by school administrations than by minority parents/communities and their children. The greater question, therefore, is whether this kind of teacher will flourish or languish. That depends on how the battle goes on other fronts of our society, on recognizing how close our neglect of minority children has already brought us to "eventual disorganization and demise."

P.S.

1

A BROKEN WINDOW

Sing a song of slum schools,
Dirt and broken glass;
Four and forty children
Packed in a class.

When the school was opened
Victoria wore the crown,
And in a hundred years or so
They're going to pull it down.
                    —Roger Woddis

SANDRA FENTON
Boston

Sandra Fenton is in her early twenties, short, blond, quietly energetic. Her education at the University of California included two terms of graduate work. She came East in March 1967, looking for a job.

All I had to do to become a substitute teacher was to get an X-ray, fill out a very short card, take an oath and mark down the courses I had taken. I taught all over Boston for two weeks and I was shocked by the buildings and the regimentation.

At Christopher Gibson I was asked to take over a second-grade classroom for the rest of the year; age range between seven and ten. I had about twenty black kids, two white kids and two children who were under psychiatric care. The class had already had three teachers that year; each one of them quit.

I had to contend with some really bad physical problems. There was a broken window, for example, right above my desk by the radiator. This was in March. We had a big snowstorm in April and I repeatedly approached the janitor and the principal to tell them the snow was coming in the room. Once the principal came in and made the children move to the other side of the room. So our children could be wet and warm by the radiator or they could be cold-dry on the other side.

Did the window ever get fixed?

Oh. At the beginning of the new school year, in the fall of '67. Kozol's book* came out and everything got fixed

---

* *Death at an Early Age: The Destruction of the Hearts and Minds of Negro Children in the Boston Public Schools,* by Jonathan

up, the windows and everything, including mine—the day before the TV cameramen came out to film the school.

Well, anyway, at the beginning I had limited teaching experience. When I took over the classroom there were no work books, no crayons, no pencils. There were some textbooks, but not enough. I tried to get some help. I knew I could be doing more if I had—something. I tried to find out what the children had been doing for three-quarters of the year but—nobody even knew. The principal came into my room just once, said what a marvelous job I was doing, then left.

I didn't have much contact with the other teachers. They were all tied up in their own classrooms. They didn't come out the door very often; two forty and a lot of teachers were gone. I can think of three or four of us who were there until four o'clock. What for? Getting the room in order so the children would come into an orderly room the next day to start over again. Make it more livable, not so sterile. Doing worksheets. Looking up things. Reading. Trying to develop alternatives, essentially.

Some of the children would stay, too—mostly, if you asked them to. Children were not supposed to be in classrooms after two forty unless they were under the supervision of a teacher. Last year I was told no children could remain after two forty regardless . . . I couldn't understand the thinking behind that, except a fear of children . . . fear of a riot, chaos, that the children would get out of hand. The big thing was control. That's what they were concerned with continually. Even if you felt the reason the children were rebelling had something to do with the

Kozol, was published in October 1967 by Houghton Mifflin and was serialized in the *Boston Globe* that same month. In substance it was an account of the author's experiences and observations as a teacher at the Christopher Gibson School during its 1964–65 year. In effect it is a damning exposé of the inhumanities of ghetto schooling in Boston and, by extension, in other cities with sizable black, Puerto Rican and Chicano communities.

curriculum, or with what you were doing or not doing, the fear of not being in control would seep in, become a part of you subtly. I felt it myself. For example, if a child got out of his seat there was just a little fear—what's going to happen?

There were about five hundred children in the school, grades K through six. We had the two fourth grades operating in the auditorium. Absolutely berserk. When I wanted to work with a small group from my class, I took them to a hallway. I taught in the hallway for most of that year and I can tell you some things . . .

There was one child, about ten, who appeared to be very disturbed. Not typical of the children at the school. He would come tearing through—he was never in his classroom—and we became friendly. I let him stay with me. One day, while running through the school as usual, he started walking on a railing that fences off a stairwell. If he fell . . . Oh, unbelievable . . . right down to the other floor! . . . It was a frightening experience. He wouldn't come down from the railing, so I went to the principal. It took them about ten minutes to come and I'd finally gotten him down by the time somebody responded from the office. I talked to him. Told him to come into the room. We had some nice things we were doing. The kids needed him to help them with something . . . he was wanted. You see, he didn't want to be in his regular classroom. He had a teacher who—I never saw her smile; old-fashioned but not that old, rigid and traditional. She was really hung up on the control thing. And if this kid was out of the room, great for her! I can understand that there are children who are difficult to work with, but there are things you can do. If a kid is really giving you a bad time you don't just get rid of him. There were a lot of teachers like that. Most of them.

This child didn't talk, wouldn't, to anybody. He liked making things the other children could use. Maybe one of those little picture books that have something that starts with the letter T and the T-sound underneath it. And if I said, "The kids are going to use this tomorrow. Why don't you come in and see," he'd watch them using it. Then it wasn't just a phony thing: "Here, honey, do this." It was something *real*, something that would be *used*. He just needed to be needed.

Reviewing her novitiate, Sandra Fenton felt she and her class had experienced "a struggling three months but I think we grew together." At the end of the school year she was asked to return. She did, but "thought it over for a long time . . ." She became one of a four-teacher unit comprising two other young white teachers and an experienced black teacher. Together they were responsible for three first-grade classrooms.

The whole year was a very exciting experience for me. It was very positive. The four of us had a pretty good working relationship. We and the children got to know each other outside of the roles we were sort of assigned. We went on trips together, to the beaches sometimes, to Harvard's Peabody Museum. Mary* has a summer cottage in Duxbury and we'd all take a bunch of kids and go down there. Sometimes we'd go to Franklin Park and play. It's in the middle of Roxbury. It's marvelous. There's a children's zoo there. They saw us in work clothes; we were on the ground, roasting hot dogs, and our clothes got dirty just like everybody else's, and we were human beings. That's what I think made the difference in our relationships. You see?

Sandra Fenton's team decided to have its own science program for their three first-grade classes. She was to be responsible for the program.

Why the administration hired an art teacher to be a science teacher only God knows. The study of gravity—

* Mary Ellen Smith. See p. 17.

the kids drew a picture of Isaac Newton with the apple! But, you know, I liked her personally. Since I was going to supplement, I had to do something, so I was just rummaging around and I found these supplies . . . a kit for each classroom throughout the whole school, with all kinds of things you can do experiments with, down at the bottom of the basement, all locked up in a room. And those kits went up all the way to the sixth grade. It must have cost a fortune and no one knew how long they had been there. Thermometers, little fossils, magnets. I hauled out one of those kits. Fantastic!

Afternoons the first-grade team would get together and talk: This kid, he's not reading. How's the science program going to work? How are we going to integrate this with other subjects? Where can I take the kids when I want to work with a small group outside the classroom? . . .

Then, some of us went home with the kids. Why? Maybe somebody forgot to wear a sweater or somebody's cousin didn't pick him up and he'd be crying. Or maybe the kid stayed after, and we were going home, so we'd give the kid a lift. I dunno, it was a big deal for the kids to have the teacher come to their home for a friendly visit. It meant something . . . and we had to take every opportunity to relate to the child and parent as human beings.

We'd drop them off. Some of the mothers would be in the yard and we'd chat. That's where I think our success was. I've seen *this* happen any number of times: a child would not do a thing at school, wouldn't read, wouldn't perform in any way, but he'd be *reading* for his mother. We'd start talking about it and I'd find that the child would be operating completely differently at home from the way he was operating in school. And it made me wonder: Why is this happening? There was this gap, again, between the schools as one kind of environment and the homes as another kind. The child's lack of desire to read in school was important, but more important it was a symbol of the gap between the home and the school. To me, the thing to do was somehow to bridge the gap.

I gather you tried. How did you go about it?

The school had a lot of hostility directed toward it. It had given out a lot of hostility. It was simply a failure for many people. A lot of parents had lost confidence in the school.

That second year I was there, four or five of us, all young teachers, none of us on tenure, felt we didn't like the role we were playing, and so we began meeting with the parents. The way it started was, some of the parents were voicing their concerns to us but not to each other. We said, "Mr. X is also concerned and so is Mrs. Y. Why don't you get together to talk about it?" They did, and we were invited to meet with them. As teachers we voiced *our* concern about things we had attempted to do but had been unable to. We had been told by administrators and other teachers: "Oh, yes, it's a nice idea" and nothing would happen. Or, "Well, we're trying our best but we just can't do anything" about the fact that the corridors are filthy, or that there've been ten teachers in a classroom, a substitute every single day, successively. And the fact that there's a teacher, on tenure, and her children are screaming and yelling all day long. And why are the reading scores the lowest in the entire district? These are the things we were concerned about.

The parents said, "Well, *we* should be saying these things." They began coming to the school in formal groups* around March [1968]. And the principal would say Yes-I'm-going-to-see-what-I-can-do, and nothing much would happen.

There'd been fires at our school throughout the year, and they were not accidents. A couple of classrooms were

* As delegations from Concerned Parents of the Gibson School.

8

shut down. In May there was a big fire and it totaled the school. Unusable. They put all five hundred* children in one old auditorium in the nearby high school, Jeremiah E. Burke. The entire school shared four toilet facilities until two of them broke down. The whole schedule rotated around bathroom times: first grade at nine o'clock; second grade at nine twenty, and so forth. At noon the second visit to the bathroom began for the school. Visits in between were officially forbidden.

The parents were extremely upset, and a lot of us were really losing ground with our kids. The kids were worried. They weren't secure any more. Little kids. Under the circumstances, the kids were great . . . We had one little disturbed boy that I held by the hand all the time.

It's a helluva way to have to run a class.

Oh, unbel*iev*able! So, we were meeting with the parents all this time, outside the school, in their community. The parents, maybe twenty or so, came down to the [Jeremiah Burke] auditorium one day and said, "Look, our children aren't going in until we can find adequate space for them." They didn't go in until eleven o'clock, after everybody negotiated. The parents said to the administrators, "We want you to call Mayor White† and get busses or whatever is necessary to give our children adequate facilities." There were available rooms at nearby high schools. They did get buses after the pressure was put on, the next day. The children were bused outside to acceptable empty rooms but inadequate educational facilities and parents rode with the children as bus aides, but when school came to an end that year the first grades were still in this audi-

* The official enrollment figure was 480.
† Kevin White, elected mayor of Boston in 1967 and 1971, for four-year terms. Both times, he defeated Louise Day Hicks, unabashedly racist member, and chairwoman for three of her six years (1962–67) on the Boston School Committee. She was elected to the U.S. House of Representatives in 1970.

torium, on the stage. They couldn't find adequate facilities for us.

In June we discovered we were getting a new principal. Also, only eight teachers out of thirty were returning in the fall. We approached the district superintendent and we said, "Look, there's only eight of us but we've had some experience now with the kids, and some successes. We know the building is in absolute chaos. (All the supplies were dropped in a huge mountain in the middle of the hallway after the fire.) Let's get the building in shape before the new teachers come in and let's have a chance to talk to them. I want to tell them about Susie, Johnny, Michael, Harry . . . Let's get some continuity here. Let's give these new teachers a running chance. The odds are tremendous in a lot of ways and if they lose it the first day it really is all over."

Newly married, Sandra and her husband spent part of the summer in California. Meanwhile, Concerned Parents requested a meeting to discuss the school's problems with the new principal. Her reply: she didn't want to start this job assuming there were any problems. Instead the district superintendent invited ten mothers (no fathers), handpicked, to a daytime meeting of his own. Concerned Parents counter-invited the Gibson School administration to several community meetings in the evening, a much more convenient time for working parents. Neither side accepted the other's invitation. The breach continued to widen all summer.

One week before school opened, Mary Ellen and I went out to the Gibson School. Some painters let us in. The huge pile of supplies was still in the hallway. Some of the rooms had been painted; not Mary's, although it had smoke damage. We discussed this with the district superintendent but—nothing to be done. The painters, though, said, "If you want to, paint it yourself." They gave us some paint. We painted. We tried also to get some of our supplies together but it was just total chaos. We came back the following day and the painters wouldn't let us in. The district superintendent said there was nothing he could do about it.

So, orientation came and people were very up in the air. The principal talked to us for an hour about teacher dress codes. She also told us that to get into the school we would have to have cards initialed by her or the vice-principal because there was going to be trouble. Little mention was made of unfilled teacher positions, lack of supplies and unfinished building repairs.

The first day of school a lot of parents and some community residents came in about nine thirty and, in a symbolic gesture, instituted their own principal, Mr. Scott.* He took a chair right next to her, Mary McLaughlin, the official principal, in the office. He simply sat down and explained how parents felt about the school—exactly what they'd tried to explain all summer. A parent came into every classroom to observe. I had Norma's father in my classroom. No problem. Lunchtime, Mr. Scott called a meeting. He reassured all the teachers, "This doesn't mean you're all going to get fired." Somebody'd asked that. He explained what the protest was about.

Twenty-two teachers. How did they react?

They didn't know what was going on; you couldn't tell too much while you were in the classroom. You could see some flash bulbs going off, from the newspapermen in the hallway. However, one teacher, fired later along with me, circulated a petition supporting the parents' actions; twenty-seven out of thirty teachers, including me, signed it. Superintendent Ohrenberger later referred to the petition

* Benjamin F. Scott, a nuclear chemist and a resident of Roxbury, who was then president of the Community Education Council, a black parent/citizen organization in Roxbury and Dorchester.

during the court proceedings as a reason for firing the six of us. There were plain-clothes men there, just watching everybody and observing you as you came in the door. Everybody left immediately after school the first day.

The second day, we had no idea of what was going to happen. Total strategy was being planned by the men in the community. Women weren't in on it, especially white teachers. Everybody came to school and it was surrounded by police, this time in uniform. It was obvious something was going to happen. All the TV cameras, everybody, poised for something. Confrontation.

About a quarter to nine all the school doors were bolted. Half the faculty was outside lining up the kids, half was inside . . . I later found out that the parents had to decide whether or not to go through the barricade to storm the building, thereby making it into a violent kind of encounter and probably getting heads busted. They decided to round up all the children and lead them away to a nearby community center. The teachers outside, in about two minutes, had to make a decision. They could either go with the kids or they could go to an empty building. Five of the teachers, later fired with me, chose to stick with the kids.

I was inside. About fifteen minutes later, the teachers inside found out what had happened and . . . after much confusion and soul-searching, I left. I went out a back door, through the basement and then over to the community center, Shaw House,* three blocks away, after finding out that this was where the parents had taken the kids. We helped set up classes and tried to make it like a regular school day.

Thomas S. Eisenstadt, who was chairman of the

---

* Named for Robert Gould Shaw, a Union Army colonel who died with many of his black troops in a Civil War assault on Fort Wagner (Charleston, S.C.) and was buried in a common grave with them.

Boston School Committee, was running for sheriff at this time. He was running a law-and-order campaign. This fell right into his lap. So he was screaming publicly, We're going to fire these teachers, blah-blah-blah.

Lawrence D. Shubow, counsel for the New England region of the American Jewish Congress and, subsequently, two Boston Legal Assistance Project lawyers, came to the assistance of the six teachers: Anne De Canio, Constance Egan, Sandra Fenton, Charna Heiko, Mary McDonough, Mary Ellen Smith. On Shubow's advice they reported for duty at the Gibson School the next day. They were met at the door and not permitted to enter.

Not being sure where the kids would be, we went back to teach our children wherever they were, at Gibson or down the block. Our feeling was that a teacher's duty is to be with the children, not with the building. The parents had called for a continued boycott. Had we been allowed into the Gibson School, we would have had to make a decision all over again. We were not in the school. After being turned away, we went back to the Liberation School and taught. The parents got a little money from organizations in the black community to maintain the Liberation School. From time to time we received small loans to help us pay rent and eat.

What would you have done if they hadn't been able to pay you at all?

I don't know what we would have lived on but we would have been there. We would have gone on. I'd been meeting with the parent group for a long time. The administration didn't want teachers talking with parents. You see, there is a sense that if you're working with parents, doing anything outside the school, you feel you have to cover up—you're forced to attend meetings at night, when you should really be having a meeting in your classroom

13

after school. It's ridiculous but you find yourself doing this because of the overriding fear and suspicion felt by the school administration toward the black community. If you do it openly you're "disloyal," and if you do it secretly you're "subversive."

The School Committee voted to dismiss the six "effective in thirty days." It also scheduled a closed "show cause" hearing within that period. Chairman Eisenstadt explained that this maneuver implied no prejudgment of the issue. It would merely enable rapid discharge of the teachers after the hearing, if warranted. At the same time he also predicted that they would be "permanently" discharged. They were. "It was completely unknown," said Shubow, "for teachers to be fired for one day's unauthorized absence. There must have been some special factor in this case."

In the meantime we had gone to the Boston Teachers Union. We felt they should intercede for us. First was the Grievance Committee. And a couple of people on that committee were talking to administration people to see what they should do . . . The Grievance Committee recommended that the union not take our case. And then we had to appear before the Executive Committee, a body of fifteen or twenty people who also voted not to accept our grievance. We were asked questions like, "Have you ever belonged to the Communist Party or to the N.A.A.C.P., or any of those other colored things?" The membership never heard our story. All they had to vote on was whether they would uphold the Executive Committee. The opponents, each side, had three minutes to argue. So Mary Ellen Smith—she was the only union member—had to get up there and in three minutes present our side of the story. She was booed and hissed—the whole bit. We were denied union support, two to one.

Court action to reinstate the teachers followed. One of the points at issue was whether the state education laws, as then written, gave nontenured teachers the right to a hearing before dismissal.

The School Committee tried to prove we had some kind of conspiracy. They had people . . . you know . . . fantastic things. Like a witness who said, "On orientation day I saw three of those six girls together and they must have been planning something." I heard one man say, "I saw Mrs. Fenton go out the first day of school and give coffee to somebody, and I think it must have been a demonstrator. I'm not sure about it."

In Suffolk County Superior Court it took the judge till January 1969 to rule against us. He said, "Those who play with the matches of anarchy are bound to get their fingers burned." He went on and on, you know, about violence and law-and-order. That was probably one of the most devastating things that happened to us. We thought we could lose, on trying to change the state law, but we didn't think we'd get that kind of a reactionary slap in the face.

In the meantime, the Liberation School . . . We had one day, initially, to get it started. We had the opportunity, which we didn't have in the public school, to create our own environment and integrate this environment with the community. The parents were really concerned about that. We could bring in new types of material, whatever we could scrounge anywhere. We had Franklin Park right across the street from us. The teachers and the children explored that environment together. And that was something different from the square hardtop playground behind the school.

We had parents in the classrooms all day long, running the school. There weren't just white pictures of white kids on the walls. The sense of the black experience was all there.

We didn't have desks. We arranged our rooms so that the children would be choosing activities. It was completely flexible. Our classroom could be inside or it could be out in the street, or next door at Aunt Janie's house. And we could bring in resource people and say, "Look, we know what we *don't* want but, dammit, we teachers and parents together have to decide what we do want for the kids. We need some help." People are hard to find. Well, we found them and they helped us tremendously. And we set up an alternative that we felt comfortable with, that we grew with. We could offset our traditional roles. I'm thinking of everything: our general approach, specific activities, the teacher's technique, how human beings learn.

We tried to find out what the children's interests were. We tried to get them to bring things in the classroom. What the child brings in is just as important as whatever I've brought in. We capitalized on that to make a learning situation for the child. If someone brought in pine cones, we *studied* the pine cones. It was a busy kind of classroom. There were some problems with supplies. We got a little bit somehow. The parents did it. There were also people in the community who made sandwiches so every kid had a lunch every day. The year before, at the Gibson, some of us on our own would bring in some crackers for some of the kids there that might have missed breakfast. Since there was no breakfast or lunch program at the Gibson, the community made a big thing of providing for that at the Liberation School. That was their business to take care of.

We had some problems with some of the upper grades. It was hard for the kids to adjust suddenly, after years of rigid and negative educational experiences. These kids did not want to go back to the Gibson School, however—so much hostility and tension there, all the time.

But they had to go back, didn't they?

The Liberation School started the second day of the school year in September 1968. It closed November 5. The parents decided that their issue wasn't to start a private school. Their goal was to change the public school they pay taxes for. The Concerned Parents were all together over here in a private school. That took many of those people who were really interested and concerned out of the public school. So they decided to go back.

What did you think of the decision?

I have mixed feelings about that. We all started out hoping the parents would win their demands. At this point, looking at it, since nothing happened after the parents did go back, I would say maybe we should have stayed with the private school idea. But, at the same time, most of the parents are paying taxes and it is their school. And most of the children in the community are going to have to go to that school. We're going to have to do something about it; that's all there is to it.

It's a difficult question. There is a long-range and a short-range kind of goal. Should the kids suffer now while their parents fight for change in the public school, or do you opt for the short-range private school approach that will do something for some kids right now? That's the question.

MARY ELLEN SMITH
Boston

I think subconsciously I knew all along that given the structure of the Boston school system I would one day have to decide: the system, or the kids? Because the system just doesn't exist for the kids. And being in the middle, a lot of teachers are going to come to this, if they haven't already.

Mary Ellen Smith, oldest of six children, grew up in Watertown, "a lower-middle-class suburb of Boston." She was educated in Catholic parochial schools, including Boston College, the latter on a scholarship. On graduation in 1965 she taught a nongraded primary class for a year at Bret Harte, an inner-city public school which is four-tenths black, six-tenths white, near the University of Chicago campus. "I had a good experience . . . There was open involvement of parents; an active PTA, free to visit the classrooms as they chose; real recognition of the parents' role. It was partly because professors at the university, whose kids were going to that school, insisted on being involved. The district superintendent was under pressure to foster this. I had a lot of contact, visiting with parents in their homes and, you know, going for dinner, and working with the kids after school. The principal gave me absolutely free rein to do whatever was necessary . . ."

Her heart set on a Boston job, she returned and taught an interim year in Bedford, Mass., while waiting for a regular inner-city assignment. "I just felt there was a greater need . . . There were things I could do that perhaps some other teachers weren't doing."

She taught at Christopher Gibson in Dorchester from September 1967 to September 5, 1968. On that day parents led their children from the school to nearby Shaw House and established a Liberation School. Mary Ellen Smith went with them.

My first experience when I walked into Gibson was one of absolute horror. I was given a classroom and the names of kids who were coming in—that was it. It was a dirty classroom. There were three windows in the room. One had been broken out and it was boarded up. The room was dark. All I could find was cockroaches and various other bugs crawling all over the place, which immediately just set me crawling. You can imagine. I didn't know where to turn, it was in such a state of chaos. They didn't have enough teachers. People running around. Nobody there seemingly in charge that I could have gone to for even such things as Scotch tape to put pictures up . . .

The twenty-eight kids came in and I somehow got started. I had a supervisor who, if I could convince her that what I was doing was valid, would let me do whatever I wanted to do. The principal respected me because I had a couple of years of experience; lots of the other teachers had less. She would also respond to ideas I had about improving the situation not only in my own room but in the school.

That October was when Kozol's book* came out. There was a tremendous emotional response within the building among the teachers. Sort of a drawing of battle lines among those of us who felt in sympathy with what he was saying, and who would even read the book, and those who took an almost paranoid approach, especially the ones who had been there when he had.

We got a notice saying, Clean up your room, don't talk to anybody; there will be people from CBS in here tomorrow. They did come in the following day but they didn't talk to any of us. They walked through the schoolyard with microphones, since the kids were at recess. I saw the thing on CBS later. It was more of a news-broadcast kind of thing, talking about conditions in urban schools and this was just one of them that was cited.

Meanwhile, how were your first-graders doing?

By December it became apparent that we had a large group who were not reading. I was going by the curriculum, very heavy on phonics, doing quite a bit with sight vocabulary, this type of thing . . . We would have to veer off the curriculum if we were going to find some success for these

* See note on pp. 3–4.

kids, so we started to group them in a different way. Those who were reading well would go to one teacher, those in the middle to another. The nonreaders I kept in my room.

I have no opinion about one method as against another. You can only try different things with different kids and you have to keep trying them until you find what works. When I tried sounding out words with the kids, the problem I had was that my pronunciation and their pronunciation were quite different. This is the problem with the white teacher and black kids . . . The whole phonetic approach for this reason is invalid for a lot of kids.

Do black teachers do better?

I would like to see more black teachers and more black principals and more black administrators in the schools simply because black kids have an easier time relating to them. At the same time I've seen some ineffective black teachers and I don't think that is any answer either. It boils down to whether an individual cares about the kids. If they do, the kids sense this right away and then the color doesn't make that much difference. And if they're white and they do care, namely, about black kids, that still doesn't give them an answer. It gives them a first step maybe. They somehow have to contend with a *system* that doesn't care about black kids, about any kids really; that functions without ever evaluating what it is doing to kids. I think white teachers have to tell themselves that they have more to learn than they can ever hope to teach the kids. They have to leave themselves open and flexible and allow themselves to relate to the kids on the *kids'* terms, not try to impose their white middle-class values . . . Let the kids *be* black. As in phonics, for example.

Okay, how did you apply this point of view in your classroom?

The most success I had with children in reading was in letting them write their own stories and then read them. There was a much better recall of sight vocabulary and everything else that way. If kids want to come in and write stories, *let* them. Don't shut them off because you don't want to hear about their problems, or because there are certain words you don't want them to use. If a kid uses words in his story that you consider taboo, that's too bad— you've got to allow the child to communicate, to relate to other kids . . .

I'll never forget the day when, right after Martin Luther King was killed, I was doing creative writing with my first-graders. We were working on colors and so we were doing the color black. I asked them to name things that were black. "Ugly," "dirty" and "witch" were the first things I got. "Okay. Let's stop. I get the feeling that black isn't a very nice color, is that right?" They weren't too sure. Nobody really responded. "If that's true, then let's take our black crayons and throw them away. They are no good to us." Of course they didn't want to lose them so they said, "No, no. We can't throw them away."

So I said, "All right, what good is black, then? Is there anything black that's any good?" So they started thinking a little more and finally they got to things you wear, to physical properties like eyes, hair, clothes, and then animals. And then somebody said, "People." It was just one child, at first, who did say it. And then it was almost as if the whole class was coming along with this and discovering that they were black, even though some of them at that time didn't want to be called black; this was three years ago. They wanted to be called colored or Negro; we had been through this before. So this led into another discussion, about black people, white people, Chinese people. We went on to something else and then this little kid came up to me and took my hand and she said to me, "I love you." And it was just . . . [A pause.] It was the kind of thing, you have to be open for that. You have to allow kids to do this. I think maybe she felt threatened by the whole kind of conversation. We were showing differences. And here was a white teacher doing all of this. She might have felt when I said, "What good is black?" that I didn't think it was much good. But the answer had to come from them. I had to wait for them to make the judgment, to come to the realization that black *was* people . . . It was only through talking about it that the kids started to develop this black pride.

This discussion happened after the assassination of Martin Luther King? Right?

Right. But a lot of things happened at Gibson before that. There were fires, obviously set by kids who hated the school. The most serious one was a month after the assassination. We had kids aged sixteen and seventeen, in grade six. There was a great deal of tension in the black community. High school and junior high school kids were demonstrating in the streets while we were in school . . . A lot of the first-graders were coming in saying things like, "I'm gonna kill all whites." We talked about that. The kids had a difficult time understanding that when they talked about killing whites they were also talking about killing me, because I was white. "No, you're not white. You're the teacher. You're my friend. I'm not going to kill you. I'm going to kill other whites."

In that case, what did "white" mean?

It was just a slogan, you know, it was a feeling of the times—"When I'm talking about whites I'm talking about the ones who call me nigger and who beat up my brother at Dudley Station* or downtown"—or, you know, whatever it is.

* A transfer point on the Boston Rapid Transit System in Roxbury.

What made you follow the kids to Shaw House that day?

When I first came to the Gibson School there was no parents group. I found myself really having to bridge a big gap just because I went out to visit the parents in their homes. I would say, "I'm your child's teacher. I just came to introduce myself . . . I would like to know what you consider his strong points, his weaknesses; whatever you feel I should know . . ." There would be a barrier there. They would hold back. I never had a door slammed in my face, but it was, well: "You're the first one; why should I believe *you?*" A few of the teachers decided something had to be done. We contacted parents and that was how the parents group started. We met with the parents group all year, though we fully realized that we were acting in jeopardy of our professional careers, just because the system is structured as such.

So this wasn't a blindly innocent decision on my part that day. As for my own particular feelings, I was upset, I was angry at the whole school department for the lack of preparation for the school, for the complete and utter racism on the part of the new principal: the way she treated the parents, refusing to talk to them, refusing even to come into the building to see if it was ready to open—it wasn't. It had been chaos the morning before and nobody gave a damn. When I was out there in the schoolyard trying to line kids up, I was angry and frustrated because of the condition of the building, the lack of materials, because the doors were locked to everyone.* I really didn't know what was going on. Somebody took the kids around to the front door. When we got around front, the line went all up the street. I stood there and I looked back at the school . . . And I said to myself, Okay. What do I do? Do I walk

* To prevent the parents from repeating their takeover of the day before. See pp. 11–12.

back into an empty building or do I go with the kids? I went. I felt that the school department had been completely lax in maintaining any kind of communication at all with the parents, that I knew a lot of the parents, and therefore I could be a vehicle of communication. Presumptuous on my part, I'm sure.

At Shaw House it started out with a protest meeting and finding out, the parents and the six of us, that we had a school to set up. The first day there were four hundred kids and they kept it running, and eventually two months later when it closed up there were eighty-five.

The parents wanted to change the public school and they were running the Liberation School only as an alternative. We didn't know from day to day how long it was going to last. But even if it had gone on only two weeks, we wanted to do the best possible job. We all had ideas about that and yet it was a real shock for us to be able to sit down and say, "Okay, what do we want?"

What encouraged us right off the bat was, some kids who weren't doing anything in the public school all of a sudden were reading and *wanted* to do things and *wanted* to learn. They had a difficult time understanding it was a school at first because they *could* do the things they wanted, because the materials were so different, because there were no desks, just chairs and tables, things they could play with, manipulate, and they could work, could sit down and talk with one another. The rooms were never perfectly quiet. We talked about what it took to make a school, and what we had here. They came to realize that this was in fact a school.

The whole attitude of the kids was one of pulling together. We had no discipline problems, absolutely none. It was an incredible thing, watching the kids in this kind of experience. There are always kids who don't get along, but after a month here I didn't see kids fight with one another. If there was a disagreement, other kids from the group would sit down and talk with them about it. It was a phenomenal thing, like they were saying to one another, "We are here for certain reasons; because our parents have taken a stand. We're special, and we can work it out ourselves." You would see a kid, somebody would go by and bump into him and he would start to cry. Immediately other kids would flock around, sympathizing, and they would get the kid who had done it and they would talk about it, all on their own. These are young kids, none of them older than eleven, and they did this without any adult intervention or anything else.

As a teacher at Gibson, you had established credibility with the black community before . . .

I don't think I really did until I walked away from the school with them. There were a lot of parents who felt, legitimately, that "whites are with us, but only up to a point." That first morning the father of one of my first-graders said to me, "You know, you're out of your mind. What the hell are you doing coming with us?" I said, "I have to." He said, "No, you don't. We're not going to hold it against you if you go back to that school. We have to have someone in that building who cares about our kids if we don't make it with this protest." So I thought about it: Okay. There's my out. They won't blame me. But I couldn't have lived with myself, having done that.

With the Gibson parents group it wasn't simply a black-white question. They weren't demanding a black principal. They just didn't want the white one the school system had assigned to them because she was totally unresponsive to their kids' needs. The night we walked out, the protest, even though it was led by the Gibson parents, all the community agencies were in on it. The cry was "Black power," "No white principals," "We don't want white teachers . . ." Then all of a sudden, here in this building they are confronted with six white people. The press was there and the reporters only wanted to know: "Well! Here are six white teachers. What you *you* doing here?" We had to handle it before the press, off the cuff, being asked questions. The whole group, maybe a hundred people, all black, were standing around and listening to us. We were being tested by the way we answered the press. When we were through talking—it was amazing. The whole place was just a dead silence and then they all started clapping. People came up to us afterward and said, "I don't know what to say. You're white but, dammit, you're cool."

By November 1, it was clear that the school could not continue in the face of its mounting financial, technical and legal adversities.

The six of us were in superior court where our case* was being tried. We came back on Friday and of course it was an emotional thing. Most of the kids hadn't seen us for a couple of weeks except occasionally; if court was over early enough we did get back. Some of the older kids had been to see us in court.

The parents had decided to end the school. The kids were questioning at first whether we wanted to send them back because we were tired of them or we didn't care any more. My class, anyway, said, "We don't want to go back if you can't go with us." I explained why I couldn't. They insisted on knowing that I would continue to see them . . .

Nevertheless, the children understood very clearly that their parents were engaged in a struggle on their behalf. They felt they had things here that the other kids of the Gibson School did not.

Bill Owens,† who had been working with some of

* See p. 15.
† William Owens, president of Concerned Parents of the Gibson School and a director of community projects for the New Urban League of Greater Boston.

the fifth-grade boys every afternoon in a session called "Man to Man," thought we should get all the kids together and talk to them, tell them what was happening. So Monday morning there was a total assembly. Bill told them their parents had made a decision: that running a private school didn't help. What they had here at the Liberation School was better for them; they had learned a lot of things here that they would never forget. But there were a lot of kids at the Gibson School who *weren't* getting anything better, and that *these* kids had to go back and help *those* kids out, and that their parents also had to go back. He asked the kids to tell what they had been doing in the school, what they liked about it, what they didn't like. Some of the kids spoke. They didn't want to go back. They tried to find another solution, tried desperately to keep the school going.

Then Bill asked them all to act—he told them he knew it was a hard thing for them to go back. (Some of the kids were crying.) But he had to ask them to do this, for themselves, for their parents, their teachers, him. The kids asked if they could sing some of the songs they and Bill had been singing together all along. He had been a professional musician for a while. They sang songs he had written himself, as well as "Lift Every Voice"* and "I'm Black and Proud,"† and songs like "I'm Gonna Let That Little Light of Mine Shine."‡ Then he said to the teachers, "They're all yours," and he walked out of the room and left

* "Lift Every Voice and Sing" (words by James Weldon Johnson, music by J. Rosamond Johnson). Since its publication in 1900, it has been known as the Negro national anthem.
†"Say It Loud—I'm Black and I'm Proud," by James Brown and Alfred Ellis.
‡ "This Little Light of Mine," a traditional song, became one of the signatures of the freedom movement of the early 1960s. One version appears in *We Shall Overcome: Songs of the Southern Freedom Movement*, compiled by Guy and Candy Carawan for the Student Non-Violent Coordinating Committee (New York: Oak Publications, 1963).

us with them. He was completely overcome. We couldn't even talk to him for a while. This break was an extremely painful thing for all of us. Some of the teachers said something at the assembly but it was very vague and general. All of us were in an emotional state. We couldn't talk much. We were pretty overcome, too.

Children, teachers and parents assembled in the Shaw House auditorium the following morning.

About nine o'clock Bill Owens said, "Well, this is it. We're going back." He advised the parents to go into the classroom with their kids to make sure they were accepted. Walking back, nobody had too much to say. Everybody was sort of wrapped up in their own thoughts. When we got to the school some of the kids cried. A couple of them turned around as they went in the door and waved. One of the kids at the school who was doorman that day opened the door, stuck his head out and said to us, "Come on in. You can come in." We didn't answer him. We just stood there, you know. We stood outside and we cried, the six of us.

We went back to Shaw House, just kind of sat around with the parents, had coffee, talked, and then we packed up stuff we had borrowed, books and materials. I really don't remember too much of the rest of that day.

How did the kids make out after their return to Gibson?

We had sent a letter to the principal asking if we could talk with the teachers there to explain the type of things we had been doing with the kids. She ignored it. But we gave the kids report cards, not graded, just progress reports . . . I know in the course of the year the kids got murdered. The other kids in the school got report cards but they [the returnees] were marked absent for the whole time. Or else they didn't get any report cards at all. Some of them were kept back. They were definitely penalized.

They were pulled out of line, sent to the office, pulled out of the class, for any kind of trouble. They were handled by the teachers as if they, the kids, were to blame for the whole thing.

What do you think ought to happen now?

There aren't any easy answers. I don't know. The involvement of parents in the education process is the only salvation for kids in urban schools. This was essentially a struggle for community control, not a black–white struggle. I think the teachers in Boston have to realize that the parents are not their enemies, that the administration doesn't care about their needs or the kids' needs and if this is going to change it is going to have to come from their working with the parents. There have to be local school boards that are accountable to the specific community which they are in.

About your role—any regrets?

No. I would have to say that I would do it again because of the principle involved. I, at the time, didn't think I would be fired. It just wasn't that radical an act to warrant that kind of action against us. But looking at it from the system's point of view, the bureaucracy and the people that run it, this was probably the thing that was most threatening to them and therefore we had to get what we did. I just had to take a chance that my support of the parents' protest might change things for the kids.

The Six were not reinstated. Sandra Fenton joined the staff of a foundation-supported ghetto school. Mary Ellen Smith became a group worker with children at a community center near the Gibson School. None of the others is working as a teacher.

Early in 1969 The Six asked the Massachusetts supreme court to reverse the county court decision. Their appeal, supported by an amicus curiae brief from the

Massachusetts Teachers Association, was turned down in March 1970. However, the association won in the legislature what The Six could not win in the courts; the state education law now protects all teachers with more than ninety days' employment against dismissal without a hearing. In September, four of The Six filed a suit for damages in federal district court contending that the Boston School Committee had violated their civil rights. At the same time, the American Civil Liberties Union in New York was preparing to carry their original suit for reinstatement to the U.S. Supreme Court.

At the Gibson School very little was changed. The principal who had roused the black community's antagonism to boycott pitch remained there. Parents of new enrollees were recruited to a Gibson Home and School Association (PTA), which, at last report, fitted more neatly into the traditional mold of PTA docility.

In Attorney Lawrence Shubow's estimation, "Their demonstration or, what shall we say, act of self-destruction was not without its positive effects. There've been good by-products of this in the school system, not far-reaching enough, of course . . ."

LOU PALENA
Boston

Lou Palena: baccalaureate, University of Pennsylvania; dropout from graduate studies in the history of ideas at Brandeis University. "I got bored. I didn't want to teach but I thought I ought to try. It was also very convenient in terms of the Army."

In January 1967 I subbed for one day. At seven thirty in the morning I didn't really know what I was getting into. I didn't know anything about Boston but I'd heard about the school.

Patrick T. Campbell Junior High is in Roxbury, which, together with contiguous parts of Dorchester, comprises Boston's major black enclave. During Palena's two years there, it was renamed the Martin Luther King, Jr., Middle School. The change symbolized a period of intense struggle dating from the 1965 Boston School Committee elections, in which Louise Day Hicks ran on a blatantly segregationist platform. Parents and community residents reacted to her presence at the school's graduation exercises in June 1966 by an angry demonstration verging on violence. The cries of "Go home, Mrs. Hicks" subsided only after she walked out of the auditorium under solicitous police escort.

"Campbell"—like, the name was ringing in my head—Where? Where . . . Just as I'm getting off the bus, it occurred to me: this was the place I'd heard about the night before on the TV newsreel. Sure. There were a bunch of teachers up there at a union meeting, complaining about teacher assaults, hollering for cops and for "combat pay"* and all this other stuff. I said "Holy cow." I went in and it was a school like I'd never seen before . . . You just walk into this place and there was this *tremendous* tension in the air that took just about three minutes for it to completely absorb you. All the teachers seemed to be very harried.

The major tension [he decided subsequently] was from the teachers most of the time because they felt they

* Bonus payment for teaching in "tough," i.e., black ghetto schools; a frequently voiced but not realized demand. "Combat pay? I think every one of the kids should get combat pay because they are, in fact, fighting for survival."—Melvin H. King, Boston Black-community leader.

were failing. This was not the way a school is supposed to be run. They were right. There were times when it would get the best of them, I think, and they would approach students very antagonistically. That's when things like assaults would come, the antagonism being a function of the teachers' insecurity. The school was a public target. Teachers were constantly criticized. They were mostly men and they wanted to make it farther up. They had a lot on the line.

The kids were doing whatever they felt like doing. Those that "behaved" did so because they wanted to, not because there was any kind of systematic behavior process in the school. But [he chuckles] they really were very good-natured. They joked and they were having a lot of fun. They could wait . . . This was a lousy school; they'd heard about it.

That first morning Palena didn't have to report to a classroom immediately.

So I spoke for half an hour with one of the older teachers. He was one of the most relaxed persons in the school, but just talking to him made me very jumpy. I said, "Hey, is this the school I heard about last night on TV?" He tried to calm me down, to explain that these were isolated incidents, that the kids were really very good, that they had a lot of inexperienced teachers, you know—"unfortunate"—otherwise things would be running a lot more smoothly. And he was definitely believing it.

The second day they offered me a long-term assignment, seventh- and eighth-grade math. I said yes. First, however, I was put into the art class for an absent teacher. Spent most of my day dodging crayons and decided at the end of the day I'd rather go into the Army. I told them this was not for me. But there was a guy they call a floater, a troubleshooter. He gave me a tremendous pitch about how the kids were great . . . and after they got to know me

. . . and they really needed it . . . nine teachers had gone through that program between September and January . . . you know? And I figured I'd give it a try. It was difficult. It never became in any sense routine, that I just got up in the morning and went to school to teach. I had to re-decide, every morning.

The kids were tremendously anxious after two or three days. They kept asking, would I stay the rest of the year. I said yes and they said, "Ah, that's what they all say." But some of them said, "You'll go, you'll go. We'll make sure you do." It was hard. I didn't understand the language at the time. I had to ask friends of mine what—The kids would say, "Man, you think you're down but we're gonna lay you out." There were two or three real ringleaders among the "baddies." They didn't do any of the childish kind of things. Basically, they would ignore me, except when I did what *they* wanted to do.

There was one very tough group of eight or nine boys, most of them sixteen, in eighth grade. They told me right from the first time they came in, "Man, we're not gonna stay unless you do some algebra." The curriculum called for arithmetic. They were older. They wanted to do what the ninth- and tenth-graders were doing. So I did it. And it worked out very well. It's a funny thing. See, they *wanted* to do it enough, so that if anyone got out of line the others would remind them: "Hey, man, let's listen. We told the cat we wanted to do this. He went and got books, so shut up and listen or get out." Sometimes they would leave. But by and large it was my most successful class my first year.

Were they capable of doing algebra?

They were. Okay, they had a lot of problems with arithmetic but I decided I could handle those through this other medium. If I had been an old experienced battle-ax, they'd have *done* arithmetic. Just that. For me, it just wouldn't have worked.

Eventually Palena's self-demand algebra group was disbanded by attrition. Nevertheless he and many of his students continued learning how to "get through" to each other as individuals. One of them was Richard Moriarty, black.

Really good-looking. Dressed very well. Really slick. He was together. Richard left that group at the end of the year and went to Northeastern University in a special school for dropouts. He told me that despite how little we had done he felt much more confident there because of the algebra thing. He thanked me and that's the last I've seen of him.

John Murray [also black], he was in another group. Had some trouble with the cops once or twice, about cars. Now he was talking up a storm about getting a driver's license. He had this little blue book from the Mass. Registry. He couldn't read well enough to pass the written test. What I helped him do was to isolate the most important questions and he just memorized them, basically. I was trying to help them learn to take tests anyway. It's funny, because two weeks after he got his license, they had a riot in Roxbury. Of course John was in the middle of it all and broke his arm pretty badly, so he couldn't drive for the summer. John used to try to hustle me all the time. His help and admonitions were always followed by something he wanted to ask me for. Like: "Hey, Teach, what am I going to get on my report card?"

"Well, John, you weren't in class the past three weeks in a row. There's not much I can do for you."

"I'll tell you what—if I get 'em all quiet will you give me a good mark?"

"Well, let me see you do it first."

"Do you think I can?"

So I'd say, "Well, I don't know . . ." It was a funny kind of thing. When I engaged in that kind of bartering with them, they somehow saw that there was a little bit of hustler in me, too. It made a hell of a difference.

I remember a fellow in another class, he came after school one day for no particular reason. I was just sitting there and he said, "What the hell are you doing *this* for? You can't make any money here, and you got a college degree. You could make *money* some place else."

At first I told him I like to teach, the usual bullshit that teachers say. I didn't have my heart in that answer. I *couldn't*, because I didn't *know* why I was doing it . . . And he didn't believe it. Every day I had to remind myself it was important. Finally he said, "Ah, you're a goddam fool." So I tried another approach: "Well, I don't know. Am I a fool, really?"

"Whaddaya mean?"

"Well, you come in and you raise hell. You play, throw things out of the window, give me a lot of lip. Everybody laughs and you go home. But sooner or later you won't be here any more. You'll be out—somewhere. Now, I go home, have a drink and forget about it. And at the end of the month, I get paid." He looked at me, shook his head, walked away. It was like: "Well, if you do it *that* way, maybe it makes sense."

During my first year I was ambivalent about it. You come home and work very hard on something you think will be interesting and you go in, and it doesn't work. This doesn't mean the kids are merely indifferent. Sometimes they'd be downright hostile: "Just get off my back, man." A lot of times I'd say, "What the hell am I doing here? What kind of a masochist am I?"

When I realized there was a hell of a lot under my control that I hadn't been aware of, that I could create the kind of climate in the room that I wanted, and really *believed* I could—the kind of climate in which I could care—that was the big difference.

The kids divide teachers into two groups—this is from

long talks I've had with kids—those who care and those who don't. There are black and white in each group. If they felt that you care about them—if that meant the rattan* or if it meant taking them out somewhere after school—whatever way you showed it, that's what was important. It was the teachers who were *indifferent*—and you could be indifferent in a lot of so-called liberal ways—who just didn't cut it. You just didn't make it.

Over the summer I came to some conclusions about how to reach the kids. One way that seemed clear was to be really hard at first. Just goddam mean. If you didn't, the kids would think there was something wrong with you. I was—what's the cliché—firm but fair? But more than firm, very tough. I learned to use my size very well, though it's not a crucial factor.

It's funny. Only once or twice did I have a real confrontation—because I didn't have as much control. Usually the way it happens is, a child comes in really feeling down. If you can tune yourself up in the morning, really very finely, to what each kid feels when he's walking into the room, those things can be avoided. They really can. And you have to do it 'cause those kids are so sensitive. They're being bombarded all the time. They have to be conscious all the time in a way I never had to be when I was their age. Anybody I've watched who has tried to ignore this, it's really been bad news. That doesn't mean the kids won't behave or anything. They just shut off. They're not themselves. They'd turn into the stereotype of a "nigger"; just very lazy and—ahh—you know.

I guess I came to terms with myself, that I really did care, a hell of a lot. I realized: "Yeah. I want to do it." I

* A switch made from the tough flexible stem of certain tropical Asian vines; the officially designated instrument of corporal punishment in the Boston public schools. An account of its use is given in Chapter Two of Jonathan Kozol's *Death at an Early Age*. A resin exuded by the fruit of the rattan vine is commercially known as dragon's blood.

wanted to do it right. And it came across; somehow, the second year, it came across.

Palena, son of an immigrant father and U.S.-born mother, grew up in South Philadelphia's Italo-American working-class enclave. In his teens the family "moved out to this kind of quality suburban neighborhood." He attended parochial schools, grades one through twelve, then earned his baccalaureate degree at the University of Pennsylvania.

In third and fourth grades the nuns were sure I was going to be a priest so . . . I did the next best thing, graduate work in the history of ideas. I wanted to teach college and I wanted to be with ideas. But I guess now I have to see very clearly how ideas are related to action. That's what was missing from graduate school.

There were eight hundred of us in my high school. It was a fantastic school, in what was one of the toughest places in Philadelphia. At lunchtime we used to have rock fights with the kids who lived in the neighborhood, but there was a kind of spirit, a kind of expressiveness that I found lacking, for example, when I went to Penn. The school was about 30 percent black. I was in the academic section and that was 30 percent black, too. There wasn't that kind of segregation by tracks. A black kid graduated at the top of our class and is now at Oxford. Out of that little high school—that's something else.

There was—I don't know—a general kind of warmth, a feeling of the existence of a future, even among the black kids. We could be anything: plumbers, musicians, lawyers, doctors. Nobody looked down on work, on being a worker, because most of us had fathers who were [Palena's father was a tailor]. But there was nothing inevitable about it. I mean, everybody was going to make it in his own way. We felt there was a lot of choice involved. Like a lot of suburban high school kids we grew up with, yeah, they had a future, too, but they felt very tight about it. For them, it had to be doctor, lawyer, professor, or some equivalent. We didn't feel that way about it.

Nobody took school too seriously. We did what we had to, to get by. We were all good hustlers and the priests seemed to understand that. I did well the first three years because we cheated well. We had really fantastic systems [he laughs, on a note of retrospective triumph]. In chemistry we had these long lab tables with a water trough underneath. We used to sit the smart guy at the upper end. When he was finished with the test he would float his answers down to us. It was beautiful. The trough was about seven inches deep and the teacher couldn't see anything floating.

There was really a kind of community spirit about it. I think maybe that was the key thing. There wasn't that kind of tense competition . . . Getting through school was really a cooperative enterprise: "We all gotta make it. C'mon, guys. Let's get together and do it."

You're talking about the late fifties. Has it changed since then?

Well, one of the things we've discovered—and I say "we" because we've been working on this quite a bit in a project*—is that this kind of spirit still exists to a large extent in the city schools and to an even greater extent in the black schools. In suburban schools it's very, very differ-

* Palena was then working with a group called the Boston Area Teaching Project. The project's goal, at the time, was to produce curriculum materials developed with the close participation of some twenty high school students. The premise for the group's existence was that "being good mechanics and using effective methods aren't enough." The group thinks that political involvement is inseparable from good teaching. In the course of the project's activity some two hundred Boston teachers "drifted in" to hear about the work, to discuss pertinent problems of their own and to participate "because they had nowhere else to go to express their concern and find a rationale for their presence in teaching."

ent, a tremendous amount of very individual competition. It's very distinct . . . We have tapes of the kids themselves explaining it.

Was there any big change, the second year, in the attitude of the kids toward you?

Yeah. The mere fact that I came back—hhuh!—an oddity. The school had a faculty turnover of 60–65 percent each year. The next year only ten out of sixty* came back. I think one of the ways kids determine who really cares are those who keep coming back whether they're having trouble or not. You're a stable feature in their lives. A fixture. You begin to become a part of a community.

I think I communicated a sense of much more confidence about what I was doing. Instead of being threatened every time a kid expressed dissatisfaction, I'd say, "Well, maybe his mother beat him last night" or "Maybe he's right." The kids were kind of young, sixth-graders that year, ten and eleven. None of them had been left back very much. It was difficult to deal with some of the stuff in a sophisticated way. But the mere fact that I was willing to listen and somehow respected their opinions—that seemed to be very important. They felt comfortable coming to me with their problems, even the first year.

In this atmosphere how did you get anyone interested in learning some math?

One of the ways was just making it concrete. I was dealing with sixth- and seventh-graders who had to learn fourth-grade math. And they knew it, just like those sixteen-year-old kids knew they were getting eighth-grade math. With one sixth-grade class, I drew a facsimile of one of my checks on the board and they copied it on mimeograph stencils. I was able to put it on the machine and make them up a hundred checks with their names on them and

* 83 percent.

stuff, and I gave them deposit slips. Now, you know, that was like a really good way. They knew about checks. They were learning how to add and subtract, how a bank operates, what it means to have a check bounce, all the other things involved. We were able to do a lot of that. Instead of just adding up columns of figures we had:

"So-and-so just gave you a check for a thousand dollars and twenty-six cents for your car. Now, put that on the balance sheet and on your deposit slip. If you write out a check you have to subtract it from your deposits." We were involved in very high digits and decimals. It made a lot of sense to them and they were very proud of it. And they tried to get me to cash it in a bank, too.

Did they ask any questions about the broader economic implications of banks?

We had a lot of rap sessions in the afternoon between one and two twenty when we went out. I always had lessons planned, but kids always wanted to talk about something that was on their minds. Some of the kids really used that. It was like a way of getting around the lesson. I had to do a lot of thinking . . . I decided it was worthwhile.

Once his pupils asked why he wasn't driving his sports car to school any more. He explained it had been stolen.

We got into the whole insurance bit. The questions they raised were more like: "Insurance is for people who *have* something" . . . Somehow it never really applied to them. They asked me if I was going to get enough money to buy a new car and I explained about depreciation. They had such a tremendous sensitivity to what they saw as injustice in a lot of procedures. Like the fact that you pay a thousand dollars for the car and they only give you six hundred dollars back on it: "That's not fair."

Something that seemed genuinely unjust, we thrashed

it out. In those kinds of broader discussions, we decided one day we were going to dissect the ghetto, and what it's like to be poor. It was just fabulous. Three or four kids, I guess it was too threatening to them, just did math in the back of the room. Everybody else was involved. We started with the whole, with what it meant to be poor, and the difference between living in an apartment in Roxbury and living like, as one kid put it, when I took them out to Brookline: "What beautiful houses you have here." (We were driving out there and he said, "Hey, man, look at these houses, will ya?" And he was severely reprimanded by another kid who said, "These aren't houses, man, these are *homes*.")

The simple economic facts—without any reading or anything—about people owning the houses in Roxbury around the school and not living there; what it meant to be paying rent and having that money taken out of the community, and how that made it difficult for people to earn a living in the community. Instead of hiring a plumber from Blue Hill Avenue, a plumber got hired from downtown. I hate that kind of thing where you just only lay everything out, so I finally asked them, "Well, what are you going to do about it?" And they came up with a whole plan.

"Well, first of all we got to knock all these places down."

"Well, where do all the people go?"

"They go out to Roslindale and Hyde Park."

"But the whites don't want you out there."

I had already told them about the [State] Commission Against Discrimination. I thought nobody had heard me. But the kids said:

"You go to that place downtown and you *tell* 'em, and *make* 'em."

I said, "You can't afford the apartments out there. Remember we're poor."

"Well, you live there for free. They're free, that's all."

"Then the old place gets all built up, and what do you do?"

"You come back now."

"But we haven't really gotten to the basic thing. We started with the question, Should blacks and whites live together?"

"Well, you don't have to come back if you don't want to. You can stay out there if you want to." Some of the kids even thought, Well, if you decide to stay out there, then you'd have to begin paying rent there. You can no longer live there free. It's very hard for me to recapture the whole dialogue, but it was very intense and, Jesus, for two hours! I was exhausted after that.

In this class I had last year two kids were particularly articulate. One, a girl; and one, a boy. Both were really struggling very hard with who they were and what it meant to be black, and stuff. Roz, the girl, came to B.U. [Boston University] once with a panel of kids. She was unbelievable. She just took over the whole thing. She articulated so well what kids want, what the parents expect from kids, and from teachers. She got right to the heart—the custodial part of the school's responsibility. Roz, she was so hip, she even had her lineage traced back to Frederick Douglass and she was really tuned in to what was happening. And whether it was true or not, I thought it was really cool that she identified herself with that line of the heritage.

In your three years at King, what was the one thing that gave you the greatest sense of accomplishment?

This'll probably sound kind of crazy. I don't fully understand it myself. It all happened kind of spontaneously. At the beginning of this year our class had to elect a representative to the Student Council. So first we had to choose some class officers. Then I explained the procedure and I said, "Go ahead, nominate." The kids got right into it and I thought, Hey, this is working. But I said to the class, "Look, we can't just elect people because they've got a name and a face. I think everybody nominated should get five minutes to make a speech." They loved that. Everybody gave a speech and I listed the platforms on the blackboard. They were really very honest and outspoken, about teachers, the principal, and all that stuff. So after about two hours they elected somebody. It was really gratifying because they had elected a guy who made the most sense. Gee, I was high as a kite for two days.

Then we began having the trouble at the school and we had some black college students come in to talk to the kids about student government and things like that. One of them questioned the validity of our Student Council. He asked the kids, "Did you really elect the people *you* wanted? Or did you elect the people the teachers wanted? This was at an assembly and I was really gassed at what went on there. When we got back to our room, I asked the students: "Do you think your representative represents *you* or *me*?" They said, "We think he represents you." So I said, "What should we do about it?" They said, "Hold another election." Hah! So I said, "How about if I get another teacher to come in and watch the election, somebody that *you'll* choose?" Fine. That's what they did, and that was that. So, who was elected the second time? Same kid. By the same margin.

I don't know—see, it's so hard, without having another person there in whom you have confidence saying, "Hey, man!" You know? But, number one was: the kids said what they thought and they *felt* they could. Secondly, they weren't defeated by it; they wanted to go on anyway and try to factor me out of the situation somehow. That was really good for me; I felt I had really grown as a teacher, to be able to do that and to accept consequences which I could not know in advance; I was really emotionally involved in it. What the kids got practically was a little experience in using democratic procedures, and the chance to call me a fascist if they wanted to [he laughs]. They didn't.

What has been your most frustrating experience?

The ones that I came home banging my head against the wall were never with the kids. They were with the administration.

Specifically . . . ?

Well, specifically they put me out of a school.

Put you out . . . ?

That's a long story. The King had been 100 percent black for eight years. Their troubles for a long while were no greater than those of many schools like it. This past year [the school year of 1968–69] the place exploded and had to be closed down three times for a total of twenty-seven days because of student disorders. The causes had been accumulating for a long time and there was a lot of unrest about the administration of the school during the summer before. Also, the black college student groups had become more interested, and had been doing a lot of talking to the kids. The unrest took a very significant turn for better or worse, whichever way you want to look at it, at the time of King's assassination [April 14, 1968]. It really made a big difference in the way the kids saw the school, and themselves in relation to it. They became much more openly antagonistic, though there were no serious incidents at that time.

The first time the school closed was after a pile of fire alarms. With each alarm the kids got progressively more out of order until they were just sort of running around the school at will. No one was hurt, no kids, no teachers. The second time, the school was closed mainly because the

School Committee* felt more time would be needed to get things settled. The third time, there was physical violence. One teacher was badly beaten up—a black teacher, by the way—and the school was closed very quickly. There was a specific incident with him and one of the more popular students that day. He was usually like that, antagonistic, and they didn't look on him as an ally in any way . . . Negro, but not black, in the language of the day.

I think it's important that there was this kind of steady progression. It was a carnival the first time. The second time it was mainly directed toward property. Then it began to be directed toward persons. The administration did nothing to respond to the real courses of the situation.

The community got kind of fed up with that. The school was never open. Their feeling was, the administration had demonstrated that it couldn't run the school. So a lot of community pressure and organization built up to actually have the community run the school itself. There was a community control struggle here around the King. Several members of the faculty—I was one of them; say, about fifteen or twenty out of sixty—took the community's part in that struggle. In fact, an organization developed out of a series of three meetings with community leaders, parents, teachers, school administration, students, everybody.

Out of those meetings a group was formed which came to be known as the King Cabinet, which consisted of six parents, five community leaders, five students and five teachers whose mandate from the whole convocation was, with the exception of the school administration, to administer the school. You know, to hire an executive director for the school, and these would be his duly elected cabinet. I was a member of that as a teacher, and a very active member. Well, the school closed down for the third time because of student riots. Teachers weren't doing any-

* Board of Education.

thing, nobody was doing anything. The kids were running around the streets. So we in the community, the Cabinet, opened up what we called King Learning Centers* and we ran the schools for the kids between December 5 and Christmas. We just did a lot of things.

Okay, so while that was going on people were doing a lot of politicking and stuff like that, trying to get some solution to the whole thing. And when the school finally reopened, those of us who had been actively involved in the community, in fact twelve of the fifteen teachers who taught at the Learning Centers, were transferred out of school—no explanation given. The way it was done technically was that since the King remained closed after New Year's, we weren't working but we were getting paid. So they reassigned every teacher from the King to be subbing at one school or another around the city. When they made the decision to reopen, they called some of those teachers back and they didn't call the others back. I was not called back. I finished out this year at the Dearborn Elementary School, which is about a mile away.

And Dearborn is now your permanent—

No. They also failed to renew my contract. I'll be teaching at a suburban high school next year.

* Peak daily attendance at the four Learning Centers was between 300 and 350. The King school's enrollment, 939 in September, had diminished by one third by the end of November as a result of transfer requests which the school was legally obliged to honor. Other students simply stopped attending.

2

THE SYSTEM

If you really want to try something new to turn your kids on, don't tell the front office; work fast and hold on.

—*a New York City schoolteacher*

WILLIAM WASHINGTON
Detroit

I'm neither fish nor fowl in this building. I'm not considered a militant and I'm not considered a handkerchief-head either. I have my own ideas. I feel strongly that we have not given the system a chance to work in the schools. I would imagine it's the same in other big cities.

"This building" is Foch Junior High on Fairview Avenue, east-side Detroit. Its seventeen hundred students come from a surrounding area of long-established black residence. To strangers merely driving through on their way to some other place, the neighborhood offers pleasant glimpses of tidy streets, substantial houses, large, grassy front yards. To sociological sight-seers, it gives off vibrations of petit-bourgeois "stability." Foch, built in the 1920s, strengthens the impression. Its spacious grounds and the romantic, Versailles-influenced lines of its façade say, Gracious learning of eternal verities available to all who enter here. Nevertheless:

There's such a huge teacher turnover, such instability in the schools, that how can we judge what we really can do on the basis of what we've done?

We have between 10 and 20 percent teacher turnover every semester, which is ridiculous. We have people who come into these inner-city schools ready to leave. They've *said* it to me, "Well, I'm here but I have my transfer already." We have been— I wouldn't say, a dumping ground —but the inner-city school is the only place where people [merely] start to learn how to teach. We have had too many of these people. Until a teacher's taught for three years, he doesn't seriously begin to know what to do without subordinating the curriculum to the discipline issues.

William Washington, chairman of Foch's English department, has taught for thirteen years in predominantly black schools, the last three years at Foch. He is dark, tall, sturdily built, conservatively dressed; an approachable man, who is informal, good-humored but entirely self-possessed.

No school should have a great percentage of inexperienced teachers. If 20 to 40 percent of the staff have been teaching less than three years, that's too high. If we could keep a dedicated, stable staff I believe we could reverse the trend [of achievement levels in inner-city schools]. We don't have enough people who want to be here, even if we pay them more to stay. Schools are people, not the building. I mean, a guy puts in one semester, then he's gone.

You say "dedicated teachers." Dedicated to what?

Well, in the first place, a teacher has to believe that this is more than just a job. I hate to make it sound corny, but, you know, if you have one of those factory attitudes about it, I wouldn't consider you dedicated. I would say: dedicated to the idea that every child deserves what you can do for him, and dedicated to the idea of quality education. Now, that's a term everybody's throwing around, but to me it simply means you do your best to teach your subject. Not just go through the motions, but see that the kids learn something. Giving the best quality that's in *you*.

I think there is a different attitude among the young teachers—a lot of them, not everybody. The unions have become so strong, there doesn't seem to be that old kind of enthusiasm for the job. When I started, it was nothing to leave at five o'clock. How do the young teachers feel about things? Many of the better young teachers reject what has been going on in the schools and they have their own ideas about how it should run. For example, during a workshop, one teacher worked out a whole new English curriculum. He had all sorts of ideas for making sure that the students knew certain materials before they went to the next step. He had his system all worked out—before a publisher hired him away to work on some black-literature anthologies. I would say that he would be typical of the bright, young teacher—especially the black teacher—who comes in with the knowledge that what we've been doing has failed.

Do you find more dedication among black teachers than among white ones?

Now, black doesn't mean dedicated. This is where a lot of people make the mistake. They say we all have to be black. I don't believe that. But given a choice between a dedicated white teacher and a dedicated black teacher in a school were the students are black, the black teacher could identify more because you have to use everything you have. I do; I use everything. I appeal every way I can. If I have to I can tell them, Do this for me because I'm black, and proud of what "black and proud" means. But—well you saw that material on the board up there about black leaders . . . The idea is that it's right to be black and proud but you got to be gifted, too. You know the song— black, gifted and, what is it?—"young, gifted and black."*

There was one student in one of my classes who was a dropout. He and his brothers—I think there were four, no mother and father—they were just running the streets of Meridian [Miss.] for two years out of school. Their married brother and his wife in Detroit said, "We've got to save one of these boys" and they brought the boy up here. He wanted a job, only when he got here things were kind of tight. He couldn't get a job, so his brother talked him into going to school . . . Now, I think, this boy is going to *stay* in school. He's changed his ideas of what success means to him. In Mississippi he didn't look any farther than making money. I've had so many cases like that . . .

* "To Be Young, Gifted and Black," by Nina Simone and James Weldon Irvine, Jr.

51

These kids have to have role models. I can remember another student; his model was the ticket taker in an all-night movie theater and that's what he wanted to be: the ticket taker in an all-night movie theater. Another youngster told me that he wanted to be like his cousin. His cousin was a pimp who drove a Cadillac and had plenty of money and all the girls he wanted. This is what the boy wanted.

When I started teaching in Detroit there were so many fellows with processes, so many slickheads. They would line up in front of the lavatory to put on their do-rags, to protect their hair. We tried everything we could to be white, you know, and we couldn't be. We're black, so why should we try to be white? I'm so glad to see this black-is-proud movement I don't know what to do. It's a wonderful thing. There's a matter of pride behind the "natural." It's saying something. Now, of course, you always have a few who are going to get onto it as a fad; not everybody who wears long hair is a hippie.

I think we've made a mistake, in Detroit and other big cities, by ignoring racial backgrounds. Dr. Conant said in *Slums and Suburbs*,* back in 1961, that the big-city ghetto schools were putting out social dynamite on the streets. That was before the first riots, and sure enough, it happened. You can't say that a black man is a white man darkened, you know. That's not true.

Some white teachers can't relate, can't appeal to black students. But you take a teacher like Karpenko, somehow that man has soul. Now, "soul" is kind of indefinable, I guess, but he has the empathy that a lot of people don't have. He has some feeling of what it means to be black, partly because he feels that he's a minority person too.

But there are some teachers here just holding on. Some people are just so completely out of their element

* James Bryant Conant, *Slums and Suburbs* (New York: McGraw-Hill, 1961).

that they really should be somewhere else maybe, with kids they can control. Some black teachers are like that too.

We're not giving the system a chance to work, you said. Who is "we"?

It hasn't been given a chance to work by the powers that be. We're looking for gimmicks. What I mean by "the system"—right now in Detroit we're talking about integrated education.* I think the black man is lost if we have to depend on integration to achieve quality education. We're talking about busing and so forth, to achieve quality education. We've got to be able to work with what we've got. We've got to do a better job so we can have quality education *without* busing. Not that integration is bad; it's good. But we can't sit around and wait to be integrated in order to do a better job. We're wasting our time.

I can't see why black people *have* to have white people, to learn. Now, I know this is the theory, that you can't learn without white people in the room. I don't believe that. [He chuckles at the absurdity of the notion.] I'm sorry, I just can't believe it. I think about my own experience of growing up in the South. I went to a school in Knoxville, Tenn., all black. With the dedication of those teachers, if we had just had the equipment we have here in Detroit, we could have put geniuses out on the street. When you think about the people who have made it—if you investigate some of the judges, the top black people in Detroit, New York—most have backgrounds from More-

---

* In Detroit, as in other cities with large minority populations, school integration has been the subject of decade-long public debate, ambivalent School Board maneuvering, ineffectual state legislation and essentially unproductive federal court litigation. Some of these activities gained momentum and stirred new public concern during 1969–71. By the end of that period, nevertheless, the strong pattern of racial desegregation in Detroit schools remained basically unchanged.

house or some Southern school. The people who have gone on and keep pushing and don't give up, they came from segregated schools. We were given something extra in those schools. We were given that desire to really excel because, you know, "You can do it!"

I have a background that would be typical of a working-class black family. I have a brother and two sisters. My father got to be a foreman in his plant. He is very proud of that and he never said to me, "You must go to college." I just felt that I had to, and I was lucky enough to meet a teacher in junior high who took a personal interest in me, who said, "Look, you've got some ability, why don't you do this?" And she followed me all the way through, gave me a lot of advice and help in getting into college. Even with clothes, you know. Like she had a brother that she got clothes from and she gave them to me. I was lucky in that regard. I don't know; maybe I would have gone on anyway.

When I was in high school I won a scholarship to Morehouse. I didn't accept it because I wasn't sure I could make it academically in Atlanta and also work. I would have had to work because the scholarship didn't cover room and board. So I decided to live home and go to Knoxville College, also segregated. Which is why, when I graduated, I said, "Well, do I know, could I make it somewhere else?" I needed to see if I could compete with white people. I went into the Army, with the idea that I was going to use that experience to parlay it into some money, to do graduate work at a Northern university. And that's what I did. They put me through the Army clerk school, and I spent two years in a medical outfit in Virginia, Fort Belvoir. It was right at the tail end of the Korean conflict. I went in in '54, when they first started talking. I was hoping they wouldn't start fighting again. Anyway, I used that time to find out what I could do.

I had my application in at the University of Michigan

before I got out of the Army. My mother's sister lived in Detroit. I thought I'd have a better chance where I knew somebody. When I got to Ann Arbor I found out what a prejudiced place that was. Wow! Really something. I guess it's a little different now. I didn't realize how segregated Michigan was.

There were maybe twenty black people that I saw in the whole school. Usually I was the only black person in the class and every time they'd start talking, they'd want to know, what do black people think about this, about that. I was supposed to speak for the whole race. That was the kind of deal that was going on all the time; it got to be very disturbing. But I had some good white friends that understood, by the way. There were a lot of veterans on campus and we felt kinship because we really didn't have the clothes, or the money to do . . . The GIs who were in World War II messed up so badly with the government's money that the Korean vets got a rotten deal. We had to go to school three months on our own money before we could get anything at all, and then we only got $110 a month. The money I saved while I was in the Army was paying my tuition. I had to pay an out-of-state fee, almost double the regular tuition. So here I am trying to make it in a place like Ann Arbor on $110 a month. I just about starved to death. The places closest to the college, to the center of activities, were places that you couldn't live as a black man. I don't think it was widely known but we found it out quickly enough when we tried to get in. I was a long way from campus, a long way. A lot of people had bicycles. I walked.

I stayed for a year and came out with a master's degree. While I was there, the recruiter for the Detroit schools came onto the campus and talked to me. I decided it wouldn't be such a bad idea to stay in Michigan. I never did go back home to live. My degree was in social studies but there seemed to be so many people in the field. I had an English minor, so I decided to go to Wayne and get a major in this too. So now I have a double major.

I started teaching at Jefferson over there on the Expressway. That was about 40 percent white, or maybe even fifty-fifty. Then slowly it started changing. But it still had quite a few white kids, Appalachian . . . Some of the schools out on the fringes of Detroit, they really have their problems. There was one school that was 20 percent black and the next year it was 80 percent or something like that.

I came from Jefferson to Foch Junior High in 1967. That was a promotion. I was in about the second wave of black department heads. I had a department head over at Jefferson who felt that you had to teach a great number of years to be qualified to be a department head. She didn't feel that these "young whippersnappers" just coming in should be promoted. But Foch has had black department heads for some time. I've been teaching, too, until just three weeks ago. When my student teacher came, about the first of April, I turned the class over to her.

Foch changed [in racial balance] a long time ago. This is not what I would call a "rock-bottom" neighborhood. Many of these children's parents own their own homes. This was brought to me very dramatically one day when we were talking—from a story—about tenants' rights. The kids in that class saw the *landlord's* point of view. They came up with all sorts of stories about how the tenants didn't take care of the property and how they had done this and that and the other and wouldn't pay the rent. Those students didn't see the tenant's point of view; I don't think there was a single person in the room that did.

There are some schools in Detroit where the adult community are "service" people who really don't have much, and there are many more problems there. You run across kids in schools like that who *really* have chips on their shoulders, you know, just waiting to strike out at somebody. These youngsters here don't seem to be that way.

About the riots in '67—I guess they told you that headquarters for some of the troops was in this area. They were camped right across in that field over there; our building had to be evacuated. Our youngsters were very much involved, so that first year I was here we did a lot of writing about the riot. I had made a collage of all the pictures I could find about the riot, on a big board, as a way to get the students to write about things they knew about. They could tell you all kinds of experiences. These kids had seen things, you know, during the riot. They write poetry: free verse, also ballads, limericks. The best of it I put together in a book. It's just an introduction, to get them interested in poetry. Most of them at the end of the year say they like this unit better than anything else they've done. And this is how all this riot material came out. It still does, now and then. They still remember. There's one poem—the boy who wrote this is not one of the better students . . .

We stop to look at a rexographed-and-stapled anthology: Poems from Room 400; 8A–211, 8A–113, and to read the poem "Negro":

> It is
> A dirty night
> When cops stop the Negro.
> It is like a black and white picture
> That doesn't come out.
> It is like balls of fire
> That will never go out.
> It is a shame in the street
> But it is the game people play;
> It is one big black truck—
> As big as a bus

> *But with more room*
> *Than you can un-soon for us;*
> *It is bad for the black*
> *And good for the white;*
> *It is more rough*
> *Than right;*
> *It is blue lights going*
> *hitting back;*
> *Red lights going*
> *As fast as they can*
> *To make it to the doc's.*
> > —Claude Ellington

He saw that, you know.

There was another poem, "Hate," reflecting Detroit's lurid nighttime skies of early August 1967:

> *With hate in our hearts,*
> *We shout ferociously—*
> *Take what you want;*
> *Burn . . .*
> *Rob . . .*
> *Kill your fellow man;*
> *Take your freedom.*
> *Destroy America;*
> *We are tired of paying*
> *For our blackness.*
> > *Lenny Henderson*

This one girl, all of her poems had a death theme running through them. When I talked to her, I found that she had had a young uncle who was killed in Vietnam. She had very strong feelings, adult feelings, about the war. "My uncle died for nothing." This is what she's feeling and she puts this on paper.

They're very socially aware, aware of what's going on

in the country. There's an underlying resentment of the police department that comes out. Any way they can put it, it comes out. They reject some of the things that we try to teach them. They want to know why they should learn certain things. And you've got to give them an answer. It can't be "because it's in the book."

After the riots, did the school administration feel that it ought to begin to do something, make some changes?

Since the riots, they've made quite a few black appointments to positions of leadership. In fact—I object to some of what they've done—some of the better of our black administrators have been moved up so high and so fast that they don't have any connection with the black community any more. You know you've got a good man; you kick him upstairs and the children don't see him any more. And they're still appointing black people as principals, department heads and so forth.

As for curriculum, we waited I don't know *how* long to get books that were, quote, relevant to the kids. A committee downtown would not approve new books until they had met certain requirements; for example, books had to have black representation in them. So we did without for a long time . . .

The teachers here are pretty free to teach. They can do things that would not have been accepted a few years ago. Take the matter of teacher dress; we have people in our building who wear dashikis and so forth and nobody says anything. One teacher wore an earring in his ear last year. But I don't believe that some teachers are using the freedom they do have to the maximum extent. For too many people, I guess, if it's not there in the book, that's it. They're not going to try anything creative at all, because "you don't want to get the kids riled up." I think we have a lot of people who, maybe subconsciously, don't believe that these students can achieve. That is the greatest problem right there.

You have to believe in the kids. At my other school the assistant principal said, "Well, you know these kids' background. This is the best they can do." He actually said that. You can see why things aren't any better than they are: if someone in authority says, "This is the best they can do."

If you believe a child can do something it's more likely he *can* do it. In fact, somebody did a study on that, a man and woman from California.* We should demand more from our students. We have things that come up, like contests where our youngsters have to compete with others in the rest of the city. Our kids can do it. And even if they can't, okay, at least they were out there trying. Two journalism students entered an area-wide competition. They both won honorable mentions. When I checked the *Detroit News* there was only one other inner-city school that won anything in journalism. If we'd let them try more, they'd win more. You don't win anything unless you try.

The D.A.R., which is not one of my favorite organizations, sponsors a patriotic-speech contest every year. This year their topic was "The Signing of the Declaration of Independence." You had to write and memorize a five-minute speech. I tried to interest teachers in our building to get involved. When they heard "D.A.R.," they turned right off: "I don't want anything to do with them. You gonna get into a contest *they* sponsor?" So anyway, our girl won the whole shebang; a girl that we teach here won the gold medal. It was a real thrill for me to see this little girl handing around this gold medal.

* Robert Rosenthal and Lenore Jacobson, *Pygmalion in the Classroom* (New York: Holt, Rinehart & Winston, 1969). The same authors presented a paper entitled *Self-Fulfilling Prophecies in the Classroom: Teachers' Expectations as Unintended Determinants* at the annual meeting of the American Psychological Association in 1967 at Washington, D.C.

Did she have any new approach to the Declaration?

No, she said what they wanted to hear. That's why she won. There was only one other inner-city school in the entire contest. And this other school was not prepared. I was really embarrassed because this little boy didn't know his speech.

I know when I was in high school, teachers said, "You can make it. You're as good as the next guy," and I wanted to see if that was true. You want to believe in yourself . . .

But even in my all-black school, there was the idea that the lighter you are the better chances you have. This is going away now, but back in the forties if you were light you got the part in the school play. I tried out for the lead and my best friend, who was real light—he looked like a white man, wavy hair and everything—he didn't even try out; he was offered the part. He turned it down; that's the only reason I got it. And the people who were the professionals, the teachers, were the people who looked most like whites. This was the kind of thing that was going on, all over. It was all part of growing up black. It wasn't easy to figure out.

There's a poem I have in a book in the office there. It's called "Black Power"* It starts out: "I stepped from black to black" and the poet is talking about how he rejects blackness in all of its negative connotations and accepts it in all of its positive connotations. This is what every black person has to go through. You can't come up in this country without having some negative feelings. It's better now, but it used to be that every time you saw somebody black it was in a negative sense—a black street cleaner or black janitor, Amos and Andy on TV. In other words there's a

* From *Twenty-six Ways of Looking at a Black Man*, by Raymond Patterson (New York: Universal Publishing and Distributing Corp., 1970); reprinted in *The Journey*, the Scholastic Black Literature Series, edited by Alma Murray and Robert Thomas (New York: Scholastic Book Services, 1970).

change that a black person has to go through. There are ways you must believe in yourself. Part of our problem in the ghetto schools is that we have people who don't love themselves. I don't think it's being racist to love yourself. We've got to get to the place where we respect and love black before we're going to respect anybody else . . . When Dr. King said, "I am black, but I am black and beautiful," see, that's what he meant. We have to keep saying it until we start believing in ourselves. Still we've got a few people that say, "Look at that old black guy, look at his big lips." We've got to learn: what's wrong with big lips? What's wrong with blackness?

I bring that up all the time. Kids used to tear the room down fighting over somebody that called them black. I don't have that any more. You know, I give James Brown* a lot of credit. That guy's done a lot of good. He can reach people we can't reach. He can reach most people really, someone like James Brown. A lot of our other black artists can do so much, you know, to help us out in this regard. People like Sammy Davis who have changed and gotten rid of that slick hair. Malcolm X, in his book, talked about why we want to wear a process, or what it *means* to wear one. Much of what he said, you know, is so true: you've got to respect your women; you've got to believe in yourself. Even if you take away all he said about white people, he's got almost a whole book of sayings that it would be good for *us* to follow now—black people.

That's why we can't just sit around crying about integration. I think we can, in our black schools, with the

---

* "[James Brown's lyrics] have often reflected the black man's intensified drive for self-pride and equality. No popular song in recent years has so thoroughly evoked the spirit of that thrust or so unanimously been adopted by the black community as James Brown's 'Say It Loud—I'm Black and I'm Proud' "—Mel Watkins, "The Lyrics of James Brown," in *Amistad 2*, edited by John A. Williams and Charles F. Harris (New York: Vintage Books, 1971).

proper motivation and the proper dedication, bring about amazing results. I really believe that, but I don't believe we've tried.

Separation has got to come first—because that's where we are; that's the reality of the situation. You've got to be able to deal from a power base; you've got to be able to talk to somebody as an equal before they accept you on an integrated basis.

BARBARA JACKSON
Boston

Barbara Jackson is a brown-skinned, middle-aged, graying Bostonian. "I'm an old maid but I have eight godchildren, four nieces and nephews, three grand-nephews . . . Her manner is informal, her competence unmistakable.

Noon. We sit and talk in a hot dusty little book room of the W. L. P. Boardman Elementary School, which she attended as a child. In 1965 it became the ungraded elementary education component of a new K-through-12 "model demonstration sub-system"* centered on Roxbury. Now Boardman's "open" program, pupil roster and teaching staff, including Miss Jackson, are about to move to

---

* The sub-system's K-through-12 structure includes the Lewis Middle School, in Roxbury, and Copely Square High School, downtown. It is operated by the Office of Program Development, a quasi-autonomous apparatus of the Boston School Department. Peter Schrag, in *Village School Downtown; Boston Schools, Boston Politics* (Boston: Beacon, 1967), describes the sub-system as "an effort to break the cycle of educational futility."

William Monroe Trotter.* This is to be a "magnet" for white pupils in sufficient numbers to prevent the racial imbalance prohibited (but not largely eliminated) under a 1965 state law against de facto segregation. Miss Jackson is a bit breathless: she has just finished conducting a long, arduous orientation meeting for the new Trotter teachers, most of them young, perhaps a fourth of them black, a heartening percentage male.

I've been teaching since 1945. I was at the Asa Gray Elementary School for twenty-two years. I've taught black kids all my life.

Would you say you're teaching them any differently here, at Boardman-Trotter?

Oh, definitely. I've loosened up so much. Before, you had to be the authoritarian figure: do it, or else! That kind of thing. Now you can let down and really get to know the kids. Before, you felt that you had your little ol' guidebook here and this guide tells you: you do *this* on a certain day; and you did it because you were learning and this guide was almost like a Bible to you. You were imposing that little guidebook on those kids not realizing that it might not meet their needs. It's like any profession. They teach you how to do a thing and, because they taught you that way, you feel *that* is the only way to do it. Flexibility comes with experience. This is what makes a new teacher different from an experienced teacher. I look to the children for direction more. I do not accept guides or people who claim to be authorities . . . Oftentimes another child's needs have been used to promote or publish materials. They're not suited to the needs of the ghetto child.

* Early-twentieth-century black militant intellectual and activist. Educated in Boston's public schools and at Harvard, he was co-founder with George Washington Forbes of the trenchant *Boston Guardian* in 1901, and its publisher and editor until his death in 1934. Efforts to name a public school for him go back to the 1950s.

What do you do instead?

If there is some sort of abnormality, some lack in achievement, I try to find out why this happened. If he is supposed to be at *this* level, why isn't he? A health condition? Or maybe he needs glasses. Or maybe he had this hearing test last year and nothing has been done about it. So you have to try to *find* where these kids are, and start from there. Sometimes it takes almost the whole year to actually get to know the child as completely as you can.

One boy was eight, a nonreader. There didn't seem to be any reason; he just didn't *like* to read. One day he told us about his German shepherd dog that was injured in an accident. As he was telling the story we copied it down and we read it in class. He was very pleased and he wanted a copy of it, so we had the story typewritten. He wanted it to be read again, so we did. Finally *he* wanted to read it himself. He virtually memorized it. We made copies and he gave them out to every child. He *went* to them. To capitalize on this we gave him a little reel of tape, and he could read his story onto the tape recorder, or any other story he knew. From his taped stories we gradually got him to read books. During that year he went two years beyond where he had started as a nonreader. He caught up with himself.

We had another boy—the same thing. Disenchanted with reading. But he liked to draw. We had a project on Africa in which he became interested. He drew a very large map and he was willing to do it again on special paper so we could mount it. He wanted to make a map of the explorations of Columbus, so we let him: "From now on you'll be our map maker because you make such wonderful maps." And then he went to the library, right up the street there. Instead of taking out a regular reading book, he took out an atlas and he made a map of Europe. For that he had to learn the names of the different countries. Then he found a map of the solar system, made one of his own and got to know the names of the different planets. He could spell out words but he wasn't interested in taking up a book just to see what was behind the cover. But now he had an incentive. He began to *use* books because he found out that this was a source of information about one thing he really liked to do. And this way we could integrate the reading with the drawing . . .

You just can't be successful if you don't know your product and your competition. And your competition is largely, for instance, television, records that the children play. I let them bring in their records, to let me know what they're listening to. Sometimes I even listen to these programs on Saturday morning, to find out. For instance, in the Apollo 10 they had Snoopy and Charlie Brown. Some adult people who came into my room and saw the diagram my children had made of that mission—they didn't know who Charlie Brown or Snoopy were. So you have to know what the children know. It starts from there.

I had a girl, about nine, who was very, very race-conscious. And we had this white student teacher that she didn't get along with. She was also a retiring girl, a slow learner, and I think she knew it. She had a "natural," so I had her make one day—she indicated that she'd like to do this—a full-size drawing of herself and put it on the front door; and she put over it: "Say it loud, I'm black and I'm proud!" James Brown, we have that record . . . This was her thing and that raised her ego, to see herself . . . Also I use this "Say it loud, I'm black and proud" to teach the *ou* sound. I take their language and start from there.

Is it unusual for a nine-year-old black child to be race-conscious?

[She sighs.] Often the youngsters are imitating adults, their parents. It depends upon their background, but I don't see anything wrong in this and I think we're at the stage where we have to . . . we've been made to feel so inferior that to have a super-ego, I think, is wonderful. It's going to be a happy balancing off, I think, with time. But we've had this *inferiority* complex, especially our males, so when they get this "*super*" complex I feel good about it. I'm sorry I didn't do that, that my generation didn't.

What would have happened if some kid had manifested any assertive race-consciousness in your classroom twenty years ago? Would you have reacted the same way then as you do now?

[A deep groan. A long pause. Then, softly] I don't know. Hm . . . I don't know. I was slapped down so many times myself. Everybody black in this business has been slapped down, in teaching, in everything [her voice regaining normal volume]. Even though I've lived all my life in Boston I've always been made to feel that I'm black and different and this kind of thing. I think I would be more sensitive to it and would react more realistically than perhaps a white teacher would. We have this chip on our shoulder, all of us have it, the black people. I'm in sympathy with anyone who shows it. Nothing wrong with it; you have to understand this.

I'm trying to understand something. The issues on which black people are speaking and acting today were there twenty years ago, too . . .

They were hidden, and we were too stupid to mention it. I was the only black teacher at my school twenty-four years ago. I'm the only black teacher in the primary grades in this school this past year. So you're always on a spot and you always have to do a little bit better, which I hate. Why do we have to be a little bit better? I think it's terrible. But it's true.

My mother and father wanted all of us to go to college, even though they only went up to the eighth grade.

My sister got a partial scholarship to Simmons. I mean, this was a family affair. We did it all together. We paid the tuition and we said, "Oh, fine. She can start her college career." And we got a bill for *five* dollars, for a gym jersey. Trying to get that five dollars was something—the straw that broke the camel's back. I remember it. This extra five dollars was a big thing in those days.

In my second year at Roxbury Memorial High they told me that Boston Teachers College, the only one I could afford to attend, was going to close down, so I took commercial courses thinking I'd go into clerical work after high school. At the end of my senior year they opened up the college and there I was, not eligible. I hadn't taken all the required courses. Since I had all A's in my commercial courses, I could take the college entrance exams. Teachers were willing to tutor me for two weeks in French, college math and history so that I could take the entrance examination. They took me to their homes and crammed all of this, and I passed.

I started college in 1941, and all during the war years it was a temptation to leave because of all those lovely government jobs but I stuck to it because my ultimate goal was this college education . . . I'd always wanted to be a teacher. I had a younger brother I used to take care of and I used to work with the other kids in school. We used to play school all the time.

And if you hadn't done "a little bit better" and hadn't worked a little harder than your classmates . . . ?

I never would have been appointed twenty-four years ago. In fact, when I was appointed, another teacher said, "What politicians do you know?" She couldn't believe I got it on my merit. Well, never mind. So being on your own you had to be so careful. You couldn't say the things that you would like to say, that you would say to your own, or now, in this kind of atmosphere, because . . . Well, I remember one white teacher. She asked why don't I go down to Washington and stay at this hotel. That was before Washington was even opened up. I didn't say anything but I thought, How stupid *are* you? because they didn't even realize, you know. They were so *stupid!* They didn't even realize the conditions that *I* lived under, that *I* couldn't go down to that hotel where she said she was having such a wonderful time. Twenty years ago people didn't realize. Until Alabama* and the sit-ins, they didn't realize the places we could not go—could not go on the trains, could not go on the buses. I mean, you go along in your own little way in your own little groups and you don't wonder, "Well, how come those black people are waiting at the back of that bus?" So now I would speak up about this. But I didn't say anything then. I just looked at her and said, "Oh no, I wouldn't care to go," and just left it sort of like that . . .

In Boston we had de facto segregation. We could go to all these places but of course they still didn't want us to go. I know a couple of times I went in a restaurant and they put me near the men's room and I'd just get up and walk out. I mean, that kind of thing, you'd expect it. Or, you come in and it's your turn, and you find out you're the last one to be waited on. Things like that, I didn't fight it. I just got up and left. I said, "The heck! If they don't want my money . . ."

But now these people are not taking it. This generation, which I admire, calls my generation cowards. So I can't say. I doubt very much that it would have happened twenty years ago [a black child asserting his race-consciousness in his classroom] because we were so . . . we were

* Specifically, the Montgomery bus boycott, December 5, 1955–December 20, 1956, inspired by Rosa Parks and led by twenty-six-year-old Martin Luther King, Jr.

such cowards twenty years ago. That child's parents would be my contemporaries and I was a cowardly Negro in college . . .

I mean, I knew about Neg—black history. I was always interested. In fact, for my master's thesis I wrote on Liberia, but these kids are *demanding* it now and it's wonderful to see references, even in second- and third-grade books to black history. We never got anything about it in school.

Has the change in the attitude of black people toward themselves and toward white America affected the tone . . . ?

The black people have lost confidence in white America. They looked to white America for answers but now they're no longer doing so. They've gained confidence in themselves. They're looking within themselves. And I think this is what I'*m* saying in a way: I'm assessing *my*self and I feel that I can speak better than some other people about what I feel is needed. I question people more. I question authority. I feel very personally involved with my kids. If I think they're being short-changed, I stick up for them and I try to do something about it. I'm more outspoken, but then I'm very unpopular because of this. So what?

The Boardman School, scheduled for closing after the move to Trotter, remained open as an annex of the sub-system's Lewis Middle School, providing a transitional program for sixth- and seventh-graders drawn from the Trotter Elementary and Lewis Middle School enrollments. Barbara Jackson is the assistant principal in charge. "Boardman is continuing the sub-system's open-education philosophy. Trotter? We haven't got all the answers but I think we're on the right track. It isn't just the new building. It's the feeling, the climate, the staff. New people have been selected for this. They're all geared for this."

BEATRICE GAVIN
Boston

I visit Beatrice Gavin's literature survey course. This is her sixth year in high school classrooms. She's personable, in her late twenties, stone Bostonian. Her skirt is mini, her teachership maxi. Students in her racially mixed class take turns reading aloud from The Canterbury Tales *in modern English. She doesn't interrupt to correct minor mistakes but occasionally provides verbal footnotes ("The age of chivalry tried to keep women on a pedestal," indicating her personal amusement at the notion). In reply to a question about the Prioress: "Well, she could be a nun who was having her fun." The atmosphere is informal, self-disciplined, brightened by occasional bursts of banter. The palpable peer-group rapport embraces rather than excludes her.*

We meet again at three o'clock. I want to know why a teacher who seems so capable of handling herself in any classroom would have wanted to change schools.

The administration at the other school was at first what you would call enlightened. We had a very good principal who wanted to innovate: "Anything you want to try, try it. If it works, good! If not, at least you've tried it." That's a wonderful way to begin teaching. You're not afraid to have your mistakes hung around your neck like an old albatross.

But then we got a typical politician of the Boston ilk. The curriculum was brought back to what the 1957 guide said it should be. I'm not just an English teacher. I think of myself as an educator, and to me these were very poor decisions. No reason for it except expediency. It didn't affect me or my department. It affected the school and it affected the kids.

I got tired of always feeling frustrated. Anything you wanted to do for the kids at that school, when you went through normal channels, you couldn't do. It got to the point where I really didn't feel that the administration was responsive to *anything* except crisis. I felt absolutely no loyalty to it, and therefore I was sabotaging administration policies to a greater or lesser degree, but it was constructive for the kids. I was getting angrier and angrier and angrier, and you can have only so much emotional tension, you know.

When I first went there the racial balance was about fifty-fifty. By the time I left, it was about 80 percent black. We had a fair number of slow-learning kids but also some very intelligent ones. Some of the older teachers would come out of a classroom very frustrated because you get kids, *white and* black today, who aren't going to just follow directions. You're going to have to be reasonable with them. They're not going to say yes ma'm, yes ma'm to everything. And these teachers, many of them, don't particularly care for black students or "this kind of student," as they kept on saying; they very seldom say "black," but "this kind." The antipathy is very seldom stated; the teacher is never really overt about it. I think sometimes they don't realize it themselves. But they don't allow for any mistakes, particularly on the part of black kids. And you can goad kids into doing something wrong. After you're with a child for a certain length of time you know what it takes to get that child aroused. I have seen teachers push and push and push, deliberately, until the child acts in an unfavorable way and they can bring him down to the office.

Why?

Some of it would be malice, some of it would be: "Get that kid out of my class. I didn't train for so many years to have to deal with this child in my class." It was mostly extended to all black kids, but usually the very slow, lethargic kids could escape this because when they were told to do something, they'd do it and it would be a "Yes, ma'm" thing. But the more intelligent black kid would be the one who would get into this difficulty. Usually we had really slow white kids, with some exceptions, and you'd get some pretty bright black ones; so it was the black kids who were more questioning and more troublesome to certain teachers who wanted blind obedience and absolutely no question or hand raised or anything of that sort.

Not all of the teachers were that way, were they?

In the English Department there were three of us and a fourth very quiet girl who wasn't . . . who really didn't like black kids and couldn't control them and was pretty miserable about it. So we didn't have too much to do with her—left her to her own devices, which was not good, not very Christian. It was a question, too, of the geography of the building. The three of us were on the same floor, and without telling anyone, we were able to do quite a bit. We would have team teaching, combined classes, independent study groups and a good many things on a smaller scale that we have on a large scale here. Anything we did about combining classes and having nongraded situations, that was marvelous with the first principal. The other people didn't care for it and they were too ignorant to know what we were doing so we went along our own merry way as far as English was concerned. But they wouldn't let us take any field trips at all because that was an inconvenience. They gave us a big run-around, saying it wasn't allowed by the city. We knew better and we pressed it, but, no field trips.

You mentioned a new teacher who couldn't control her kids. How was your first day?

It was scary. The first time I was ever alone in a room with black people . . . [she laughs] in my whole life.

Because I had gone to parochial school and then to college and occasionally you'd be in a *room* with a black person, and you'd kind of look, and satisfy yourself that he was safe [she laughs again] and you'd proceed . . . The group was half and half and I really didn't think I'd have much trouble. I brought them up to the classroom and sat them down, and I looked—and my stomach just dropped. I got panicky because I couldn't tell one black face from another and I—oooohh—I just got this big feeling, you know—fear. It was really fear. I didn't know how they'd react, and how you should talk to them and what you should say. It was a scary situation. And yet now I would not want to teach in any school that has fewer than 50 percent black kids. There's very little phoniness about them. If they don't like you they're going to let you know . . .

My first and biggest problem was that I was too authoritarian. You have to learn that just because you're the teacher, kids aren't necessarily going to say it's so; nor are they going to do what you ask; that cooperation has to be built on a mutual respect, and it takes time to build that. One particular group of kids were coming in late because they were going to the ladies' room and there was a rule about it. I was within legal rights but I was chewing at them and it got to the point where we were yelling at each other. I sat down and I said, "Gee, what do I look like to these kids?" The next day I dropped the whole teacher role which was actually a defensive thing. I started talking to them as people: "Hey, look. Do you realize what we are doing to each other? You came in late; you're wrong but, I mean, what's *your* point in this thing? You're in school because you *want* to be. I'm certainly not in school to fight with you. All right. Now, I'm going to chalk this all up to misjudgment on *your* part, and misjudgment on *my* part." I'd had them lined up for a series of punishments, staying after school, and going down to the principal and all that stuff. I canceled all that. Amnesty. Just by talking about it person to person, we ironed out the whole thing . . . When we did run into difficulty afterward it wasn't two parties geared for battle. There was a *ground* set, so you could talk about it.

What did your students like about learning English?

They loved grammar. These were kids, white and black, who chose to deal with specifics in the language. If you don't teach them grammar they don't think this is real English. They couldn't do it very well, but it warmed their very soul because they felt you were doing a good job and they were getting what they were supposed to be getting. Children of that age can be very conservative.

They loved plays, too. This was something you always knew would grab the kids, acting things out. I'd put on an occasional play; wrap them in sheets and stick 'em on a dingy old stage down in the cellar auditorium. It really came out very well. It improved their reading, their speech, their motivation. They learned how to analyze language. Very few times were we so formal as to have them memorize parts. When they did, it turned out very well. Most of the time I let them have their book. They'd work, and have their props set up and then we'd rehearse with them and get them all excited. They loved Shakespeare—*Romeo and Juliet* and *A Midsummer Night's Dream*. We also did *The Devil and Daniel Webster, I Remember Mamma* and *Riot,** a play about a race riot which went over very big with the kids. We were working on *A Raisin in the Sun* but we never got to the point of putting it on stage for people to see. We had begun it before Martin Luther King was killed. After he was killed there was just this terrible feeling that nothing the play said was really applicable or relevant,

* By Julia R. Piggin, in *Practical English*, Vol. 44, No. 13, May 9, 1968 (Scholastic Teacher edition).

that it was much too optimistic, generally, for what was happening today. We started out thinking it was a good play. The kids thought it was. The assassination changed it for us. Instead we decided to have a symposium on race relations. We dealt with the issues that the kids thought were most important: integrating schools, integrating neighborhoods, mixed marriages, busing, what the white people think of the black and what the black people think of the white, separatism versus integration; the issues that were tearing people apart. We had a panel of kids who rehearsed roles: a black conservative, a black liberal, a radical, right down the line. We gave them questions and we worked out how each would react, and we polished it. It was based on some of the experiments that were going on in the theater at the time, of trying to involve the audience so that they would become part of the production. This was toward the end of the school year and the teachers were very busy doing inventories and all such. So we just sent a note around asking the teachers to release these students to attend. We didn't take any kids unless they were released by a teacher. There were about a hundred and fifty.

The panel was up on the stage but what I did was to plug in a microphone down in the audience. The panel were fighting with each other and expressing all these extreme views. And then we had people planted in the audience who would stand up and scream things like, "The only thing for a nigger is a shot in the head . . ." Because one problem I saw with these kids—they never really confronted out-and-out prejudice, either black or white. And it got to the point where the kids in the audience were standing up and just screaming out, so then I said, "We can't have this. We'll give you the microphone. If you want to say something, you tap the microphone and you can say it." That was the only time I interposed myself. I had this terrific little lady up on the stage who moderated, a freshman. She'd cut somebody off, you know, and she'd say, "All right, I see somebody over here," or "somebody over there" . . . This was really run by the students. It went on all afternoon. This was two or three weeks after the assassination.

The kids left, very disturbed. Not in the usual way of going, seeing something, and then leaving. They were taking it out with them but they were also taking out a good amount of understanding. Not only that, they were made to take a stand of one sort or another, and that was my purpose: "No matter what you feel, if you make a stand, although it may not be *my* stand, I'll *listen*." Then the kids came after me, black kids I'd been friendly with. They'd say: "I hope you're satisfied. Look at what you've done . . . all the trouble you've made . . . people yelling at each other . . ."

Good! This is what I mean. People are too apathetic to want to question. They don't. They might feel something inside but they don't speak up. So I was making them "make a scene." They did it.

What was the reaction in the front office?

They didn't know. There wasn't any rule about getting the auditorium for any particular thing because it was such a small auditorium, never used as such, and we were always down there anyway, using it almost as a classroom. They were just never aware of it. The doors were closed and they couldn't hear anything going on in the auditorium. I really don't think they would have paid much attention to it if they had known. We didn't deliberately hide it but we didn't go out of our way to advertise it either. If you ask permission, people can say no but if you don't ask . . . hah! . . . *fait accompli*. It was legit. I could have explained it very well if they had asked me later.

The thing we had in that school: I could talk about pretty nearly anything and we could do pretty nearly anything, and it was kept among ourselves. We had great battles, I mean ideological battles, teachers and kids, because I never made any secret about how I felt about this, and you know, I learned a lot in that school.

Kids would come in and say, "We're going to have a riot." This was the day after Reverend King was killed. And I got angry because many of them were just playing and I said, "*What* kind of black people are *you?* You're not the black of Martin Luther King." It takes an awful lot to say that to an all-black class and by that time I had all-black classes except for a few white seniors. And you can say something like that because we have kids saying, "Well, I'm black." Right? So you have to be pretty honest with these kids but you have to lay down the ground so they can answer you. You can't crucify a kid in a discussion and let it stay just because you're the teacher. If you're going to say something like what I said about their reaction to Reverend King's death, you're going to have to defend it and you're also going to have to accept whatever answer you get back . . . They could say, "You're nothing but a white honkey . . ." and so forth. So I said, "Here is a man of peace who was devoted to showing you how to get what you wanted by peaceful means, and all you think of is violence. If you felt bad, you'd cry. *I* cried when I heard about it. I'm disgusted." I walked out of the room, for about five minutes, to let them calm down, because it looked as if we really were going to have a riot and some of the other teachers were kind of afraid. Then I went in and gave my same speech in a couple of other classes and some of the other teachers went *Ooh*-hoo-hoo-hoo [a ululating sound]. Actually, the majority of them stopped to think, but at first, as any kid would, they were carried away by the excitement of the moment.

What would you have answered if one of these kids had said to you, "Bull, Miss Gavin. My people have been crying about things like this for three hundred years and we're tired of crying. To hell with it. We feel like busting windows"?

[A short sigh, a long pause.] I would have agreed with them. It's very hard to say. There were some kids who certainly felt that way, and yet—I don't know . . . These kids, many of them, later did go out and get into riots. They didn't make any secret about it. They'd sit down and discuss it.

I remember one girl coming in and telling me, "I was real excited. We got all kinds of rocks together and went down to Blue Hill Avenue and we were stoning cars; yelling and screaming and running around and there was this car, and we finally got it to stop. That was fun, getting cars to stop. A woman got out of her car and she was bleeding, and she was alone with her little boy and he was bleeding. And you know, it didn't make any difference if she was black or white or anything. I just felt awful. My friend and I, we kind of went home. The others stayed. I didn't do anything any more."

The thing was, no matter what kids told you, you didn't start condemning them. You just talked to them and they might come to the point where you could say "That was wrong, wasn't it?" You can't just moralize from a dead start.

Right after the assassination, you know how they had these television programs that went on and on about it? They allowed us to watch it. And there were a lot of these talk shows on radio, people calling up to give their opinions. We were letting the kids, if they wanted to, call up and give their opinions, too. The front office didn't know the kids were phoning. They're not supposed to use the phone.

You have to keep all the lines open but . . . a phone was unofficially available to the kids that day.

Any of the students from your old school keep in touch with you?

Oh, yeah. Kids keep writing to me and I went to their graduation and I always see them because I shop in the same stores they do. They tell me who's had a baby lately and that type of thing, so you keep in touch. I felt bad leaving them and I still miss them. But teaching is teaching and kids are kids. There are kids over here and I care for them, too. Here I have a better chance to do *something* for the kids' education.

3

THE
CHILDREN

he talked revolushun
in a pea-green cap
shoving his hands
thru the air fingers
grabbing
he talked liberashun
in sneakers with
holes in the toes
and frayed edges at
the ankle part

he talked freedom
with a quiver in
his voice and his
tee shirt pulled
out of his pants
at the back the
belt didn't fit
right

and i listened
smiling
nodding my head in
hearty agreement
he was 9 years

old
and his paper from
school said
we want freedom
and liberashun
and revolushun
NOW!!

with exclamation marks
painted carefully in
red-black-green
drippy paint.
he talked revolushun
in a pea-green cap
hanging precariously
on the edge of his
glasses

and i smiled
and knotted my fist
to him as i left

wondering
will he ever see
the day?

—Lyn ("For That Little Brother
Whose Name I Never Got")

ALFRED AIELLO
Cleveland

We happened to be the only Italians in the block in the whole area, so we were the dagos, the little wops. That helped me understand what was going on . . . I can recall incidents in my youth that really bothered me, that I became emotional about. Ridicule. I had empathy with the person who was being ridiculed . . .

Fred Aiello values the sensitivities he developed as a featherweight ethnic rarity growing up on Cleveland's (white) West Side. They were strengthened by benign interracial contacts not uncommon for native Clevelanders, and by his service in the World War II Marine Corps. He has been principal of John W. Raper Elementary School ever since its opening in September 1962.

Raper stands on East Eighty-fifth Street in Hough Heights, one of the city's high-compression black-poverty areas. Aiello, light-footed, nimble-minded, stands in the middle of everything, to the best of his ability, which is considerable. In the opinion of Clevelanders who have written off school integration: "If community control really happens around here, Aiello won't have to worry about his job." Or, "If the time ever comes when there are enough black teachers . . . Aiello will be the last to go."

He doesn't theorize about integration versus separation. And he doesn't worry about keeping his job but about doing it, in concert with the parents/community he serves.

The school? What do we want it to be? Hmm . . . We'd like it to be [he sighs deeply] a place where youngsters can develop their potential. That sounds "canned." We'd like it to be a place where children can feel free, can find warmth; a place that stimulates youngsters, a friendly place and needed. This is what we try to be. By doing that, we feel we can turn the youngsters on. That's what is needed to do the job anywhere but particularly here, with youngsters who have a whole spectrum of learning inhibitors operating on them. All the problems that you identify with the poor and with the victims of prejudice, I consider to be learning inhibitors. So, they have to be compensated for, and part of that is meeting physical and human needs. This means we operate as a social agency whenever it's necessary.

We're in the business of raising funds here, not only for supplies [beyond the limits of his official budget] but for shoes and clothing and things of that sort. Our children operate a store for supplies, and our parents operate a clothing store on Wednesdays. Just for shoes [to supply to children who need them] we collect between twelve and fifteen hundred dollars a year. We have a shower program and we've gotten an okay on a washer and dryer from the Board of Education. We intend it for the use of the community as well as for our own children. Our library we use for the breakfast kitchen, too. We want a partition. That'll take time. We have about a hundred volunteers who come in during the week, in every category, tutors primarily, aides, enablers, money-getters. Most of our help comes from outside the district, from the churches that are involved.

Kids who want to avail themselves of the shower facility may do so once a week. The school provides "towels, soap, supervision and instruction." At the same time, the children's clothing needs, especially undergarments, are checked out and supplied. Since the clothing demand is far in excess of the school's supply capacity, Aiello wanted to use the washer-dryer for the first step in re-cycling children's clothes from a stockpile to be built up by donation

*and/or low-cost purchase. A year and a half after he ac-
quired the washer-dryer unit, Aiello has written me, it was
still lying inert in the school basement.*

*Red tape and the possibility of hassles with local
union officials often make it inadvisable for spirited school
administrators such as Aiello to call for the help of technically qualified volunteers from the community.*

Our concern for the youngsters must be primary. Secondary is the development of the academic skills. The two
are closely related. You can't really divorce them. So we're
heavily committed to involvement, anything it takes to be
a neighbor in the community.

What other kinds of involvement . . . ?

To whatever extent we can do it, we have a free exchange between school and community, people coming in
and going out. We give our community as much control as
we're allowed to give. That's part of it. We have a Parents'
Advisory Committee which is very, very effective. They
meet monthly and have real advisory capacity, authority,
responsibility. They holler at me and I bring problems to
them. Our understanding is that if they have a concern
about curriculum, practice or procedure of any kind and I
can't justify it to them, then I have an obligation to change
it. If I can, they have an obligation to accept. So we work
on that basis.

And we have a Representative Council of parents,
teachers and our own children. This is kind of an experiment with us: Can elementary children relate to school
and community problems? So far we've found they can. Up
to this point we've allowed the children to initiate the
discussions. They're concerned with why they can't have a
lunch program, why they can't use the school in the evenings, and one question— the kids raise this—is: What are
parents doing to improve the behavior of our children?
They're just great. So that's another involvement.

Then, we invite the parents of each grade in turn for coffee on Friday mornings at ten o'clock for a weekly grade meeting, just to talk to me and the teachers about anything that's on their minds.

We also have a couple of programs that force our teachers to get into the community on an individual basis, in what we call a reverse open house. We close school early once a month and the whole staff goes out on coffee klatsches with parents and others. The effect on the community is great. Then we have a few friends who provide the fifty dollars it takes to keep the school open one evening a week for sewing classes, a buyers club, physical fitness for women, teen groups, that kind of thing. We operate a fathers club, which is struggling but at least we have one, and they meet regularly even though no one shows up sometimes.

There is also a bigger, broader community which includes all of the militants, the verbal people, the spokesmen. We bring in leaders in the community to relate to our youngsters and to our people whenever something's come up. When community control first became a national issue, we brought in people who were espousing that, to talk to our faculty: "What do you mean by community control? How can we get together?" Same thing with Black Nationalism; we brought in spokesmen for that point of view and we have a good relationship with the Afro Set.* In

* A grouping of youthful black Clevelanders, militant and nationalist. Regarded with chronic suspicion and hostility by the police department, the Afro Set has a more positive image among large segments of the city's black community. On the evening of July 23, 1968, a shoot-out between policemen and black militants left seven dead and fifteen wounded. During the week of intense civil strife which followed, Harllel Jones, Afro Set leader, played an outstanding role in Mayor Stokes' emergency committee to help bring about a "cease-fire." Nevertheless, the Set's craft shop and meeting hall were twice invaded and vandalized by white policemen that week; Jones was arrested, but later acquitted, on a charge of having a revolver in his car. Subsequently he sued for false arrest. A full

fact, one of them sits on our Parents' Council. And so we've gotten a reputation for being willing to explore. Our staff is willing to sit and listen, then we have several meetings, depending on the interest, to try and find ways that we can get together.

Does that mean you get along pretty well with the whole spectrum of Black Nationalists and separatists?

Oh, yes. We have no problem with them because we've been very open to their suggestions about what they think is necessary and we find that we have very little to disagree with. All of the problems we've had in schools, the riots and so on, everywhere, has resulted originally from a reluctance on the part of the people in power to sit and listen. When we've listened we've found we have much in common on many of the things we're doing in some of our programs.

Black studies, grades one through six, have been taken seriously in Raper's curriculum from the school's very beginning in 1961, several years before most big-city school systems began to feel intensive pressure from Black communities.

At first we taught it separately because the children need to know the importance of what they are studying. Then we tried integrating it for a couple of years because there was some strong feeling that we were isolating the subject. After the Black Nationalists became prominent we found out that what they were doing [as teachers of black history] was very effective, so we decided to go back and teach it specifically. We integrate it whenever we can, but it ought to be taught specifically.

---

account of Cleveland's week-long state of civil insurrection, prepared as a report to the National Commission on the Causes and Prevention of Violence, is accessible in a paperback: *Shoot-Out in Cleveland*, by Louis H. Masotti and Jerome R. Corsi, published by Bantam Books (New York, 1969).

You keep saying "We are involved." How about you, individually?

I started out knowing that if you're going to be a neighbor, black or white, you have to be concerned with what concerns others. So after a number of years of passive participation, knowing my place, not offering advice unless I was asked, not pushing myself but being visible, there has developed the kind of relationship so that I'm involved in everything. I'm *invited* to be involved in everything. It's very time-consuming, four nights a week and so forth, but that's been important. Whenever there is something the community is concerned about, Aiello is visible.

Where would you be now if I weren't in your office?

I'd still be here. The meeting doesn't start until seven thirty. What meeting? Oh, I'm secretary of the Area Council. It deals with everything—community problems. This is really the most influential group in any community, at least in Cleveland. They were formed a long time ago, I guess by organizers in the welfare department, but now they're self-perpetuating. They're incorporated and they run their own organization. Anybody can join if they work or live in the community. There are representatives from all groups. [Only about half a dozen whites participate. Aiello is the only white officer.]

Are you and your school committed to any particular educational philosophy, right now at least?

We're experimenting with Glasser's "schools without failure"* approach. We're trying to make children respon-

---

* William Glasser (M.D.), *Schools Without Failure* (New York: Harper & Row, 1969). Psychiatrist-educator Glasser says that "the problem of failure" and its massive incidence is the built-in result of education which does not guarantee initial experiences of success to schoolchildren and which obliges them to measure their performance by rigid, competitive norms rather than against their in-

sible for their own behavior and for their schooling. We've eliminated the grade cards. Hopefully we'll eliminate grades, and we eliminated corporal punishment. It's a whole involved program but it's based on respect for the individual and getting the youngster to deal with his problems. I hope you can see examples while you're here of the feeling our people have for children. It's not all great. We don't do all that much, but it's in the right direction, I think. Here children are human beings. I know *I* treat them that way, and I'm allowed to do this; they're important people.

On corporal punishment, the parents are split. We've had about fifteen meetings this year to get them acquainted with our new project [the Glasser program] and it's been very difficult. For the youngsters, too, because corporal punishment is what they're used to, and when they don't get it they've had the tendency to feel that you don't care. Now after three or four months it's getting across to them that when we paddled a child, *we* were assuming responsibility for *his* bad behavior; paddling didn't make *him* assume it. When we've had real problems, parents would say, "You're not doing your job. If you'd only beat them that would take care of it, so don't keep asking me to come in."

We still do have one rule. When kids are involved in a fight, even on Sunday, in church or somewhere, both parties get paddled. The standards we have in this building are carried on twenty-four hours a day, seven days a week, which is maybe a little unusual. The law says that after children are dismissed from school and on their way home,

---

dividual sense of self-esteem. Key words in his treatise are "involvement," "relevance," "thinking," "responsibility," defined in relation to learning and teaching. The body of the book comprises Dr. Glasser's proposals for the practice of these concepts "combined into a total program" intended to reverse the failure/low self-esteem /failure cycle. The atmosphere of such schools, their curricula and their populations would be recognizably "open."

we don't have any responsibility for what happens on the street, but we deal with it all the time. I think this makes a difference. They get paddled not for fighting as such but for breaking the rule that says, "If you have to fight, you come in and ask to put on the gloves and we have the fight, if we can't settle it any other way." I'm the referee and nobody watches, you see. They can get out of being called chicken; they can give in if they want to; the crowd doesn't keep them fighting when they shouldn't be. This works. The girls, we expect them to be ladies, so we suspend them immediately, until we can have a conference, and this works, too. Last week I refereed half a dozen fights but usually it's about one a month.

Who does the paddling?

Either I or the assistant [principal] or one of the three administrators. It doesn't happen very often.

How do you feel after you've paddled a kid?

Very poorly. I get angry and really it [the paddling] is of no help to me. It's therapy for a person who's a parent. It's what the normal parent, the concerned parent, does with his own children. We're not talking about eliminating every swat on the back but about punishing a child for doing a particular thing, with a beating as the answer. When you have to do it, that shouldn't be taking the entire responsibility away from the youngster.

When I do have to paddle a child, we talk afterward, quite a lot—about why it was necessary, what I expect of the youngster, how he's capable of doing a great deal more, and what it is that I have to admit when I resort to paddling him, namely, that we weren't able to take care of it—he couldn't, and I couldn't. So we generally leave with my arm around him. It doesn't always work, either. But we do talk. This is the pacifier . . . [He lifted the lid of a leather-covered box filled with hard candy.] It helps when we're talking . . . It's *how* you lay the hand on.

You try to meet the children's "physical and human needs" to compensate for "a whole spectrum of learning inhibitors." Have you been able to measure the effects of this kind of effort on the kids' achievement levels? I mean, how do they test out?

Everybody asks that . . . They want to have something they can put their finger on and say, "Show me! *This* is the progress curve." I tell them, "No. Our goal is more complex than showing achievement in academic areas." But I think we can see differences in our youngsters. Everybody who comes in here tells us that. There *is* a difference. Our youngsters feel a little bit more comfortable, a little bit better about themselves. If we continue, we should be able to see some general achievement . . . I think our youngsters are better off now than they were. Our children getting out of sixth grade probably do better on achievement scores than a lot of kids from schools in comparable areas. I think our children stay in school longer, after leaving us, than children coming from another situation. A lot of them keep in touch with us . . . As much as I believe in compensating and removing the barriers to learning, I haven't been all that successful . . . It's being done, let's say, by *this* teacher, and three more aren't really *actively* doing this kind of thing at all . . . That's not enough to make a whole big change in a kid's academic achievement record.

Does that mean your staff suffers from some "teaching inhibitors"? How do you compensate for those?

Even though I have many concerns about their depth of commitment, their willingness to adopt our philosophy, I'd still have to say that of all the staffs in the city of

Cleveland, pound for pound, ours is the best. Maybe that's not saying much, but it's a good group.

The last couple of years I've refused to take any experienced teachers, not because I don't need them but because they wouldn't fit into what we wanted to do. They were too traditional. So there are some hang-ups by taking only new people. We lose them. They're always getting pregnant, and many new teachers aren't really teachers. But I just made up my mind I prefer having a young person who is willing to change, to be innovative. The experienced teachers who can "do the job" are dedicated to teaching the skills, without recognizing that they have to open the doors first. You have to get children to open up, to be secure, to have a good image, to love you. Magic things happen to people through love. You'd do almost anything for a person you admire and love and respect, so—why not do that? Doing the job in a traditional way has been a failure here.

And so we're trying to train our own, and all of these young people just may blossom. By the end of the year, I'll have to see how many of them made it. If I have a high percentage who are limping along, I may have to take some experienced teachers just to maintain some control . . . With a higher percentage of young teachers who are having problems, we have a building atmosphere that is not as positive as we'd like to have it. The building atmosphere determines what the children do. See? New people come in. They feel what's going on. If they come into an atmosphere that's productive and positive and children seem to like each other and are open, the newcoming teachers move into it, too. If it's one of hostility, if children are always being yelled at, young teachers who are having problems with their classes develop an antagonism that becomes part of their teaching personality.

You have to demonstrate a concern for our youngsters, to be human with them, to show respect, but you still have

92

to dig like the devil to get the skills. You have to be relevant and you have to motivate, but that doesn't mean playing games all day, either. So we've had some real discussions over this . . . A lot of teachers haven't lasted here too long because children find them out too easily; all fun-and-games and very little teaching substance. The teacher who comes in saying, "I don't care if they like me or not; I just want them to learn" doesn't come through as a mean teacher, if he really means that. He's the person who's innovating anyway, who's working hard to make things successful. Children can tell whether you're for real or not.

Our teachers are pretty free and open because they have plenty of opportunity to be. We run our school a little bit differently from maybe other schools. We organize the staff like secondary schools. We have grade rather than department chairmen, not paid, but I give them what free time I can. When special-subject teachers come into the building, the chairmen get their services first, so that they have some released time, and I use them as administrator-supervisory personnel. Right now I also have an assistant principal and an administrative intern. Then we have our elected six-teacher Staff Council. They meet with me monthly for dialogue, communication, developing programs and so on. We have a union conference committee, elected by the union members. This also meets monthly. We do about the same things.

We have a variety of committees that generally operate. We have a Project Committee; we sell candy or we have pictures. or whatever. Forty percent of whatever we earn on any project the teachers are involved in goes into a kitty and they determine who's to get that. The teachers apply to the Project Committee for funds. These are very, very mini grants.

Then we have our Human Relations Committee, which meets in staff members' homes once a month. We also have weekly evening "pot lucks." We get some great food and it enables teachers to get together. Teachers never have an opportunity to share experiences or to dialogue . . . We have weekend workshops, too, occasionally. And we've been operating an in-service program two evenings a month to develop this Glasser project. We're all involved in the determination of policy. The teachers have some say in what goes on here. But, like our community, they're reluctant to pay the price of involvement, which means assuming some responsibility . . . Our women teachers don't get involved in the evening to the extent I would like them to. Their husbands demand them at home. Some of our men become involved, but mostly during the day. It hasn't been easy getting teachers voluntarily to move out of the classrooms and into the street, not easy at all. They're afraid; they're defensive because it's been in vogue to attack schools. Well, many of our people who are successful will accept it. After all, it's criticism, and we have to admit that there's reason for attack. We've had several community meetings that developed into that kind of thing. When the Black Nationalists come in, our black teachers get *very* defensive. When Afro styles first became popular we brought somebody in to talk about hair at our PTA and our parents became defensive. Some of the teachers don't really believe this is necessary, becoming too familiar, too involved with our people. See, "I'm here to teach these children and not make them happy. I don't need to know."

Does this reluctance to circulate in the community involve any physical fear?

Our new people, yes. Some of our white female teachers who haven't yet made it here have had an unconscious fear. We have it come up all the time with our volunteers. We have teenagers bused in from the high schools to tutor our youngsters and that's always a concern. But we've *never*, in eight years, had any physical attacks on any of our people. Even though our influence doesn't extend too far—our district is only three or four blocks long and a block wide—and even though a lot of people *don't* know us personally, the word apparently gets around. And Raper is open one evening a week to adults. But our teen-agers have come in and wanted to play ball, so we've established discussion groups on sex and drugs and things of that sort, as well as basketball. Generally community people and some of our staff plan the programs and we meet with the teenagers to help them develop discussions and so forth . . . We started with adults and allowed teenagers to come in but now my children, the Raper children, want to be here evenings, too. *"It's our school! Why can't we come?"* So it's more than I can handle. I pull my hair out every Thursday: "I've got to have more *volunteers.*"

What were the black teachers being defensive about?

We have the black *middle-class* teacher who has a bigger hang-up than our white people . . . sensitive to their background and the fact that our children are poor. They're nonaccepting of children who are dirty and vulgar, some of them; and so on. Our black teachers have a tendency to be more traditional, unwilling to try new approaches, unwilling to be warm with youngsters because the way to "get there" is you got to put your nose to the grindstone and if you mess up you get beaten. They're the ones who have the most difficulty giving up corporal punishment. That's the way *they* made it. They had to work hard. Second, black teachers are apt to be sensitive because the white community has always held blacks to be lazy, so they want to dispel that idea. There is also a feeling that to be innovative or to be human . . . the children have too much fun. Our white teachers are the ones who have been the most innovative. So there's a hesitancy now because Whitey is here and *he's* doing this and he doesn't really care. They feel that Whitey doesn't stay long enough and so he wants them to like him while he's here [it makes his job easier]. He's not really concerned about getting those skills. Time *is* too often wasted in innovation for innovation's sake.

Do you think of teaching primarily as an art or a science?

It has elements of both. I would think primarily it's an art. I can teach a person the techniques of teaching, the science of it, but that doesn't assure anyone that learning will take place. It will, if we have children who are open, comfortable, who have good self-images. Under those circumstances learning takes place without any special kind of technique. We can enrich it, make it happen faster, but real teaching is an art. It's the ability to recognize what children are thinking and doing, what they're sensitive to, the nonverbal clues they give. You know, you almost have to be born with that kind of thing. You have to be sensitive yourself.

Our children, especially, can read another human being quickly and accurately because of a skill they've had to develop to survive. A good teacher has to be able to capitalize on that. They have to have techniques, I guess, but the ability to use them to the best advantage, that's a real art. You have to be a showman, to begin with. You have to be willing to get next to people—how to win friends and influence people. That's an art, isn't it? It's a feeling; it's the compassion a person has, and if they have the science—boy!—they're really tremendous teachers.

Some who are lacking in the art can develop it; they do. You can't be with human beings as intimately as a teacher is with young children without having them affect you. There're constant emotional experiences going on in the classroom. These are what produce changes in teachers, and if it's possible to make them negatively different, it is certainly possible to go the other way. So, constant confrontations, exposure—it's a learning situation, and the teacher is constantly learning. My experience—I'm *constantly* learning. The things that I get, along with the frustrations—I haven't given *nearly, nearly,* as much as I've taken and I think that's the way it is with everybody on the staff. Children sure have taught me about people . . .

I've heard very enthusiastic comments from individuals outside the system. What do the people "downtown" feel about it?

We've had our problems. We weren't very well accepted in the early days. Until just a few years ago we had no autonomy in Cleveland. We had to follow general policy. I have never done that in the eight years I've been here. We've just gone ahead and done what we thought was necessary. Well, a couple of things happened. I spent a month in New York one summer at Bank Street College in an integration workshop which had great impact on me. I started this buddy program. It was just taking classes, white [from other schools] and black, and having trips together, spending the day together and so on. Well, then all my problems began.

Then, after the riots* here, the U.S. Commission on

* Between January 1964 and the July 1968 shoot-out there were several major episodes of antiblack violence. On January 29, 1964, a mob of whites tried to push pickets at a "white neighborhood" school off the sidewalk into the path of oncoming automobiles. The next day a crowd at the intersection of two main streets in "little Italy" attacked black auto drivers. On April 6, the Reverend Bruce Klunder, white, died under the treads of a bulldozer during a nonviolent effort to stop the construction of a school building at a site which was the subject of community protests. A night of store looting and clashes with police followed. On June 22, 1966, a crowd of blacks threw rocks and bottles at police because they refused to investigate an attack on two black youths by a gang of whites whose car was still on the scene. On July 18, 1966, a sign, NO WATER FOR NIGGERS, on the door of a bar at Seventy-ninth Street and Hough Avenue precipitated "the Hough Riot," a week of mass

Civil Rights had a hearing in Cleveland [April 1–7, 1966] and I happened to be one of two principals who were asked to give testimony . . . All of a sudden the things we were doing, at least the philosophy and the intent, were the accepted thing. It was the only thing in Cleveland at the time that the Commission could point to and say, "Hey, there's something going on." So instead of a liability we became an asset but we've never been any kind of a "fair-haired" school. Right now it's a kind of "hands-off" policy; we don't get any special considerations but nobody bothers us any more either. You know, there's scuttlebut and rumors about what our status is and what my status is. I'm pretty well convinced it'll never be any different from what it is now. But at least they [the upper levels of the Cleveland schools administration] aren't negative. They don't put stumbling blocks in our way any more. The last year or two there's been a big push on involvement and so it's changing a little. We no longer stand out.

You said before: frustrations. What are the satisfactions?

The relationships, obviously, not only with my youngsters but with the staff and the community; the things I've been taught. I'm working with people and children who are more open than anybody I've ever been around. They're more exposed to life. They're more realistic about it. They're people who have been able to handle massive kinds of problems and still exist. Just communicating about that kind of thing, I've been richer for it. And if you have any successes here at all, then your successes are beautiful. And when your concern and love is returned, it's returned like a thousand percent and it's warm and sincere, not the phony kind of thing. When a youngster comes up to me and he or

---

civil conflict approaching the intensity of Watts and Newark. Aiello could not recall this sequence off the top of his head but he understood why I asked, "Which riot?"

she puts his arm around me while we talk, you know, that's—that's just great. Most teachers experience this. In our community, when you're walking down the street, everybody knows you, all the children do. And the young adults, who would normally ignore you in this day and age, they identify you, and it's ju-u-ust—kind of nice. When they see you in a crowd or at another school and they say, *"Hey, Mr. Aiello!"* [he chuckles] there's some human feeling being transmitted.

And when we get into trouble there are people who come to our defense. We've had a couple of incidents here . . .

To be accepted, to be given responsibility, to be given trust . . . What else does a human need but to be recognized by other humans and to win their respect?

HARRY FINKS
Cleveland

In the center of Harry Finks's sixth-grade class, Room 229, at John W. Raper Elementary School, five students are on their feet, engaging in a mute exchange of contacts, gestures, gyrations, grimaces. The group is followed by two others, each performing its own set of antics. The rest of the class watches intently, appreciatively, laughing at the performers' occasional difficulties in giving or getting the message. What these kids are up to is revealed in a duplicated briefing sheet headed "Mission Impossible?":

"Your task is difficult. You have only thirty minutes left during which you may speak or write in your own

language. At the end of thirty minutes you must be able to communicate with your group but without either writing or using your voice . . . one of you will be called on to demonstrate how well you understand your new invented (unspoken) language. Work wisely and be sure each of you masters the following in your group's own language: "a name for each one in your group; a list of seventeen concrete verbs, verb phrases and nouns, plus any 5 other words your group selects."

Okay, these are exercises in nonverbal, nonliterate communication, but what for? What does Finks hope his pupils will learn?

I just have felt a need, always, to get to where students can cooperate; where there is something in which they need to organize themselves, to evaluate themselves individually and as a group. The whole purpose has been to come up with tasks that to be completed, everyone has got to be involved, and involved enough so that there is a group result. We do these "Missions Impossible?" once or twice a week.

How did you arrive at this conviction? That you need to work as a group?

Well, to me it's basic that people *respect* people. The ugliest thing I have ever watched in any situation anywhere is places where people have no respect for each other. I have watched a number of classes be very negative and bicker and fuss back and forth constantly. If you'd say, "You two work together" they would never get past calling each other names. I've had this same class for, well, this is its second year. [Finks became their sixth-grade teacher when they moved up to the fifth.]

I found that working as a group and accomplishing anything was very unusual, so I decided that was going to be one thing I attacked separate from the "Okay, now you'll do this assignment or that assignment." If they can work on some task with just the idea of coming together and working together, then we can do better in things like social studies. They get used to the idea that a group is more than just one person, that to be a part of that group you have to contribute and also you have to lead and be led, receive and give and all that. Understand? I do find a carry-over in it. I think the children have developed a respect and, well, a kind of sympathy toward each other that I have not seen in classes I dealt with before. I admire them very much for the fact that they can laugh, and not laugh *mean* at somebody who says something kind of dumb, and that if Arthur's group doesn't get there, they're all not harassing: "Look, they can't do anything." Which is something.

Other "Mission Impossible?" tasks:

Using a selection of foreign postage stamps to develop geographical, political, historical and aesthetic information and "creatively think of other ways mail systems could work with no postage stamps (. . . with short explanations");

Conceiving of ways to improve seven common objects: pencil, banana, automobiles, bicycles, fried chicken, hallways, watch dogs; diagramming and writing out the improvement for each;

Producing a folder of plans, in complete detail, for the group's idea of a "perfect school camp." (Many of Finks's students were familiar with camps operated for Cleveland public school children, from experience or hearsay.)

Every "Mission Impossible?" briefing sheet begins: "Your task—should you decide to accept it . . ." Each member of the group is provided with a small form on which to evaluate himself, other individuals and the group as a whole in their performance of the task. There are also class discussions immediately afterward.

I'm kind of proud of the way they *are* able to function together, and it certainly has not been an accident. I've worked with a lot of beginning teachers whose classes are constantly at each other, and because there is no "we" feeling, no inner strength, the classes kind of go sideways, whereas most of the time we go forward—certainly not all the time.

You put a lot of emphasis on cooperation, on commitment of the individual to the group, et cetera. How does that equip your kids for "making it" in our highly competitive society?

It doesn't. It just helps. We do a great, great number of things that are strict competition, except I can't believe that a person is going to function totally as a lone competitor out for himself. I definitely have never let a child leave the sixth grade if I didn't feel he was able to cope with competition. I think all children need to be able to function alone, with groups, and in all kinds of situations. I use any kind of situation I can put together. The sad thing is we have to resort to so many "put together" situations instead of things that really come up. But in racial situations as well as social situations I'll work as hard as I can to provide everything that I believe a child needs to have. This particular class is going to spend twelve days in Wyoming at the end of the school year. We've worked on it the whole past year. We'll work on it for the rest of this school year until May 31st when they go, with the idea of really preparing for the social experience of staying in a home with whites who live there, the idea of being on a float trip down a river in the complete wilderness, this type of thing. I'm trying to find every type of experience that people like to call normal and give it to children who wouldn't ordinarily have it. They went last year to Washington, D.C. The trip itself is not the thing as much as the preparation—where they know what it is like to be in a motel and when they know what it's like to order food in a cafeteria; where they know what it's like to be in situations that ordinary middle-class people, so to speak, give their own children. You know, the home provides its curriculum.

What's so great about knowing how to order food in a cafeteria?

Are you really seriously asking that? . . . I think it's just part of—of *living;* that as long as there are going to be cafeterias . . . on television they watch people walk down cafeteria lines, taking and filling a tray and going to the end of the line to pay. And if it's still as unreal as seeing movies of Chinese people planting rice, then there's something kind of wrong. This is part of America, certainly not a huge beautiful exciting part, but it is assumed to be common in ordinary life. It's *not* ordinary to these kids . . .

A friend of ours who was a volunteer in my class three years ago was transferred to Wyoming—she's the wife of the Episcopal bishop there—and she said, "If you could get money enough to bring them, we'll host them." They'll be doing a lot of things that are, to me, beyond what ordinarily would happen with a person. Yet I really believe you've *got* to go beyond that because very little distant traveling ordinarily *ever* happens for these kids the way things are now. Their family is not going to Yellowstone next summer, or the *next* summer . . .

We'll bus from here to Chicago and take a train to Laramie from six in the evening until twelve noon the next day. I want them to get the size of the country into their heads. Probably that is as clear a way to do it as any. In Laramie we will be met by people in the Episcopal diocese. As good as it is for the children, the different people who are hosting us are going to get maybe more than the children do from the trip. They're not that used to inner-city children. Also these are not really typical. They've already experienced more than some children in their community ever will.

They'll be taken out to a ranch with all the horseback riding just immediately to get something very active. Then they'll spend the night at homes in Laramie. Then we'll start crossing the state and go into Thermopolis which has a very large hot springs which I didn't even know existed. Then on to Cody, where there will be ceremonial Indian dances, stopping at an Indian reservation to spend the night in Indian homes. From there, on to the Yellowstone–Jackson Hole area, where they will stay in not just cabins but really a nice place. After about three days in Jackson and around in there, back through Buffalo, which I know a little about. There's a ranch they'll be staying at there. Then we'll take our bus back to Denver and fly back to Cleveland. The adult complement will be my wife and I and two parents and a teacher's wife plus adults working with us out there. It's a six-or-seven-thousand-dollar undertaking and we have the money already.

During the full school year, 69'–70', Wyoming was the learning axis on which much of the curriculum and dozens of worksheets turned. The children learned to use topographical, population and route maps; studied Indian history and culture; heard guest speakers on the American West; read the daily U.S. weather maps for Denver, Cheyenne or Cleveland; learned to use movie equipment; participated in working out the itinerary, clothing lists, finances and parent-class relations. They briefed themselves on the identities of flora, fauna, towns, and the individuals they were to meet. Some of them also spent a night at the Finkses' home in sleeping bags on the floor as a training exercise.

Private foundations and the Rotary Club provided substantial sums for the Wyoming expedition. There was also a strong trickle of small donations, plus income from school-sponsored fund-raising projects and from the "Tiny Tiger Co.," a school-supplies store stocked, staffed and managed by the children in the class. "It took a lot of begging on my part and a lot of hard work on the children's part."

It's a reasonable guess that Finks's success in financing the Wyoming trip is related to the "home curriculum" of his own growing-up years.

. . . I'm from a very rural Missouri background, a town of seven thousand people, south of Kansas City. My father is a banker in a small-town bank and this is what I always thought I would do.

Teach?

Be a banker. I went through college [Westminster, a Presbyterian men's school in Fulton, Mo.] in economics, planning still to go into business with my father when I got home. I finished school in '61. Right after college the Peace Corps came out and my wife and I immediately applied. She had just finished two years of college and I was at a point where I really wanted to do something like the Peace Corps. We applied and weren't immediately accepted because it was just barely in the planning stages and they didn't really have one. I had a fellowship to George Washington University, in government—I had business and government *both* in my head. But I still hadn't turned toward teaching.

We had been in Washington for one semester of graduate work when the Peace Corps notified us there was an opening in the Philippines for teachers . . . So we had three months of doing nothing except Peace Corps training. Then we had two years of probably the happiest life we'll ever have, teaching and living in a very, very rural town that we just loved. I would go back there right now; I would live there my whole life if I could, if they needed

American teachers; but they've got a surplus of teachers. Anyway, we taught for two years and enjoyed it very, very much. You see, I have some skill as a teacher and I really like teaching children. True, it was a deprived situation where there were no supplies and just very crude things to work with, but we devised many things that worked very well and, there, discipline was not a consideration.

So after extending a little bit of overtime in the Philippines, we went back to Missouri. I went into the bank and was totally unhappy. I could see immediately that I just cannot sit behind a desk. I gave it enough time that I knew it wasn't just a reaction, then I went back to school and got myself certified to teach. My wife finished her last two years of school and we got through her student teaching, and were all ready to start. We wanted to go to the city because we thought by now that America's area of need is the city.

We read about Cleveland trying to get returning Peace Corps people, giving them some kind of support, some personnel who will help you begin. I was doubtful . . . but the last five years we've been here.

For a lot of college graduates in recent years there have been only four immediate choices: the Peace Corps, graduate work, teaching school or military service. What were your feelings about that?

I have very strong feelings against military service but that was not why I went into the Peace Corps. I suppose it was still hanging over my head when I came back, but for some reason there didn't seem to be any pressure on me at that point and I don't know, being married or something, or the age I was in, just didn't seem to hit, which I was very glad of. After I had gotten married they passed something which changed . . . married men not being drafted . . . Anyway, I have very strong feelings of people involving themselves in other ways instead of military services.

My wife, for the past couple of years, has taught. This is my fifth year. My first class was not as unified as this one but I worked to get them that way. I didn't struggle too terribly much as a beginning teacher. But I did struggle quite a bit to find ways of working with children, to find things that were relevant, ways of relating. I supposed, when I first started, I would be really good, and I wasn't; but I didn't fold.

What was the extent of your contact with black people while you were growing up?

Not much. Where I grew up, there was a small part of town that was black, a very small part. School integration began there when I was in high school. I don't think there was a black person in any class I had in school. I guess never, until I was in graduate school . . . When I was a freshman in high school they called us up to have our pictures taken by the papers, standing in the doorway holding the door open, black and white walking through together. I found the picture last time I was home. And I only remember one incident that came up: one of the teachers was very angry because her daughter was dancing with a black boy. The students all thought that was very bad, that there was any kind of complaint. I don't remember it being much of an issue because there were very, very few . . . nobody cared that much . . . My feelings have definitely grown and my understanding has really changed since I've been here.

What's your feeling about the old familiar statement: "I'm color-blind"?

I've no opinion of that statement at all. I mean, I don't think anyone is really color-blind. I'm certainly not. I have developed a lot in my thinking on this. I have gone through a childhood of saying everyone is the same inside. From that I went through college thinking of other issues, very removed from racial thought. The Peace Corps did help me see that the differences in people are beautiful things, and the whole set of cultural thoughts began there for me.

As far as blackness, I have thought a lot about this, too. I started out saying what was at the time right to say and think—"equality and rights, etc." I still believe this, but the difference now is that I have been fortunate enough to really know people, most of these, children. Now I more than believe, I *feel*. I am not color-blind.

I know much better now that I am white and the children are black. Through a wealth of experiences and five years of schoolchildren, *plus* the conditions of the society and the progress that is so slowly being made—I know where I stand. I don't prefer separation. I don't like violence. But I understand both. I have not had to experience the violence of going to a junior high where I was more a prisoner, insulted and punished, than a student. But I have been fortunate, and unfortunate, too, to know deeply and care much for children who have had that experience. Therefore I have the right and the obligation to feel violent, too.

I explain it poorly, but people have shared enough, and have accepted my attempts to teach, well enough so that now I can think black. Of course, I'm not, and I don't experience the fullness of this. I might be a better teacher here if I were black, but I'm not. Therefore I have a great responsibility, as a teacher in charge of black children. I have to know and do more than *care*. I have to help them prepare to change things. And I also have to take my stand and know how I look at things.

Sometimes my color has held me back from saying some things that need to be said, from complete openness in a couple of areas.

If we're in a situation and they build these situations often for inner-city schools, where they mix a black school and a white school together, a lot of times there are unpleasant things being said, especially by white children . . . to black children. My being white puts me in a position where I can express my opinions of what has happened, why it's happened and talk about it. In some ways I'm more effective because I am white, and in other ways the children I'm teaching may not *fully* know what I'm trying to say. That's hard to explain but . . . like the school camping is generally set up where black and white schools of equal economic levels go out together and there is often great, great prejudice in that type of white person and they immediately insult the children. You know, my children. I am in the bind of having to calm the children I am teaching, and sometimes I can deal with it very well because I *am* white and have known white children all my life; and yet the type of white children I lived with are not the type my kids are dealing with . . .

There are just occasional things . . . but it happens every year going to the Supplementary Resources Center downtown. They take four classes usually, one from a school like ours and a couple from the near West Side. Very often in the lines there's bickering back and forth and tongues stuck out through the windows of buses, and usually it's not our kids instigating it; it's usually being done to us. We just went back and factually talked it out: exactly what did happen, what did get said and then tried to figure out why it happened. It's not too hard to talk about . . .

How do most of your kids do on standard tests, or doesn't anyone here care?

I'm interested in how they do. On the whole, last year, their reading improved a good year from what it was before. Recently several of the children tested seventh, eighth grade in two or three things. In math, I think the class will average sixth grade; in reading they'll average about fifth. I don't live in fear of tests. For the child's sake, I hate to see them test poorly, a lot of times much more poorly than they really are doing on their daily work.

What was that thing I saw on your board about the "Top Ten"?

Oh, they have a behavior contest in the classroom which is teacher-judged. I have always made it a point to take children extra places out of school, like I take three of them out to the house to play in the snow sometimes, or take them to a good movie, or bowling. My wife and I will take them out together; we've done this all along. Getting in the Top Ten is the way a person would earn some of these extra things they do. Each child takes a secret name that's known only to the child and to me. For like a couple of weeks, I'll list the ones that have really excelled in trying to be considerate of people and good behavior. The real names get revealed eventually, but by then very likely every one of the thirty-three names has been up there some time during the duration and it's never really caused that much upset. It gives me a system rather than just randomly selecting people to take places and I've done it hundreds of times. Everybody does go some places at some times. Some of the children have been with us to my wife's parents' farm in Missouri.

Which kids in this group have impressed you the most strongly?

There are several I know pretty well—Arthur, for instance, but I can't really explain much about him. He's an extremely intelligent boy, a very, very good mind. He came to me in the behavior modification class* three years ago, completely sloppy, ill-mannered. That first semester he never did take much shape. He never would find a project to do; he would always be just on the edge of anyone else's

* See p. 122.

activity. He was very nerve-racking to everybody, very quick to fight. I would really talk with him and get nowhere. He'd get very mad at me. But during the course of the semester we developed feelings for each other which neither of us knew we had until we stumbled into them, you know. It was not a smooth-operating thing at all. But some way we got to the place where we could understand each other. We don't grade, but if we did, he'd be doing almost entirely A and B work. He is still sloppy, has the most beautiful sense of humor I have ever seen in any child and yet he's really a hard one to deal with. He cannot relate to any adult that he has contact with, yet . . . as long as I'm in control, I'm the adult who's supposedly teaching, I'm the one that's supposedly leading, I've kind of got him. When he switches over to anyone else, music, art, whatever he goes to, he completely crumples. His work has taken shape, which is progress. He does get along some of the time, which is progress, and yet . . . He's got all these other things, and I don't even know exactly what they are, that operate so fully on him. [An undertone of anxiety became audible in Finks's voice.] He does well in my setup but that's not saying I'm good or bad or whatever. It's not devotion to me. In some way I have come up with a way—a structure—he can work within. I seem to have enough respect for certain things he *has* to do, enough awareness that he is kind of nervous and he's got to move, that I cannot say, "you've got to sit still all day long." That's not very well explained but—the reason he registers with me so fully now is, I don't know what happens to him next.

In my first year I had a very large boy, fourteen, who had been sent away to Harbor Creek*—I guess was the name of it—in Pennsylvania, for some robbery or something. He saved me as a first-year teacher completely. He was big and he looked like he should be just awful. Everybody said, "Oh, you've got *him* back." For some reason he

* A Catholic school.

lined right up with me. When the class would be kind of playful and try me, he'd stand with me. He pulled the whole class of thirty-nine kids with me that first year and he did all right himself. He was such a leader for the other children that because he wasn't against me, nobody was. It was amazing. And I really felt obligated because he was so good for me to work with. He improved in a lot of *his* work too. He's on my mind now because he's in his tenth or eleventh grade, at Boys Town in Omaha. He writes sometimes now, and he really has come through. The reason is that he's been put in situations where he was not just shut off, that had a positive atmosphere. He's gonna finish high school in a year or two and—be a pretty good man. It's a good feeling . . . The children here [in Finks's class], the ones with the strongest personalities, are definitely the ones that were in that behavior modification class.

This is your fifth year and the difficulties of your job are pretty clear. But haven't there been any moments of elation, when you could say to yourself, Boy! I'm really doing it!

Well, I always feel like I work hard. Then there're certain times when I feel like it's going all right. I really don't know. What we're doing is just a tiny part of something so big that for us to say, "Look what I've done"— why, I've done nothing! . . . A moment of elation? It could be all of a sudden when the writing is really great: I've worked with them for a long time to get it at this point and—there it is! I don't know. I think there have definitely been moments of success, so to speak. Like, if last year you taught a child to use a map and all of a sudden this year they pull out a map and know how to read it. Or a child who hasn't read for a whole year all of a sudden calls you aside and starts reading to you. I mean, there's been *that*.

Arthur, for example, was third or fourth grade in reading all along. This year I scored him and he tested ninth

grade in comprehension. That's a success but I don't light
up and say, "Look what I'm doing!" It's happened several
times. The child maybe has known how to do an awful lot
of things that he won't *do*: "So what?" you know.
"School's so horrible anyway, why waste my time reading?"
Yet, you find out that a lot of things are already there . . .

I have made my approach to the class quite flexible.
There are some lessons which I purposely make as a lecture
where they have to sit and pay attention. There are so
many things that if you can expose the kids to them, in a
way that will allow them to think: I've seen that, I know
what that is, I see why things are falling apart, then, as a
teacher, I may have done something. If I can go ahead and
give them a little bit of strength inside . . . When I think
of junior high coming up—I kind of shudder . . . They go
to a pretty bad junior high.

*The Wyoming expedition (May 27– June 7, 1970) was
accomplished according to plan, though eight of Finks's
thirty-five sixth-graders were unable to go. In December
Finks was still quietly ecstatic: "It was beautiful. Everything went right. The children were amazing."*

*In the fall, the thirty-five were dispersed among three
junior high schools but a number of those who had made
the big trip continued to work together. They were editing
the extensive footage they had shot for a documentary film
of their class's culminating elementary school experience.*

*Finks himself is no longer at John W. Raper. He is
director of the Experimental Learning Center at Baldwin-
Wallace College (current enrollment, twenty-four hundred) in Berea, a Cleveland suburb some twenty miles
from Finks's own suburban driveway. Why did he leave
Raper? "I've had the same class for more than two years.
They had done so many things, I kind of felt I was burning
myself up. I miss being at Raper very much. It's been part
of my life for five years. I'm hoping now to some day*

uncover a junior high that really wants to do some changes. Soon as I find that, I'll be teaching again. Directly or indirectly I've managed to keep in close touch with the class. Whenever anything appears in the Cleveland newspapers about Wyoming, his phone begins to ring—young veterans of the Big Trip are calling.] I've lost complete track of only one. So far junior high is not too great an experience for some of these students."

RICHARD LODISH
Cleveland

John W. Raper Elementary School feels like a livable place even this gloomy late-February morning. The kids at a table in Richard Lodish's third-grade class make room for me. Caroline Wright, nine, clues me in by pointing to a line in the lyrics of "Friendship Train" which the class is following on rexographed* sheets as we listen to a recording of the song by Gladys Knight and the Pips. Her finger traveling under the printed words, Caroline softly sings up a storm in unison with the record. Occasionally, without losing the beat she makes little comments to herself about what's happening:

It don't matter what you look like,/ People, or who you are/ If your heart is in the right place/ . . . ("*I like this*") . . ./ This train stands for justice/ This train stands for freedom/ . . ./ ("*That's good*") . . . Come on get

---

* Trademarked name (Rex-O-Graph) of a device for printing multiple facsimiles from a master copy. Similar to the Ditto. Both generically known as "spirit duplicators."

on the friendship train.* *The pleasure of concentrating on a freely chosen activity is clearly shown in her earnest, lively eyes. But she's working. She knows Mr. Lodish will ask questions about the words. Equally important, she knows he will not only answer but will welcome any questions she feels like asking. And most important, she knows nobody will demean her if she chooses to sit at a corner table to do some arithmetic instead of joining the reading lesson. The song ends. Most of the kids in the room have a satisfied look on their faces. What this whole exercise means is something to go into with Mr. Lodish in due course.*

I was teaching summer school and something came up about Martin Luther King. I wanted to use a recording of his "I have a Dream" speech, so I transcribed the words and put them on an overhead projector, played the speech and the kids pointed to the words as they heard them. Then I got the idea to do it with other records. It just kind of hit me. It's great for motivation. All the kids listen to soul or rhythm-and-blues radio stations. They all know the current songs. I felt a lot of times they wouldn't know what the songs really meant. They just kind of sang along. So I've been getting this method together for two years now. To me, anyway, it's a fairly consistent way to teach new vocabulary and reading.

There're certain classic rhythm and blues songs that carry through over the years liks "My Girl"† sung by the Temptations and "Little Green Apples"‡ by O. C. Smith. Each of these introduces good vocabulary. As the song is sung, the children point to each word and this, of course, reinforces what reading is. You know—speech written down.

* "Friendship Train," by Norman Whitfield and Barrett Strong. Copyright © 1969 by Jobete Music Co., Inc. Excerpts used by permission of the copyright owner.
† By William Robinson and Ronald White.
‡ By Bobby Russell.

I develop different ways to approach it. Like the way we did it today was taking out specific vocabulary words that I want to teach. Sometimes we play a game, the boys against the girls. They listen to the record without the word sheet and tell me where I've stopped. If the girls get it right they get a point. Again, it's reinforcing the spoken with the written word.

I make it my business to listen to rhythm and blues stations. I'm interested in black music. I buy a lot of these records for the children, and for myself. I like a lot of different types of music. Jazz, for example. Sometimes during reading I'll put on some jazz, just instrumental, of course. I'm also a kind of a student of old blues—Leadbelly, Blind Lemon Jefferson. I've been wanting to put together a lesson about old blues singers, and where a lot of the rhythm-and-blues music came from. Bessie Smith, Billie Holiday, Ma Rainey, people like that. The children'd probably think it was strange at first because they sing different from the current singers. But approached the right way, in historical perspective, you know—this is what people used to sing—they might appreciate it.

Certain songs seem a little too heavy for third-graders. I try to get those across the best I can simply because I like them. Nina Simone came out with one called "To Be Young, Gifted and Black" and she had a song: "I Wish I Knew How It Would Feel to Be Free."* I played it for the children. We talked about it. Me, I could almost cry when I hear a song like that, but you know, children are different . . . If they want one I don't particularly dig myself, I'll still use it because I'm teaching for *them*.

Teachers should hip themselves to the things going around in the community and this includes music. To teach in *any* school you should be familiar with the environment the children come from. If it's so alien to you that you don't know what music, for example, the kids

* By Billy Taylor and Dick Dallas.

listen to, you shouldn't really be at this school. Conceivably you don't have to like their music that much, but to be effective you should be hip that it's a part of their culture, for these kids a big part. If I were teaching in an all-white school I might choose different songs. In a West Side School I might use something by the Beatles.

We've done a lot of creative writing about the songs. A lot of them have a message, like the "Friendship Train" today: ". . . What the world needs now is love and understanding . . . harmony is the key, my brothers and sisters . . ." We haven't really discussed the meaning of that but we'll get around to it in a group discussion. Sometimes they bring in their [song] reading book, and, seated in a circle, talk about what the song means to them and the specific things it says. What the words mean. For example, in "Message from a Black Man"* it says, "Move on aside because I'm coming through . . . you can't stop me now." Who moves aside? What do we mean by "coming through"? It brings up a lot of black-and-white issues. There really is this overall feeling now of black pride. It's like a changing of psyche almost . . . About the line "You can't stop me now," they said, "We're really pushing ahead now to be free, no matter how hard white people try to stop us." It's funny—I don't think they really consider me in racial terms.

Richard Lodish, twenty-three, stands five foot three, square-built, in his suede desert boots. His long blond hair, bushy beard, luxuriant mustache, would deter only the more captious among his parents' generation from describing him as "a very nice-looking boy." A psychology major at Washington and Jefferson College, he lived the last three of his undergraduate years in Washington's (Pa.) central city area: "One, it was very cheap and, two, kind of for the

---

* By Norman Whitfield and Barrett Strong. Copyright © 1969 by Jobete Music Co., Inc. Excerpts used by permission of the copyright owner.

experience. A lot of my friends were not really from the school but from around the city." His apartment was three doors from a black Elks Club. "They had great jazz and things, good entertainers from Pittsburgh. I used to go there, drink with people. I really became—I guess—accepted, you know. When I go back there, these are my friends. That kind of accustomed me, maybe, to black poor urban life."

In his junior and senior years he was director of a tutoring program for some seventy city schoolchildren at LeMoyne Community Center. He also spent one summer in research at the Yale Psycho-Educational Clinic on a National Science Foundation grant. On graduation—"Phi Bete; I studied hard"—he abandoned his plans for graduate work in child development.

This whole draft thing came up [in 1968] . . . so I kind of started looking for alternatives. I applied to the Peace Corps; I was going to teach English in Turkey; all kinds of things. Then I heard about this program at Case-Western Reserve University where you get a master's and you teach at the same time. I really liked it. This was something I could really get into. If it wasn't for the draft, I'd probably be at Cornell, as I'd planned. I'm definitely staying in education. It's really changing rapidly. It has to. So many things are being questioned that should be questioned—people like John Holt and Jonathan Kozol, Edgar Friedenberg and people. It's very heartening. I just really dig what they're saying. But putting ideas into practice—really doing, letting children create and be themselves—this is what I'm all about.

Overall I see the school system like it's really bad. A lot of kids are really having death at an early age. The whole structure, the way freedom is stifled, and kids don't have choices, and this whole age-grade promotion thing.

I like to see kids cooperating among themselves,

choosing something, and really being active in class. Really using their hands and their voices. You go into some classes and they're so quiet.

To me one aspect of learning how to read, learning how to learn, is talking about things, discussing. You have to make some noise when you do that. When my class is all quiet sometimes, I feel like shouting or screaming to get them to do something, like they're not learning when they're not talking.

If you really look at why kids talk—you know, a kid'll have trouble with a word; he'll say, "Jimmy, what's this word?" A lot of teachers would say "Turn around!" He's asking him about a *word*, for goodness sake. Most of the talking is *like* this. Quite often it's perfectly okay to ask someone a question, to work together on something, to write group stories with someone. Sometimes we'll have four kids sitting around. They'll all read a story and they'll all contribute. This is *learning*. This is what it's all about.

We had a good discussion on "What Is Reading?" and we made a whole list of things you could read. A lot of kids in elementary school have the idea that reading is just reading Alice and Jerry books.* This is what's thrown at them. But reading is reading comic books, cereal box tops, TV commercials, stop signs, library books, anything. We made a whole list of them. If they want to write a story on the board and then read it to someone, they could. This is

* *The Alice and Jerry Basic Reading Program:* twenty-seven volumes, pre-primer through Grade 7. Published since 1936, with various changes and revisions, by Row, Peterson, in Evanston, Ill. The series is a counterpart of the older, more widely-known "Dick and Jane" series, pre-primer through Grade 8, published by Scott, Forsman & Co., in Chicago. This latter series has undergone several changes of overall title since it first appeared in 1931 and is now identified as *The New Basic Reading Series.* Despite more drastic change since the mid-1960s, both the Row, Peterson and Scott, Forsman series portray an idealized, essentially white middle-class world totally alien to minority group children.

reading. We do that from nine o'clock till ten o'clock in the morning.

I'm concerned about content too. For example, the library books that I choose. We have a lot of city-oriented books, things like *Snowy Day** and *Who Cares?*† books written by themselves, a lot of black history books, and books about cars and Indians.

Content is a funny thing. I don't know if there's that much good content written for elementary schools kids. Like I'm supposed to do a unit on Indians. I look at the books written for kids about Indians. It's like you see on TV, the cowboys and Indians and Custer's Last Stand. I wouldn't teach that type of thing. They don't go into the real exploitation of Indians and how we literally murdered them. If I see a book that tells the truth, then I would use it.

Of course, sometimes a good way to teach things is by taking a book, let's say a book that justified slavery or something, and teaching that and saying, "Well, what do you think about it?" or "How do you agree or disagree with it?" Basically a lot of content comes from discussions. I just can't see teaching two weeks of South America and two weeks of Venezuela and the Panama Canal. For me, it'd go in one ear and out the other. I don't want them to know just facts, that the Panama Canal was built in 1903. I just don't care! I want them to learn how to think, how to conceptualize things, how to compare, contrast, how to be themselves and think for themselves. And I want them to learn how to read. I have friends in the junior high schools here. They're teaching social studies, and the kids can't even read the books at all. They seldom even read on fifth- and sixth-grade level in ninth grade.

Different kids learn how to read by different methods at different times. Okay? According to their unique devel-

---

* Ezra Jack Keats, *The Snowy Day* (New York: Viking, 1962).
† Virginia Brown, *Who Cares* (New York: McGraw-Hill, 1965), Skyline Series.

opment. You have to present these methods to them and, in a way, help them make the choice: Which way could I read better? For example, using a book like *Through the Green Gate*.* A couple of kids might be able to read by using that method and a lot of kids definitely don't. Some children, I think, learn to read by writing their own stories; by doing that, they pick up vocabulary. Some children learn better by reading their classmates' stories. Some kids have to touch the words to read. Some kids have to hear the word and correlate it with the written. Almost all my children are improving in reading. But just as important, they are learning to love books and to express themselves through the written word.

I don't think children really learn in a real strict environment. It just isn't organic or natural for them. Like I was talking last night with a student teacher. She was saying the kids don't seem to be themselves in the room she's working in. They're real uptight. They get out of line and the regular teacher might whack them with a ruler. They couldn't express themselves. I see this so many times. You know—the kids are a little noisy and the teachers turn out the lights and make them put their heads down on the desk. It's crazy. The kids just aren't learning when you're sitting up there and trying to put information into an empty vessel. It just doesn't get in there, though you might think it does.

You give your kids a lot of freedom but there's got to be some kind of adult control and directiveness, doesn't there?

I guess I operate a kind of democratic class, with mutual respect. This is the overall attitude. We all try to cooperate with each other—a small community.

They have freedom to talk and work together most of the day. I have a maths area with all kinds of materials,

* Book One of the Grade 3 level in the Alice and Jerry series.

including puzzles, bottle caps they can count, graphs they've made of things in the neighborhood, number games, tape measures and a lot of homemade things. But I also introduced language skills in this area, starting with words about whatever a kid may be working on. Behind the bookcases is the reading area. It's comfortable, a place where children can relax and really *enjoy* reading. They can do hundreds of learning things here. But sometimes, for about twenty minutes, I want not a chair moving, not anything. This is a time when I want their complete attention. It's really distracting to me when the kids are talking during that time, and they know it.

When we finish group projects, kind of for my own sanity I want it quiet in the room for like ten or fifteen minutes where they sit down quietly and work in their reading books.

See, now, at the beginning of the year, I kind of wanted it quiet all the time, playing the traditional rules. There's definitely a time when they should be talking and working together. I tell the children, "I think you could learn better by talking together, by figuring things out together, by having a choice. There's also a time that you should listen to me and it's not going to be that *much* of the time."

This is your second year at Raper and your first year with a third-grade class. What did you do here last year?

I taught the behavior modification class. Mr. Aiello decided that since each class had one or two children that were disruptive behavior problems, it would be good to put these kids in a class where they could kind of get themselves together—kids who couldn't get along in our prevailing classroom environment. So he wanted to set up a type of free environment where the children have choices, where they could do mechanical things, work with wood and paint. They could talk about their problems with the teacher and with psychologists and tutors and get a lot of individual attention, then gradually get back into the regular class.

I have a psychology background; I've worked with emotionally disturbed kids before. So I tried it for a whole year and there was a lot of ups and downs. Toward the end of the year I came to the same conclusion as Harry Finks had done: this wasn't really benefiting the kids that much. In a way it was hurting them because when you take a behavior problem out of a class and say, "You go into the special class," no matter what you call it, the kid realizes that "I'm bad and I'm in this class with other bad children." By the end of the year I definitely concluded that it just reinforces their badness. I think I helped them in some respects but overall not much. The way you have to approach this is: the teachers have to learn how to handle it.

Like in my room I have a little boy, Bertram, who was in my behavior modification class. He's eight years old. I let him out of school at four o'clock. He comes back to school at twelve o'clock the next day and hasn't been home yet. In winter, *now*, he sleeps in the street, in apartment buildings. Boy, this kid's really tough. I mean I could never, never stay out in the freezing cold. I don't know where he gets money. I can always tell when he's run away. He comes in and he looks so disheveled, with water in his boots and his shirt open. The last time this happened he came in and he was physically shaking, from cold, from nerves—I mean like this—[he simulates violent trembling]. I took him down to the basement and I gave him a shower. We have showers. Then I gave him food, and after he quieted down I took him home and we sat down with his stepmother.

See, what happened: the first six years of his life were spent with his mother, who was a prostitute. Then he went to all these foster homes and then his real father wanted him back. So now he's living with his father and his stepmother. You know how important the first six years of life are, and this is how he lived. His stepmother would call me: "Bertram isn't home. What should I do?" She'd get really scared: "Where is he?" I used to drive around with his stepmother and help look for him at two o'clock in the morning but he would dodge us. He didn't want to be found. Now she doesn't look for him; I don't, and the police won't look for him any more because it's happened nine or ten times . . . He never goes home. He wanders back to school in the morning.

He's a real good reader but it's hard for him to keep on one thing. He used to have a tendency to run out of the room. Now he's in my regular class, working much better because we talk about behavior and feelings in the class meetings with Bertram: "How could we, as a class, help Bertram?" So now a couple of boys are appointed to help him. When he gets out of that room they bring him back and we talk about it. I think it's a much more positive thing than me sitting up there as some kind of authority thing in the old behavior modification room.

I think he *feels* they're helping him. If I thought he felt they were policing him I wouldn't do it. It's just not that type of atmosphere. Let's say someone is working quietly and Bertram starts hitting someone with a pencil. George, one of my leaders, will say, "Bertram, don't do that. You're hurting the class. Be quiet!" Bertram will say: "We-e-ell, okay." We always talk about helping the class. Let's help the class to be better. Like if I'm talking and a couple of kids are throwing spitballs, I'd get really angry. (This doesn't happen much any more.) The reason I get angry, I mean: "How is that helping the class? How is that helping anybody? Is it helping you? Is it helping James? Is it helping me? Is it *helping*? It's not helping anybody!" And they *conclude* that.

Setting up a good classroom where these kids could function, not taking them *away* from the classroom setting, is more beneficial. I just feel more comfortable in a regular class with the behavior problems in the class. I felt, a lot of times, really uptight in that other type of class because I couldn't argue against my own feelings that it was no good, that you shouldn't isolate behavior-problem kids. I think it carried over to the kids that in a way I wasn't truthful in what I'm doing. This year I feel really good about what I'm doing. They used to say, "If we all go back to our regular class, you'll be out of a job, Mr. Lodish." Isn't that something? That wasn't far from the truth.

I had some real incidents in that class—and some beautiful moments, too, where I thought I was accomplishing things. I had this kid, Paul, who was diagnosed as brain-damaged and I really think he was. He was a beautiful kid. He'd open the door for you and say Thank you but sometimes he'd just get violent. One time when this happened I got everybody out of the room, except Paul and a little boy, Roger, whom I didn't notice was there. Paul all of a sudden just beat the living hell out of him. Finally I got Roger out and I tried to settle Paul down who was just waving his hands like crazy. Mr. Aiello tried to talk to him. Paul ran outside and threw three bricks through my window. Then he ran home and his mother came back with him. *She* was stranger than Paul. She kept taking his side, you know, that Paul was right. Maybe once every two or three weeks I'd have a day like that.

But some days everything was good. For example, the room was set up kind of like mine. We had a workbench, typewriters, a whole stage with carpets, library books. We had a painting corner, a puppet corner, really lots of things to do in that room. And some days, you know, one kid would be making a boat with wood, another typing a story. A couple of other kids would be getting the words to one of the rhythm-and-blues records. A good day. The next day there'd be a fistfight. They'd be working at different groups and all of a sudden *boom, boom, boom!* and that was the end of the day. I couldn't really plan things.

I had first- to sixth-graders in there at one time. I tried having the older kids tutor the younger ones. We did this for three or four months with kids from Mrs. McGriggs' kindergarten class who were working on reading, beginning sounds and things. I explained to my kids that these kids are having a little trouble: "Let's try to help them," and that worked really good. I bought them all pre-primers and they would prepare a lesson plan—these kids, these so-called behavior-problem kids. Then every other day they would go downstairs and take the little kindergarten kids by the hand and bring them up to their "offices." This was a cool thing I set up. It worked good: I had about twenty bookcases in my room. I put two against the wall to form three sides of a cubicle and that would be an office, in between the two bookcases, with a little desk in there. They'd take the kindergarten kids into their offices, sit down with them and really help them read. Like there'd be a picture of a boy and the little kid would have to cut out the word "boy" and paste it on. And they'd really—sometimes, for hours! That would be beautiful, really cool.

I had one kid, Victor, a real creative kid. He used to think up his own methods. He'd bring the typewriter over to the little kindergarten kids and he'd type *a* and he'd say "a." He'd type *b* and then he'd say "b" and then he had the little kindergarten kid press the *a* on the typewriter. One time he cut out all the numerals, 1 to 20, on a piece of cardboard and he'd give them to his student who'd have to sort them out, and he cut out the alphabet and the kid would have to put them in order. Some days I'd just sit by and say "Wow!"

This year instead of the behavior modification, we have the Opportunity Room, a place for the kids to get themselves together so they can function in a regular classroom. Let's say a kid is throwing spitballs and you say, "Come here. Are you supposed to throw spitballs?" and he says, "No." And you say, "Well, could you *not* throw spitballs for half an hour and the kid says, 'No, no. I gotta throw . . .'" This is the type. Then, if he really can't make a commitment right there, instead of being suspended or going to "the office" you send him to the Opportunity Room, to work it out for himself. When he feels ready, he comes back.

In the beginning of this year I'd come home and I'd say, "Gee, this was a lousy day. What could I do tomorrow?" I'd call up maybe Harry Finks or someone and I'd kind of complain and get a little catharsis, you see, and then I'd say, "Well, I'll try something new tomorrow." And now I feel like things are really happening and it's good. The kids like me; I like them . . .

I bought a micro-bus to take my children on trips. Mr. Finks has one, too. It was an impetus for me to get one. I take the kids on hikes and to museums. Like sometimes if we need books from the library, I'll take them with me and have them pick out the books. I live in the attic of a big old house, with three other teachers. It's a very big attic room and I have lots of games and things for the kids. Lots of children's records, too. They play the records; it's fun for me. See, at this point in my life, I have so many different things: meetings, and two courses at Western Reserve. I don't have that much time to devote to extracurricular activities, so I just take the kids home after school sometimes. And I make it my business to meet the parents. A lot of times I'll go to their homes and stop in just to talk.

A few days before I met Lodish, his class gave him a party. He was apprised of their intention by a note which said in part: "Do you want it or not. You deserve it."

It was beautiful. They told me at twelve o'clock, when they were going home for lunch: "Don't come in the room. Leave the door open.* We're going to come in and do

* In most big-city public schools, these days, teachers are expected to lock the doors when their classrooms are unoccupied.

something." While I was in the teachers' lunchroom a couple of boys came up to me and said things like, "Oh, Mr. Lodish, how was your lunch?" to kill time, until a messenger came to tell them it was okay, so they said, "Well, do you want to come up to the room now?" I did, and all the lights are out and all the kids are hiding behind their desks. They jump up and: "SURPRISE!"

They had two long tables all filled with food and— Oh, it was great. They got all these bottles of pop and mixed them together, grape, orange, cherry. Then they had this big bowl of potato chips and stuff, and one girl baked a cake. There were all kinds of food and candy and gum. So all afternoon we ate, and I played music and we had like a dance contest and games. They set up the whole room, moved all the tables around. They really got it together. We didn't do any work that afternoon. I goofed around and it was a lot of fun. I don't know what the specific occasion was. I guess they sensed that the class was going good and they just kind of wanted a little break . . .

A couple of kids in my room are real leaders, like James. In a way I'm real nice to him, go a little overboard, 'cause he kind of has his finger in a lot things in the class. When he says, "Mr. Lodish is trying to talk now, be quiet," there won't be a sound in that class. At the beginning of the year he'd do some bad things. I talked to him and I went to his house, too, and I talked to his mother, "James is definitely a leader. The kids look up to him. Try to use it constructively. Try to work together." And he's beautiful in that respect.

He writes plays, a lot of good plays. I'd be sitting up there working with a kid and I'd see James pass around little note cards to everybody. What he did, he wrote a whole play and then he put each part on a little note card and gave it to the kids and that afternoon they gave a play.

Don't the other kids think of him as "teacher's pet"?

No, uh-uh. He's liked. The kids look up to him. See, some teachers might say, "James, sit down. You can't talk with the other kids." They might resent his overstepping the teacher's bounds. But I see him trying to help the class. I guess what I did is let the class pick the leader and I go along with it as long as he is working constructively and we're not at cross-purposes. I just realize his power function and let it be. It just so happened that I liked James and the class liked James, so it's a good thing.

A lot of teachers wish they had the kind of freedom you have here.

Yeah . . . I've always wondered what I would do in a real tight school where the principal comes in your room and says, "You're not teaching reading at ten." I'd probably go berserk. Like what happened with the leadership-development lady. It upset her that kids in my room were able to talk and things and she just really was getting on my nerves. She circulated a long note about ways to set up reading groups and it said, "Sign here." So I put on it: "Don't bother me."

She called me to the office and said, "What's this all about?" I said, "Don't send me a note like that; that takes ten minutes to read. I'm trying to teach and this note comes in and I got to read it and answer it." The other teachers patted me on the back. They had seen the note, too, and my comment next to my room number.

I've been doing a lot of work in organizing teachers, to kind of fight the system. I consider myself a good teacher, but I'm only doing 60 to 70 percent of my potential because there are certain institutional things you can't cope with that are operating against you—age-grade promotions, class sizes, not being familiar with a lot of the equipment. We formed this thing called Teachers for Action in Education—about a hundred teachers in the Cleveland system now, black and white. Basically it's an organization that's child- and student-centered rather than wage-oriented. We're trying to work through the union to change its priorities, to be more child-centered, to improve the curriculum, to involve the community more. It's not like a revolutionary group but we want a lot of changes in the schools, to operate more effectively, to turn on the children.

Basically there's not enough people like Mr. Aiello around, working with the community instead of against it, for the kids instead of against the kids. The administration's not like this, you know, from downtown . . . At our school we have people from the Afro Set* helping out. The way a lot of my children view it, the Black Nationalist is a kind of gang leader. If you're in a group of Black Nationalists or Afro Set or something, then you're tough and you can hit other people. They don't get the political essence of it, you know, the positive aspects about pride and this type of thing. The Afro Set explain that they try to police the neighborhood, stop purse-snatching, prostitution, gambling . . . So I think we should bring members of the Afro Set to speak in the classes, to clarify exactly what they do stand for.

You can give so much time and effort to your job not just because you enjoy it but also because you don't have many personal responsibilities. What happens to your way of working if you get married?

Get married? And have five kids or something? Fantastic! I think the person I would marry would have to have an outlook similar to mine, and would want to help children.† I think it could possibly accentuate involvement rather than detract from it. Like in Harry Finks's situation.

* See note on p. 86.
† From a subsequent letter from Lodish: "So much has happened since I talked to you last . . . I am now married to the student teacher we talked about who was having trouble with her class."

I think he is more involved because of his wife than he would be without her. It's kind of a reinforcing thing. Let's say, like I enjoy bringing kids over to my house, but it's not really reinforced. My roommates enjoy it, I guess, but if I had a wife it'd kind of be a little easier. Like when I took kids to the museums. I had a date, a girl I see, and it was really nice. Know what I mean? So it depends on the circumstances and it depends on how many kids of your own you have and things. But it doesn't have to detract from involvement. It could increase involvement depending on your responsibilities. I have to think when I start getting involved in teacher organizing: "Gee, I can't spend this time maybe preparing for my kids and taking them on trips." But then you have to weigh certain things. I think you have to approach, and constructively, the system also, the kingdom versus the castle in your room. So this is the way it is; you have to budget your time. I definitely have time enough to do what I want to do. I still go out and things. I enjoy being with the kids. I also enjoy being by myself listening to music. I enjoy being with people. And a lot of times you can kind of combine all these things.

For example, like on a Sunday—let's say it's a nice day out—I've done this a lot: get a date and then pick up two or three kids. We go out in the country and go for a walk, holding hands with the girl and yet the kids are having a good time, we're all talking and—it's just a beautiful thing.

Several months after our conversation Richard Lodish sent me a seventy-two-page anthology, I Said Hello to the World: *written (in their own handwriting) and illustrated by third-graders from John W. Raper Elementary School— the ones I had met in Lodish's classroom. The thirty-one children and their teacher had published it as a group enterprise. At a dollar a copy it was "a hot seller at avant-garde bookstores and specialty shops downtown," the* Cleveland Press *reported.*

"The most rewarding aspect of the whole thing," Lodish wrote to me, "has been the parents' and children's reactions . . . The money we make (I've printed 1,000 copies) will all go back to the kids probably for an end-of-the-year camping trip . . . School is terrific. The kids have been so excited lately. The book was a perfect project to end the year with, especially since all of my students were finally in the book."

What is the "free writing" these children have produced? They are genuinely poetic expressions of encounters with reality, of perceptions, sensitivities and of intellectual and spiritual gropings by no means blind or directionless. The title of the anthology comes from Ruby Gant Smith's poem:

> One day i saw the world
> and the world were very pretty
> . . . So i went out and i said
> Hello to the world . . .
> And when it were time
> for me to go i said
> Good-bye to the world.
> And the world said Good-bye to me.
> And i said i will see you in the morning.

The most prolific contributor was Jose Tate, who wrote, among other things:

> Black and white have hands
> Black and white friend.
> no war
> I said no war.
> But freedom got it baby
> Yes it do . . .

JAN DE CRESPIGNY
Cleveland

I came from South Africa originally. I was born there and I started teaching straight after I finished college. I wasn't allowed to teach in a black school. I wanted to, but they said teaching was one of the few jobs educated Africans could do . . . In a black school I'd be depriving a black person of a job. And I said, "Okay, why don't you let blacks teach in white schools and then there'll be . . ." HAAAH! HOOOH! In South Africa that was as good as saying you were a Communist.

Margaret Ireland Elementary is one of Cleveland's newer buildings. The teaching staff is two-thirds black; the school's enrollment, almost totally so. From the doorway, looking into Room 122, Jan de Crespigny is not visible at first glance. She must be descried as a larger body in one of several constellations of first-graders variously engaged in painting, looking at books, trying out math games or, in two or three cases, just unobjectionably goofing around. Her crisp, distinctly British accent is as unlikely a sound as one would expect to hear in the neighborhood of Chester Avenue and Sixty-third Street. Her class, seemingly, has no trouble with it.

A little later, the kid-clusters coalesce. They become a unified group of some thirty black children, ages six to seven and a half, sitting in a semicircle they have formed with a minimum of fuss at their teacher's request.

It's conversation time. The day's topic is bluntly introduced by Mrs. de Crespigny: the relative merits of being smaller/younger, remaining the same or growing bigger/older than they are; and what do they look forward to when they grow up? In its first moments the occasion seems con-

133

trived, but the children's responsiveness gives this colloquy all the validity it needs. Their statements overlap and flow through each other like signals from a poorly tuned radio. From the teacher there's none of that "Let's talk one at a time, please" flak but when she calls on children by name the hubbub subsides, reactively, and the single voices come through loud and clear: I'd like to be my age till I'm thirteen . . . I'd like to be big . . . I'd like to be tall . . . They [littler children] can get just about ANYTHING THEY WANT . . . WE CAN'T . . . Yeah . . . That's true! . . .

And, when they grow up? Raymond: I'll be looking forward to a car. Margaret: I want to be married. Rosemary: A nurse. Darrell: I want to be a Black Nationalist. Cornell: I want to be a doctor . . . One little boy, with clearly mischievous intent, calls out that he wants to be a pimp.

It's noon now, no children in the room, but the feeling of liveliness remains. Mrs. de Crespigny looks pleased with the way her morning has gone. So? What happens here, ordinarily, that doesn't happen in a conventional first-grade classroom?

Actually, you saw this culminating part where everybody was doing what we call "free study." But early in the morning you'd see that certain groups as they come up to read, or for math activities, are engaged with me. The rest of them will choose what they want to do—which may be making puppets or painting, writing stories, using magnets and magnifying glasses. But when everyone has finished doing his formal work for the morning, and they do tend to sort of hurry through it because they want to choose their own activity, they all pretty well do their own thing. I am then involved in guiding and suggesting rather than in directive teaching.

They have at least thirty minutes of reading in a group

and they have twenty minutes, approximately, of math in a group. They have an oral language program which is very good. We use cards and tape recorders, intercom equipment, anything to encourage them to verbalize. We have a science program, too, but that's particularly for my room because I wanted it. It's mostly just discovery and investigation—nothing formal. Emphasis is on silent reading, comprehension and a very strong phonics background, but not overpoweringly so. It's a basal reading series, but they're not confined to that because they also read individually at their own speed from library books. . . . After all, people read silently, you know. But I do check them orally—listen to them—and I check their comprehension by asking questions about the content of what they're reading. But they also do a lot of oral reading at this stage because they're fairly young and they like it.

What *doesn't* happen here is—very seldom are they addressed as a class because they're grouped flexibly, so that I can teach skills, you know. If a child is weak in a particular thing, or if several children are, then I'll pull them out and do things with that group individually. But, now, I almost never address them as a whole class; perhaps *that's* different. The fact that they're allowed to move around freely is different, too. Most first-graders are confined to their seats; they don't move around.

Reading tests? Yes. These are supposed to be diagnostic, but are not marked on their official records. They do very well. They have a high scoring rate. This year, the class has turned out to be a fairly homogeneous group, just accidentally. It wasn't last year, at all.

One of the boys said he wanted to be a Black Nationalist. What does that mean to a six- or seven-year-old child?

They're not sure what it means but they know that's something they want to be. I've tried to get them to be more verbal about it, and they'll say, These are Black Nationalist gloves because they're black leather. I really don't think they've got it at all, at this age. But they do know the Black Nationalists are people they respect, and that they're doing what they should do; and they want to be like them. And that's as far as you can go. They sense an image of manliness and dignity in this—from the way they say it, you know. They don't laugh at each other when one of them says, "I want to be a Black Nationalist." Unlike the one little boy who said, "I want to be a pimp," and everybody laughed.

What does that mean to a six- or seven-year-old?

I don't know. But I've talked to them about what they think about love. The word means only sexual love to them and they get very giggly and silly about it. It's been a matter of the different meanings a word can have, depending on usage. If I ask, "Is love a good feeling?" they say, "No, it's a bad feeling; you shouldn't love someone." If you say, "Do you love your mother?" then they'll think again and they'll say yes. And they'll begin to wonder about the fact that one word can have a variety of meanings.

Why have you always wanted to teach in a black school?

It's a guilt feeling, I guess, about being a white South African, for what my people have done to Africans. And also a personal sort of thing, of wanting to make up for a personal lack in myself: I just had no idea of how Blacks thought or felt. I had lived so close to people but knew nothing about them, and *could* know nothing about them. In South Africa it's almost impossible, you know. I mean, we were arrested in Durban for having a party that—just because there were Blacks at the same place; for having a multiracial—I mean, it's so very difficult. And we can't go back. My husband is not allowed to . . .

Jan was already married when she left South Africa, to the man in whose political science course she had enrolled as a university student. He was English, so England was where they went. She taught there for three years "in very progressive schools."

London County Council schools, in the poorer suburbs again. There—that's where I really got interested in children whom I suppose one calls "deprived," because they were so exciting and fabulous to work with. I taught a lot of West Indians, East Indians and Cockney English. They're just so much more interesting to teach because they're so excited about everything that happens. And they respond to affection so marvelously.

My husband got a job here. He's chairman of the political science department at Case Western Reserve University. I've been teaching ever since I got here three years ago. And I've been doing a master's degree at Case for the same period of time because I'd had no education courses at all. This may be the only school that would have accepted me. Downtown they thought this was such a wild lady that they'd have to find a school where I wouldn't be thrown out too soon . . . It was my background, I guess. The fact that I had no American teaching experience; and teaching in England in very progressive schools. And I came from South Africa, which was risky. I guess just the way I talked made them think I wouldn't fit in.

After South Africa, how and what did you feel when you faced your first all-black class in this building?

Terrified. Very scared. I felt very inadequate because I suddenly felt strangely fraudulent. I wondered what my motives were and whether I thought I could *give* these children something, whether that was in the back of my mind somewhere . . . It's amazing how soon these black children's faces become just children's faces and one is not really aware of the difference. But initially there was a feel-

ing of vast difference, exaggerated by my cultural background, my voice, this sort of thing. This blank look of
astonishment on the children's faces which they wouldn't
have produced if I had spoken with an American accent. So
there was a terrific wall for a long time, because they
couldn't understand what I was saying and I didn't know
what *they* were saying. I don't know that it ever did give
way that first year for me, except with certain children. It
was very hellish, I think, both for the children and me.
That was my fifth year of teaching but my first year in the
United States, my first experience with a different sort of
method, in a different environment. It was a very, very
unhappy year. The next year was better and this year's been
just great. Beautiful.

The children learned the basics, that first year, but not
by the methods I would have wanted to use because I was
unsure of myself. I was much more authoritarian than I
would have been normally. Much more control and structure and—you know. It was nervousness. Toward the end
of the year the children began to trust me. That gave me so
much confidence that I was able to relax. It was when they
first began to talk to me that I began to revert to my old
teaching methods. And then I was happier, so *they* were,
naturally. They always reflect your moods so much. You
start grouchy and you've got a bunch of real miserable, bad-
tempered kids in no time.

Now, there are things like absolutely no corporal punishment in this school and a child knows that he's not
going to get beaten if he is sent to the office. This sort of
thing has made a fantastic difference to the children's
attitude.

*What do you think about—Now, wait a minute; you
mean to tell me kids this age get beaten in classrooms?*

They *were* the first year I was here. Sure. Knocked
about. The second day I was in here, I saw a child picked up

and shaken. By the then principal—not this principal. Apart from what it did to the child, it was so horrible for me because if I had not permitted the child to do whatever he was doing—which was being a snake or something on the floor, something not very complicated or harmful, you know—he wouldn't have incurred the wrath of this lady. I think she was trying to show me that I should be firm with the children or something like that.

What did you do?

I left the room with her and said I couldn't possibly teach if this was going to happen. And she said, you know, the usual line: "You've got to accept the fact that these children will take advantage of you. You're going to have a chaotic classroom unless you start firm. I'm just trying to help you." [She subsides with a sigh, laughs, and sighs again.]

Okay, the kids trust you now. How do they show it?

They're very open. Children will tell you things that you—about stealing and things they've done, which I think is terrific, that they'll trust you to that extent . . . How do I react? I generally sort of ask him what he feels about it. Does he feel bad about the fact that he's done it? And why does he want to tell me? He will frequently come out with: "I'm worried," or "I feel I shouldn't have done it" or something. Then I say, "What do you think you can do about it?" I'll leave it up to him to make the decision, and he'll say, "Well, I could tell my mother," or "I could give it back" or the like. If he decides that he wants to keep it and he thinks it's the right thing to do, I mean, I'm stuck. I'm not going to tell him he *must* do this or that about it. Most of these things that children have told me about happen outside of this building . . . They don't always respect each other's things in here either, but that's different because, from living in large families, they're used to sharing.

And they just expect that things that are around are theirs to be used. They don't regard them as somebody else's property.

And there's a little girl who saw both her father and mother shot, about a year ago. Her father died but her mother recovered. She talks about that, and how she worries about her mother. Her mother drinks a lot, and she doesn't know what to do about it, and that sort of thing. She's seven. Apparently she carries the whole household. She's very tiny, about this high. And she's very independent and she obviously feels a responsibility for the family because her mother's just fallen apart after this. But this is fantastic. To think that a child can come through, you know, and succeed in school and in practical things with this traumatic event behind her. And she does.

And there's another child who had a twin in this class. The twin had a cerebral tumor in October and has completely regressed. And this child is very frightened by the fact that she sometimes feels that she is the twin as well as herself. She's sort of absorbed the twin into herself. And she'll say things like: "I'm going to read for me now. And I'll read for Gloria in a minute. And I want you to hear us both read." And she talks a lot about that. She'll stay after school . . . This sort of business, of identifying with the twin, is very alarming I find. I'd really like to talk to somebody professional about it . . .

I've never managed to get that sort of help and I've felt that a lot of the children I've handled in the last three years have needed it, some of them badly. That's one of the worst aspects. This school is so good from so many points of view but *still*, if you have a very seriously disturbed child you can be pretty sure you're not going to get any help for that child, before it's too late anyway. The school psychologist will test him, but getting outside help is a long, slow business. . . . Assume the child is seven, then you have another couple of years when you go through all the forms and things and the child is nine. It may be too late by then.

To go back a little: Is the wide disparity of cultural backgrounds, yours and the kids', still much of an issue in your classroom?

Now that they hear me around the building, they've gotten used to me. I'm just the teacher who talks with the funny voice, you know. In fact, you should hear them reading, and they read with my accent. Mrs. Tebelak is always debating whether they're going to pick up my accent before I pick up theirs, you know. It's quite a thing. The children are very patient and very kind to me. They explain about all the things I don't understand, and I love them to do that. They talk about all the different foods they eat and sometimes I say, "We happen to have that in England" so that it won't be so *wide* a difference. They explain to me about dressing and chitlins and greens. I'm still not sure what they mean by greens.

Greens can be anything: mustard greens, collard greens, turnip greens—

The tops of underground vegetables, eh? . . . I've tried a lot more food now, so that it's not so strange as it was in the past. I think the children understand me and I understand them much better after three years of it . . . I've taught at private schools in Australia and I didn't enjoy it nearly as much.

Do you think these kids are brighter or less so than the white kids you've taught?

Certainly many of them are just as bright and some are brighter. I mean, it depends on the measuring sticks again, doesn't it? In many ways they're much, much more interesting to teach because they respond, you know. And they're not oversure of themselves. They don't feel they know everything. Brighter? Heavens, I don't know. I wouldn't think there was that much difference, really. They certainly have more learning disabilities. From the fact that a lot of them don't get as many books or get taken to as many places. This sort of thing. But if you open up a world for them, they grab it so eagerly, they plunge right in. And they're so courageous. They're so unintimidated.

How do you get along with the black teachers here?

I found in my first year, that was a bad year, you know, there was a bit of constraint. I came from South Africa and they didn't know how I felt. But I don't have this problem any more. I don't think so; I hope I don't. I know some black teachers now, out of school, on a personal relationship—go to a party, have dinner together once in a while, so I shouldn't *think* there's any constraint.

4

THE NEW WAVE

*Young teachers are the best;
they are the most energetic,
most intuitive, and the least
resented.*

—Jacques Barzun

PAT KOSKINEN
Washington, D.C.

First of all there's the whole self-image business. A child has got to feel good about himself, that he's somebody, and can learn. Like the words "stupid" and "dumb" many of them have heard from their parents, from society, from our culture . . .

I start with something I know the children are going to be successful with. Many teachers start testing within the first couple of days to see where the children are but you can learn a tremendous amount just by watching them instead. A test is the most threatening thing to a child. I save it for a little later. Get the child's confidence first of all. Get him with some vested interest in you. Let him know that you care about him. The work is not all going to be inner-motivated by the material itself. Many children have to have an outside reason, possibly their desire to please you.

This school is K-through-6. The program I'm working in is K-through-3. Last year I taught second grade; two years ago, third grade here at Grimke. I don't have a class of my own because I'm a language arts teacher. I see six classes a day. Some classes twice a week. Generally I have them for only thirty-five minutes. This program was developed to be in-service training for other teachers here. So part of our job is working with the children. The other part is showing teachers new and different ways of working with children. But our work is scheduled for these other teachers' planning periods, when they can't be in the classroom. And the label we get as "relief" teachers stops all communication. The regular teachers generally aren't there to see what we're doing. This prevents them from being involved and making it a continuous program.

We're an all-black school. This neighborhood was designated by the President's Commission on Juvenile Delinquency as having an extremely high crime rate. We're four blocks from where the riots were last summer. In impoverished areas where I've been working, second grade means only that these children legally have to be in this grade. At the beginning of last year I had no children that were on a second-grade reading level. Some were non-readers and some were pre-primers. They were at least a year behind . . .

Pat Koskinen has honey-blond hair, country-fresh countenance, mini-skirted shapeliness. She's twenty-six and as unmindful of her beauty as Snow White. She is artlessly cordial, reassuringly direct. That, and her obvious enthusiasm for moving small kids toward proficiency in the Language Arts, compel instant attention to a deeper aspect of her identity. She's an open teacher running an open classroom at Grimke Elementary School* in near-Northwest Washington, D.C.

Inside and out, this building has had it; it's a depressing sight. Mrs. Koskinen's room is another matter. The walls and extensive floor space accommodate an eye-bewildering, color-splashed jumble of adult-originated artifacts in aid of education and the creations of young children caught up in acts of learning. A big sign says, "Read a book and share it: Paint a mural / Paint a picture / Make a puppet / Make a diorama, a bookcover, a mobile." And there is a mural: figures from "Hansel and

---

* Built in 1887. Renamed, posthumously, for Archibald H. Grimke (1849–1930), black member of a white Charleston, S.C. slave-holding family. He was a Lincoln University- and Harvard-educated journalist, lawyer, consul to Santo Domingo, civil rights advocate, a biographer of William Lloyd Garrison and Charles Sumner and, latterly, a president of the N.A.A.C.P.

Gretel," "Jack and the Beanstalk," "The Gingerbread Boy," etc., on a big sheet of tan wrapping paper, in crayon, water colors, Magic Marker ink.

A long wiggly craft-paper creature stretches horizontally above the top of one blackboard—the Bookworm. Every kid who reads books of his own choosing is represented by name and titles on a separate segment of this cryptozoic honor roll. The more readers, the longer the Bookworm grows.

There's a panel of color photographs the kids have taken of their teachers, each picture bearing a caption thought up by its photographer: "Mrs. Green ain't want her picture." "Miss Downs looked at the camera and the picture snapped. Miss Downs had on her shades."

There's a cardboard carton crammed with stick and hand puppets and props for dramatized storytelling. And a magnificent sequence of photographs of black urban life called "The City." The work of children, evidence of their willingness to learn, is salient, visually and atmospherically. In twenty minutes or so, the visitor's bewilderment wears off. The room makes excellent sense. So does Mrs. Koskinen, explaining her relation to it during a walk-around.

You want them to learn to read? You have to learn to speak first, to be comfortable and free in using speech. Many of my kids aren't, at least not in the schoolroom environment. I do a lot of language development, a lot of dramatics, with props and puppets that encourage the children to talk . . . This gingerbread house is one of the few things they didn't make . . . Who? . . . I did, for a prop when we acted out "Hansel and Gretel" . . . I make all the visual aids I can . . . You have to provide enough motivating circumstances to aid the memory . . .

Wanna see the puppets? Now, puppets, even if the children just do creative play with them, like pretending they're mother and father—it gives them a reason for speaking, a form, and something to speak about.

These are things the kids wrote, on this board here. I just typed them as they talked . . . You know, there's a tremendous controversy over using children's language. The old-line educators say if a child sees his words in writing exactly the way he speaks, he'll think that's the way he's *supposed* to speak and this will impede his development . . . I don't believe it will. Not at all. You should use his speech. Kids *should* see their language in writing. After we visited a farm, one kid said, "Me pat a rabbit." If I write it down as "I pat a rabbit," he's going to read it back as "*Me* pat a rabbit" anyway. But that doesn't mean he's going to say "me" the rest of his life.

All these papers are really part of a book that *they* have written and they will read it over and over again. Much of the language in trade books does not sound at all like the children's language. I don't think it hurts to have a few books *they've* written, in *their* language, and keep them around where they can get at them. These stories are being written by a slow first grade. Right now they really want to talk, but believe it or not, *they will read.*

At floor level a flannel board* leans against the wainscoting. It bears a huge color picture of the Apollo 9, cut into its component units: Saturn V rocket, command module, lunar module.

I knew they'd be hearing a lot of new words about Apollo 9 on TV, so we started with the assembled spacecraft. After "blast-off" we pulled off the first and second stages of the rocket. Next we uncovered the command module and the lunar module, separated them; then we "docked" again. After they had seen what happened they

---

* A display board surfaced with flannel to which flannel cut-outs—numbers, letters of the alphabet, other flat shapes—will adhere on contact. Used as a visual aid in elementary schools.

simulated the whole thing with body motion: lift-off, separation, crawling from one module to the other, orbiting, splashdown. I wrote the words on large sheets of paper for them to take home, told them to watch television and listen for these words. Some children collected newspaper pictures that demonstrated these words; some wrote stories using these words . . . a developmental process . . . I'm not a science teacher but whatever turns the kids on, I teach. I think children learn by doing. Physical involvement has a tremendous meaning for them. If you're going to talk about docking why not physically do it?

The only visual reading aids I can remember in my K-through-3 years were the alphabet on the blackboard, and those dopey little drawings in the Heath Readers, which I hated, by the way. Why do these kids need such elaborate techniques? Cultural deprivation?

What's cultural deprivation? It means many things to many people. To define it doesn't mean that's going to solve any of our problems. Cultural deprivation can mean the lack of the basic necessities, of constantly being worried about where the rent money, the gas money, is going to come from. You can have middle-class deprived homes just as well. A very disruptive family situation—two parents who pay really no attention to the children, don't give them any really basic consistent affection. Middle-class kids can be culturally deprived too. So can teachers who don't look at the children, don't see their problems, and don't adjust to them.

These children have responsibilities like taking care of younger brothers and sisters and making dinner, and this is way beyond children of their age in other areas of the city. But many of their interests are not academically oriented. Of some you can say they're bright, or dumb, or much slower than others in their class but it's a matter of potential.

Last year I had little Rosemary, whom you met, an absolute doll. I just—you know—if you ever think of adopting anybody, I would *really* like to take her home. She didn't read very much at first, obviously hadn't been taught. She has a memory like you wouldn't believe. You read to her, she will memorize the book. She's a real smart child. She tried to steal some gloves during the winter; it was very, very cold. I found out and I brought her mother some gloves to give to her . . . Her mother works from nine o'clock to eight o'clock or something like that. They live in literally one room, with a hot plate; the bathroom is down the hall. Her father comes home occasionally. I said to her mother, "I can just tell you really work with Rosemary because she's such a delightful child and she tries so hard." And she said, "No, I don't. I come home and I'm too tired. I just go to sleep." And here's this little girl just literally *thriving, entirely* by herself. She's just a beauty! You see, you don't know what the potential is, you really don't.

Your first impulse is to shower the children with love and to let them run all over you as a sign that you love them. I learned very quickly that that's not the way. I give everybody a good dose of tender loving care, but at the beginning I'm very stern (but kind), not very open, I'm not very loving. I'm precise, I give children definite boundaries. White teachers in impoverished areas, this is the one singling-out item: whether you can control the children. And it doesn't matter how young the children are; they can be out of control—a very big problem for white teachers.

What about black teachers?

Black teachers have problems too but it's usually the white teachers. This is why many of them can't teach in the ghetto. They come from a different kind of background. The way they talk to the children, their tone of voice. They come to a black school and they're not used to being precise, spelling out things clearly. Also sometimes the teacher can't understand the language the children use.

I had difficulties, too. But one thing was a real saving quality: I did a tremendous amount of home visiting at the beginning, because this was where I felt a tremendous lack. And I listened very closely to what other teachers said to children.

The black teacher I was working with when I started —she was very strong, very authoritarian, but a nice woman. All she would have to do was say "Boo" and the kids would sit up straight and be quiet. She was very fine in making a good disciplinarian out of me. She had so many things that I could parrot, so many things that I could say to the children. Some of her teaching techniques were very different from mine but I couldn't be teaching unless I learned how to handle the kids.

Do you ever have to whack a kid in the interest of "control" or use physical force of any kind?

That's one thing I don't do. I don't condemn people for doing it, but I've never hit a child and I don't ever plan to. No doubt about it; there's a lot of hitting. Teachers hit with rulers . . . It's a way to control children. That's not my style. To me, it's not a legitimate style. But it's also not fair to say this is an indication of a poor teacher. Some teachers, when they hit a kid, can get away with it.

Is it possible to hit a kid without giving him the idea that you have no respect for him and that he's no good?

I think it is. I've seen a couple of teachers do it, but it's the exception rather than the rule, like a mother spanking her child in an ideal circumstance: "I've told you, this is a serious rule, and if it is broken you are going to get a spanking." The meaning of this act depends on all the other factors in the relationship. Many teachers hit kids in an act of desperation and some are sadistic. You just have to establish other avenues of discipline . . . Some children don't think that much of being hit . . . If you are hit so often [outside of school] and you always see children fighting, it doesn't have the same significance that we attach to it. Physical punishment is so misused that I'm violently against it. I try to set the children an example of a *different* way of resolving situations. It sounds corny to say that kids learn by what they see, but this is how kids *do* learn. If you're going to hit kids, then it's perpetuating something I don't believe in. The children would just *die* if I hit someone, they would be so shocked. It's not my style and they know it. The main thing is to establish rapport with the children—Listen, do you want me to tell you about a few things that I think are a necessity for a teacher in this kind of area?

Sure. I want to know what you think.

Well, first of all, getting to know the community is absolutely crucial. Some teachers see a sleepy child and they get mad at him because he's not paying attention. You've got to have sensitivity as to why the kid is sleepy. Maybe the family moved the night before, or maybe he sleeps with three other kids, etc. Or why he's belligerent: because he didn't have anything to eat that morning. If you don't know how a child is living and surviving in spite of many things, you don't have an appreciation for this. But if you do know, you get a tremendous new respect. A lot of people are apt to look only at the bad things of the culture. It's so important to have a feeling of admiration for what the kids are doing . . . I've had discussions with kids about what *they're* fixing for dinner tonight, and this is a second or third grader. I mean they bring a tremendous sophistication and worldliness . . . And many times you'd never find it out because they don't talk about it.

The real Waterloo for many teachers is not knowing

the environment of the child. I mean, you know what a middle-class child's environment is like because you come from it, but you don't, for a black child, usually, and you really have to *get* out there and, I mean—I went to social service agencies last year; I took a couple of parents down to Welfare. I've had success in my relations with the parents because I go early, before the child has jumped out of the window or done something terrible. I'm big on preventive work so the catastrophe doesn't happen. Many of the parents have not been used to fair treatment in the schools. They're used to very condescending behavior from the teachers, black or white. A teacher's visit in the past always meant something bad was happening.

One crucial element in home visiting is that you come with something planned. I've always been on the lookout for children's clothes and getting them on the free lunch program. Like they have this stupid rule that the parent has to come to school to sign up for that, and many of the parents are at work, they don't even realize it's available. So I would go out and ask them, saying that we have this marvelous program of lunch and would you like to have your child come and have lunch? To begin with, I might tell them something nice about their son. It's really kind of plain tact, just ground rules with anyone, not especially with parents. But a lot of people forget this when they talk with parents.

Tell me about some of your visits.

There were two children I had a tremendous discipline problem with, at the beginning, so . . . I asked them if they wanted to go on a little trip with me. And, where? They said the zoo. So off we went one Saturday. This gave me an opportunity to speak to the mothers in a positive way. If you go to the parents with complaints, they're used to complaints and they're defensive. But telling them we were going on this trip built up rapport, and the next time I had problems I had the mothers' confidence.

I remember that first visit with one of the mothers. She was sitting on the porch. She knew me by sight because there were only three white teachers in the school. I just said it might be fun to take Tommy to the zoo if I had some time; that I wanted to get to know him a little better in hopes I'd be able to help him in his studies; and possibly if I got out and talked with him and we were sharing something a little bit different . . . She thought that was great. She said, "Fine," and I went around in my little VW picking up the kids that Saturday. I took three of them.

Tommy was third-grade, couldn't read, had a tremendous inferiority complex, lived in a condemned house—well, that's not so terribly unusual. But he was an inventive child, terribly clever artistically. He really started working after that, because the zoo trip helped us change our relationship a little. He made some just beautiful art objects. One of the greatest things . . . we were working on musical instruments at the time . . . He took a bike handlebar he'd found, bent it straight, pounded holes in it, and made a clarinet. Isn't that beautiful? He could blow on it, make a few sounds, but it needed some refinement. He also brought in a banjo he'd made out of a box, a piece of wood, some nails. *That* he did play quite well and we sang along with him. All of this made him really special and this is what he wanted. He didn't succeed in the normal reading and math avenues but the kids would really admire what he did. His whole self-image began to change.

Here's a good example of what you sometimes have to do to win a child's confidence so he'll start working. David, second grade, was literally out of class all the time. Hyperactive. He was supposed to be on drugs, tranquilizers, but he wasn't . . . He literally could not sit in his seat. Instead of sending him out immediately or calling his parents in, I had something called a play frame. It's made of pegboard and has no top on it. The child can go into it like a little house. He needed to work with his hands, so I let him. The minute he'd walk in, he'd go back to the play frame. He'd make all sorts of marvelous things with Tinker Toys, like a little car, and he'd run the thing down the middle of the aisle when I was teaching and I would pick up this thing and say, "Goodness gracious, David, that's a marvelous car . . ." It was just using good psychology.

David would constantly hit people. The only way I could survive was, we discussed one day when David wasn't there *why* he hit people and what *you* were doing if you hit him back. And I made it really almost under penalty of death: *nobody* was to hit David back. People don't give children enough credit for understanding, but they *realized* . . . And after six weeks of doing no work, he worked happily the rest of the year. He'd maybe play with the play frame for an hour, come back and do twenty minutes of math, then he'd go and work off his tensions, come back, and work again. He still got into a few fights but not with his classmates. He was just delightful, a lovable child.

His parents were very belligerent. His father had a heart condition and he taught David that it's a dog-eat-dog world; therefore you hit, you do whatever you feel like doing—and don't bother with the teachers. Yet, the father was impressed that I came to tell him not that David was so horrible but that he was improving a little bit. You kind of have to get personally involved. It worked the same way with this special teacher whose class David went to. (He definitely had a spatial disorientation.) He would sit there and put his coat over his head and throw shoes at the board . . . I told her that, possibly, if she gave him something successful to do when he first came in—and believe it or not, he started working for *her*. This is not only with him but with a lot of children. Success really breeds success.

Do you have any discussions in class about what goes on outside, about what the kids do, about their families, their neighborhood, that sort of thing?

We do talk about what they do out of school but without stressing the family problems. I don't know whether it's right or wrong not to, but more than half don't have fathers and *they're* sensitive on this issue. Maybe if the children were a little older we'd talk about the more personal problems. But we have all sorts of school problems that we discuss. About fighting, for instance, acting out how a situation could be worked out in a different way.

After Martin Luther King's death we talked about the looting and rioting. It was very frightening for some of the children. Like when there were shots outside their window and one little child fell to the floor. Many of them said that the tear gas came in and burned their eyes. Some talked about the belongings their uncles got. They saw the window and it was open, and people in the supermarket were taking things. They drew pictures of what the people were doing and things that happened to them.

We talked about Martin Luther King and Rosa Parks, kind of a historical thing on the sit-in movement, and what a soul brother was. That was just kind of exploring—very, very elementary. You know, a soul brother was nice. Did it mean he was black? Could a white person be a soul brother?

Many children said no, that a white person couldn't be a soul brother. Then one of the kids said, "But Mrs. Koskinen is white!" From that point on, the discussion altered slightly. Most of the children, because I was there, thought that a soul brother could be white. But they didn't think that my intern teacher, who was white, was a soul brother. The thing is, it's still second grade and this is a very difficult concept. In the third grade everybody knew I was white, but a lot of the little children don't think some-times that the teacher is white.

At the beginning of the term we were doing autobiog-raphies. To start the children, I told them about myself and my family, and I brought in some pictures of my family. This was to let the children see me as a person, to notice detail, to lead them to tell about themselves. So they got to draw me, however they saw me, what I looked like. At this point a lot of the children drew me black. I think this was just because they're used to drawing people black and most of their teachers have been black.

Pat Koskinen was born in Santa Cruz, Calif. She spent most of her first seven years in San Francisco. When she was eighteen months old her mother died of polio. Pat, stricken at the same time, needed a long course of surgery (functionally successful and cosmetically faultless) to cor-rect muscular impairment of one of her legs. "I think that made a difference in my life; you get sensitive to other people's difficulties when you have problems of your own."

Pat's family background could be called enriched multi-ethnic. Her mother's origins were Scotch/Irish/ French. Her father, German-Jewish, was remarried to a Japanese woman in Hawaii when Pat was about eight; Pat grew up there with several half-Japanese brothers and sis-ters. She also has three black cousins, children of her father's sister's husband. As a child she accompanied her father, an official of the International Longshoremen's and Warehousemen's Union, to the homes of low-income dock workers. She reacted with empathy because of what she knew about her stepmother's growing up on "a rather poor plantation place in Hawaii." She regards her father as having always been very civil-rights-oriented, very aware of people: "He hasn't just talked it; he's lived it." He subse-quently switched from trade union administration to the practice of law.

It was a great background, a good family. When I went to college, my father went to law school, a year ahead of my husband. I went to Oberlin from '60 to '63, married in my senior year. My husband was at Yale Law, so I transferred to Connecticut College for Women. Then we went to England for a year, and then we came to Washington. I was a psychology major and I was planning to work for an M.A. but I heard about the Cardozo project* here, so I thought I'd try it for a year. It was on-the-job training, where we immediately went into a classroom and worked with an experienced black teacher. We had outside help and consulting as far as technique was concerned but no regular teacher-training courses. I just went into the classroom and started teaching. It was the sink-or-swim method. I really enjoyed myself. I've never found something that, as they say, turned me on so much. First of all, there's a tremendous need, there's no doubt about it. And it's very rewarding to work in an area where you are *needed*. I had no idea I'd ever stay in teaching but I feel I'm going to, believe it or not.

Then that summer I worked with a group called Innovation Team, teaching in an impoverished area in California. Then I came back here and taught second grade and trained teachers in the Cardozo program. What I'm doing here now is part of that. There are several other Cardozo interns here. And last summer I taught interns from the graduate program at Antioch here in the city.

I must admit, I've been a detractor. The idea of the Cardozo Project, of on-the-job training, is fantastic, but I think it still needs a lot of refinement. During the past

* So called to identify Cardozo High and several lower schools in its vicinity, including Grimke, as part of the District of Columbia Model School Division instituted in the mid-1960s and embracing fifteen elementary and four junior high schools. Its purpose has been to establish the use of materials, techniques and teacher-pupil relationships associated with the (widely variable) concept of "the open classroom."

couple of years they've had a chance to practice at it but they still do it sink-or-swim. They just throw teachers into the classroom.

I'm not sure teaching children in this neighborhood is so different, but in teacher-training colleges, you're taught only the basic, dull, middle-class things, not how to teach in impoverished areas. I think the major reason we have more trouble in our inner-city schools than we do in other places is that we get many of the most poorly equipped schoolteachers. If we had the best teachers they would be smart enough to say, "What's wrong with *this* child?" and would be able to adapt. Elementary education hasn't been attracting the best talent mainly because the ed. courses are so mundane and you're having to give up the *exciting* things that you learn in college, so . . .

I think that there's a whole new wave now, and education *can* be exciting but it needs people to *generate* this excitement and to carry it through. I think you can see it in the new crop of teachers that's coming up. It's more social-action-oriented, more socially conscious. I think a teacher's role *has* to have much more community involvement in it, especially with children who are oppressed by poverty.

SUSAN HARRIS
Detroit

I have this wig; it matches my normal hair. I don't wear it too often, but one day—it was so funny—I was leaving early and, in front of the building, off goes my wig and off I go chasing it down the street. Usually there aren't too many kids outside, but all the kids seemed to be there that day. They were laughing at me and I had to start laughing. The next day I never heard the end of it. "Your wig blew off, didn't it?" "Hey, Miss Harris, did your wig blow off?" Some of them would just go by and start laughing. And they don't always call me Miss Harris. Sometimes its Scaly Sue or Big Mabel or Hey, Susie.

"Scaly Sue," that started last summer, in Operation Go. That's a federal program for potential dropouts—small groups of kids each with three adults. We did everything with the kids, took them to museums and beaches. I have a skin allergy, and when I got sunburned my skin was all dry and flaky. One of the teachers gave me this name and the kids picked it up. So I was SS and Scaly Sue.

"Big Mabel" came from *The Learning Tree.** I took a class to see it last semester. She was a prostitute in the film and they started calling me Big Mabel. I get Hey baby, too, when I'm walking down the hall. It makes no difference, this kind of thing. It depends on the situation.

Some of the big kids talk about my legs, but the only time I really object is when a kid in the class calls, "Hey, baby," and makes a big thing out of it and the class wants to make it an excuse for goofing off. In the hall it doesn't bother me. I turn around and call the kid a nickname: "Hey, Chi-Chi." I figure if they think enough of me to tease me, I should be able to take this. They like me and they show it. If they didn't they wouldn't pay me any attention half the time.

Susan Harris teaches reading and speech (in the teachers' lounge they call it "reech") at Miller Junior High in Detroit. The school has an integrated enrollment, with whites in the minority; for example, her 7A class has six white, twenty-five black students. She's twenty-three,

* Movie version of a novel about black childhood by Gordon Parks, directed by the author and released in 1969.

blond, lissomely medium tall, personable. Indianapolis-born, she lived her first decade there; her second, in Columbus, Ohio, and in Worthington, a suburb thereof. How did she happen to come to Detroit?

That starts back at Bowling Green [Ohio] State University, in the College of Education. For two summers while I was there, I was a tutor-counselor in Upward Bound, which tries to motivate students from low economic areas to go to college. We lived in the dorm with the students—high school students, mainly black, from the surrounding counties. I lived in with the girls as a counselor and I also went to their classes, for which there were certified teachers, but I wanted to know what was going on because it helped my counseling. I also had my own class where I taught geology, sort of an experience in teaching. I really became involved with the students. They were the cream of the crop from low economic backgrounds, but they had so many problems! They needed understanding, good teachers, teachers that were concerned. This was what made me want to teach in a city school.

With the exception of one or two black kids in my high school, I had never associated with blacks before. Not only with my students but my peers with whom I worked in the Upward Bound program—we became very close. I'd say there were eight or ten of us at Bowling Green. We had the same concerns; it was a rich experience for me. One black girl, we graduated together and came up here together, lived together here in Detroit. I still write to the others, call them. In fact, I have a huge phone bill. This was where my involvement began, at college.

I started out in biology and ended up with English and French but I had planned to teach. I didn't know where. I didn't want to stay in Columbus where I lived. I wanted to get away. Chicago and New York were almost too big for me, I felt. I had thought of Cleveland, Philadelphia. I interviewed here. Detroit impressed me, and I feel they were impressed with me because they offered me a contract on the spot. I said no, I want to interview with the other schools first. I want to have time to think about it. This was in February, before I had done my student teaching or anything. I wasn't going to graduate until August. But in March I signed my contract with Detroit and specifically asked to teach in an inner-city school because these schools, traditionally or historically, have been a place where they throw anybody. Nobody wants to go there. This is where the most rapid rate of turnover is, especially in junior high. The best people get to choose where they want to go. The inner city gets what's left over. You see this in supplies even, in the Detroit system. I know people teaching in Detroit schools next to the suburban areas who have all the supplies in the world, and we don't have any. I'm not talking about paper, chalk and ditto paper, things like this. I'm talking about machinery, automatic duplicators, tape recorders, what have you, that they have more of than we do. I wanted to use a film strip projector last semester. We didn't have one in the building that worked. When you get ready to use the tape recorder, you have to go find the reel, then you have to go find the microphone from somebody else. We have *some* things, but in comparison, if you would go from Miller out to Murphy Junior High near Redford Township on the northwest side of town, you'd find four times as much as we have.

Inner-city schools are short-changed. Blacks are short-changed. They're short-changed in education, therefore they are short-changed in jobs. They can't get jobs, then their children can't be educated. A vicious circle.

As far as my formal education courses in college, they were nothing, except my philosophy-of-education class. I had a beautiful professor—free, not requiring anything. He suggested reading for us to do. There was free discussion in class. He believed that what you were going to learn you would learn, regardless. He asked, "What grade do you want?" I said, "I don't care. I feel as if I learned a lot and the grade is not important to me. I have a B average; give me a B."

The education courses, per se, didn't prepare me for teaching in an inner-city school. That came from my experiences with people, especially my black friends. I learned a lot from them as far as being honest with one another. They express their feelings, their thoughts. Some were a bit older. They came from inner cities but they had made it, they were going to college. One guy had been in the Army, was going to school on a GI loan. A very well-read person with a C average in college. He was more educated than I am, from his experience and his own reading. He's in grad school now, University of Cincinnati, working on his doctorate.

When I knew I was going to Detroit, I had this brainstorm. I went to my philosophy-of-education teacher thinking that maybe I could get my student-teaching requirement waived and do some independent study on black history, black literature, instead. But the university requirements were set up by the state and the supervisor of student teachers sent me to a school in the middle of the corn fields, Lakota High School, about fifteen miles from Bowling Green. I had no problems. I taught in the spring, April through May; just came in and took over—three classes of French, three classes of English, all ninth grade. I enjoyed it but . . .

If you're going to teach in a black school you should know something about black history, black literature. Now I'm teaching reading and speech and we use, you know, a basal-skills reading book. It's sort of irrelevant. As far as I can see, it's sitting down and doing exercises. If a kid likes to read, it's fine, but I should be teaching reading in a context that they are interested in. If a kid is interested in black history, okay, let that kid learn to read by reading that.

Today I tried an experiment with a class that—oh, they could drive me crazy. They are a very talkative class, very immature. I have them late in the morning. I don't eat lunch until one-fifteen and my energy level is down because I'm hungry, you know. This has a lot to do with how I react. I was feeling very frustrated. I thought, Why, they're not *learning* anything. They are *failing*.

The kids read comics. Every day they come in reading comics and I say, "Got to put that away. Got to get to our work." This time I said, "How many of you have comic books today?" Some of them raised their hands and I said, "Okay, would you like to read them?" Some said, "Okay," so I said, "Why don't you sit over here by the window. What I want you to do later is to tell in your own words what you have read. Also I would like you to make a list of the words you're not quite sure what they mean."

Then I asked how many wanted to work on their SRA* kits because some kids really like to do this. "Okay, you guys move over there too. And the rest of you, would you like to read the controlled reader?"† "Yeah, we want to see that today." So, "Okay. I'll be with you in a minute because I have these kids over by the window to straighten

---

* SRA = Science Research Associates. The kits are designed to move users from lower to higher reading-ability levels expectable within a bracket of two or three grades, for example, grades seven to nine. Physically, the kit consists of short selections from a fairly wide range of subject matter, questions, and answer keys, printed on separate sets of cards; plus a record book in which the student can write his answers to the questions.
† A largely automatic projector designed to illuminate reading material, usually brief stories, one phrase or one line at a time, at a rate of speed set by the teacher. Its purpose is to make consistent left-to-right eye movement, without backtracking, which is a strong habit. The teacher uses a printed test manual to assess the students' comprehension of what they have read.

out." Then back to the controlled-reader kids: "What would you like?" They finally chose "Rumpelstiltskin." So I wrote our key words* on the board and: "Let's see if we can tell what these words mean, in our *own* words." They didn't know what a miller was. I explained . . . Then: "Okay, we're set to read." They went at it and when somebody started to read out loud, I said, "Read to yourselves, you guys," and I explained why . . . Also I could circulate on the other side of the room. Somebody was playing with the shade; I looked at him and he got back to his comic book. I had to go over mainly and help students and maybe ask questions but I was really amazed. Some of these kids, they were beautiful. And they were all *doing* something, most of them. The kids that had the comic books, some of them said, "Miss Harris, could I finish tonight and bring in the words tomorrow?"—the first time that somebody wanted to finish something at home.

If they're interested in comic books, let them read comic books and then work into the other contents of reading. But first of all they have to master the skills of reading. What I was doing before wasn't working. It was failing. Why can't we try something else?

Wait—are you telling me you feel that you must accept the children's choice of content?

Yes, to a certain extent. Now, I have to place limitations . . . oh . . . a sex book. I would have to be very careful and it's obvious why—parent reactions. But if I had a child who had run away from home, okay, I'm gonna get him to read by reading dirty parts in a book if I have to. I admit it. I haven't actually had any kids reading pornography, but I would accept it. No qualms about it. If that's how they're going to learn to read, that's what I'm interested in. So I had success today and I hope to have it

---

* Words essential to a clear understanding of the story or to development of the students' vocabulary.

tomorrow. Carry-over. And if it doesn't work, I'll try something else.

On a real bad day, sometimes, I think: What else can I do? Be a secretary? No. I'd be bored to death. Be an interpreter? I'd need much more skill and background in French. But I *have* a skill now—mmm—I think teachers need to be more professional than they are . . .

You've been teaching at Miller for not quite two years. I watched you yesterday. You seemed like an old hand. Do you intend to go on teaching?

I just started working for my master's at Wayne, taking courses in linguistics of reading and in core curriculum and this is where I have gotten a lot of my ideas about learning—that you don't learn anything unless you really want to. No one does.

My professor, Dr. Clute, started out the class by asking, "How do you feel when you have learned something?" I took it back and we did this in class; they discussed how they feel when they have learned something. That question turned these kids on. It was hard for them to get started—they're immature—but it was very successful. This was in an English class. I had been hearing them say, "We don't like what we're doing. We're bored. We just sit and discuss this book." They liked to read the stories but they thought we dragged out the discussions too long. This gave me an idea. Why not pursue their own interests as far as English is concerned? I didn't propose any projects. I said, "What do you want to do?" and they came up with some ideas. A group of them read the same book and discussed it. Some of them said, "I don't know what I want to do." I said, "Isn't there anything you want to learn about English? If you're not interested in English for itself, are you interested in something in science? Do you have any pets at home? Or do you like music? You could write a research paper on this."

Some of them didn't think of a project because, for example, they didn't see any connection between science and knowing English. There's this boy, Gerald. Other kids pick on him, call him names and he gets violently angry. I try to watch how things go in the class, to keep him from getting upset, to keep the other kids from picking on him. He's very interested in technical things, cars and engines, building things. He wrote a beautiful thing on cars. This was something that he was *interested* in.

Now we have a discussion group, a playwriting group, creative-writing students. I had this one girl, Alberta, who had been turned off. Up to the time we started doing this individual learning, she never had her books; somebody broke into her locker and stole them. She lost her paper. She didn't have a pencil. She slept in class. Very seldom did she enter a class discussion. She has a home experience that is very unfavorable. I think she lives with her grandmother. I don't know all the ramifications of her background, but it definitely comes through that she has a temper. This winter she called me everything but a child of God—you white bitch, you asshole. One day she accused me of being prejudiced because a girl was crawling across the floor and I sent her out of the room. She said, "You sent her out. Why didn't you send that white boy out who was talking back there?" Another time we discussed poetry by Langston Hughes and she said, "You're white. What right do you have to teach about black people? You don't know what they feel. You haven't experienced these things."

I said, "Right. I can't experience the same things that you have because I am white and you are black. I agree with this. But I can present poetry to be discussed. If it were Walt Whitman, you would interpret it according to your background as I would interpret it according to my background."

I felt she was trying to back me into a corner and I was trying to be rational with her. Some people agreed with her and some disagreed, but it was very interesting. Usually the student at a junior high school doesn't attack you that way. They accept you because you are *you*, white or black, if you are sincere, if you are fair; they see right through you if you are phony. She had a lot of bitterness; and I didn't wholly answer her. But when we started this individual learning she began to turn in poetry. Yesterday she gave me this poem, "Hey Black Girl."

She came back this morning to pick up her notebook and I said, "How would you like to publish this poetry? It's very good." "What did I get on it?" she said. I said, "A, of course. It's excellent." Her face! I can't describe it. The look of success. She was pleased, elated. It made her feel so good. I'll talk to her more about publishing it. I don't know how . . .

How do you teach creative writing?

I don't know, really . . . This is something that stems from what a child wants to express and I let him express it.

I noticed in one of Alberta's poems she misspelled "communication." I was thinking last night how I could suggest, for example, that she misspelled the word. Maybe I would ask her if I could make suggestions on one or two points of spelling or grammar and *not* on her ideas. If she would say "Yes," okay. If she said, "No, I like the way it is; it's mine," then I wouldn't say anything to her because I wouldn't want to destroy what I've seen come out in her. She was so turned off before.

Our schools are stifling creativity. We say, "Come in, open up the books. This is what we're doing today. Don't stray from the course. Maybe we'll get into a discussion. Fine, express your points of view, but that's it."

Your tone—you sound so concerned that—

I am. You have to be in order to really teach, do a good job. You have to be really concerned. Otherwise you're just going in and drawing a pay check. We have teachers down here that are doing this, and they do it everywhere, not just in inner-city schools.

I try to be involved with the kids after school, too. I feel I'm single and can afford the time, whereas married teachers cannot. Like chaperoning dances or being a lifeguard at splash parties, or this variety show I was helping the kids with last night. Not really helping, just being there. They were running the show themselves. My homeroom is a ninth and they're graduating. What they're working on is to make money for their prom. They don't want to have it in the gym. That's the same old thing—they have dances down there all the time. They want to have enough money to rent a hall and have a band. They've got high school friends that play in a band and won't charge them too much. So, they've had a bake sale, dances, and sold things. This variety show is another way of raising money.

Then I'm co-sponsor of the Girls' Athletic Association and sponsor of the cheerleaders. The girls approached me. The sponsor they had had to give it up. I said, "Sure, I'll take it." The kids do everything, except I unlock the gym door. I have a good time. I bought their sweatshirts for them; they partially paid me back. They were yellow and I got some blue felt to sew on—M's for Miller. Cheerleading is a wonderful activity. The kids have to get to school to practice, you know, meet certain standards. This is good self-discipline for them.

I enjoy being with kids outside the classroom. Last year I took kids home to stay all night with me. They really enjoyed it. They played records, talked, washed their clothes, did the dishes and had a good time. I loved it. I wouldn't make this an everyday practice, but once in a while it's enjoyable. You learn a lot about the kids; they sit and talk and they're very free. I'm also in this Curriculum Committee which was set up this fall by our assistant principal. He's new and he's very concerned about relevant curriculum for the kids. We've been doing a sort of self-study; questionnaires to staff, first of all, to get their views. Part of the problem in the junior high school is the rapid rate of teacher turnover. So many want to move up to the high school and then stay there until they retire. We discussed incentive pay for junior high so you might be able to be more selective in hiring teachers, really look for them instead of just getting the leftovers.

Then we asked the kids, each homeroom, to elect two representatives to come to our meetings. We said, "Now, we're here to listen to you. We don't want to talk. We want you to talk." They were very honest, expressed themselves very well on things they thought should be changed and on things they liked at school. A lot of them felt that they should have more black literature and Afro-American history classes. One student said they were tired of doing dictionary work in English. They wanted to learn how to write research papers, term papers, that will help them when they go to high school. Some kids brought up things about having the lockers broken into, books and belongings stolen.

They also brought up the honors program. Our school has a unique situation. Part of the enrollment comes from Lafayette Towers, the Lafayette Park area—middle-class, professional people. This was supposed to be an urban renewal area but it didn't turn out to be that for the people who used to live there.* Then, most of our school population is black and poor. So these honors classes were mainly designed for the middle-class children, the more highly motivated children. They are not any better—in fact, sometimes they're spoiled brats. Their parents are pains sometimes. Yet they can be very helpful and can push for things like a new cafeteria that Miller needs.

So we have these honors classes and the kids feel that

* Lafayette Towers is a high-rise, high-rent apartment complex.

sometimes the people in them are rather snobby. The students, in general, feel there shouldn't be honors homerooms,* but maybe an honors class in English. All students that have a particular interest or do better in English should be in this class. If some students do better in math, they would go to an honors math class.

Many staff members are against the honors homerooms too. There should be more mobility. Some children are slow in reading, but not all of them. You can have a fast kid in a class with slower students. You could have the faster kid help a slower student while you're over helping another one. This technique works quite well. Sometimes it depends on what two students you put together, you know.

It's perfectly natural for people, including teachers, to be more attracted to the bright kids. Are you?

In a sense, yes, but also I'm attracted to the others. For example, this one child, his name is Hubert, and I had him in a 7B "reech" class. He did absolutely nothing but cause trouble. Then, in the summer, I worked in Operation Go. The main goal of the program—a very difficult goal—was to change the attitudes of these students from negative to positive, toward school, adults, peers. The students we selected had to meet three of these criteria: police contact, constant counseling referral, low grades, at least one or two grade failures, low scores on tests of mental maturity, truancy—quite different from Upward Bound.

Hubert was one of these underachievers. He failed the semester I had him. He was doing nothing and he certainly qualified for Operation Go.

We had a very unstructured program—from nine to twelve-thirty five days a week. The kids came in, sat around and ate breakfast first. Three days a week were for academic work and the other two for trips—education trips,

* In practice, the honors homerooms are a tracking device.

fun trips, to museums, beaches. And we horsed around, rolling around on the grass, throwing it in each other's faces, down our backs. This was a very personal thing. We were human beings and the kids saw this. These kids especially needed somebody to relate to. They needed to know that you cared about them—they needed to play around with you because this is part of human interaction.

To get back to Hubert. All summer he was actively involved, rarely missed a day. When we had written work he would write almost a whole page, which was progress. After the summer, I had Hubert again. He was back in 7B for the second time. I could see him influencing the other students, especially the boys, in a negative way. He was very sneaky, would do anything but his work. I talked to him constantly: "Hubert, I'm behind you," but Hubert was failing again.

The class went to the library one day. Library cards are issued to the students free, of course, but if they lose their card they have to pay a nickel for another one. Hubert said, "I never got my card. I wasn't there when my homeroom teacher was passing them out." The way he looked at me I felt he was communicating to me, like: "Let's *see* if you're behind me, Miss Harris." So we went up to the librarian and I said, "Mrs. Clements, Hubert was one of the students who didn't get his library card when they were passed out. May he have one?" She said to him ,"Okay, I'll get you one. Miss Harris has vouched for you." Hubert looked up at me and there was something in that look that said he now trusted me because I had trusted him. I wasn't sure that he was telling the truth, but I *took his word*.

Now I have him in English—the third semester in a row. I don't know what's *happened*. He's been to class on time. Usually he has a notebook, paper, does his work, doesn't throw things around. The other day I said to Hubert, "Do you know what you got on your report?

You're going to get a C1." The numbers 1,2,3 after the grade mean citizenship: 1 is outstanding, 2 is average and 3 is below average. The kid was a constant troublemaker. So now he has moved up from a totally failing grade, E3, to C1. I'm so proud of him.

I had been over to his home several times. His mother tries very hard, but Hubert has older brothers and sisters that he is influenced by—they dropped out of school. She explained this to me. She said, you know, "I can beat Hubert and beat him but it don't do any good." And I said, you know, "Sometimes this doesn't work at all."

Does it ever work?

I don't think so. I don't know—it depends. Paddling is legal in our school. A lot of teachers use a paddle. They make a joke of it; call it a "board of education." It depends on the personality of the teacher, how it is done.

If I paddle a student, I usually take him out in the hall where no one is watching. Sometimes I just go out and talk to a child and the other kids don't know. Sometimes I pretend like I hit him. I say, "Now, look, I'm going to hit the lockers and you [she giggled] pretend like I hit you when you walk back in so nobody knows what really happened." I don't like to use the paddle . . .

I think you can show you care in other ways. What methods you employ depend on your personality.

What's the extent and quality of the school's relations with the community?

We have a very active, a very concerned community. We have to learn to get along with them. We have to be sort of professional advisers, explain things so they understand. They have to feel that we think they are important. And I do. I respect parents and the community people. There are people who are working as aides in the building and I feel that I have a good rapport with them. I have visited homes to talk with parents of Operation Go children. Also we have parent-teacher conferences and two or three times a year we go out to homes. This year my aide went with me. She is also a parent, concerned. When I take kids home from basketball games I run up and say "Hi" to the parents or I make contact with them through other extracurricular activities. I also phone parents. If I'm having a problem with a child, I call and say, "I'm concerned. The child's not doing his work. Could you possibly help in some way?"

Have you ever heard people say, with a touch of self-satisfaction, "I'm color-blind"?

In a sense, they aren't being very realistic. I mean, you *see* color. I myself wouldn't say "I'm color-blind." I would say to the kids that I don't care what color they are. They're kids to me. But I'm to the point where I don't always notice color. A friend of mine is doing postgraduate work in the field of special education. She asked if she could come and give my children a self-esteem test, and have them draw pictures of themselves. Later I went over to her apartment to help her get her things together and to tell her who was black and who was white. Next day, I had to call her and say, "Wait, I made a mistake on one girl"— I had told her the wrong color. So this is an example. I really don't pay that much attention to white kids or black kids.

Some people have argued that it is not the role of a white person to be in a black school any more, that blacks should be taught by blacks. I would not agree with that. I would say it depends on your personal desires, where you want to be, your interests. There are some—they are good teachers, but they have limited experience with black people and people of low economic backgrounds. Okay, they don't need to be in an inner-city school, because of their attitudes, because of the nature of our society, the way people are brought up, the way prejudices are passed down from generation to generation.

I would say not only to white teachers but to *any* new teacher that you have to be sincere, honest, you have to be concerned about any child. You have to live through the hard times because it is going to be hard in an inner-city school whether you're black or white. You're going to fall down and you have to get back up. You go through so many times of being frustrated, so much feeling of being inadequate. But this is just something that you have to live through and in time it comes—learning to communicate with your class. You have to go by the trial-and-error method as to what will work for you, for your personality, in your specific situation.

In an inner-city school you have to be dedicated, concerned about the students today, 101 percent. I'm always trying new ideas. Like, I just started having the kids make progress reports on themselves. I want them to evaluate themselves and get away from this teacher evaluation, these tests . . . I'm not trying to teach something, because you don't really teach, but to try to motivate students, try to find a student's interest and guide him so that he learns. That would be my definition of a good teacher. If you could make it in an inner-city school, I think you could make it anywhere as far as teaching is concerned.

Sometimes it seems impossible to change things, but we can't give up. *This is the future of our country.* We have to keep on trying. Trying new ideas and seeing how they work, starting a mood of enthusiasm that runs through a building . . .

So myself, I think of friends, people that got married right out of college, even out of high school. How much they have lost as far as new experiences. There are so many things to gain here—the teaching, the different people that I meet. I look forward to each day. It's never dull. It's always exciting. What if I was tied down with kids of my own?

STEVEN DANIELS
Philadelphia

You have the feeling that it's kind of like the witches scene in *Macbeth*; that maybe two thousand years ago some people sat around a table and tried to figure out a way to purposely destroy people, especially kids. And the best thing they could come up with was this educational system. Right down to the minutiae. I can conclusively tell you, as can anybody who spends ten minutes in any classroom, what's happening now doesn't work.

Teaching in a ghetto school is fantastically difficult. A teacher goes in there every day, drags along and sees his kids are falling farther and farther behind every year. Now, subconsciously or quasi-consciously (but never consciously, right?) a teacher has to say to himself, "Probably something's wrong. The kids are failing and here I am. Either: (a) I'm a crummy teacher or (b) these kids aren't teachable." Right? Now, *given* that, what is *any* human being going to say, except the more exceptional ones?

It's bad enough you have to put up with all the crap—I mean all the administrative shit you have in any school—the endless forms and routines, the pencils and erasers . . . which in the suburbs you can put up with to a degree because at least, in the forty minutes, you're dealing with various kids, as I did, who jumped on me because I confused the words "libel" and "slander," right? Whereas in the slum school, you've got troubles with the administration and you've got troubles with the kids. You have six hours a day of sheer hell. Most people who teach get zero satisfaction. And up until just about today, zero money. Today's starting salary in this town, $7,500 or $7,200, ain't bad, but then you get the take-home, $5,000, $4,950; so you don't even get the satisfaction of a pay check.

So it's easier to say, "Listen, I can't teach these kids. *Nobody* can teach these kids. These kids can't be taught." And that's the end of the story.

You may think it incredible but I can't find three effective teachers, and I know easily a hundred and fifty, two hundred. There's just so much *crap* that goes on, and these kids are systematically beat over the heads. In the suburban schools you're likely to produce a maladjusted kid who'll try to be happy with his job or maybe he won't. But at least it's only him. When you get a maladjusted kid out of my school, he isn't going to commit suicide until he's bumped off half a dozen people.

These kids get shot—thirteen, fourteen years old. A kid I taught two years ago was knifed to death. The injuries are pretty systematic. Over the last six months, I've had two kids who've been clubbed, half a dozen who've refused to come to school because they feel that their life is in danger.

That's not an exaggeration. Gang warfare in Philadelphia is the worst in the nation. And North Philly, the area of this school, has its own reputation. The only kind thing you can say about North Philly is that Bill Cosby*

* Bill Cosby flunked out of tenth grade, joined the Navy and finished his high school education by taking correspondence courses. Subsequently he attended Temple University on a scholarship. He emerged as a major television personality in the mid-1960s. Over the years he has drawn extensively on his background as an urban black child and adolescent for his characteristically low-key, self-

177

was born here. He's a source of great pride. Otherwise, there's not much to be said for it.

So the teachers get zero. They get zero coming and zero going. It's amazing that more of them aren't embittered. It takes an exceptional person to keep his equanimity, you know, just to maintain your cool.

So, how is it for you? How do you stand it?

Well, I started out badly. There are certain classical mistakes that everyone makes the first year. Then the question becomes: either (a) you quit, which many people do, (b) you become embittered and continue, and therefore embitter the children or (c) you try to revise whatever the hell you're doing so that something works. I tried the third. I wasn't going to come back; when I left that June, that was it. But for me, as well as for hundreds of thousands of other kids, the alternative was the draft. So I figured what the hell, let's give it a go. We'll go back to Stoddart-Fleisher and see what we can do.

Why?

Well, there were two questions. First, is it possible to educate these kids? Then, if it is possible, can I do it? . . .

Steven Daniels' reading room at Stoddart-Fleisher is furnished with orange crates for make-do library stacks: hundreds of paperback books; salvaged chairs, mostly hard, a few overstuffed; a magazine rack holding copies of Ebony, Black World, Sepia, Soul, Life, *others. The décor is Open Classroom Random—pupils' drawings, pictures and text material clipped from publications, a composite chart recording the students' individual progress, by name and reading achievement.*

---

respecting though unmilitant humor. In his performances, with stabs of sudden earnestness, he has occasionally urged on youthful viewers the importance of not dropping out of school.

Daniels' clutter-topped desk, obscurely located, looks as if it's in the room only because he might want to use it some day. He stands, walks, sits, with and among his students.

He is twenty-four, dark-haired, with some of the supple, symmetric handsomeness of Classical sculpture. At college his major was television production. "Then I looked at it; I thought it was, as a way of life, pretty grim. Television seemed to me—not a question of just having skill but of having all the skill in the world and then having a break. Right? Whereas in a field like writing, whether it sells or not, if you feel it to be a great work, it's a great work to you, and it's not up to Joe Slob whether it gets on the nine o'clock slot. Or if you decide to play the violin, you may not get a job at the Philharmonic but you still play a pretty good violin. Or if you teach, teaching is a positive skill and if you do it well, it's because you've done it well."

. . . So I went back and the second year went fantastically well. I picked two objectives; more than two is absurd; *two* is a lot. You know? I have ten months with a hundred and sixty kids. What do I want them to get out of having known me or sat in my room?

Reading, first. Because if you have the ability to read you can do whatever else you want. If you can't read . . . you're dead. I mean in terms of negotiating your way through life. Like picking up *TV Guide* to find out what's on the tube. That's what affects a kid directly now, as opposed to, like job applications five years from now. Five years from now for a thirteen-year-old kid is like forever and then three weeks.

And second, self-esteem. The kid's got to see himself in a different light.

All right. A person reads because he wants some information. Or because he *enjoys* reading. In a suburban school, a kid has to find information about—who knows?—Latin-American history, point A, B, C. He knows he can read a history book to get it. He has the motivation to sit through it because he knows he'll get a home, a car and a whole life. And he gets that by sitting through all this crap.

We take a slum kid—he has no motivation. He's not gonna get a Mustang, he's not gonna get a good job—the whole bit—whether he does or does not do the work. So he's not seeking information.

You can get him to read, however. You say, "Hey, kid, here's a good book. You want to read it?" And he'll say maybe yeah, maybe no. So you sit him down. It's a lot more structured than that. There's a lot of complexities in it, but basically you give the kid a book you want him to read.

I'm a salesman. I'm selling this book. I say, "Look at this great story." Or "A guy spent a year of his life writing this. You give him five minutes. You give him the first two pages. You want to throw the book on the floor after the first two pages, throw it on the floor. Or read a little more if you want."

Some kids, I can look straight in the eye and say, "Read the first two pages of this book," and they're going to. They're going to read the whole book if I say it that way, right? Or I can say "It's pornographic," or "I'm selling rubbers under the counter," or "I got a great misprint here." It's a totally individualized program. One hundred percent individualized. To the nth degree. Each kid reads any book that he wants to read. Period. End of story.

I say to the kids, "Give it a chance. You can run through the room and scream and yell and antagonize me; or you can read this great mystery story. You can hit Joe anytime. And you can antagonize teachers all over. You *do* from nine to three. But how often do you get a chance to read this great story?"

Also there's the physical arrangement of the room. There is no front; there is no center. The things that might be the most centered are the bookcases. I've subdivided them into six sections, six levels of difficulty, loosely structured because the kids need a little structure, but not a lot. I'm not going to bullshit the kids They've got a pretty fair idea of where they're supposed to be, and by telling them— instead of saying Levels One Two Three Four Five Six—if I divide it into, you know, apples and oranges, that doesn't fool them for two seconds. I mean, everybody knows the Robins are smarter than the Bananas, even first-graders.

Each of these sections has like fifty books in them. I have two, three copies of each book except for the real expensive $4.95 ones. A kid goes to whatever level he's in, which is determined (a) by reading tests and (b) by talking to the kid. If he doesn't feel he's in the right level, he can move down or up at his option. In general I say, "Here are these great books, see. And you can read by yourself, to yourself. You can read with a friend out loud. You can read with a friend quietly. You can stand on your bloody head and read the book. I don't care. I don't care whether it's noisy. It should be quiet enough so the guy next to you can read, but if you want to say three words to your neighbor about who's your date for Friday night, that's your business, not mine. You learn to read, you'll be in better shape. You can't learn to read, you're going to be in very bad shape."

But aside from moralizing, the whole bloody thing comes down to: "Gee, here's a good book."

I don't teach. I'm providing a classroom and more material than I'd imagine you'd ever see in another classroom and I say, "Kid, here are all the materials. Do it. Do what you want to do." This releases me. I can spend maybe a whole period with one kid. There are kids that need my attention and there are kids that don't need it at all. I have a couple of classes where I don't have to say four words to anybody about anything at any time. They don't want to know and I don't want to know; I decorate the room.

I have a kid write down on a card which book he finishes reading, which date. I can look that over and see how often a book's been read. If the book has been read to the end, it says something for the book. I mean, there's been no pressure in the world to make him read it. I know what sells. *The Wizard of Oz* doesn't, but *Ellen and the Gang* does, big. *Charlotte's Web* is universal, and *Stuart Little. Run, Westy, Run,* by Gudrum Alcock, and *Durango Street,* by Frank Bonham, those are great books. Now, *Durango Street* is great because it doesn't moralize, like a lot of the gang books. You know, the killer ends up being a cop or something like that. Whereas in *Durango Street* the story ends like it began, the kid's still in the gang.

Books that sell deal with the school situation, about gang wars, divorced families, no fathers, and so forth. Also books with black characters—biographies of Martin Luther King, *Black Like Me* [John H. Griffin], *Manchild in the Promised Land* [Claude Brown], *The Contender* [Robert Lipsyte], *The Soul Brothers and Sister Lou* [Kristin Hunter]. But those are hard. They automatically exclude about 75 percent of the class.

I think to a degree that kids are probably getting tired of "the black kid integrates the white school" books. *Mary Jane* [Dorothy Sterling] was the predecessor for most of those and so that's kind of valid, you know. But now there are half a dozen . . .

You're limited on a lower level. There are only so many first-grade books you can get that would appeal to a kid. Dr. Seuss is the best around. And the Random House Step-Up books. Ezra Jack Keats' *Whistle for Willie.* And the Bank Street series. That's a program designed for a kid of fourteen who can only read second-grade material.

Initially a kid's going to say to me, "Man, I ain't going to read no second- third-grade books." And I say, "Well, jeez, you know, it's a pretty good book. Why don't you give it a try?" What I'm saying is, Kid, you read third-grade, you know? Tough crap. And it's really bad news, for you, for me, for everybody. You're five years behind in reading. You got crummy instruction in school. You had crummy teachers. It was no good and it was not your fault. Right? And I say, But kid, you're fourteen, and you're old enough to make your own decisions. If you want to continue reading on a third-grade level, it's your business now. Right? From now on I hold *you* responsible. For *before* this, I hold somebody else responsible. But if you don't want to do it now, *you're* going to be the gunkie, not me. ("Gunkie" is a Bill Cosby expression. Fat Albert and Harold: "Harold, you're a gunkie.") I put it very straight: Kid, you're reading, according to this test, two-point-nine. This is the way it is, kid. It hurts, but let's talk about it."

About "gunkie"—do you find yourself lapsing into the language your kids use?

There *is* a speech gap. The kids have a whole lexicon of expressions of their own. Like "mole," which means "Ah, you stupid idiot." Or if you "drop dimes" you're a stool pigeon. Or "foxy momma" instead of "beautiful girl," or "tackhead" for "ugly girl."

I'll use one of these expressions sometimes if I want to make a point emphatically, but I'm not going to prove to a thirteen-year-old kid that I'm a good Joe because I say "foxy momma" or "tackhead." I'm not being paid to teach them that. I'm being paid to teach them conventional English. I speak conventional English. It would be pretty corny to do otherwise. I'm not a thirteen-year-old black. I mean, everybody knows I'm not.

There *are* teachers who do it. Always saying "Baby

183

this, and baby that." That's all right if you feel at home with it. If it's natural, it's okay. But it's not okay, you know, to be natural and still be a barbaric son of a bitch.

Is there any discussion with the kids about what they read?

No, not a discussion. I pass words with the kids. He finished *Charlotte's Web* and I say, "Hey, pretty good book, wasn't it?" and he says, "Yeah." Or "How do you feel about the ending of *Stuart Little?*" Kid wants to talk about it, I'll talk with him. Kid doesn't want to talk about it, he won't. Most conversation, most talk, in fact, is to check up, did the kid read the book.

Some books in the room I haven't read. I see a kid reading one of these I'll say, "Tell me what you think of it, will you?" The kid says "No good," and you ask why, you usually get a one- or two-word answer. "It was corny . . . I didn't like . . . Didn't make sense." I get enough "No good"s and I get rid of the book.

I don't bring out the fact that *Alice in Wonderland* is really on a deeper level—or that *Animal Farm* is really on the Russian Revolution, because, you know, when the learner is ready, the lesson is there. Meanwhile, it's a good story. Remember I'm dealing with eighth graders who can only read on a third-grade level. Before I start with the whole gamut of intellectualization, comprehension and so forth, let's get the kids' reading level up to at least sixth or seventh grade. Then we'll talk about all the tangential intellectual skills.

But kids do ask questions. They're curious about a lot of things. Don't they ever come to you with questions?

Well, I'll tell you a story. Okay? My first year, I'm doing mapping at the board. I'm well into this—a map lesson, legends, scales, direction, which street and which boulevard— really into it. Kid holds up his hand, and I say,

"My God, I've got a question." The first one all period, you know, an honest-to-God bona-fide question. I mean every teacher wakes up in the morning and says, "My God, if I only get some honest questions." Right? So this kid holds his hand up and he says, "Will you die if they cut your penis off?"

I said, "I don't know." (And I really didn't know.) "I'll have to look into it and I'll tell you."

This was a mixed class. Hysterical laughter greeted the question. Well, I had to find out for him. I asked some guys. Apparently you can live without a penis, but if you really get shattered, you die.

How do your students react to poetry?

Poetry isn't popular. Some things in Nancy Larrick's *On the City Streets* sell. That's pretty good. And a very popular poem is "Life for Me Ain't Been No Crystal Stair,"* which is a Hughes poem. Hughes sells when read aloud.

Now a bunch of teachers up there are pushing black stuff at the kids. For thirteen years the kid didn't know from black or white and now they want to ram it down his throat. "Kid, you've got to learn everything about Crispus Attucks." The kid's been going through life happily or miserably without Crispus Attucks. And all of a sudden life revolves around Crispus Attucks, or Matthew Henson. If you push these black guys with your old teaching techniques, using an old curriculum and old everything else—and illogically, it doesn't matter what the hell you're shoving at the kid—he's not going to learn it.

Then do you think Kozol was exaggerating when he told about his class's reaction to "Landlord, Landlord" in Death at an Early Age?

* "Mother to Son," in *The Weary Blues*, by Langston Hughes (New York: Alfred A. Knopf, 1926).

No. See, you have a different situation. In Boston you get fired if you *read* "Landlord, Landlord." In Philadelphia, George Fishman* is in trouble for *not* reading it, so to speak. The difference is the advent of a new superintendent of schools here [Mark Shedd] who has been, if not effective, at least brought a liberal atmosphere The atmosphere in the schools now is one of, you know, you must innovate. If you're not going to innovate, get out.

Dr. Mark R. Shedd was chosen superintendent in November 1966, with a mandate from a new Board of Education to reform an undeniably moribund and oppressive public school system. In Philadelphia, whose 654,000 black inhabitants comprise one-third of the total population and more than one-half of the school population, this meant change of quasi-revolutionary scope and quality, particularly in administration, curriculum and community relations.

Shedd's bold exercise of his office and his responsiveness to ideas of decentralization and community control aroused Philadelphia's reactionary (and essentially white racist) forces to powerful resistance. On November 17, 1967, Police Commissioner Frank L. Rizzo interdicted Shedd's community and student relations policies by ignoring the superintendent's request to keep uniformed policemen away from a demonstration of 3,500 black high school

* George Fishman, a teacher at West Philadelphia High School, became the center of a controversy which reached gale force between spring of 1969 and the year's end. The issue was his often vague, perfunctory treatment of the black presence in American history—the central and active role of the freedmen in Reconstruction, for example—and his extreme reluctance to permit challenging questions or debate on such matters in his virtually all-black classes. Following a student boycott of Fishman's classes, corridor sit-downs and auditorium assemblies, the principal recommended a transfer, which Fishman, momentarily, seemed willing to accept. The forceful intervention of the Philadelphia Federation of Teachers (AFL–CIO) persuaded the Board of Education to overrule the principal and restore the teacher to his classroom at West.

students at the Board of Education. Instead, Rizzo personally directed a massive and brutal attack on the demonstrators outside the building while their delegation was conferring inside with Shedd and the board president, Richardson Dilworth, Philadelphia's reform mayor from 1955 to 1962.

Rizzo, a high school dropout, with a wide reputation as "the toughest cop in America," ran for mayor in 1971, pledging, incidentally, to "get rid" of Shedd if elected. He was. Faced, additionally, with a Board of Education majority reconstituted to assure a majority favorable to Rizzo, Mark Shedd resigned early in December...

If Shedd was "not effective" it was largely because Philadelphians arrived at no clear choice between two alternatives that Shedd posed: "Either we follow a course of reason [in response to the demands of the black community] or we follow a general policy of suppression." Seemingly, it was not his ineffectiveness but his show of effectiveness that majority Philadelphia found intolerable.

This pressure for innovation isn't making itself felt in the ordinary classroom with the ordinary teacher, but the young teachers are for it, for the most part. A lot of the guys who came in to get out of the draft have found it good work and are sticking with it and God bless every one of them. (Hear, hear!) There was a big stink a while ago with newspaper articles or a magazine article about people who teach to avoid the draft and doing it to half-lengths and ruining the kids. My point is that so many people are ruining kids anyway that it's good to get ten good teachers out of the whole batch. So these are the people who are willing to experiment, you know. "Let's give it a go. Let's see what the hell happens."

In an article I read about school decentralization—they'd try anything. Give the whole goddam school system to some militant and see what he does with it because he can't do any worse . . . Take the garbage man off the street and stand him in the classroom because he can't do any worse, and maybe he'll do a little bit better.

The way money is spent now is hysterically macabre. I mean, people on the school system level are taking money and building for two million bucks here, a million bucks there—showcase progress—the results of which never get disseminated anyway. Right? Which brings in more federal grants for more showcase progress while, by Christ, I'll bet you five dollars *cash* that you can't get a roll of Scotch tape tomorrow in my school. And if you can get Scotch tape, you can't get a ruler or a pencil.

Have you ever put in for a mini-grant from Mark Shedd's special fund? You're supposed to be able to get up to three hundred dollars to finance an innovative project in your classroom.

I've poured well over five thousand dollars, my personal money—honest-to-God personal, Boy Scout's honor —into my classroom the last two years. A lot of people do that. What I'm doing works, statistically. It massacres the school norms. I have all the tables and so forth. In point of fact, the kids gained 61 percent over what a control group gained. That was last year and I expect that what I'm doing this year should result in a gain of well over 100 percent of what their past performance had said they would learn. And the kids are really alive and they don't hate it. They may not love it, but they don't hate it. Well, I've got the application for this special fund sitting on my desk. This is the third year I have submitted for it and it has been rejected outright each time. Now my contention to the administration is: I spent all this money and I'm broke. I don't have any more, and you're going to have to kick in. It's *your* bloody school system. And I've gotten zero dollars and zero cents . . . They're big on sympathy . . . The point is, it's either their three hundred dollars or mine. For a change, I'd like it to be their three hundred . . . We were going to do a photography project; we were going to go out and do some taping. The ideas are good; and three hundred dollars is not a fantastic amount of money. I personally resent the hell out of it that I haven't gotten it. I mean it's a straight case of bitterness, subjective in part, and it's partly objective bitterness. I know that what I'm doing works, and when they refuse it, it hurts.

What do you picture yourself doing, say, ten years from now?

That's the $64 question. I don't think I'll be teaching. I think four or five years of teaching is enough, pretty much. Otherwise I'm doing the same repetitious stuff year in, year out. The kids change, and that gives you a little something. But after a while, it just doesn't have the same excitement. There's got to be something in it for the teacher.

There are teachers who've been in for twenty years. Mostly I've found the kindergarten, first-grade, second-grade teachers have been doing it for twenty years and they're great. I mean, they really know kids and they *feel* the whole thing and they do very, very well. But I couldn't see like—senior-high history, just going over the same old stuff. If you're not discussing Chicago, you're discussing Saigon. And if it isn't Chicago '68, it'll be Chattanooga '72.

My school . . . I interviewed at various schools before I picked this one. It has a fairly liberal administration. I'm allowed as much freedom in the classroom as I want. That's why I work there. Otherwise I couldn't put up with it. I mean, you have all the trouble with the kids; if I had to turn around and get a whole bunch of crap from the administration, I'd be pushed in and in, like Bel Kaufman,* you know, until I gave up. But this way I'm only faced with one set of problems: kids. I don't get much support from the administration. You can't expect everything . . . I mean, they leave me alone. I was left alone to make my own mistakes and I was left alone to fix them.

Is it as bad as Bel Kaufman makes it seem?

You can't appreciate the humor of it when you're doing it.

Early in 1971, the Westminster Press, Philadelphia, published Steven Daniels' comprehensive account of his classroom techniques, practices and results in a book titled How Two Gerbils, Twenty Goldfish, Two Hundred Games, Two Thousand Books & I Taught Them How to Read. *In the fall, Daniels started on a new job, director of curriculum planning in the Ann Arbor, Mich. public school system.*

CHERYL GREENE
Detroit

In her mid-twenties, white, unmarried, Cheryl Greene has been teaching English at Cooley High School since September 1966. She grew up in a small, very white town near Rochester, N.Y., went to a Catholic girls' high school and to Marygrove, a Catholic women's college "which is in Detroit; that's how I got to Detroit." She had considered other occupations. "I thought teaching was what a woman

* Bel Kaufman, *Up the Down Staircase* (New York: Prentice-Hall, 1964). Also published by Avon Books, 1966.

did if she couldn't do anything else. But I was more interested in English than in most other things, so . . ." She entered the school system on trial, calmly resolved that if she found it distasteful or inwardly unrewarding she would not remain.

I like it very much. There are times when I get very excited about being here, when things look very, very hopeful. Then, sometimes I get downright discouraged. At the beginning of this semester I saw some positive things coming across, especially like individual discussions with students. They were coming to ask me if there was something they could do for a particular project, or how they could get certain courses [mostly, black studies] incorporated into the curriculum. They were showing that they wanted to do something very positive.

And of course, when we had the disturbances—everybody for a couple of days afterward just is hurt. I think that's the inward reaction, although we go to objective things to discuss, like security in the building, student committees and things like that. But we're all dealing with it at such a time from a very subjective basis, just a personal kind of discouragement. It hurts. It's disappointing.

"The disturbances" at Cooley erupted, as they did in many schools throughout the country, immediately following the assassination of Martin Luther King on April 4, 1968. At Cooley, the black students were obliged to confront an aggressive white youth group, Breakthrough,* from outside school. In the course of the year, black students reacted by organizational effort to deal with issues directly affecting their lives within Cooley.

I have thought of returning to do some more graduate work but the fact is that, no, I don't want to go to a suburban school. I really don't. I like this school. I think this

* See note on p. 237.

is very exciting. I don't mean because of demonstrations and fights; I mean exciting when good things happen, and there are many good things. Name some? Yes. Being able to take something like *Othello* in a very contemporary situation, even though maybe Shakespeare didn't mean it to be; taking it from two points of view and having them vocalized in the classroom.

Or coming in from a false alarm [an aspect of "the disturbances"] and having a black student come up to you and say, "That upset you, didn't it?" And I say yes and that student says, "Let's go for a walk around the halls and talk about it."

There are learning experiences here for me, too. Like being able to say to a black person when something (a conflict of some kind) happens: "I feel very prejudiced," and having that black student say, "Yeah. I know what you mean. I do too." To me that means we could both recognize we weren't being objective and we trust each other enough to say so.

Or today. I just came back from the post office with two students, one black, one white. We were driving along, looking for the place, and I saw a mailman. So I pulled up and I called out, "Sir . . ." and that didn't register. Oliver, he's sitting alongside me, says, "*Hey*, brother." I was embarrassed . . . Later I said, "That man must have thought it was *I* yelling 'Hey, brother' and he was probably wondering 'Who's she trying to kid?' " but Oliver said, "Well, what were you calling him 'sir' for?" That Oliver, he's really something—and it was just an awfully good moment, an awfully positive thing. Something like that out there, that workshop, that gets me excited.

"Out there," is the spacious sunlit library beyond the door of the small conference room where we are talking. A constitutional convention of student delegates is deciding the forms, functions and powers which it will propose to

vest in the Student Union which is undergoing a long, controversy-laden reorganization.

I've listened all morning to what's going on . . . Many students out there will be graduating in four weeks. They could say, "I don't care. I'm not going to be here." Yet they're *in* there, talking about things that will concern other students next year. They're dealing with issues, and very logically. Many times we do them an injustice when we simply say, "Give us your ideas," instead of "How would you put your ideas to work?" Because then they're involved in the real practical aspects of it. The idea of a student council sounds great but how are you going to make it work? When they start talking to each other about this, they realize it isn't easy and yet they're trying to be really fair about it.

This problem of student representation within the school is really difficult. A student council should be fully representative and yet it is so easy to charge them with *not* being so. How *should* it be? Students who are elected may not necessarily be involved themselves in extreme movements or extreme ideas. They can be, but they should be knowledgeable of every element within the school. They should be able to go through the halls and talk to somebody they wouldn't normally talk to and find out how he would vote on *this* issue and what he thinks of *that* question. If he is a person who is from the extreme, in one corner or another, he should be able to approach the person in the middle and find out what that person thinks, and vice versa.

What's extreme around Cooley and what's conservative?

I guess I judge it by the means which are used to achieve what you're asking for. I think some of the people who form demonstrations out in front, who are very much concerned about it being orderly but effective, are not extreme. They are taking a direct, perhaps very dramatic way of showing something, but they do not necessarily, to me, form the extreme elements, those who seem to have lack of consideration for any of the other elements involved.

What is there here to demonstrate about?

The Student Council, if they didn't think it was representative . . . We have a group formed by some of the very concerned black students, Black United Front, which has proposed several lists of demands to the office: incorporation of black literature in the English courses, various workshop projects, including sensitivity workshops for the faculty. Some faculty members favor it, some feel it's a complete waste of time, some are reticent but willing to try it.

Then there are proposals for changing the cultural orientation within the building, that the names of some of the study halls should be changed to represent black figures in history. The art work in the halls could be changed because it's antiquated anyway but also because it isn't representative of their own culture; many black students feel it should be. And many of them aren't simply saying "black-oriented" but more of an international flavor [with Third World implications]. And they want more of the students' own work represented on the walls. One student who graduated from here is doing murals at the request of black students in another school. This kind of thing is, you know, an excellent idea for their own relationship to the building . . .

One of the main issues is student representation: What is the role of the student in determining the direction of a high school . . . I think the demand is voiced more strongly at Cooley than in predominantly white schools. They are asking for a more immediate proof of these things coming into action, in a reality . . . You also might find that financially there is a greater need here for an immediate answer than in a school where the money is there and the parents want it and know they can get it right away, whereas these students feel they're really going to have to speak up to get the sort of thing they need.

We had one Saturday workshop, on a voluntary basis. About thirty-five teachers were involved in that, which is about one-fourth of the faculty, plus a few parents and students. I thought that was a very good kind of workshop. I enjoyed it very much. Another one was for the entire faculty and more students, on a much larger scale. I think everybody found it unsatisfactory. That could be because you got people who didn't want to attend. I don't know, maybe faculty people and students who were not as cooperative as they should be. Also, we had people in large groups. I'd rather see three teachers and five students go out and have a hamburger together, you know, and sit around and talk . . . There should be more of that than there is.

Okay, you get along well with the black students. But would you say that expressions of hostility, suspicion, by black kids toward white teachers is not uncommon?

Yes, that does happen. It's happened to me. It's a very difficult thing to deal with. If someone says you're prejudiced, what do you say—"No, I'm not!"? You can't prove it any other way than the way you act and believe. I was also accused once, by a white student, that I was "prejudiced in reverse." Prejudice—it's a charge that once made cannot be really properly refuted. How? Not by giving a better grade if it's undeserved. A person who leans over backward to prove that he isn't prejudiced is obviously probably more prejudiced . . . It's a really delicate issue, especially for a teacher who has worked to relieve that kind of issue . . . It's a very delicate thing . . .

Are there any prejudiced white teachers here? I would guess that that is true. But I wouldn't say it exists any *more* in this building than in any other. I would think that for a person who is prejudiced this situation would be extremely uncomfortable. Because certainly students are well enough aware of that kind of tendency. They have been schooled well enough in the reactions of a prejudiced person to identify it and react to it.

Teaching language and literature, what are your general goals? What are you trying to accomplish with your students?

First, clarity of thought: absolutely the most important thing, in the students' interpretation of literature and in the presentation of their own ideas. If they're going to be involved in things that are at *all* controversial, and they *are*—that's what almost every part of life is concerned with now—they've got to be able to look at something and ask, What is the basic thing that is being said here? . . . If it's an idea, then I've got to look at the proof and see what *is* proof. And, am *I* saying something when I explain *my* point of view? Or am I so subjective about the fact that it's my idea that I'm going to assume that everybody already understands it? Am I really trying to *communicate* and prove it? . . .

In our college preparatory English course, twelfth grade, this semester the students have done research papers on subjects of their own choosing. We've read Thomas Hardy's *Return of the Native*. Then we took *Black Voices*,* principally the short stories and poetry. Now we're doing *Othello*, for two reasons. One, because of the idea of a supposedly tragic black figure, and secondly, I like Shakespeare. I try to get them to like it . . . It's too bad we

* *Black Voices: An Anthology of Afro-American Literature*, by Abraham Chapman, with an Introduction and Biographical Notes (New York: New American Library, 1968).

can't do more with the crossing of time barriers in literature. I read them a passage from *Les Miserables* about the
French Revolution: "This revolution is based on two
mounds, one of suffering and one of ideals . . ." and I
said, "Date this. Where would it be?" They had no idea.
They were very much surprised at the date of it because it
sounded so contemporary. They were surprised how phrase
after phrase in the whole passage seems to be reflective of
things they hear today. I said, "Relevance does not necessarily mean that it has to be written in the last five years.
Relevance does not necessarily have to do with the date of
the work" . . .

I'm concerned with form to the extent that your work
should reflect what *you* value in yourself, *how* you value
yourself; that it has some kind of dignity about it, that it
shows what *you* think of what you think. Content should
be varied; it's a kind of intellectual diet. If I concentrate
too much on one area I'm doing students an injustice, even
though a teacher's got to realize that not everybody is going
to like everything . . .

Sometimes I wish we had a setup where a teacher
would teach a certain specialized area, somewhat like the
college setup, partly for the students' sake but mainly for
myself, selfishly, because there are areas—I teach Shakespeare better than anything else; and the essay, maybe
because the concentration in thought and presentation
interests me. Also American literature, but poetry is a
difficult thing for me to teach just simply as poetry, from
an anthology. I'm sure every teacher has his or her prefer-
ences about this kind of thing. I like Sandburg and Whitman, for example, because they are so people-oriented . . .

*You've got a big population of black students here
who are hollering for relevant—*

Black literature? Yes . . . I think Richard Wright is
really fantastic in his understanding of the psychological

197

reactions in a man. I've read Wright more than I have any of the other black writers. I think this is something that is absolutely going to have to be incorporated into college curriculums. When I was going to college there were no courses in black literature. It would have been very pertinent for me . . . People don't seem to study things like that independently when they're busy accumulating credits toward a degree. And there simply wasn't an accredited course. I feel handicapped in my own background. You can bone up on something because you know it's important but that's not quite the same as having it taught to you in a classroom two or three years before you need to use it. I need a period of assimilation so that I can *bring something* to the material, to make it relevant.

There is some form of black literature incorporated into each semester here. This has taken place in the past year, maybe a year and a half . . . There were no real examples of black-literature study before that time [the period in which black students learned to press for curriculum changes]. Part of the problem was that the teachers were not prepared, were not that knowledgeable themselves in some areas of black literature, and I'm not saying that we are now. It's a slow process* . . . I feel there is a great deal I'm not familiar with in respect to black literature. I think there are other teachers who know much more than I do. Two or three of them are white and a couple are black.

As far as black writers are concerned, most of the students tend to be interested in the novelists rather than the poets. The poems in the anthology we used were, I thought, a little outdated. Quite often the poets' tendency was to portray a situation and their own reactions to society, their feelings about the situation, but then counter with the idea that "this is something I must accept or that I will suffer through." I'm not saying this about the whole

* Beginning in September 1971, Cooley planned to offer an elective course in black literature.

body of work by any poet but only of the selections in the anthology. I found in the prose writers a little more bitterness, a little more of the sense of struggle than I found in the poetry. Of course, you're dealing with the difference in approach between two types of literature. I guess the prose is just a little more effective, maybe because you become attached to a figure more closely. And maybe this is simply so for me, as a white person; I can see it better because I've been given more time to associate. A black person may be able to respond immediately to something a black poet says because he may not need this kind of building up of an empathy; it's already there.

I'm not saying that poems we took were not relevant but prose selections like Richard Wright's "The Man Who Lived Underground" or excerpts from *The Invisible Man* made a much greater impression.

I found the first time that I taught *Black Boy* there was much more response from the white students than the black—discussion, interpretation, questions. I was surprised. But this semester I'm getting equal response from the black students.

I gave them reading assignments in the book, and study questions to be discussed in class the next day: What was Richard Wright's first reaction to the sight of the prisoners as they came from a distance? What were the motives that went into his burning the curtains? This type of thing. Then the discussions grew from that, so we could follow the theme from the beginning of the book to where it narrowed down toward the end.

They were very honest and direct about their answers and I don't think that any of the questions skirted issues. What was Wright's own first experience of racial prejudice? He stood in line with his mother . . . You know. Why was his grandmother considered black when she looked as white as any of the other people he saw on the train?

Of course you have some students who are very vocal anyway and they are going to be quick to raise their hands. Yet, I think the [white] student who found black literature the most revealing might be the one I never got to know about. Many of those students who are sitting there very quietly are seeing things they never saw before. They wouldn't be comfortable enough to discuss it . . .

Do your students show any independent curiosity about literature?

I know I've had students who looked through my bookshelves when they stopped over at my house and who became interested in a book just because it was there. And they'd say, "Hey, can I take this?" I think this is the best way to instill an interest in literature, this casual kind of thing: "Hey, did you ever read such-and-such? Because it's a little like, or very different, from something else, with which both of us are already familiar."

Are these visits from your students casual, too?

I had one class for two semesters at Cooley. After they graduated I said I want to have you all over for dinner, so they came over one night . . . We sat around and talked for four hours and I'm sure I had a better time than they did. I thoroughly enjoyed it. I have had on occasion somebody call up and say, "Would it be all right if we stop over to see you?" Well, "All right. Fine." I'm not married, which makes my schedule more flexible, of course. I don't think that the hours I spend here can be spent with total informality, but I've always felt that my free hours are their hours and that's a time to talk, to fool around and they can just come in here; that's fine. The paperwork I can always do at home. It depends on a teacher's personal life. If she's married, with four or five kids, that's something else, and it doesn't mean she isn't a good teacher. But much of the contact, like going to the post office with those two students today, that was more a part of the whole thing of being a teacher than any formal class. I have found that personal feeling is—*so* much.

Usually the kids call me because they're involved in Student Council work which takes place after school hours. Sometimes it's kind of like being a parent. You drop 'em off at a meeting and then they call you up when they're ready to come home and you pick 'em up and take 'em home. There was a time at the beginning of the semester when it was not unusual to be in the building from seven A.M. until ten thirty at night. Maybe go home and get something to eat and come back. But a person can't do that every day.

Personal feeling counts for so much in what respects? How?

We've had a Community Council here, comprising representatives of the teaching staff, the Student Council, the student newspaper, the parents, the community. It's not functioning now. One of the meetings—it was re-e-ally involved. There was so much conflict. It was just very disturbing and I thought, Oh, I want to leave; but I had to take some of the kids home afterward. I got in the car feeling almost hopeless about the general situation at Cooley High School: I just don't care. It's so sticky. Why get involved? Then the kids got in and we started talking about the value of the faculty workshop, about the suspension of a student, about the representation of students before the administration and the school board—many points. We talked. And my attitude changed entirely, toward teaching, toward the issues. At that big meeting, where you'd think there would be the most objectivity, people were just making their own point. But when we got together in a small group where we knew everybody liked everybody else, we just dealt with the issues objectively. We [Cheryl Greene and the students in the car] had opposite views. Both sides, if you want to call them sides, stayed with their own opinion, but the thing was that each side could *see* there were other points of view that had to be dealt with.

Is the division of opinion on the issues in and around Cooley mostly a racial division?

There is obviously an element of race involved. But I don't say, and I've really talked to lots of students about this, that the division was that clear among the students. The *issue* can be racial but the people who are taking sides don't necessarily take sides along the racial division. We [the Student Council] were talking about the [established] school paper and the [new] Student Council newsletter.* Is the newsletter going to conflict with the paper, compete with it? Some people made the charge that the paper was white-oriented, therefore the newsletter should be black-oriented. Now, this is a racial issue. But at the meeting a white student came to talk for the Black United Front, and a black student who was on the paper talked for the paper . . . These situations are never *simply* racial. They aren't simply one issue. There's so much division within a person about what he thinks is right, or what he believes or how he would react to a certain situation. The fact that you've got a friend, you take gym with her or something. And then you're thrown into a demonstration where the black students are outside and the white students are inside . . . The kinds of decisions that these students have to make place a great deal of pressure on them to know themselves, and what they believe in and *how* they're going to react in a certain situation, and dealing with things that I *never* had to deal with. I mean, it's just unbelievable, the kind of issues and the kinds of contradictions they face every day.

* See note on p. 237.

What is the essential contradiction at Cooley, and at similar schools?

I'd only be guessing. I would say [a twenty-second pause] maybe [another pause, eight seconds] present situation versus past situations—uh—for everybody.

REBECCA STAFFORD
Detroit

I'm thinking of transferring. This is my seventh year at Avery Junior High, but this last semester has been more difficult than others. I've been hearing it expressed by some people—colleagues in the building—that a white teacher really can't do a job in this type of school. And I began to question whether I could or not, so I requested a transfer. In general I have a good relationship with the people I work with, but, for example, at a faculty meeting the statement was made that white teachers could not be—quote—adequate role models and that perhaps they didn't belong here. Two-thirds to three-fourths of the staff is black now and I think this feeling is getting stronger. I have close ties with some of the teachers but you don't see everybody every day. It depends on who you're thrown in with on your free hours in the lounge. Some black teachers aren't going to give you a "Good morning" unless they happen to be in the mood. But they're in a minority, naturally, and I don't think they're accepted by all their black colleagues either. A couple of years ago, I worked very closely with a black teacher. He had all kinds of dreams about what we were going to do when we revamped the curriculum. Anyway, he said he resented the fact that certain people thought, because he was black, he should hold certain notions; he resented the pressure put on him by some of the black teachers.

When I first came to this school I never felt any racial tensions at all. But of course seven years ago they weren't that many and they weren't expressed, as they are today, that in some black people there is a certain quality of hatred toward white people—like whites have toward Blacks. I sense that they feel that I think I'm better than they are and that their reaction to me, accordingly, was, "You're down here working, but that's it. That's the limit of our relationship." I should have kept count several years ago—it would have been interesting—how many times people around here wanted to know: "Do you live in Grosse Pointe?"* Kids and teachers have commented, "Well, *you* live in Grosse Pointe." And I *don't* live in Grosse Pointe. But they seem to think white is rich: you have it nice, you're living in Grosse Pointe. And I tell them, "My father was a factory worker. I had to go to college on scholarship." I mean, I didn't exactly have it soft either. I guess maybe I resent that some of the teachers imply that because you're white you don't have *any* problems, but it's a little hard to take when it comes from the adults.

In the first moment of meeting, Rebecca Stafford gives off "vibes" of competence, self-possession and of a distaste for pushing or being pushed; alert but not uptight. She's an unmarried not-yet-thirty, substantially built woman who walks with a purposeful gait, comes to rest in a sturdy stance. Her speech is low-volume, even-toned; her formulations direct, uncomplicated.

* Detroit's wealthiest suburb. During most of this century it has been the closely held residential preserve of the city's industrial/financial power elite and its managerial seniors.

A great number of the kids here are from welfare families, ADC. I know kids who have to arrange for free lunch, kids who are out of school because they don't have clothes sometimes. People don't own their homes. The kids are not living with mother and dad. They're staying with their aunt or they have a brother on the west side—someone else is in the South. They don't have a stable home situation, which I think accounts for some of the discipline problems here. But they shouldn't think that all white people are rich and living well. My being white doesn't mean I'm rich.

From their point of view, is it so unreasonable for them to think you're rich?

I guess not. Probably the kids are as unknowledgeable about me as I was about black kids when I first worked with them at the "Y." Neither of us knew how the other lived.

One time I invited some girls to my home for lunch over the Christmas holiday. It was a class I had been particularly close to. They were graduating and we had worked together closely on the school election campaign. They were to come to my house by bus. They didn't come and they didn't come and I thought, Oh, they got lost or something. Then about six girls came on my porch at one time.

"Did you get lost?" I asked.

"No," they said. "We walked around the block." They wanted to see where I lived. They said, "You have a nice block." My, it was quite a revelation to them.

I can accept this from the kids—thinking I'm from Grosse Pointe and all that—but it's not so easy to accept when it's your colleagues in the faculty lounge. They make little slurs, you know . . . It's never anything directed to *me*. I'm probably supersensitive. It's possible the criticism isn't being leveled at all white teachers and maybe I just put myself in the category of white. But when you hear people who are knowledgeable in the area of race relations, people who are the proponents of our Afro-American studies program, which I think is great—these are the people who are speaking against the white teacher. So maybe it's true. Maybe the white teacher can't function here.

I sense some hostility in the kids now which I never did before. I feel I still am able to win them over, but it takes longer than it did at one time. And sometimes it's discouraging to spend your entire day working for acceptance. Why should I have to *prove* every day that I *respect* them as human beings and getting them to accept me? Because I don't think I can do the job until they do. And certainly it's a lot more pleasant. If they're coming to just sit there and say "I hate white," then I'm not going to be able to teach them anything.

I had always felt that what I wanted to do should not be based on or limited by my color. These kids need so much basic knowledge—skills more than knowledge—and I don't really think that my being white should interfere with that. I still feel within myself that I am doing as good a job here—and in some cases a better job—than many of the black teachers. That's why I've stayed. But this year—I have a class, and it's getting toward the end of the semester, and I don't really feel I've done what I want to do with the class.

But why did you and why do you want to teach in a black inner-city school?

Because in the past six years I thought I could do it. The kids need so much and I could see I was doing it better than other people. I wanted to do it. That may be selfish; because it made me happy doesn't necessarily mean it's good. I'm not saying it's a breeze. It's never been an easy job, but when you really feel you're getting to the kids and they're with you regardless of any color jazz, it's very, very rewarding.

But why here? You're a teacher. You could find rewarding situations in other places.

I don't know if I would find the same kind of reward. Maybe I have a sort of tendency to—to champion the underdog [she chuckles apologetically]. I really had had no contact with black people at all. I was raised in a white neighborhood in Detroit. I went to white schools. My father was a factory worker. He worked with black people and we were taught that they were just like we were. When I was quite young I went to the South because my father's relatives lived there. I can remember seeing the separate drinking fountains. I was only about eight at the time and it never occurred to me that you have separate drinking fountains. And there I was in line with all the colored kids. People were laughing and my aunt from the South ushered me away with a flourish. That made quite an impression on me. And when I was fourteen, fifteen, visiting my father's parents, they would point to "that dirty nigger" and "that nigger's Cadillac" and I used to really get upset about it. Of course I didn't argue with my grandparents, but it used to bother me.

The first time I had any contact with black people was with students in college. I was going to Wayne, right here in Detroit, and I did some work with the YMCA at a day camp. For ed. credits you had to put in a hundred hours with kids. So I had it figured, you go a few days, you work ten hours a day—a terrific way to pick up your hours rapidly. But I found it such a great experience that I went the entire summer. I found that I was able to get along with these kids and have fun with them, talk to them, listen to them. One of the first days in the camp, we had to go quite a distance by bus. The bus was very crowded, so this one little girl—she was about ten—was sitting on my lap. And she was positively *thrilled* because their family was going on a picnic to Belle Isle, which is a little park in the Detroit

River. This was something I had done all my life. You go to Belle Isle maybe every other weekend. But she had never been there before. And she was thrilled because they were going to have hot dogs. That's what made me realize—wow—what this kid had was nothing compared to the things I had experienced.

What did you feel about it?

Compassion. I don't know. Guilt. Right, yes. Guilt because, I guess, I had so much, and she, nothing.

I can remember another time going on a hike with the kids. This little boy about eight or nine said, "Are you afraid to go into the woods?" And I said, "No, are you?" And he said yes, he was. He'd never been in the woods before and he was sure he'd get lost. He asked me, "Could I hold your hand?" After he saw we weren't going to get lost, he felt a lot better. He had never been away from the city. And it wasn't real woods; it was a state park.

All summer, working with them at the crafts table, I was always impressed with how thrilled they were about small things, really insignificant things, I thought, that were important to them because they had so little. You'd see kids coming to camp who didn't have shoes. I thought they just wanted to be barefoot in the summer, but they didn't *have* shoes. They maybe had some of those 29-cent rubber things, which were not too good for hiking, but that's all. It really opened up a whole new world when I realized how some other people lived, what they have, what they don't have. It kind of turned me on. You know, you read about it in school. You listen to the ed. professor and everything. But it was not until I was with these kids in a very informal situation that I realized what it was like for them.

That was long ago, about ten years ago. But that's why I was willing to take an assignment here when I finished college. People who had substituted here at Avery said,

"Don't go, don't go." There are a lot of white people who don't think it's a very good place. But I don't think some of these people know what a school's like inside. At the time I was offered the job here, I heard all kinds of bad things, but a beginning teacher wasn't offered one of the prime silk-stocking schools anyway.

The first year was very rough. I probably would have quit except I—I don't like to quit. There was a lot of crying the first year.

And now?

Not as much crying anymore. Questioning, but not crying. You learn that you're going to have bad days.

Do any of the kids you've had in your classes stand out especially in your recollection?

I can think of so many. There have been a lot of kids I've felt close to. Just today two girls came back to see me. They're seniors in high school. One I had in 7B. She was a very nice kid and now she's quite the young lady. And another girl, we were maybe kindred souls or something. She used to hang around here quite a bit after school. I took her out for lunch when she graduated from the ninth grade. She still calls me and keeps me posted on what she's doing. And a boy who was in my homeroom. He was not a good student but I got along with him real well, I guess because I didn't have to get on him for some reason. And he comes back. He's so proud that he's still *in* school because everyone had told him he was not going to make it, that he's gonna be shoveling the streets and all that sort of thing.

I think it's the kid you have trouble with and then win over that really is the reward. Right now I have a boy in my class who's just been a constant irritant all year. He *wasn't* going to open a book, he *wasn't* going to bring supplies, *I* wasn't going to make him do anything. I was *after* him and *after* him. I felt sure he was capable or I wouldn't have hounded him the way I did. He's really working now. He comes by maybe two or three times a week after school, to ask, "Am I doing better? Want to give me some extra work? Am I going to pass?" He's really concerned now and I'm sure he's going to pass. Of course there's some I don't reach. And it bothers me a lot.

You talked about discipline problems. What happens?

It's mostly kids talking when they shouldn't be. Very seldom does it get to the point of fighting. Sometimes it's a student who's belligerent, resenting your authority. I feel sure that the problems I do have are because I don't use corporal punishment. Corporal punishment is quite popular. The kids themselves tell me I should paddle them. I've had boys make paddles for me at shop class. But I don't think you're teaching the kids anything with this type of punishment. They need to learn how to function without someone standing over them with a stick. I just can't do it. Some teachers use it. It's effective for them, I suppose. I'm completely against it.

Some kids seem to think that that's what they need to be quiet. The other day, just kidding around, I picked up the yardstick and tapped one boy on the seat of his pants, and he blurts out to the whole class, "Hurray, Miss Stafford finally paddled somebody." They respect the stick. The class will be noisy and a man walks in with a stick—silence. But to me, this isn't really teaching any type of behavior. I'd be quiet too if someone was standing over me with a stick.

I'm quite convinced that the teachers who don't paddle in this school have a harder time because there are teachers who do. The kids come to look on that as *the* punishment. That's why, perhaps, it takes me longer to get the kids to where I like them to be working.

In the last year, maybe I've been overlooking too

much. There are behavior things which should be corrected, but if it doesn't cause a disruption in class, I overlook it. I don't do this all the time. On a good day, I'm on top of things, but some days I'm not. It bothers me because to the extent that a kid feels he's getting away with something, that diminishes his respect for my authority as a teacher. Sometimes it's not that vital. You see paper on the floor now. Two years ago my room was spotless—just spotless. And I should be after the kids saying, "Pick up the paper there" and so forth, but I don't.

I want the kids to respect me as a person who's there to teach them. And to respect the rules which should be mutually agreed upon. At the beginning of the term I explain to them that since they're going to be here for twenty weeks, we're going to have to get along. There are all kinds of rules, simple things which should include picking up paper, rules for discussions. I tell them that these are the rules and ask, "Are there any objections? Any you think are unfair? Any reason why you can't go by these rules?" And of course there's no complaint—until someone breaks a rule. But as I said, I let things slide, and I shouldn't.

Recently I had an incident in the hall. I saw a kid throw a jar at a girl. It had some kind of cream in it that splashed on the walls. I grabbed this kid by the arm and said, "Before you go to class you have a mess to clean up."

"I ain't cleaning it up," he answered.

I didn't know this kid. I'd never seen him before. I told him to get some paper toweling and clean it up, but he refused.

Now he was getting mad. "Take—your—hand—off—my—arm!" The tension is mounting. It's like this kid and I are in an arena. The other kids are gathering and watching this confrontation. Teachers, men teachers are watching.

One man said, "Hold onto him. I'll go for help." I said "Thank you." And I told a girl to run to the lavatory to get paper towels. She was so flustered that she forgot there was a lavatory right there and went running around to the other end of the building. When the incident was all over, she brought this big wad of paper towels.

So this whole time the boy is saying, "Take your hands off me!" I said, "You're not going anywhere till you clean up this mess." "Take your hands off!"—that's all he kept saying. I—I was a little uneasy because the kid's the same height as I am and he's going to hit me any second now. He pulled his arm away but luckily by this time the principal had arrived.

This one teacher said, "You shouldn't have bothered about it. See, you got yourself all worked up. You should have just let it go." So I said, "On some days I would have done that, maybe." But I don't think you should let it go.

Did you wonder afterward why the kid was so unyielding?

I tend probably to be too idealistic. I would think it was resistance to Authority. Maybe I'm saying that because I don't want to face that the kid felt any special way about *white* authority. Because I always like to think that white and black are going to get along.

I've actually had only one kid where there was a racial clash. He was a boy with a lot of problems. He was in with a very bright group of kids and he couldn't cut it. So to compete he did things to get their attention. He would make a big display of going up to sharpen his pencil, hitting a few people on his way. Or else he didn't have a pencil and would holler out, "I need a pencil," every day. It got to the point where I sent him to the counselor and said in an after-school conference I wouldn't take him back in class till I had achieved some sort of understanding with him.

So the kid came down to me and said, "The counselor's going to put me out unless you give me another chance. Please, please give me another chance." So I said, "A chance to do what? A chance to continue acting like this or a chance to try to do better?" "Oh, I'm going to try," he said. But next day it was the same old song: he's loud. He's walking around the room bothering other people. I said, "Paul, don't you come after school begging me for another chance." And that was the wrong thing to say because he answered, "I don't beg a white person for anything." He left the room and he never came back to my class.

It was upsetting to have a kid say that. Luckily the class was on my side. If they would have all felt hostility for the white teacher, I would have been finished. Because he brought it right out: "I'm not going to beg a white person for anything." But the class was quiet and when he left the room we went on . . .

I guess you want to think you're going to get to all the kids. I take defeat very badly. That's why, I think, I've hung on here—because it's very hard for me to quit. I shouldn't have felt any great personal defeat because Paul was a problem in every class—with black teachers as well as white.

That encounter with Paul was the first time that anyone brought up the white thing overtly. But kids have mumbled under their breaths sometimes. I can remember my first year here, I reprimanded a girl and another kid said, "You never say anything about Susan." Susan was white. And I heard one little girl, Rosa, say under her breath, "That's 'cause she's *her* color."

I let it pass because she didn't mean for me to hear it. And I didn't want to make a whole big thing because when I first came here I shied away from talking about race. I find it much easier to discuss racial issues in the class now. You learn a lot, you know. You learn what sort of things the kids need, what sort of things they react to, and some of this is color-oriented.

To come back to Rosa: she was very homely, a pretty miserable kid, but by the end of the semester I doubt if any kid in the class was closer to me than she was. After school she would hang around, straighten up my desk, do anything she could to help. And I went out of my way to give her attention. We were talking one day and I said, "I'm really lucky to have a good friend like you." And she said, "I really help you a lot, don't I?"

"Yes, you do," I said. "But I don't think you wanted to help me in the beginning, did you?" She didn't answer—just a sheepish grin. "It took you a while to get to know me," I said, "and it took me a while to get to know you. Sometimes it's hard for people to get to know each other. And maybe it's harder because you're a Negro"—at that time we weren't saying "Black"—"and I'm white." And she said, "Yes."

Most of the students in Rebecca Stafford's brightest eighth-grade English class must have had some teachers who did something right before they met her. Their reading out loud from "Patch," a short story in their literature anthology, is lucid and knowing. They make cogent comments on the plot, characters, viewpoints and values of the story. The serious-minded mood of the group is somehow accentuated by the lurid color drawings of amorphous creatures, half comic, half nightmarish, on the classroom walls. These are visualizations of the Bottle Imp in Robert Louis Stevenson's story.

"The Bottle Imp" is rather difficult reading. Some of the kids really couldn't manage it. So for the kids who can't read it, I *tell* them the story and it's a story they enjoy. There's no detailed portrayal of the Bottle Imp, just minor description, the fact that it's very horrible-looking. So I suggested that whoever wanted to should draw his or her own idea of what the Imp looked like. They welcomed the opportunity to do something besides write, and to make something as ugly as they possibly could. The art teacher came down to see them. She thought some of them were quite good.

I spend a great deal of time on literature because reading is such a problem in this school. We're supposed to be putting in time on grammar, but I cut that to a minimum because I'm anti-grammar. My college English instructor thought grammar was more or less instinctual. It was nothing you could learn. I think this is very true.

There's a new scientific approach to grammar which was supposed to be used in the Detroit schools, but it was never followed through with any consistency, so now it's no longer used here at Avery. This particular school of thought also says that grammar is instinctual. Like, these kids do have their own grammar. It may not be the King's English, but it's theirs.

We should have more individual teacher say-so in selection of textbooks. They have a system now where certain teachers sit and look at books and choose for the whole system. The same book is put in every school. Fortunately we have a fairly adequate book for a change. It has a nice variety and it has some black writers included, which is fine. For all these years we've been having to do without that sort of thing. Some schools have reading rooms where kids can go and read. I'd like to see us have a room like that, where kids can read books that appeal to them. But that takes money naturally.

I use the stories we read in class as a jumping-off place for discussion, for compositions. We have been reading *Manchild in the Promised Land*. Something like that, or some of the other black lit. gets the kids writing what they really think. Every once in a while it will come out, how greatly oppressed they feel, how antiwhite a kid will be. It's refreshing to get this honesty, to get them to say some of the things that they won't say in discussion. They're not just writing what the teacher wants. It's upsetting, because they have such hostile feelings. But it's good, because then it gives them a chance to bring these things out in class discussion. I can say, "I'll read what someone in the class has written," without naming a kid. Then we discuss it or argue about it.

Of course they never direct their hostility to the teacher who's going to grade their paper. Last year I had a very, very militant kid in my class. It took me a great deal of time to get him to understand that he was going to have to curb his behavior while he was in here. Now I have him again and he's a great buddy of mine. But that's me. He still has his hatred for whites, I'm sure.

What would you like to see happening in this school or in the Detroit system?

Number one, smaller class sizes. When you have thirty-five, thirty-six kids in a class, there's very little time for individual attention. That's my number one gripe.

There are changes that need to be made in the teachers too. We really need some good teachers. I do think kids get a raw deal very often with teachers, black and white. Teaching can be an awfully easy job; once you get the kids in line so they're going to sit down and be quiet, you can really just sit back. I have kids come and tell me they're not doing work in a class; the teacher is sitting there reading a magazine; the kids know if they talk they're going to get whacked. I take what they say with a grain of salt, but some of these things I see myself.

Aside from technical requirements, a teacher needs something intangible—concern for the kids, respect for the kids. And they're not just kids. I mean, they have opinions. We read something the other day from *Manchild in the Promised Land* about the probation officer. The kids really liked this man because he treated kids as people. That's the way they want to be considered. Respecting them goes a long way, and it's the best way to earn *their* respect . . .

When they find that I don't hate them because I'm white and they're black, it works the other way too; not automatically. There are some kids you don't get through to and some that—they're just there; they've got to be in school, and that's it.

I know people, teachers in this building now, who should not be here because of the way they think about the kids.

An incident like I had in the hall, an incident like that could not make me reverse my thinking and become negative about black people. But I know people who after being in a situation like that are just confirmed bigots now. They say to themselves, "Well, that proves it. I was right about those people all along." We had a teacher here one time and it really threw her. She told me she found herself writing on a sheet of paper, "I hate Blacks, I hate Blacks."

This school has never turned my feelings around that way. I have days, you know, when I say, "Is it worth it?— trying to prove my acceptance of these people. Why should I have to be on probation every day? Then I have days when I don't think that way. I have a really great day and I don't want to leave.

I thought I'd like to try teaching in a senior high, but I don't know. Maybe when the time comes and they offer me another school, I won't take it.

When the time came, she chose not to transfer but to remain, "still endeavoring to do my job and endeavoring to get along with my colleagues." Which is why Rebecca Stafford and Avery J.H.S. are pseudonyms.

5

THE VISIBLE MEN

Somehow, I happened to be alone in the classroom with Mr. Ostrowski, my English teacher. He told me, "Malcolm, you ought to be thinking about a career . . ."

"Well, yes, sir, I've been thinking I'd like to be a lawyer."
He kind of half smiled and said, "A lawyer—that's no realistic goal for a nigger. Why don't you plan on carpentry?"

—Malcolm X

Cooley High School, standing in a middle-class residence area of northwest Detroit, was 90 percent white in 1964. Since then, its enrollment of three thousand has swung to 65 percent-and-rising Blacks.* In the same period, 1964–1970, the proportion of black teachers has climbed no higher than 20 percent—twenty-seven in a total of 136.

    Eugene Cain is one of the twenty-seven. His casual manner, unsimulated smile and trim physique on a five-foot-nine frame give him an air of undergraduate youthfulness. He's thirty. For three years before coming to Cooley, he taught at predominantly black Foch Junior High. There he was one of a small cadre of young, new, black teachers whose sense of personal involvement and creativity gave Foch a noticeable degree of de facto "openness." It was one of the first Detroit schools to add Afro-American history to its curriculum, a program Cain was instrumental in setting up. When he left, his students gathered for a mass farewell. "All of my kids—that was from a three-year period—as many as they could pack into that room came back. It was a surprise going-away party. I cried. Man, did I cry."

Tuesday Afternoon at Cooley H.S.

Cain and his eleventh-grade Afro-American history class, mostly black, are reviewing nineteenth-century slave revolts in the United States.

* By June 1971 Cooley was 85 percent black.

CAIN: If we look at the classical definitions, we would have to say the revolts led by Denmark Vesey,* Gabriel Prosser, Nat Turner turned out to be failures. But we're gonna have to look beyond that. These revolts demonstrated—what?

STUDENT: That black people were not going to accept being slaves without some kind of resistance, you know . . .

An interchange follows between Cain and a few students about slavery as a system in which social, political and economic goals were determined by the slave owners, the power-holding class . . .

CAIN: Let's bring it on home to 1970. Are there things you all think about? Is everything just okay with you; everything breezin' along? What is it you're uptight about?

VARIOUS STUDENTS: The educational system. Checking ID cards. Law enforcement, primarily the police department. The war in Vietnam.

CAIN: Now I've asked you all this because what's involved historically as well as now is the question of authority, the question of who determines who is gonna do this, that and the other. That's what you're telling me. Now, as a group of students, what power do you have [to change what they are dissatisfied with]?

* Denmark Vesey, himself free, formed the most elaborate and efficient insurrectionary organization of slaves in U.S. history, in and around Charleston, S.C., beginning in the winter of 1821. It was betrayed, in May 1822, by Peter Devany Prioleau, a house servant. Gabriel Prosser's revolt, around Richmond, Va., was aborted by a combination of betrayal from within and a hurricane on the night appointed for the uprising, August 30, 1800.

In August 1831, Nat Turner, slave and preacher, stormed through southern Virginia with seventy followers, killing masters and their families and freeing slaves. It took three U.S. Army regiments to stop them. At least 120 blacks were killed in reprisal. Turner and his lieutenants were executed.

STUDENTS: None. The power to protest. We can think about it and figure out something to do, etc.

CAIN: Do you think these persons, Prosser and Vesey used their power effectively? Or did they have any power. Remember, the slaves were in the majority in Virginia at the time of Nat's revolt, and in Charleston at the time of Vesey's. Now let's go back to what Charles said before that in order to take effective steps you must be organized. Now when ol' Tom came and he spilled the beans on these other guys, Tom was not dedicated. In terms of his make-up, he was consistent. He didn't feel he needed an organization. This dude could see how he was getting along. And he was gonna use this primarily as an opportunity to get closer to his master and say, "Well, look at them out there. I don't have to undergo the same kind of punishment that these other guys . . . If I'm close to the master, what's affecting them won't affect me . . ."

Now, Vesey's solution to the problem was armed revolution. Carl, what's your solution to the war in Vietnam? [No answer.] Del, what's your solution to the educational hang-ups? [Del's answer is vague and general.]

Now, Charles said before that organization is necessary. He comes to you and to me, Shirley, and says we got to organize some pickets, do this, do that, come up with some political demands or what-have-you. Would you be game to go along with him?

Shirley says yes, if she could be sure that a lot of other people would, too. There's sophisticated laughter and she defends her position: "What can I do by myself?"

CAIN: Say! That's a good question. I can't answer that by myself. And I also want to raise the question: Should you be concerned about overall numbers or dedication to the cause?

223

A general, inconclusive discussion follows. Cain, re-urning to one student's dissatisfaction, voiced earlier, asks, "How many of you have ever had run-ins with the cops?"

There's a sprinkling of laughter. Two or three students ell of incidents they've observed or experienced. Their one is matter-of-fact, unemotional, though laced with rue-ul humor . . . The consensus in the class is clearly that policemen, including black ones, are hostile, club-happy.

STUDENT: I know this policeman, he's an old friend of the family . . . He'd give his mother a ticket.

CAIN: Now, suppose this man was a problem in your neighborhood. He's causing all kinds of trouble, knocking heads. He knocked your sister's head last night and what-have-you. What can you do, as a citizen in your community, about him?

STUDENT: [Placidly] Kill 'im.

CAIN: No! No! Seriously—and I'm going to ask this question of Lonnie over there who's sleeping and every-thing . . .

STUDENT: He's nodding.

The class relishes the joke. None of them would be careless enough to make it in the presence of an un-hip teacher. And Lonnie wasn't sleeping, just daydreaming. He has no answer.

CAIN: In your community this Man is a problem. He's causing all sorts of trouble. How do you deal with him effectively?

STUDENT: Zap 'im, that's all you have to do.

Cain interrupts, not to express horror or to moralize, but to debate the practical realities of such a solution . . .

CAIN: Do you realize the number of cops you'd have to zap or vamp all day? Okay, and suppose [even] three are killed in your community, what happens to your commu-nity in the long run?

STUDENT: I *know*. Everybody suffers for it because they're gonna be coming down, jacking up people, finding out who did it and if you *look* like you might have did it they're gonna kill you.

CAIN: Well, don't you think this is something you should at least think about seriously?

STUDENT: No, but look here . . . Okay, seriously. In a case like this, like the police jumped on my sister, I would probably do the same thing [to him] he did [to my sister]. If I was the kind of person who *did* do that stuff. You know, it's exactly the same old thing that everybody else does when they get misused. You know, you ain't gonna let it happen . . .

Cain and the student are at an impasse. He changes the direction of discussion:

CAIN: Oh, now. Misused. Hey, Charles, do you feel you're *using* the educational system?

STUDENT: I'm just here. As a black man, I'm just here. To a white man I'm here to be like him, to learn his stuff, you know, and to hate my own.

Another student agrees. She comments that she found the legend of George Washington and the cherry tree uninformative, unimpressive. She thought it had been silly for her lower-grade history teacher to make such a big deal of it. It is clear from spontaneous comments which follow hers that some of these students entered high school with a less-than-reverent attitude toward the traditional heroes of American history.

CAIN: Are you saying Georgie-boy* is not so relevant? . . . Now, you know, in this society, we hero-worship.

* In the comic strip *Peanuts* (November 23, 1970) the following dialogue occurs between a little black boy and a little white girl sitting just behind him in a schoolroom.
Boy: What did you write for Question Number Five?
Girl: I said that he was one of our greatest Presidents and one of our most beloved leaders.

Malcolm X, Mohammed Ali, what-have-you, these are *our* heroes . . . And when we get through writing about them hey will still be our heroes. Got it? So when white folks write history books, I'm quite sure ol' Georgie-boy will always come out a hero. In other words, every time we write, I don't care who we are, we come out with our own little prejudices . . . I cannot write like a white man. No white man can write like me, because no white man has had the same experiences that I have and I haven't had the same experiences as the white man. Therefore we write with two different feelings. So what's heroic to you might not be so heroic to me. Let's look at it.

Most of our textbooks . . . *have been* written by white authors, and so what would we expect? . . . But history gets periodically rewritten. You always have a group of historians come along—revisionists—and they try to get the record straight. Haven't you heard people say, "Oh, you really won't get a fair evaluation of John F. Kennedy until twenty or thirty years from now"? They're coming out with all kinds of evaluative books about Franklin Delano Roosevelt, especially here of late . . . But the guys who were writing, say, five or ten years after Mr. Roosevelt died, most of that stuff was highly so-called partial, in his favor . . .

Okay, here's a good example. You know what? The wife and I went down to see this, oh, freaky movie—what was its name?—*The Liberation of L. B. Jones*. I was so mad at that movie. Because, now in this day and age, dig? They portrayed L. B. Jones as a man who has no power. He was supposed to be in the upper echelon of the black community. He had an undertaking business and what-have-you. And his wife was making it with this white guy who—I don't know what he was. To me, he seemed like an illiterate but he *controlled* L.B. He would walk into L.B.'s

Boy: Do you really believe that?
Girl: No, but I've learned never to bad-mouth a President in a history test!

house and go into the room with L.B.'s wife, and L.B. would just get in the car and look back at the house, you know, and drive on. [The students laugh at this implausibility.]

Okay, it happens. It's *been* happening . . . And the guy who comes in and more or less saves the day is some big black guy who has nothing but brute force and strength. [Charles chimes in: "And no intelligence."] It was trash as far as I was concerned. At this point I feel that we don't need any more of this. We need better image-building pictures for our black people. It was sickening! *I wasted five bucks for that movie.* Actually, five bucks and forty cents; we got a popcorn.

CHARLES: Only one box for you *and* your wife? [Laughter.]

Some class discussion follows about the persistence of the pejorative Negro stereotype on television in the showing of such ancient films as the Our Gang *comedies . . .**

CAIN: Now, the paper we're taking home, will you kindly read it? We'll be discussing, primarily, the methods used by Nat Turner to liberate his people . . .

And I don't think any of you should go out satisfied and feeling as though we've solved any problems or what-have-you but these are things in which you should constantly use your reason. You should constantly question the things you are subjected to, and not only question but come up with some sort of reasonable and rational manner of solving problems.

* The series, produced by Hal Roach, began as a silent film entertainment in 1922 and persisted in the sound era until 1939. The juvenile cast of presumably lovable (but actually repulsive) brats included a classic Hollywood stereotype in blackface: a pigtailed pickaninny named Farina. In more recent times *Our Gang* has emerged from the film storage vaults as a regularly scheduled anachronism on scores of TV stations across the country.

Sunday at the Cains'

They live in a small yellow brick-and-wood-front building on a neatly kept street, with grassy strips between curb and sidewalk. The room we sit in holds an inviting, comfortable clutter of communications media: books, records, a player, a TV set. Poster-size photo portraits of black liberationists are taped to the ceiling and high on one wall. They help Cain to keep his perspective when he stretches supine on couch or floor to review his day's events or plan tomorrow's activities:

"When I want to look beyond, I look to Malcolm. When I want to look for rational thinking, in the conservative manner, I look to my man here [Frederick Douglass]. When I want to look to the left, I look to Rap Brown. And when I want to look for defiance and people taking a stand, I look at that." "That" is a photo of Tommie Smith, gold-medal winner in the 200-meter dash, setting a new record of 19.8 seconds, and John Carlos, who finished third in that event at the 1968 Olympic games in Mexico City. On the winners' stand to receive their medals, they responded to the raising of the American flag and the playing of "The Star-Spangled Banner" by bowing their heads and raising, each, a black-gloved fist in a salute to the concept of militant black unity. It was also the climactic gesture in a tentative campaign for a boycott of the Olympics by black athletes.

Mary Cain comes in with a bag of groceries, says hello, chats a moment and leaves. She has business of her own, even on Sunday, with the students in her junior high school science classes.

The word "education" implies change. To be educated is to be more or less reborn. My job as a social studies teacher is to look at our society with complete emphasis on the need for change. I care less for what-in-the-hell they did fifty, sixty, seventy years ago. Although I do believe that my kids need historical references to relate present to past ideas, to see how archaic they were, and are . . .

We shouldn't tell them about the Constitution: "Man, the thing is beautiful." In an ordinary civics class, when they say that, they're talking about structure. I care *less* about structure. I'm concerned about *process*. This is why I go to no end to find my own material and present it in my classroom . . . We've had to argue back and forth on some of these issues. I've read them some case histories of the use of police power and some of the white kids didn't believe this stuff actually happened. So I took the kids downtown to Recorders Court [Detroit's equivalent of Police Court]. They came back and: "Gosh, there's no justice down there, Mr. Cain. It's just like you were telling us." I said, "Okay, I was showing you what the deal is. Now, what are you going to do about it?" I wasn't expecting an answer but I didn't want those kids to forget the *question* I was raising. I believe that their role should be to realize the need for social changes, you see.

Over here at Cooley High School, I had a friend who was assistant principal. He said, "Man, they need you." At first I didn't want to come. I had a nice program going at Foch. I was instrumental in setting up the black history program; that was my program and it was really running beautifully. Plus, the climactic thing was the "Wall of Respect"* the kids built, and that *was* beautiful. I'm so proud of that school.

* The first "street" mural and the term "Wall of Respect" by which many similar works have since been designated, were originated in Chicago by the artists, Bill Walker and Eugene Eda. Their two-story-high, eighty-foot-long painting at Forty-third Street and Langley Avenue was formally dedicated in 1967. Since then, publicly visible walls of ghetto buildings have become a communications medium for artistic messages, of which the walls themselves are an inseparable part. In Chicago alone, at last count, there

A year rolled around and my friend invited me again to visit Cooley. I went over and I talked with the kids and I saw what he meant . . .

I transferred and I began to get very active with the kids, black and white. There's such a big need for persons with that humanistic spirit for those kids. And pretty soon I was looked upon by the faculty as being a troublemaker. I was called a black racist. The kids wanted to walk out about it and stuff like that. How was I a troublemaker? The kids were around me all the time; they were fostering some of my ideas of coming together, of questioning some of the things that were going on in the classroom, such as this: A teacher comes in and does absolutely nothing. He just sits there and takes down bets for the track, you know, and runs out. Tells the kids, "Turn to such-and-such a page, read the Constitution, underline such-and-such a thing." I was looked upon as Threat Number One. I *will* speak out, you see, any time I can, as to what we're doing wrong . . . Kids come and tell me, "Mr. Cain, Mr. So-and-so said that we have different blood" . . . "Mr. So-and-so says that we are baboons and that we're lazy" and what-have you. We've had stuff like that going at this school since I've been here. I've been the so-called hell-raiser, you know, because I refuse to let those kids, black and white, be stepped on by some senile old lady or old man. I got the kids to do some critical thinking; evaluation of self, of the community, *their* role, their teachers' role in society. And, man, for some reason people don't like that.

You see, this has been a haven for white teachers who wanted to escape the city—the system. Well, the school in the past three years has gotten a large number of black kids.

---

were thirty-two, with such titles as "Wall of Brotherhood," "Plight of Black Men in America," "Black Women," "Urban Scape," "Rip Off," "Wall of Choices," "All Power to the People," "Environment." Some, like the one Eugene Cain is talking about, are smaller, indoor creations.

And teachers talked down to the kids, really nasty: "Hey! Where are you going? What're you doing in the hallway? Get out of there!"—stuff like that.

And usually the issue is—authority. This is the whole problem in the high schools: "You'd *better* do such-and-such a thing, or else you will not pass this course!" and what-have-you. I have no regard for rules that are set up for me to harass a kid. If a teacher can go out of his classroom and go to the john next door and take a smoke, I think damn well the kids can do the same. This is how I feel; I might be wrong. See, I don't smoke* and I seldom drink. But I do believe that if we are educating kids to be adults, we must be the models, living examples. We shouldn't be hypocritical, say one thing and do another. And—I'm caught in the middle. I tried very hard to show the people in faculty meetings what is wrong. Every time I stood to speak, I lost one more so-called friend . . . Black teachers? Most of them are afraid to move. You see, high school for black teachers has been looked upon as a step up . . .

Well, what is it? Do all of these teachers feel you've undermined their authority?

No. They have this idea that they're professionals; most of them have master's degrees, have done additional studying. They feel that I have more or less upset the pattern of learning around that school—the curriculum, in the sense that students are questioning some of the things they are doing in the classroom. Really, that's the whole thing with these teachers. Their little playground is open now and the kids want to play on the swings, too, and they want to ride the seesaw—together. You know: "We can learn together." And we do! I don't believe I have a monopoly on knowledge and the kids know this.

* "My excuse for not lecturing against the use of tobacco is that I have never chewed it, that is a penalty which reformed tobacco-chewers have to pay; though there are things enough I have chewed which I could lecture against."—H. D. Thoreau.

The kids—these are my friends. They call up: "Hey, what are you doing?" and they come over. My place has become a haven for kids . . . They come by for constructive things. And if they want to hear Blood, Sweat and Tears, the Beatles, or James Brown, fine. And I have just as many Beatles albums as I have blues . . . and we can sit in the classroom, too, and talk about that. Yet and still, we learn, regardless.

I feel as though teaching goes beyond the classroom. . . . The wife and I have had a little campaign for about two years. Anywhere some kids want to go on the weekend, if we aren't busy, we take them. We've been to basketball games, baseball games, concerts. They've got to go out and get their ticket money. We'll supply gas and the chaperones. She'll try to borrow a station wagon and I'll get my car . . .

Sometimes Mary and I get jealous of one another, like yesterday. She wanted to carry her kids to some pond to get pond water and was hoping the kids would catch a few bullfrogs. And I said, "Oh, why don't you stay here with me," because we seldom see each other . . .

Here's a letter from a kid: "Say, Gene, we had a great time on the road rally, didn't we? Seriously though, I'm glad to say you are one of my friends and not just a teacher." [Cain, explaining]: We took a bunch of kids on a trip that time, and we ran the car into a ditch. That was the "road rally." The kids paid my towing bill. This guy is at Harvard now, and he's on the dean's list. He's also teaching black history at a reformatory up there, using notes he made in my class.

. . . And to teach kids that they have some of the same frustrations and what-have-you that I have—that makes them respond to you. Like Friday, you know what I did? Hell, I didn't feel like teaching. The kids had assignments to do and I just hate to sit there at my desk. So I stayed outside the classroom and called them out one by one. What did we talk about? Ruby's mother is in a mental hospital; I wanted to know how she was doing. Grace (white), she's afraid to take the giant step, to go to college, although she has a 3.6 average. She's afraid of competition and I'm trying to get her into a school. H.H., a basketball player, is having difficulties with *The New Industrial State*, the book they're reading, so I gotta review the book with him. Kenneth has this problem that, you know, all whites are no good . . . Sometimes I take the kids out and we have classes on the lawn.

I find myself shaking some of the grass roots that the teachers before me laid down. They're not so sturdy, I can see. Nate [a black former colleague at Foch Junior High] was like this, too. And boy, I wish my friend Fred Jones were here—a white guy, a Southerner, from Virginia. He was teaching stone, stone in the ghetto. I mean really. This is a boy whose relationship with the kids was something beautiful to behold. I've never seen anything like it. But he's on the West Coast now. *He* was *so* real. He worked at Spain [Junior High] with my wife. And Cheryl Greene:* She is really honest with the kids. They love her, black and white. And that's a beautiful thing.

So, this is the stuff, man—that I try to go with the kids. But I know I have a job to do as a teacher. This is my responsibility. The kids tell me I am hard as hell. Oh, man, do they have to do their work. No foolishness! I don't give conditional passing grades, which put them right in the middle. Either you make it, or you don't; that's my philosophy.

How does the Cooley administration feel about him? Detroit's black population is statistically imposing: 660,000, comprising almost 44 percent of the city's total. It has a correspondingly formidable capacity for pursuing goals of interest to the Black community, peculiarly so because of

* See pp. 190–202.

its comparatively strong employment and trade union membership base in the automobile industry, and particularly so in the years of heightened civic "sensitivity" following the Insurrection of 1967. So Detroit school administration is apt to adopt a "hands off" attitude toward "far-out" young teachers, such as Gene Cain, in black districts.

. . . I've organized things like this political seminar. This is a noncredit course, meets on Tuesday, not every week. Average attendance is about a hundred and fifty. The kids come in and they feel like staying. It's in the afternoon. They talk . . . I've invited people from all facets of the community to speak on various questions: a guy from the Civil Liberties Union, about the rights of teaching the students—academic freedom; a discussion about black economics based on the Black Manifesto;* a guy from Lafayette Clinic to speak on drugs and narcotics (an addict, a junkie, also came along—he was a friend of Claude Brown's referred to in *Manchild in the Promised Land*).

But—

We have an organization in this community called Unicom—United Community—which has been instrumental in getting kids to think politically. This is a black organization, although it was founded by the Catholic Archdiocese. I've been working with Unicom establishing a Freedom School. That's why I have all this stuff here about the Street Academies in New York. My job was establish-

---

* Adopted by the National Black Economic Development Conference in Detroit in April 1969. The manifesto demanded $500 million as reparations from white Christian churches and from synagogues to finance such undertakings as a Southern land bank for dispossessed black farmers, a new black university, black publishing houses and television networks. It was dramatically presented to the world a few weeks later by James Forman, one-time executive director of the Student Non-Violent Coordinating Committee; he interrupted a Communion service at Manhattan's Riverside Church to read the document.

ing a curriculum . . . Well, the school board somehow infiltrated the meeting that I chaired. And, they had their spies—black spies—who went back and told the principal about my role. I was called in by the principal and one of the assistant superintendents downtown. And the principal's question was: "Gene, why do you go outside of the school to solve school problems?" And I told him, first, that I live in the community; and, number two, I am black, a black man; and, number three, I'm a concerned teacher. I told him this was the decision that I had to make for myself.

We've had about twenty kicked out of school* and I saw the need for those kids and others to continue their education. So, I messed around and got a group of my friends, who were going to help me teach this thing . . . they can't teach free there every day. But my wife, she'll be teaching math and biology there. And I'll be running a political seminar on Saturday mornings plus organizing this stuff through the week. And I've been, you know, pretty busy . . .

See, this is another thing. Not only do I sit and talk, listen and participate, with kids in groups; I try to reach all of them, those who have and those who do not have academic talent because I see them in the long run not as students of Eugene Cain but as functioning individuals.

Tell me about some of them?

Okay. Roger. One of the nicest kids you'd want to find. White. His mother is Establishment, all the way. His parents are very prosperous. They have told him in so many words that he is shit . . . because he had his hair out to here, and a beard. His father calls me and says, "Mr. Cain, talk to my son." Roger wants to join a rock band as a drummer and he has this idea he doesn't want anyone to

---

* In connection with black-white student conflicts and black student–school administration controversies.

give him anything. Like he's been accepted at Michigan State and he's going to pay his own way . . . And the parents have more or less come out and castigated him as being of no value, a nothing, because of the way he wears his hair. He won't accept *their* values, this is it. And, by the way, this is one thing—my wife doesn't know this. The kid was over in Canada* with his girl and a bottle of wine. He called me around three o'clock in the morning. I had to get him out of jail, and it (whatever it was) came to about four hundred dollars. I didn't have the money, so I got on the phone calling everybody I could. We got the money together and I went over there . . . The kid has paid me almost all of the money back. And this is the stuff—it's BEAUTIFUL, man! [Cain is giving off an almost visible glow.]

In the course of the afternoon Cain shows me a bewildering collection of photographs inscribed to him by students and former students, exemplary pieces of their course work, mementos they've made or bought for him, and a fat file of letters from students, former students and adults . . .

. . . They always send you these things. We try not to throw away anything that the kids give us. It's pretty interesting around here . . . This is Lola. She's at the University of Detroit on a four-year scholarship. And this is a short story she wrote, really beautiful. There's a good chance I'll get her [another photograph] into Syracuse on a scholarship. I've got one kid, Norbett, into the tool and dye business . . . And Mary's kids, they're equally as nice and as alert as my students . . . I have so many sons and daughters; I mean, when I say children, *we* don't have any kids . . . I've had many, many trying moments in making decisions about what to do. Right now, it's Felicia. I've *got*

* Just across one of several bridges spanning the Detroit River.

to see her this week, find out what's wrong. She's still at Foch. For a junior high school kid she can really write; I recognized the talent there. She's going to high school next year at Southeastern but her grades have been dropping something terrible. I don't know what in the hell is wrong. I've got to go over and find out—there are so many Felicias around. And Roger is on my mind now. He was supposed to call yesterday but he hasn't.

You're leading a pretty strenuous life . . .

Yeah. The doctor told me, "Better slow down." The kids tell me quite often, "Hey, why don't you take a week off?" but the only time I take off is when I need off. A lot of times, in my situation at Cooley, things can happen that I regard as critical. Just recently we've had—oh, man, we've had all kinds of difficulties. School was let out for three or four days. We have interracial fights* and what-have-you . . . these fights have been by a minority of the students, however. I've stopped a number of fights. I stopped a fire-bombing of the office, and the office doesn't even know this.

A fire-bombing?

Oh. At the height of the frustrations at Cooley some of the kids felt as though the administration was dealing with them in a very, very unfair manner, that it was simply the old white paternal attitude: "Hey, you're lying. You don't know nothing. The administration knows it all." Some of the kids, the radical wing, who are politically and socially active wanted to fire-bomb the office. A kid called

* *Fact Sheet,* issued by the black student union at Cooley in April 1970, listed three major clashes between Breakthrough, a "white racist group," and black students ("no police action taken") on April 5, 1968, and on September 19 and February 21, 1969. A series of tensions and specific points of controversy between the black student organization and the Cooley administration is also summarized.

my wife about it to see what I could do. I met with the kids. I usually know where they hang out. And I asked what the deal was. My thing was that they would do more harm to the movement—we refer to this thing as "the movement" at Cooley High School—than good. We argued, we cursed one another back and forth. I was called Tom, and I called *them* Tom, and what-have-you. Tell me to go to hell and I tell them to go to hell. With those kids, the extremely radical ones, this is how a typical conversation will go. But they respect me because I'm willing to come and listen; because I've agreed on some of the [reasonable though unorthodox] procedures that they have taken. They knew I was there as a *personal* rather than as an "official" friend. And I told them, "No, I will not tolerate this." Finally, after about a couple of hours, I said, "Okay, dammit! Just take a vote right now." (We don't believe in Robert's Rules of Order, and whatever, stuff. I think that has been used to keep people in their places, keep them from speaking out.) But they showed hands and it was a tie. I didn't vote. So I said, "Now, you know that the leader can always cast the damn deciding vote." So one of the kids said, "Who in the *hell* told you *you* were our leader?" I felt so funny. Oh, man, did I crack up! They laughed and I laughed, and I said, "Okay, we're split fifty-fifty. Now, what can we do, on a fifty-fifty basis? The pigs can always get us when we're divided, you know." Then I left. I didn't know what the deal was going to be the next day, but nothing happened. Nothing happened.

Gene Cain also has a more formal role in student affairs at Cooley, as co-sponsor with Cheryl Greene, a white English teacher, of the Student Council. In the spring of that year the council was reconstituting itself in response to the widespread feeling that it had been ineffectual as an instrument of student power which might have prevented or mediated racial and student-faculty antagonisms in the school. A *step in this democratization process was the publication of a newsletter, the first issue of which contains such statements from students as the following:*

"*. . . I also suggest a judicial branch of this* [student] *government . . . there will be students to pass judgment on lawbreakers . . .*"

"*. . . the Political Seminar showed us that people really care about Cooley. Blacks, whites, faculty, and administration were united in defending Cooley against outside critics . . . Cooley is our school . . . We can find fault . . . We can denounce Cooley, but . . . you'll find that Cooleyites know how to unite and how to stick together . . .*"

[*Excerpts from a poem:*] "*I hate Cooley High School . . . I hate almost all the teachers . . . But Mr. Cain know what's happen, He definitely knows where it's at . . . I've heard him talk his business, but we've never even met! . . . Though I can dig the students, / The teachers are too uptight.*"

Cain tries to be loose.

I use the same vernacular as the kids—"Hey, what's happenin'." Kid called me Cain the other day and a teacher said, "Why do you let him call you Cain?" Well, this is our way of communicating. Why should I be concerned with him calling me *Mr.* Cain. He respects me; I know this. I've had that kid in one of my classes. We get along beautifully. People are so hung up on tradition and—I knock tradition. Like my free period I will go outside and walk around the periphery of the school trying to find out what's going on.

Cain's urge for "openness" as a teacher has earned him a certain amount of Klan mail as well as fan mail. He holds out an envelope sealed with blackberries, addressed to "Eugene I. Cain, Negro teacher," and signed, "Long-Time Native Detroit Taxpayer." It contains a lengthy outpouring of xenophobia. Excerpts: ". . . your great leader, Martin

Luther Coon was the biggest trouble maker of all . . . Negroes are similar to savages or cannibals; they are totally unlike decent typical Caucasians. Their very thoughts are completely different so there is little use in preaching 'integration'. It only makes matters worse. Northern cities are to be pitied these days . . . Our White brothers to the South know how to keep colored people in line. Unfortunately we up North haven't learned the secret yet . . . You complain you were stopped* while going out the entrance of Cooley. Well why not? Negroes look all alike. We good folks can't tell one of you from another, the bad from the 'good' if indeed there are any good among you . . . Crime, crime and more crime being committed daily by niggers isn't doing your image any good . . . You are a school teacher, Gene, and ought to know better . . ."

All of these letters I get, I share them with the kids. I tell them, "Hey, class, dig! This is something that you are born to be faced with in life. What are you going to do about it? How do we deal with persons like this?" and I get answers like: "Oh, Mr. Cain, don't pay them no never mind. They're going to die off pretty soon; ain't but a few more of them left." Some of the kids say, "Who in the hell does he think he is?" "I wish we knew who he was." "Why does he bother you?" "Who can *we* write to?" "We'll fix it; we'll fix it" and it gets to be really funny, you know.

What do the radical kids in your class say?

They say, you know, "We need the gun . . . Off him." What happens is, with this spectrum of opinion you have a basis for discussion. We keep it within the frame-

* The black students' *Fact Sheet* said: "On April 6, 1970, Black students and community leaders were stopped and questioned at the north entrance . . . by members of the Detroit Police Department and Board of Education security forces. White students and white community persons entered . . . at the south door without any questions."

work of what's going on in the class, but a letter like that does take us back into history.

Russ Gibb, part-time disc jockey on WKNR-FM and a former ninth-grade history teacher, spent two weeks as a student at Cooley, disguised as an eighteen-year-old ultra-hippie. In a subsequent article in the Detroit News (January 29, 1970) he wrote extensively about his experiences in Eugene Cain's classroom:

"I learned an awful lot about black culture in that Afro-American class—things that I, especially as an American history teacher, should have known but didn't . . . But it wasn't so much the details that impressed me as it was the realization that the black man has not just been sitting back and taking his fate. The stereotype didn't fit.

"I thought Cain was a good teacher . . . He injected excitement and enthusiasm into a subject. He was alive . . . Obviously he liked kids . . . Casual in his approach to the classroom, Cain wasn't hung up on discipline . . . nor on course content. If the kids wanted to take him off the subject, he . . . would allow them to go where their natural curiosity took them. He didn't play the role of the god-teacher, but treated education as a joint process. In a McLuhanesque way, it seemed to me that Cain was teaching more about democracy by the way he taught than a textbook ever could."

Talk about letters! I have one that was gotten out of the teachers' lounge, and here's a letter from a kid who wants to quit the Student Council . . .

What about the letter from the teachers' lounge?

Well, here was a person saying that I was the leader of "black violence" at the school. Some of the kids went down to the office. They wanted the principal to find out who wrote the stuff. It was in the teachers' lounge being distributed to teachers, and the principal went up and got the whole stack. It was duplicated on school property—paper and everything. Unsigned, except for "The White Racist Faculty Members."

What got you into all of this, the whole thing, to begin with?

I guess the thing that prompts me is that I came along during the Freedom Rides. I grew up in Birmingham [Ala.]. I went to Talladega College.* I had a great-grandmother living at the time and she was an ex-slave; she died at one hundred and fourteen. At college I was overwhelmed by the amount of history around me, but I couldn't relate the stuff to anything. My adviser was a Nigerian, Mr. Anonye. He asked me if I had thought of taking a real in-depth look at my own history. I guess that's what got me going.

You know, it was funny. Talladega was a very small, small old town and it really wasn't nothing downtown. But we came along during this wind of change. Everybody else was doing it at every other black college campus and we fell right into the groove. We wound up downtown, five students, sitting-in at the local pharmacy. And we tried to integrate the Trailways bus stations and what-have-you. We had a few of us beaten; our dormitory was harassed. We didn't reach the national headlines but we raised enough hell—the student body and some of the faculty

* Talladega College, forty-odd miles from Birmingham, was founded in 1865. Its tradition embraces the historical memory of a successful slave mutiny aboard the schooner *Amistad* in 1839. Arthur and Lewis Tappan, New England businessmen and abolitionists, were among the organizers of the Amistad Committee, which conducted a successful three-year struggle for the mutineers' freedom following their seizure by the U.S. Navy off Long Island. The Tappan brothers subsequently (1846) became founders and leaders of the abolition-oriented American Missionary Association, which, since 1867, has given its auspices to Talladega. On the lobby walls of the school's library building a mural sequence painted by Hale Woodruff circa 1938 commemorates the *Amistad* event, and a representation of the vessel is inlaid in the floor design.

with us. That campus represented economic power; we bought a lot of stuff from those merchants downtown. We organized a boycott and they began to feel the sting of it. And pretty soon they came around; they opened up these places for us.

No longer did they tell us we couldn't try on a pair of pants or a dress in their stores. This was a victory for us, a big victory. When we left we felt damn good. And the funny thing about it, we're still working. It wasn't but ninety-nine of us who graduated that year, but every now and then I hear about guys like Ulysses down in Charlotte, working his butt off with these grass-roots efforts, and Charles down in D.C. These are the small things, you know, that we have forgotten and I don't think any of us will forget . . . I got a long scar on the back of my head for this stuff. I spent five days in jail, in Talladega . . . We know what it means to be fed mush, or being taught by your teacher on the other side of the bars; the frustrations I felt as a person; the fear I had of these big burly white guys just waiting to kick my ass, and how all of us were afraid and we were acting out of fear . . .

Is the kind of resistance you've been getting from uptight teachers and parents characteristic of what happens to a teacher like you in other urban public schools?

Yes, I think so. Any time you have someone come in and address himself to the issues. It's gotten too hot at Cooley. Since I got my master's from Wayne State I've been teaching down there part time—new perspectives on the black experience. And Dr. —— said, "When it gets too hot at Cooley you can always come down to Wayne." That's where I'll be teaching next year. The school administration, when they found that I was leaving, they almost cried. But some of the teachers, *are they glad.* And one guy had me laughing: he told me he overheard a conversation between two teachers and one of them was saying, "Oh! That Cain is leaving, he's *leaving*, baby! Whoopee!" . . . I won't be leaving. I'll be working with the kids in the community, in Unicom. I'll be right here. They don't know that. They'll find out.

What is your feeling about white people?

I've had some very, very nasty experiences with whites but I've had some damn good ones. Probably the best was in a summer music work camp in Stockbridge, Mass., right around the corner from Tanglewood. I was straight from the South, although I had been North many times because my father worked on the railroad. But I still had this fear of people, white people. This was a Jewish family running the program. And, man, the closeness of these people, their family, to me. I'll never forget it as long as I live. I was still at Talladega but most of the other camp staff members were from Harvard, Radcliffe, what-have-you. I was almost afraid to hold conversations with people. And they used to talk to me and I learned that I could talk to anybody.

I think it's the small efforts that can show these kids they can really make it in society, that they can ultimately look beyond those little boundaries of color, that we can get something going. I have so much faith in this generation right here because I steadily see these kids bridging the gap. Take this white kid here [he pointed to a photograph]. His father is a policeman and, *boy*—now, there's a generation gap! The father talking about "off the niggers" and the kid don't go along with that . . .

I just have the firm conviction that we can really make it, black and white. This is my whole thing: it's not necessary to go around and hold hands and say, "We shall overcome, we have overcome." What's going to bring people together is just open honesty. Be honest with us. And this is what I've been trying to get the Cooley administration to do: be honest with the kids. They want the kids to know the rules about the small things, like not being out in the halls. But what about the stuff like, Why is it that most black kids are channeled into the so-called non-college-oriented programs? Why is it that the black kids are more or less talked to like dogs in the hallway? Why not explain to the kids that Cooley has been a haven for white teachers escaping from the inner city? The kids understand this stuff in *my* classes.

And the kids don't like whites coming up grinning and patting their heads, patting them on the back. This has been the administration's approach . . .

Yet and still I tell my students—I let them know—that out of all this doom I still believe that this society can make it. I don't know why I believe that. I guess it's the small, small experiences I've had with people. You'd be surprised at the direct influence a teacher has on a kid. And if I can get a white kid to see the need for—"Hey, man, stop running. What in the hell you got to run to the suburbs for all the time . . . ?"

After one of the interracial fights, there was this girl—mother's white and the father's black. They've been together for eighteen years. A *beautiful* family. She was crying in class—*boy*, was she crying. So I told her, "Stay after school, I want to talk to you." She did, and she told me, "Mr. Cain, where do I stand? I'm right in the middle, fifty percent white, fifty percent black. Now, where do I stand?" And, here again—I've had to talk to them so often about looking beyond this thing called color. And I said, "You stand where most of us would want to stand in the long run. We're all human beings."

Excerpts from inscriptions on photographs of themselves given to Cain by his students, some black, some white, at Foch Junior High School and Cooley High School:

"You are one person who isn't afraid to commit himself. Many students will remember you for that." "If all the teachers were like you, there wouldn't be any drop-outs.

Keep on doing your thing." "I hope you'll keep your swinging personality, along with your dedication to the people." "One of the hardest but nicest teachers a person could have." "You are the coolest teacher and hippiest soul-brother I have ever known." "I've had a lot of fun listening to your funny stories. Beside the coolest teacher, you have got to be the hardest. But at least I've learned something."

JOSEPH B. JONES
Philadelphia

Tall, lithe, purposeful, he strides to the front of the room. Facing his seventh-graders, he spreads his arms wide and lets his warm baritone roll out:

"Young friends! Time is our enemy!"

Joseph B. Jones is thirty-five, black, unpretentiously bearded and conventionally dressed, except for the brimless, inch-high Guinean hat closely encircling his scalp. (It's the kind newspaper readers have seen in pictures of Sékou Touré.) Jones is a teacher at the Sayre Junior High enrichment center, in a former parochial school some twenty blocks from the main building. Buses bring a weekly total of five hundred children to the center's classes in African and Afro-American history, math, science, French, Spanish and communications. The place is largely free of official requirements as to curriculum, materials or method. Standing at the edge of the University of Pennsylvania's enclave, it draws on the academic population for two dozen tutors and other volunteer personnel. The university's lecture halls, labs and libraries are available to Sayre classes as the goal of field trips to dig the scene of higher learning. This relationship gives the project a name: Sayre Cooperative University Center. Jones and his fellow teachers give it vitality.

Jones is saying, "As usual, we do not have enough time to do all the things we want to do. Today we must go over our notes. Then I'm going into your living room. I'm going to find out where your mother shops on Saturdays. I'm going to find out about your television set, your favorite movie company and some of the girls' favorite hair pomade. Now, young people, let us hurry . . ." The kids have no notion at the moment, much less do I, of what their Mr. Jones is up to. It becomes clear as the session rushes along, vociferous, ebullient, to the unwelcome end of its allotted forty-five minutes. The class adjourns reluctantly. Several of the students show signs of wanting to hang around. Jones eases them out patiently, lovingly . . .

I'm teaching Afro-American history, a two-year program beginning in the seventh grade. This year I started from the development of man, in the sense that Africa is the cradle of all mankind. Currently we're talking about the kingdom of Cush, when the black-skinned kings of Nubia sat on the throne of Egypt . . .

He points to a sentence chalked large across the front blackboard: "At the height of their power, the Cushite kings ruled over a kingdom which extended from the Mediterranean Sea to the borders of Ethiopia."

But along with that, I also teach a "key word" concept. I believe that seventh-graders should be expanding their vocabulary. That sentence on the board—the word I embraced was "height." Now, "height" is a third- fourth-grade word. I try to extract from them related words they already know but are not certain of the meaning.

For instance, today, I asked, "Where does your mother shop on Saturday for her groceries?" Many of their parents go to the Acme Market, but I doubt seriously if they know what acme means. Or they look at Paramount movies, like *Mission Impossible*. They see the trademark, the top of the mountain in a circle, but I want them to know what *that* means. So I erase "height" and put in "acme" or "paramount." Then I asked "What brand television do you have at home?" Someone says "Zenith," and I write that down. Or "Apex" which is the name of a hair pomade. Acme, paramount, zenith, apex—these are their key words for today. This is association, so they will understand and remember.

I have pupils tuned in to expect to learn new words. They look forward to it. Generally, I want them to look up the word at night and then come in and read it in context. It's not just memorization I want. They should be able to develop and use every word. Their vocabulary can help them widen their horizons.

What made you want to teach?

I'm a product of the Philadelphia school system. Twenty-one years ago, a high-ranking administrator was ready to send me to Daniel Boone, a special school for discipline problems. I was raised without a father, by my mother only. They separated when I was sixteen months old. I'm the youngest of three and I have an older brother who is a teacher, too.

I was a bush-burner in junior high. Now, reflecting back . . . maybe I wasn't understood . . . What saved me was, I always had a knack for reading. I worked for a movie theater Saturdays, delivering circulars. A black man there—he's the manager now—used to give me books. *Knock on Any Door*, for instance, by Willard Motley. Here I was associating with a black author, a rather successful one. Then, I had some fairly good teachers in the ninth grade—Mr. Sack, who's now at the University of Pennsylvania's Graduate School of Education. In 9-B, the teacher, named Mr. Fineberg, thought he detected a raw talent in me. He put me on the honor roll and told me that I really had what it took . . . I left Barry Junior High School in January 1949, and went on through high school . . .

I was lucky. Many of my junior high school friends died in Korea. You see, the big thing in 1949 or '50 was to join the Army. It looked great. Join the Army! See the world and make a lot of money! . . . With the present-day militancy, the thing now is *not* to be in the Army, to duck this Vietnam war. Who wants to get shot? But in the early fifties, in my low social-economic neighborhood, the Army was an escape for many of my friends. It was either that or they were going to go to jail or turn into dope addicts. Some of my friends are junkies, out-and-out junkies, two steps from the gutter, in the literal sense that their life is meaningless, it has no meaning. My very good friend is an alcoholic now, my very dear friend, my closest friend in life at that juncture. These are the realities.

After high school, in 1952, the military became Jones's escape. He attended Washington State University while stationed at Fairchild Air Force Base. Mustered out in 1956 with the rank of staff sergeant, he worked in the post office, studied for his B.A. in history at St. Joseph's and Cheyney State College and began teaching in 1964.

What *really* made me want to teach was living directly across from Sayre Junior High School. I moved there when I came back from the service. I used to see the touches of unruliness and it made me reflect back on my personal experience . . .

The discipline problems stem partially from self-dislike perpetuated by the system, by the racism in our society. The kids have been taught that black was bad. This is one thing that I do early in the school year. I completely destroy this myth about "Black is bad."

Next week, in Cush, we'll be studying about the great black Pharaoh Piankhi, and I've already told the children,

"Now, I don't particularly want you to be warriors, but if Piankhi conquered most of Egypt by the time he was twenty-two and sat on the throne, a black Pharaoh"—we know there was such a man; his grave site has been unearthed in Egypt; there's a stele in Cairo—"there's no telling what you can do when *you're* twenty-two. Oh boy, you've got about nine years to prepare yourselves. We're starting now!"

Time is our enemy?

Time is our enemy! Right!

Undisciplined behavior can also stem from weak parental control. The parents are out working, struggling to make ends meet. The Sayre community—I would say 85 percent of the parents are buying their homes. It's good for black people of lower middle class to want to own something, to leave some legacy. But oftentimes the parents work two jobs to support their children and then there is a breakdown. Another probable discipline factor is the desertion ratio in some black communities. That's why it's important that we have male teachers, black and white, especially at the elementary levels.

Very seldom do I have a discipline problem. I try not to have students suspended because the black parent can't afford to miss a half day's work to come and see about a bad child. I try to handle the problems here. When I first started teaching, I had to learn the ropes, how to handle the children. Now I think I'm halfway home. It took me about a year and a half to understand how to point on children, how not to point on them, how to get around them. But if you hang in there you'll learn.

For instance, just a little trick I've developed about breaking up fights, especially if a big boy is picking on a little boy. I run up to the little boy and say, "Stop picking on him or I'll suspend you." Generally they will break out in laughter and a bad situation can turn into a joke.

Or, take Evan Wray. Evan is one of eight children. His mother works long hours. I don't know if father is there or not. He tended to cause quite a bit of trouble when he first came here in September. But I say, "Evan, you'll never get into medical school if you holler out in class." It's bantering but he likes it and I'm getting to him. Evan is a good student and he's going to get better. But, if you noticed, there's respect between us for one another, even with the bantering.

Another thing I tell them is about the size of the brain, the general weight of the brain. How it was developed about 75 percent when they were five years old. I say, "You're thirteen now, twelve or thirteen. Your brain has grown eighty-seven and a half percent of all that it will ever grow. You're ready to run!" You can call it brainwashing if you want, but I want them to know that they are ready, they are ready to learn. They know that they can pass.

These students here—I see nothing but future lawyers, engineers, physicians, nuclear physicists. This is my hope and my dream because, again, I see *myself*; and I tell them that. In the last four or five years this school's become predominantly black. Before, many of the white students were going on to Central or Girls' High. They're college preparatory schools. But many of the black students that graduated from Sayre six, seven years ago, they're not on their way to being internists, lawyers, engineers. Some of them have died in Vietnam because they were dropouts. And many of them drop out because they can't read and they're embarrassed, so what is left for them to do? Trouble on the streets or a menial job. That's not our purpose. Our purpose at Sayre is to develop these students to reach the highest level of life they can.

Fine. The kids at Sayre seem to be getting the benefit of a lot of effort, concern, imagination. But what about the vast majority of kids, in the vast majority of inner-city schools? What's the answer for them?

I really don't know. But the answer might lie in a situation like this one, here. Do you know about this building? How it was born through community involvement, community concern? Well, Sayre was overcrowded and threatened with a double shift. But the parents said no, this time. They'd had enough of this dual business, some children getting out very late, et cetera. About eight or nine parents under the guidance and leadership of Novella Williams* and Mrs. Shultz and Mrs. Lofton, they walked through the snow to find this building. This is an old Catholic school, St. James. They told the Board of Ed., "We'll find a building. You just set up the funds. You rent the building for us. We know what we want for our children."

This is why Sayre is a community-controlled school to a degree. There's a close relationship . . . The community offers advice and is asked advice. It hasn't been formalized; there's no local school board but there's a mutual understanding, a mutual respect.

The parents thought up the idea that they wanted something like an enrichment center. We were getting kids moving up from the sixth grade who were out of contact, who'd only been in the Center City once in their lives; kids that couldn't communicate. That's why we changed our format here. This is a unique school. We have a communications classroom, a math laboratory, a real science lab. The seventh-graders are exposed to Spanish, French and Latin so they can make a more intelligent choice in the eighth grade. I told my students the other day that they could speak German too. They said, "Oh, we speak French

* President of Citizens for Progress, Mrs. Williams is considered a formidably effective organizer and spokeswoman for black-community action on issues involving the well-being of Philadelphia's "one-third of a city."

and we're going to learn Spanish, Mr. Jones. Now you're telling us we can speak German."

I said, "You can already speak German."

"How?"

I said, "What was the first class you were in in school?"

They said, "Kindergarten." So I explained *kinder, garten,* et cetera.

We're in our third year. This is my second year here. I was at the main building but I was aked to come here to set up an Afro-American history program. Here again, Mrs. Novella Williams and Mrs. Lofton, Gerald Klein* and Oliver Lancaster† and several interested people in the community who had seen me work with children, they insisted—to the administration—that I come to the school.

I want to say that this is one of the most enjoyable teaching experiences so far in my life. I have a tremendous amount of freedom. I develop lesson plans, and use them as I see fit, according to the needs of the children. For instance the hieroglyphics that you saw. A young lady from the University of Pennsylvania, a volunteer, did those for me.

Jones had shown me a beautifully drawn set of hiero-glyphs resting on the chalk rail of a blackboard: "Can you read these?" Of course I couldn't. "Well, my kids can."

I have a tremendous amount of room here to experiment, to work and to use all types of resource materials.

"What does Egyptian history mean to black people today? How can you relate to it?" If I were teaching a class of Italian students, I would expect them to be proud of Leonardo da Vinci, Christopher Columbus. If I were teaching a class of German students in the Midwest, I would

---

* Vice-principal at Sayre J.H.S.

† Assistant director of the Office of Integration and Inter-Group Education. The O.I.I.E. was one of Superintendent Mark Shedd's administrative agencies for implementing various aspects of school reform especially affecting Philadelphia's black population.

expect them to know about Einstein, Schopenhauer, Hegel. The Chinese, they would know about Confucius, about the Boxer Rebellion. But until the last five or six years, black children here in America—their heroes were the standard fellows, Booker T., George Washington Carver and maybe Crispus Attucks.

But let's go beyond that. Let's go to the great black warrior Chaka, to the six black, distinct black, Cushite kings. I want these people to be their heroes. I want them to know that black men sat on the throne of the oldest civilization in the history of the world. I want them to know that Mansa Kankan Musa traveled from West Africa to Cairo with hundreds of servants, each carrying a staff of gold. These are heroes that have *not* been brought to their attention.

How did you equip yourself for teaching African history?

I've done a great deal of reading on my own. I *am* a history major. There's very little in standard textbooks on ancient history. I like to rely on men like Basil Davidson and John Hope Franklin. I use Dr. Eric C. Lincoln's *The Negro Pilgrimage in America* and William Katz's *Eye-Witness* quite a bit for Afro-American history.

I ran a sample test on the children just to find out what they know about their background. About 85 to 90 percent of these black children, when they come into school, are not aware that their ancestors came from west Africa. And some of them who are aware but do not want to identify because they've seen the Tarzan movies . . . Many of them thought that most of Africa is jungle. These children didn't want to identify with that because of the negativism of the mass media. That's why I wear an African hat in class. I have a couple of dashikis on order and other African-type artifacts that I will use when we start on Ghana.

Now if you were to ask my children, "What do you know about Greek civilization?" do you know what they'd tell you? What the Greeks learned, they learned from the Egyptians. Because that is historical truth. The interchange between the Egyptians and Greeks was tremendous.

Do you think black history ought to be integrated into regular history courses or taught separately?

Until textbook publishers can spend more than two pages on Ghana in a ninth-grade world history text, I think it should be a separate area of concentration. Until the textbook writers familiarize themselves with it and give the history of Africa its just due, I can't see integration at the watered-down level. My experiences on the city-wide book-listing committee have shown me—many of the books that I saw, they hurried and found out something about Ghana and treated it very surface-wise and that was it.

We take field trips with the children. Beginning of the year when I talked about Africa as the cradle of all mankind, I told them about *Australopithecus* and *Zinjanthropus* but I never wrote the words on the board. The other day we were at the Civic Center and we walked by a model of *Australopithecus* and some of the students called it to my attention. This is when I find my teaching is rewarding.

It's nothing for me to gather up thirty children: "Come and let's walk to the University of Pennsylvania." I'm brainwashing the children there too. I kid them. I say, "Yes, there's a class, there's a seat waiting here for you," as we walk through the campus.

I went to New York last year with eighty-two children. Other teachers went with us. I chaired this program. We went to see *Hello Dolly!* on Broadway. I wrote Pearl Bailey a letter, so she came out and talked with the children for twenty-five minutes. Then we went out to Yonkers to have dinner and the waitresses out there loved them so much they gave them extra milk and everything. All for $13.60, the bus trip, the show—direct immediate identification with black people on the stage—dining out, complimented by white and black diners. June 14. One of the greatest days in my life.

How many classes do you have?

Quite a few. Four classes in the morning and four classes in the afternoon, except Tuesday (then we teach half a day because of the faculty meetings). Eight classes a day. You can become a little weary. Like, the lesson I was teaching today I taught to my morning and my afternoon classes, hopefully with as much enthusiasm.

Now what I'm doing with the slow readers— We make a little profit selling cookies to the children but we take the profit and the children get it back. And I went out and I bought *The Negro Cowboys*.* The boys are fascinated; you know, it has authentic good pictures. I haven't really made up my mind what I'm going to do with it. I might try to get some inexpensive cowboy hats, maybe a six-shooter or a gun or something. Maybe we'll work out a little skit or have them give a report. "All right. So you're Deadwood Dick" or "You're Nat Love." These were Negro heroes.

I don't know if you noticed the artwork around the room. I have an annual Afro-American art contest. [For prizes] I will buy a four-dollar transistor radio and I'll get a couple of books. We'll make a big to-do at Christmas time about the winners. In my heart they're all winners, but there's a competitive spirit.

These are things we can do with a small center. This is why I'm saying this might be the school of the future. You can work with the smallness. One of the greatest assets is the outside exposure they get. The big classroom is outdated unless every teacher has at least one teacher's aide.

* By Philip Durham and Everett L. Jones (New York: Dodd, Mead, 1965).

Teaching thirty-five, forty-five children, one teacher—that's very difficult.

Another thing. Many students leave the building without their schoolbooks. The lockers in a large public school should be open at night and nothing should be in them. If they take the books home, these children might dip into them at night . . . But they have to be responsible to someone who'd check their work. This society we live in—oftentimes black parents just don't have the time . . . Now, if we get the books home, let's pay interested parents in the community two or three dollars an hour and call them Home Visitors or the Homework Brigade. Pupils who are not doing their homework—let the interested parent knock on that door: "Mr. Brown? I'm Mrs. Jones from the Sayre Home and School Community. Your son's name is on my visiting list because he's not doing his homework. Now, what can we do about it?"

Generally when I visit a home it's not for discipline. It's for academic efficiency. I just get sick and tired of this "discipline" business. If a child is involved in a vicious fight, he's suspended, and I guess rightly so. But a child can come to school without his book for a year and he's not suspended. I question that. I question teachers that make a big to-do about collecting money for a lost textbook in June when the book was lost in October.

True, teachers are overworked, definitely. I haven't mentioned anything about pay . . . I need money, yes. I would be fibbing if I said I didn't.

It took me a long time to make up my mind to teach. I worked for the federal government in the post office for thirteen years and five months. I taught school during the day and worked at night and I made more money in the federal government than I make now teaching. I had to moonlight. I needed the money. I just left the post office last September and now I'm working on my master's in teaching at Temple.

One thing that's bothered me is that some of my black brothers have had to desert the teaching ranks for economic reasons. A very good friend of mine just recently took a job with [a textbook publishing company] because of the pay. Many black students that are teacher-oriented and certified are taking jobs in industry. I'm not saying they shouldn't. But a black person from the ghetto with something to offer—and I kid them when I debate this—on their way toward their first million, they might pause for two years and give it all they've got and *then* go on.

What are the chief obstacles now to the improvement of education for kids of the Black communities?

The vast bureaucracy and money. If people that can pay taxes flee to the suburbs, there's no money for new buildings. *This* can be an obstacle. There is resistance from the middle-class white and the middle-class retiree. Their children might be grown . . . I guess many middle-class white men say, My taxes are going for those black children who are rioting and they don't want Fishman* to teach them, et cetera, et cetera. The bureaucracy—you know, decentralization might be the answer. Those administrators, you couldn't get them into a classroom with a shotgun. They might have taught for one or two years, then fled. I'm just saying that a lot of good teachers become administrators, for more money. Why not find a way to reward a good teacher, financially, to keep him in the classroom? Once they get in the Board of Education, you can't get them back in the classroom; they don't *know* what's happening.

The teachers unions, economically they have helped a great deal. But here there's a moral issue now that black teachers must address themselves to. Black teachers in the city of Philadelphia have talked about leaving the union. If that were to happen, I guess I would have to follow along

* See p. 186.

although it would hurt me in several ways: insurance policies through the union, etc. Economically the unions have helped us.

I've seen some white teachers who just didn't give a damn. This bothers me. When I detect this in a white *or* black teacher we're generally not friendly. But there are white teachers—like a young lady came to Sayre Junior High School about three years ago. She walked in the *door* teaching and she's been teaching ever since. She has a great concern. And that's what counts.

A couple of young girls who had gotten jobs down at City Hall, where my wife works, asked, "What does your husband do?" She said, "He's a teacher at Sayre Junior High," and one of the girls said, "Your husband taught me in ninth grade, and we knew he *cared*." Knowing that a student can say something like that about me, I just try all the harder; I give it everything I've got.

When I look at these seventh-grade pupils, I often think of Joseph B. Jones, who was going straight to Boone, the special school for bad kids, when *he* was in the seventh grade. My children have got to learn. This is their only salvation. That's why I say to them, which is my slogan for the year: Time is our enemy.

CECIL WHITING
Cleveland

Cecil Whiting, Jr.: twenty-seven, married, a native Cleve-lander; Bachelor of Science in music education from Central State University. His grandfather brought the family

North from Alabama in 1920. "Back home, he'd taught school. He couldn't get a teaching job here at that time. He was sweeping streets for a number of years." Whiting's father, a high school graduate, never went to college, was a commissioned officer in World War II, retired from the U.S. Army Reserve with the rank of major; he manages the meat department in a chain store.

What drew Whiting to teaching was "basically the idea that I could make a contribution to the Black community." There was also the matter of occupational security, of knowing he could readily find a job.

. . . I wouldn't have thought so much in those terms if I had known what teaching in the public school system was like, because I threatened my own personal security in some of the things I did later on . . .

Last year at John Hay, I was adviser to the Afro-American Culture Club. At the first meeting, about eighty students, I spoke on racial differences, those that are more than skin-deep. Some of them are obvious. Take hair. If it has a greater surface area on one side than on the other, it curls very tightly. Or, a doctor giving a physical examination to a black person checks on things like hypertension, sickle cell anemia, so forth.

Now, on the standard mental tests available today, black people average fifteen points or greater below white people. And this is a fact, on *those tests*. Then, we have people who say, "Well, intelligence is not the exact measure of a person. We have to think about creativity and adaptability too." So our school systems say, "He can be creative with his hands and he can adapt to being a carpenter." And black people are going to be relegated to industrial arts, to vocational courses. And that takes us back to Booker T. Washington and what we fought long ago. You are really creating a racially identifiable servant class.

I, as a black person, can't accept the premise that black people are mentally inferior. We have to find out exactly what is wrong—why it is that black youngsters score lower on intelligence tests, why they are generally more prone to drop out of school. And when we deal with *this*, a lot of teachers have a tendency to recoil. It means condemning the educational system, criticizing their employers. It indicates to them that they have been on the wrong track—an insult to their professional pride.

When I spoke to the students I didn't try to negate the fact that there are also some nonphysical differences. I tried to redefine them by explaining that, basically, European society was very competitive. The people in that particular society had to compete to survive. In African society they didn't have to compete. Without this feeling of competition, black people, you know, developed a particular mentality.

Potter—he's a black social studies teacher—sat in on the talk. Afterward he came up to me and said, "You know, Whitey, we can't perpetuate hate." And I said, "Does that mean we have to suppress truth?" His rationale for any of the things he does in his class is based on that same idea of "not perpetuating hate," even if it means the suppression of the truth. This is what I refer to as the ostrich approach in education.

It's not a question of encouraging hate but of making sure that youngsters are prepared to enter the real world. You have to be honest about the society that we live in. If black youngsters are going to face racism after they graduate, they have to learn how to deal with it. To me this is the best way of eliminating the frustration that culminates in rage, in senseless violence.

And speaking of frustration, John Hay offers plenty of them to a teacher. I went there straight from college in September 1966 after substituting for a few months.

John Hay High School stands just outside the six-square-mile area cordoned and occupied by hundreds of cops and twenty-six hundred Ohio National Guardsmen for five days following the shoot-out of July 23, 1968. It was built in the late 1920s as an architectural/academic showplace of the Cleveland school system. The natural tributaries of its enrollment were tree-lined streets of decorous white upper-middle-class homes radiating from the outermost circumference of University Circle. Little more than a stone's throw distant from the Case Western Reserve campus, it had the outward appearance and the internal atmosphere of a "feeder" school for the university. Today that campus seems as remote as Tibet to most of John Hay's seventeen hundred black students; they suffer one of the system's highest dropout rates, year after year.

An even closer neighbor, physically, is Cathedral Latin, a Catholic high school but: "The relationship has been very poor . . . It's been such that if John Hay is dismissed early for any reason, Cathedral Latin is dismissed earlier." The principal and faculties of the two schools seem hardly to know each other in any real sense. Between John Hay and Cathedral there have been a few tentative efforts to develop interschool relations, such as exchange of visits and building tours of Student Council groups. The most ambitious project was Whiting's, an interchange of concert band personnel—". . . at least we had the kids playing together, if nothing else." The effort was quickly phased out because John Hay's then-principal, white, was uneasy about it: "He didn't like the idea of our youngsters going over there, across the street." More recently these efforts at "cultural exchange" have been resumed on a very modest scale.

Musically, the school had never been anything to scream about. They'd had a mediocre band. Never entered a city-wide contest. No orchestra to speak of. They had four good string players—all members of the all-city orchestra—but I was only able to work with two of them because of scheduling difficulties. We had uniforms that were purchased in 1947. 1947! Almost twenty years old!

We had to start right in with the marching band for football games. I spoke to Mr.——, who was head of the music department, about new uniforms and he said, "Well, we don't have the money now, but we can start a candy sale." So the kids in the band put on the old raggedy uniforms and they stood out in the cold downtown. They played and sold candy to passers-by, collecting money in their hats. They sold quite a bit of candy.

They did this in '66–'67, again in '67–'68 and in '68–'69. At the end of each year I'd ask the principal to get our uniforms now. And at the end of each year the reply was "No, we don't have enough money."

They finally bought the new uniforms last year. A few days before the band contest I asked the principal if we could use them. He said, "The band hasn't paid the money they owe for the candy." The uniforms remained stored in boxes. We entered the contest anyway. We were the only school there without uniforms.

Even worse was the lack of instruments. So many were stolen one year that the band was almost wiped out. I called the Board of Education inspector downtown and he came out and made some recommendations. He pointed out to the principal that in a building that size we ought to use fifty different keys instead of one general master key that fit every door. For the youngsters' own instruments we got a metal cabinet and I had the only key to it. That stopped the private instruments from getting stolen, but I couldn't get the locks changed on the cabinets for the school instruments, so they continued to be stolen.

The first year John Hay ever entered the band contest

was in '67, during my first year there, but we didn't enter the orchestra contest because we had, basically, no orchestra. I had no cooperation from the guidance department in scheduling anyone into orchestra or band. Finally last year I went to see the principal. I had gone through all the permanent record cards and found that we had sixty-six people in school with instrument experience. So I arranged to be there at the beginning of the scheduling period when they were making out the cards so that I could write "Band" in the space allotted for that on each of the youngsters' schedules. I did this in pencil, so what happened? Rather than consult me, they crossed out or erased "Band" and wrote another subject on top of it. You know, music is secondary. We did have maybe thirty-five in the band that second semester, but still not as many as we could have.

I also had a music history and theory class, but this basically became a haven for seniors who needed five points to graduate. I accepted these students, understanding the situation, but it did sort of reduce the class to one in elementary music fundamentals rather than something to help those youngsters who were interested in continuing in music.

Was there anything you could do to spark the students who came in just to cop the five graduation points?

Yes. We used basically a lot of material from *Blues People* by LeRoi Jones [Imamu Amiri Baraka]. And to add a little shock, I started out by saying, "Did you know Beethoven was black?" It was a device, really, to stimulate black students into finding some identification with the subject, particularly when you start talking about Western classical music. J. A. Rogers' *One Thousand and One Amazing Facts About Negroes* not only points to Beethoven but to Haydn. I don't go along with his documentation on Haydn, but the facts about Beethoven are found in other sources, too.* A couple of kids did a report on it.

Did it work?

Yes. It was something that I could use to make them enthusiastic: "What's next? Tell us something else."

And we drew a parallel between the history of black music starting, say, from 1770 on Congo Square in New Orleans, twenty years after the death of Bach, to the present. We talked about periods of jazz and compared them to periods in Western classical music. We talked, historically, about music evolving from folk music to the church and we spoke about black music in the same light; in our case, folk music being in the fields, moving into the church and eventually moving out and becoming jazz. And in the case of Western music, moving from the church into the concert hall. We covered the parallel lines of evolution of Western music and black music pretty extensively. The comparison created an enthusiasm that would normally have been lacking. There are a great many techniques to help black youngsters identify with Western classical music, to find some *use* in it.

At this particular juncture, because Western music has abandoned form, it is completely in a state of chaos. I really personally can't consider it art because it's dropped out of

---

* J. A. Rogers (1880–1966) was a self-taught historian, author of ten major volumes and copious periodical writings over a period of fifty years. As such, he was a major influence in popularizing the importance of black history among his largely black readership. Best known of his works, which he usually had to publish himself, are: *One Hundred Amazing Facts About the Negro, with Complete Proofs: A Short Cut to the World History of the Negro,* 24th rev. ed. (New York, 1963) and the three-volume *Sex and Race: Negro and Caucasian Mixing in All Ages and Lands* (New York: J. A. Rogers Publications, 1940–44, 1957–61). His illustrated feature, *Your History,* appeared for many years in the *Pittsburgh Courier,* a nationally distributed weekly newspaper.

art altogether. Karlheinz Stockhausen said in '58 that form is dead. But, you know, musicians, to be really artists, have to—you have to demonstrate your wares, and you can't eliminate form altogether and still have some basis for judging art . . . But of course, electronic music is a whole new medium.

How much did the development of jazz forms come up in your class?

Quite a bit. Especially, there were kids trying to imitate John Coltrane or Archie Shepp and finding out: "I sound just like Shepp"—just by playing, you know? This game sort of inspired them. At first they thought, Well, I don't need to know any more music to play what Shepp is playing, or Trane," but in realizing *that*, they tried to *figure out* what they were doing. So we began to examine a book, a small collection of Ornette Coleman's compositions and analyzed them according to the music theory we had learned. The kids understood then that jazz was very close to Western classical music, with the exception of improvisation. We used the *Journal of Ethnomusicology* for a couple of reports handed in by students on African elements in jazz, but that's rather advanced reading for high school students because it gets into some very technical terms . . .

That reminds me of another report we had, on Ravi Shankar. We discussed the sitar and related instruments, and the koto from Japan. And seeing how complicated non-Western music was, it turned them off from Western music—"No, let's go back to India, we're not finished with India yet." And in such cases it was very difficult to stick to a lesson plan [he laughs].

The difficulty of sticking to lesson plans was pretty universal at John Hay last year. Why did the school have to close down. What happened?

Well, there were a lot of controversies. One was associated with John Hope Franklin's book *From Slavery to Freedom*, which was the text for the black history course. The youngsters said it was too hard. It was basically a college-level book and they wanted one like Lerone Bennett's *Before the Mayflower*. Charles Leighton, the editor of the school paper, he's also class president, took a petition to the principal, who said, "You're a student. How can *you* tell me anything about a textbook?"

The students came to me because I had agreed to be the adviser to the Afro-American Culture Club, and I suggested that it might be a good idea to write to Franklin. So they wrote and got a reply that substantiated what they had said. Okay . . . Then they took Franklin's letter to the principal and to some of the other people who were giving the black history course and suggested that since Dr. Franklin had said the book was not high school material, a change should be made. But the faculty response was, "Well, texts have been ordered for this year. We might do it next year."

Then there were complaints about the cafeteria. At Cathedral Latin, an almost-all-white school a block away, the students were boycotting the cafeteria. But when our students came to me I tried to counsel them not to engage in disruptive activities. I tried to think of an alternative. Like passing out questionnaires. So their first one consisted of three questions: What do you think of the food in the cafeteria? What would you do about it? Would you be willing to participate in a two-day boycott of the cafeteria?

When we tried having Afro-American Culture Club meetings, the principal laid down a rule that the youngsters were not to wear dashikis. Immediately, several students were suspended for violating this edict. This one boy, Ron, was the center of controversy because he's the type that wouldn't back down on any position he had taken. He said,

"I'm going to wear my dashiki. If I'm coming to school, I'm going to wear it."

Now, I'd known Ron before. My first year at the school he had been a discipline problem for me. Not the type that he's going to knock your block off; he was the playful type. But I had a long talk with him about his particular role in the school and sort of turned him around. So I felt personally responsible for what happened to him after that.

Okay, Ron was suspended for wearing a dashiki. He was over eighteen and could be kicked out for any minor infraction. So, after suspending him for wearing dashikis, they kicked him out of school for being absent too long. Downtown it was listed on the record as "over age."

I talked to Ron's parents and his sister. She's a scholarship winner with a tremendous average. She really talked to his homeroom teacher and he said Ron was unteachable. Now, I know Ron would learn, if the material is presented to him in a way he could relate to. So a lot of the trouble centered around what had happened to Ron.

Then the administration decided to get after the students who were roaming around in the halls. On one particular day they rounded up thirty students, brought them into the Student Council office and suspended them right then and there. Almost immediately a rumor started that the Student Council had been disbanded; that supposedly was why the administration had used the room for its roundup.

The day after the roundup two council members, very conservative students, passed out a leaflet saying there would be an emergency assembly during the third period.

Now Jerry Mitchell, the basketball coach, went to the principal* and said, "We have a serious problem on our hands. The students think the Student Council has been disbanded." And the principal said, "No, they don't. I

* An earlier one, not the incumbent at the time of this interview.

don't believe that. It's just a rumor." He rejected it, you know.

So just about all the students in the school showed up . . . The principal and a couple of the administrators, faculty people, came down and tried to terminate the assembly but the students wouldn't leave. Emily Carter and two other band members were on the stage. (I think most of what happened was done by band members.) There was no way they could get the students to leave besides letting Emily Carter speak. So they started to speak about some of the things they thought were wrong with the school.

Now I had made the mistake of saying in the Afro-American Club—well, I don't think it was a mistake, except maybe tactically—that when a teacher opens a book and says, "Today we'll read from page 139 to page 159," when he tells you to do that while he reads a newspaper or does other work, he's not teaching class. Emily quoted this [without attribution to Whiting]. She and the others raised some legitimate grievances. The principal agreed that these could be taken up through the Student Council. Some rejected this because the Student Council had traditionally been dominated by the administration, but all the students went back to classes. There was a minimum of trouble, but still, that undercurrent—you know? The students had gone to the PTSA [Parent-Teacher-Student Association], and after they met with them, the parents decided that what the students were saying was absolutely legitimate and they were anxious to find out exactly what was going on. Okay. Things were quiet until the change in the semester when Emily Carter was suspended, and transferred to East High School. Now, this was the culmination. The students met away from the school on three successive days at a place called the Performing Arts Theatre. They had gotten to the wire services to say that they were going to do this, so it was announced on all the radio stations that morning. They had about eight hundred students there. Parents came and then they went down to see Dr. Briggs,* the school superintendent.

After the third day, the students decided to come back to school. They all congregated in the principal's office, waiting to see him. I don't know exactly what happened there, but the rumor circulated that the principal had jumped out of the window [his office was on the first floor] to get away from them. Which, you know, reduced his position.

Meanwhile the *Cleveland Press* published an article that was attributed to the principal. He said he couldn't relate to the youngsters at John Hay because he didn't have—this is a quote—"an Afro haircut, didn't wear yellow pants and couldn't soul-talk." After that the school was in turmoil. The students went down to the Board of Education and Dr. Briggs signed eight grievances, including the reinstatement of Emily Carter, and admitted to the press that the board had made a mistake. When they came back, they demanded an assembly in school. They said they had been given permission by Dr. Briggs to have one to discuss exactly what happened. Everyone gathered in front of the auditorium, but the doors weren't opened. So the students started roaming through the halls. And some who were less contained started kicking over things and burning things in the halls. So they closed down the school.

The school was closed for a week. Some of the parents went to the Board of Education office and confronted Dr. Briggs, so that was when he guaranteed that the administrators would be changed.† Now, I think it's important to say that from what I observed, the principal was a liberal educator and a very sincere person, but he was the victim of

* Dr. Paul W. Briggs, Superintendent of Schools since September 1964.
† Subsequently, there was a change of administration at John Hay.

some bad advice from less liberal faculty members, including black teachers.

I can give you a specific example. I attended an in-service course for band directors. The man who was teaching it said that the best way to save money on valve oil for trumpets and trombones was to use kerosene with some valve oil added to it. Okay, now, what I did was get a gallon of kerosene and put it in my room. I came into the room the day the fires started, and the kerosene was missing. I asked Mr. —— where it was and he said, "Oh, I took that down to the office." Later I heard that another black teacher had gone to see the principal and said, "Did you know that Whiting has a can of kerosene in his room?" As if I was the fire bug that had been setting the fires, or I had been assigning kids to go down and set the fires.

That teacher was ambitious about getting an administrative position. But he wrote himself off by making a couple of statements downtown in regard to student activity. He referred to the youngsters that we were supposed to be educating as "dirty little Black Nationalists." The board people didn't like that. They knew that the type of person in an administrative position would be very dangerous as far as alienating the community was concerned.

During the week that school was closed, the teachers met downtown and decided to do nothing—as they had been doing all along. And I stood up and told them that they were being reactionary, that they should be responding to what the students were doing and that they should formulate their own proposals. At another meeting some of the teachers were trying to get a petition around to have certain parents barred from entering the school. I was trying to be at my conservative best and not rock the boat. But when they started talking about this I couldn't keep my mouth shut. So I said, "You can't keep parents out of school. This is a public institution. Public education can't be selective." That started off all kinds of name-calling, shouting at everybody else. Two weeks later I was called down to the Board of Education to explain why my work had been deficient this year.

I don't mean that all the teachers are reactionary. Some of them are very dedicated. But there are two types of dedicated teachers: those who get frustrated and quit; those who stay in and quit. There are black people at John Hay today who will close their classroom doors and teach like the world was coming to an end and try to convince the kids that their lives are at stake, you know. But when they leave the classroom they assume the attitude of some of the other members of the faculty. They don't emphasize their own personal convictions.

Like after I spoke up in the faculty meeting, about five of the teachers came up to me afterward and said, "I go along with what you said a hundred percent." But the few who did speak up were subjected to the same type of harassment that I was. For instance Mrs. —— spoke out in the meeting when they said that students shouldn't wear dashikis. She said, "I don't see anything wrong with a dashiki." So the next day the head of her department called her in and said, "Are you a Black Nationalist?" They had all kinds of accusations going around about any black teacher who spoke out.

And there's another thing. Some of the most radical teachers in the Cleveland school system—particularly those with a strong education background and who are on permanent contract—instead of suppressing these teachers, they promote them to higher positions, so they're part of the administration.

They hadn't really prepared a case against me. They brought me downtown on such short notice that they had no documentation as to my deficiencies. That's one reason I'm still here. Even though they transferred me from John

Hay, I'm still working for the Cleveland school board.* If I had really been deficient all through the year, they would have been able to prepare a case against me in time, you see . . . The can of kerosene never came up. To this day I've never even seen it again, but I think that had a lot to do with the sort of forced decision to bring me downtown on such short notice. But I think this might be my last year. I've been thinking about doing some graduate work and perhaps becoming one of those people who make those policies that make people mad. Seriously, I think the trend now is to think of creative alternatives to public education. I think there are going to be a great many private schools coming about because people are becoming frustrated with the public school system. For instance, my son is six months old now and I'm thinking about his education already. I sent to a private school for a brochure and found it cost $695 to send him to kindergarten for one year. And I'm seriously thinking about that.

Have there been any benefits as a result of the student movement last year?

Minimal. The only benefit, really, is a greater understanding of what the problem may be, a greater awareness that there *are* problems. The curriculum hasn't changed, nor have student-faculty relations.

The new principal is black. What about him?

From what I know of him he's the type of fellow who can say, "Hey, man, what's going on? How you doing today, chief?" They placed him in this situation because they thought that his attitude, his approach, might sort of pacify the students. As long as principals receive their pay checks from the Board of Education, they will be loyal to the board. You can't expect a principal to take a stand for

* Assigned as a music teacher to a circuit of several schools on a weekly basis.

the community unless he's receiving pay from the community.

Schools have to be accountable to the community which they serve—to the people, the patrons, the consumers. And until there can be established maybe a private school system, or some other method for financing education, education won't move.

Short of community control, what do you think is the most urgent need for kids in a school like John Hay?

I think education is basically preparation to survive in our society. It has to be survival-oriented—basic down-to-earth pure survival. Physical education should be thrown out and you should institute a course that might be called "environmental mastery"—or something like that. Considering the pathology—in quotes—of our community, the kids would learn how to defend themselves physically. They have to know how to hustle for money that they need. But more than that.

The school has to become the source for expertise that the community needs. For instance, a businessman is trying to get his business started on 105th Street. The nearest high school is John Hay. So he comes to John Hay and says, "I need to know something about bookkeeping." "Fine! we'll send three students right over." And this will be those students' task, to help with his books.

The school has to become the source for special skills the community needs, like the Masotti Report* was made by Western Reserve. Schools should be making reports on

* A report on the July 23, 1968, shoot-out and subsequent events, prepared by the Civil Violence Research Center at Case Western Reserve under the direction of Louis H. Masotti and Jerome R. Corsi, with the collaboration of three reporters from *The New York Times,* Gerald Frazer, Anthony Ripley and Thomas A. Johnson. It was prepared with the partial but not initial support of, and submitted to, the National Commission on the Causes and Prevention of Violence. It was published in June 1969 as a paperback, *Shoot-Out in Cleveland,* by Bantam Books.

their community. They should use the expertise that's there, for the community's benefit, in relation to the community's needs and the community's will. Schools hold a lot of manpower. If it wasn't for the labor unions, you could have classes in home construction from the ground up, teach the highly skilled trades from which black people are still kept out by the unions. A class in heavy-equipment moving . . . classes in plumbing, in electrical wiring, in carpentry, bricklaying, interior decorating, landscaping. And after these classes built houses you could sell them at a low price to the people in the community.

You would want to teach the students the legalities of police work—what you have the right to do and say. I have a friend who teaches at Glenville High. He's now suing the police department for false arrest, for two hundred thousand dollars. You know it's been estimated that over 50 percent of the males over twenty-one in the Black community have some type of arrest or conviction on their record. With those arrests, *without* a conviction, there should be a lot of suits for false arrest. There should be channels open for people to make complaints.

In Environmental Mastery we would teach a student, basically, his rights in dealing with the police department. We could have a policeman come in and reinforce this belief. Then there should be a man they would know at the Fifth District police station whom they could go see if they felt their rights were being violated.

And the course would teach practical home repairs, how to judge the quality of furniture when you pick it out. You could have a course in black economics that would teach the basics of the credit system, to show people how they get hung up in it. Courses on housing and health laws, scientific pest extermination.

The kind of "survival" courses you're talking about would educate kids to adapt to life as it is. But a lot of the theorists and practitioners keep talking about "education for change." What possibilities do you see in this respect?

The changes that are made now are basically accommodations. It's like turning down the heat under a boiling kettle instead of turning it off. It builds back up, they turn it down a little bit more. The problems in our schools have really transcended the problem-solving abilities of the current educational hierarchy. Soon the schools are going to become so unmanageable that nobody can handle them. At that time the parents or somebody are going to have to move in and say, "Well, we'll take over now." . . . If we were going to get community control, it would have to be total control, however, including finances. That means changing taxation power, school laws. And that requires legislative power . . . If you're speaking about *total* change of a school system, the system will have to become a significant part of a whole revolution or it will become part of what the revolution is *about*. Is it possible, or impossible, to conduct any education for change within the present school system? That's a hard question. I really don't know. I can't say . . . The schools will change, but *education* for change will not take place within the school system as it exists today.

6

THE LOVING WOMEN

The first school that I went to was operated by an old woman in her home. She had great pride and demanded that her school pupils have pride, too. If we should purchase something from the grocery we could not eat it from the bag while we were on the street. Such a thing was a violation of her rules of culture. If you missed a word [in spelling] she would whip each letter into the palm of your hand. But I remember her as a great teacher . . .

—*Septima Poinsette Clark*

EUGENIA CLARKE
New York

Eugenia Clarke is a social studies teacher and "resource person" at Arthur A. Schomburg Intermediate School (I.S. 201). At other schools, where she had been one of very few black teachers, or the only one, she became convinced that most white teachers were unable or unwilling to bridge the race/culture gap between them and the black children in their classes. In those earlier years she doubted the value of taking the initiative to overleap the same gap, which existed in adult and professional terms, between her white colleagues and herself.

At that time I was not confronting people openly. I was not yet at that point in my own development.

What made you change?

I think Nzingha had a lot to do with it, my four-and-a-half-year-old daughter. Having a child makes a difference. The things you have to do, maybe you have more reason to do them. But this was before Nzingha—the sit-ins. I was very saddened about that whole sit-in scene [in the early 1960s], seeing black people spat upon. I thought it was terribly degrading and humiliating. These students could accept this vile behavior because of something they felt. I could not have done it. I remember watching some of this stuff on TV and just burning with frustration and anger. This was when I began to be more outspoken, so much more that I said something at the time of Kennedy's assassination that I might not have said earlier.

I had a class of disturbed children and someone came in, interrupting the class. I was annoyed because what for did they come in to tell me Kennedy had been assassinated? That was the way I felt. I was *annoyed*. I just said, "Oh, okay." Then somebody else came in . . . I said, "Oh, all right." So everybody's getting upset. I said, "Six children were killed in Birmingham, so what is the problem?" You know, this was after,* and they're getting so upset. And—o-o-o-o-oh! I was like—burning! I didn't hear all of this from the white teachers, you know, when these six kids were assassinated. No-o-o. Nobody was upset then. It so happened that Friday we were going to a meeting— with the psychologists, a social worker and that sort of thing—and everybody . . . really, I was amazed . . . here they were, deeply moved. You know, this man, this was *one* person, assassinated. All I could say to them was, "Well, what in the devil do you expect? Six children killed and nobody's alarmed, so this is what you're saying, 'Go right on. This is an invitation.' " My verbalizing this would not have happened earlier. I mean, I would have just sat there and looked at them. Just sat.

Most of my confrontations have come in school situations. I worked with emotionally disturbed children about three years. In one school there were only two of us, Katherine and I. We were the only black people; she was a psychiatrist. And there were a number of things the other teachers just didn't understand about the children. These were things of social grouping and racial difference. There were many times when I had to assume responsibilities about this lack of understanding. So a lot of it has been that. In recent years it has been Nzingha. Like once, we

* The assassination of John F. Kennedy occurred on November 22, 1963. Two months earlier, on September 14, a bomb thrown by white-supremacy terrorists, killed four little girls and injured twenty other black children in a Sunday School class at the Sixteenth Street Baptist Church in Birmingham, Ala. That afternoon, John Robinson, sixteen, was killed by a policeman's shotgun while he was running from the scene of a clash with white youths; Virgil Ware, thirteen, died of a pistol shot fired from a passing motorbike ridden by two white youths.

were on a bus and a white woman sat on her. Instead of saying to me—

Sat on her?

Sat on my child, instead of saying to me, Would you please move your baby so I can sit? And all I could do was to push that woman. I couldn't get to my hatpin fast enough. This was a woman obviously of some means. She assumed that she could just sit on my child. First of all because Nzingha is black, but it was a class thing, too, you know. She didn't have to respect someone like me. Well, she got off the bus after I finished with her. My sister was with me; she was whispering—good Christian woman— "Eugenia, stop!" I said, "Listen, this is my child here." You know, I had to go through. I had to perform because my daughter had to understand: No one does this to you; you do not let anyone do this to you. So this—yes—I think she learned something positive from this.

In school, do you go to any pains to teach the kids that they must not permit—

Well, I can think of an example. We were visiting the museum at Fifth Avenue and Eighty-sixth Street. I was the only black woman teacher. There were two men along. So I was standing somewhere in the Egyptian Room and then I heard a guard speaking harshly to the children. The children were behaving beautifully, really, but you know how boys are . . . The guard was annoyed because he had spoken to another teacher, before, about some of the children and it seems she hadn't done anything. I waited to see if either of the white young men teachers would say something. They didn't. So I said to the guard, "Listen here, don't you speak to our children like this." I had to go into a whole thing with him, because the children could see and hear me do it. I couldn't have him talking to those children like that. You know, once more somebody was going to step on them and it wasn't necessary. So when I can, I do defend the children.

What do you think about the white teachers you've worked with?

In my experience there have been some basic kinds of differences. The first group I encountered were older, domineering, very rigid in their classes. I'm sure they had always been that way, even with white children. In their behavior with black adults, this was obvious, that they were what you might call "prejudiced." Yet and still, some of these teachers *taught* the children. But their manner, you know—they were condescending. And children, being what they are, were aware, I'm sure, of some of this. Most affected were these very aggressive little boys, the little imps. These were the children most likely to be classified as retarded when they were not retarded but had become behavioral problems and could not be handled.

I would observe younger teachers, in mixed classes, overreacting to the behavior of some of the more active boys when they would not react the same way if it were a white boy. These little black boys were not attuned to the kind of social behavior the teacher wanted. She wouldn't realize that she was always picking on this child and therefore his negative behavior was being provoked by her. She was creating it, you know—her attitude. In classes for brighter children, this was very often the teacher's attitude: "You've been put in this class" (and the condescension came through again), but some of you don't belong here. But since you are here, act like you appreciate it. Don't give me such a hard time."

Teachers will put a child out of the room, send him to a teacher who they believe can "control" the children. I've had them sent to my room, and one teacher, when she discovered I was giving the child work, decided she wasn't going to send him to me anymore because I didn't just have him sitting there. She'd rather have him standing out in the hall . . . Why would she feel that way? At that time I was not facing up to people so openly. I only said, "It's all right if he continues to come to my room. I don't mind." I didn't go up to her and say, "Why don't you send the child in any more, you'd rather have him out here." I had no difficulty with the boy and maybe she resented this.

Then what do the young teachers amount to, in your opinion?

The most striking thing is that many of them do make an honest, a real human effort to understand how the children see things and what life is like in their community. They try very hard, unlike some of the older white teachers. But they're rather weak. Our children don't need weakness . . . Many of these teachers seem to think that just love will work wonders. They seem to forget these children are terribly handicapped because they don't have the skills. They have not been taught to read well. Fifth-graders are still counting on their fingers. Ask "Five plus six," and you wait ten seconds for an answer. They've got to go out in a world which is demanding much, much more. I'm not saying love and affection has to be equated with weakness because some of the black women have been very loving but strong. There's no need to be weak.

We've got some black teachers that are goofing off, too, but black teachers by and large do not mistake *loving* the children for *teaching* them. I think this is especially a white teachers' problem. It's a condescending kind of thing, really. I'm watching and wondering when it's all going to backfire. Children do catch on. That's why they give these teachers such a hard time.

The black teacher usually knows when the black child is putting her on. She is not caught in a bag where she feels sorry for the child. Very often she's come from that too, so: "What are you feeling sorry for? Get up and let's go!" She's not wallowing in anything. She does not have to contend with the personal problem of many of the young white people who are trying to be honest, like—I've played a part in what's happened to you; you are crippled and I've participated in that.

The guilt feeling is quite real with a lot of people.

Probably. Black teachers aren't caught up in that. I think they can say things to children with much more credibility like . . . I do live in Harlem. I have to shop in the same stores. I mean, it's not just that I'm black. If they know I can't control my own room: "What are you going to do to me? I'm already in the hall and I can run." But I follow through and: "If you get fresh I will speak to the AP [Assistant Principal]. And if you're close enough, I will catch you . . ." But there's catching and catching. And if you're going to be abusive when you catch a child, oh-ho! then you better not catch that child, you see.

What do you think about whacking a kid who gets really troublesome?

I have on occasion used a ruler. This was a kind of environmental thing, a school situation where teachers were doing this, and out of my own frustration I picked up the habit. When I realized what was going on, I had to stop. The children are embarrassed. It's not a *teaching* experience and it's not a learning experience, where you stop and work out a problem. You see, a spanking [she slaps her hands together], it's supposedly finished, but it's not. You haven't talked it out. There's no understanding. I was disgusted when I did it and more so afterward. I finally felt that if this is what I do to a child, this is all he's going to understand.

I'm not really as much of "the old school" as I was in the beginning. There's been so many changes in working with children, so many things that I've learned and understood. It might even have been better if I had worked with younger children earlier.

Do you think white teachers who have been teaching for any length of time are capable of real change in the quality of their teaching relationships with black children?

It depends. There are white teachers who have been teaching as long as I have (eight years) and they are— white teachers. Steeped in their own beliefs about the inferiority and the inability of our children to be really good students. They can't change. I can also think of a former co-worker, same age, same length of experience as mine. She has been trying to change, and I think she can. So I'm sure it depends on the person.

What differences have you found between teaching at I.S. 201 as compared with other New York City schools?

At 201 there's one of the youngest staffs in the city. Really, I just marvel at some of these young people. I've been very saddened to see some of them leave the classroom for one reason or another. They're young, not quite sure they're in what they want to do. But their whole attitude toward the children, and the way they try to relate— they're fantastic. I feel this way because I'm of "the old school," very sort of set in the way my class is supposed to go. That had a lot to do with prodding me out of the classroom; I can work much better with the teachers, helping them to become better informed. I'm not being pressured by my feeling that "I *want* these children to learn *this*," you know.

It would be beautiful if most of the older teachers could just sort of let the younger people take over. But it's not realistic. A lot would be lost. Experience, expertise. Very often the older teachers are better, but who's to say? Are you a better teacher just because you know the subject matter? Time will tell. Hopefully a lot of these young people will develop expertise. Many are experimenting. Perhaps they'll come up with things more meaningful to our children.

But you think a lot of them aren't making it?

Yes. You see, you've got your good points and your bad points about being 201. A lot of serious, earnest people have been attracted to 201 but there are goof-offs, too. A lot of people have gone in because of two months' paid vacation, all these holidays and, you know—nine to three. And some of them work just nine to three, believe me. I know I sound terribly old but I really, really—they don't work like we work. And the complaints they make: "The union says we're not supposed to do this." The contract, you know? The contract! They're supposed to be *teachers*, and they sound like they're working out there in a factory somewhere! These are *children* they're working with, but the things they scream about. It's very interesting. So, many of them come and what do they want to teach? Social studies, African and African-American history, and if you talk to them they don't know *but anything* about any kind of history. Yet they feel they can do this at 201. You see, that's it; they aren't serious. You know, the African studies are just beginning, so those who are teaching them have to dig. I mean, *I'm* digging like mad and I've had an interest in this for some time.

As a social studies teacher at I.S. 201, Eugenia Clarke feels free, productive. African and African-American history have a legitimate, equal footing in the curriculum. At other schools any such teaching was a matter of her own initiative and ingenuity supported by the hope that no one would mind.

I had made attempts to teach about Harlem in previous school experiences. This woman from the guidance office always made it a point to come in at the time I was doing the unit. I don't know what she was doing or who she was. I guess she was observing all of us. I didn't object to people coming into my room, but I didn't want, first of all, to have my unit stopped and I didn't want her to make the children self-conscious, so I just changed the time for instruction. I didn't invite a situation where I had to even find out what would have happened. I just avoided it. She finally stopped. She didn't ask me about it. I said nothing about it. There was no confrontation on the issue at all.

This, by the way, was just a unit on Harlem with third-graders, but a lot of current things would come up because the children asked questions.

What kind?

It's interesting what comes to mind. Taking them on a trip. We were on the bus and this little boy said, "Wait till we get downtown. You'll see. There's lots of lights and the streets are clean." I said to myself, My God, look how early it begins. He had already discovered the differences between Harlem and downtown. Eight years old. That's not so early. I know that now. They would ask things like why only black people live in Harlem. They were most aware of their immediate neighborhoods, you know, the trash, and they were concerned about the winos on the street, what they do, how they ruin the apartments, stay in the lobbies, how they ruined the sandboxes and left glass scattered in the park.

What else is different at 201?

It's great to have a black principal, the first time I've had one. The assistant principals are all black. Many of them don't have the experience because in New York City it takes quite a lot. But the things that they're bringing to it help to make up for the inexperience. I mean, a simple thing like getting materials: they don't know anyone down at the board to call, and like, push something through. But their interest and their concern for the children, the way in which the principal tries to give as much time as he can to the children and to the parents of the community . . . There are people on the staff—I don't know, I just find it really beautiful, the way they sort of open up to the children. The children of 201, I've seen them come back, and a lot of them have given a lot of trouble but there's something about the warmth at 201—a human kind of thing, people trying to relate to them—that brings them back. There's a fantastic woman at 201, Chris Phillips. She is fantastic. She's the assistant principal. They come and they do bug her. Goodness knows. They're always in the office. But there is such a warmth. I had never seen this in a school. Her whole attitude towards the children, the teachers . . . 201 is quite different.

Does some of this quality belong to the concept of the school itself, with or without particular persons?

I really don't know that that can be. I think the people in charge have a great deal to do with this. The Complex itself contributes in that people see 201, first of all, as an experimental situation in which black people are trying to do what many call a "black thing." Trying to put some soul into it. Educating children not in a kind of sterile situation, but trying to make it relate very closely to what life is all about, how we get along with one another, what our responsibilities are, the whole interrelationships of people. I think it depends to a great degree on just who the principal is. Teachers are not going to do it by themselves. One thing about 201 is that you have had a gathering of people of similar minds.

You've been both critical and complimentary about teachers, especially the young white ones. What is the dominating idea among teachers at 201?

I think there is an attempt on the part of the staff at 201 to develop an increasing respect for the children for what they are. Many teachers do all these nasty little, disrespectful things to children, and that has to stop. So much of this has been inflicted on black children; they really get the burden of that. It just has to happen if there's going to be a real change . . .

What has to happen?

Oh, respect for children. Oh yes, it just has to be.

This is what teachers are going to have to have?

Oh, definitely. Oh, yes. Or you just aren't going to be able to teach, because the children are demanding it. It's happening in the society. See, many of the older teachers had to leave 201. It's not just the breakdown of discipline which is horrible for a teacher of the old school; they just naturally feel children must march in lines and *they* must be respectful, but children are saying to themselves, Why must they be when people aren't being this way to them? And they're picking it up from the larger society. The young people are rebelling, you know: Why are we killing people all over the world? It's because of the lack of respect, and the children are demanding more and more of this for themselves or they aren't going to give it.

INEZ SMITH
Brooklyn

Basically, I'm an old-fashioned teacher. I like the room to be relatively quiet, rather structured. I like to write things down, have the children copy things in their notebooks, learn how to take notes just for accuracy's sake, and to help them remember. But I would hope I'm not a strict or rigid teacher, even though I'm old-fashioned, because I don't think the two are synonymous. Many people think if you're not a "progressive" teacher your room is stagnant, and nothing is going on . . .

It's shortly before three o'clock on a mid-June day in Inez Smith's second-grade class, P.S. 137, Ocean Hill-Brownsville. "Old-fashioned," "strict," "rigid," or their opposites are soap-bubble words here. Touched by the turbulence of twenty-six children's speech, movement, willingness to know and to learn, such words pop into nothingness.

Any stranger walking into this room while these kids are in it must be prepared to satisfy their curiosity about him:

"Are you the dentist? You gonna check our teeth?" Several kids stretch their mouths wide and tilt their heads upward.

"No."

"Are you a doctor?"

"No."

"What have you got in that bag?"

"A tape recorder."

"Can we see it?"

"If Miss Smith says it's okay."

One kid, pleasant but implacable: "What do you do?"

"I'm a writer."

Chorus: "Yeah? What do you write?"

Kids deserve thoughtful answers to their questions, especially to personal ones. The effort to answer this one in terms that might interest them is a pitiful failure. In less than one minute, they're turned off as completely as a delinquent subscriber's telephone. This non-dentist, non-doctor, non-whoever he is, has failed to pay his dues to their curiosity. Their attention goes temporarily out of service.

Inez Smith intervenes. She's in her early twenties, a supple, dark-skinned, Brooklyn-bred embodiment of the "Black is beautiful" statement. This is an "old-fashioned" teacher? If so, there's nothing happening between her and the children to indicate it. Very much but easily in command, she puts an end to the happy little mob scene at the front of the room with benign, big-sisterish authority. Her tone is good-humored, despite a touch of afternoon tiredness in her voice. The bell rings. The room empties.

This is their classroom. They know who belongs here and who doesn't. They see medical personnel come in here: the dentist, doctor, nurse. They were just being curious, the way kids should be. Sometimes I have unstructured lessons, talking about whatever comes up. Their minds are acute. Even the ones that are slow in reading. After we went to the Aquarium, we talked about it. And their questions! "Miss Smith, how did they get a whale from the Pacific Ocean to the Aquarium?" I said I would find out. I did. When I told them, they said, "Well, how do they catch them?" It so happened that the following Sunday, on *Wild Adventure* or whatever it is, they showed how you catch a whale. So they watched it on TV and found out for themselves. Something that I know they're going to be successful doing, I have them do on their own: "Well, *you* go and find out." Sometimes they'll ask me what a word means, and even though using the dictionary isn't supposed to be a second-grade skill, I'll say, "Most of you have dictionaries at home. You go home and you find out what that word means."

During class I was sitting with Steven and Troy. At one point Troy said to me, "You have very nice hair," and they both ran their hands over it. I don't have nice hair. I have hardly any. What could they have found so interesting about it?

It's different, that's mainly what it is. They like my hair too. At the beginning of the semester, they'd come up and all they would do is touch—touch my hair. Most of the girls have their hair straightened. The boys wear theirs cut close. They didn't know what in the world I had done with mine. We talked about it.

"Miss Smith, why do you wear your hair like that?"

"Because I like it this way. This is the way it naturally is."

"Well, do you come from Africa?"

"No. I was born here in Brooklyn, like you."

"Were you in Africa?"

"No. I've never been to Africa."

You know, they see an Afro haircut and you must be an African. Finally I said, "Well, why *is* my hair like this?" I got some of the strangest answers: "You don't wash it." "It won't grow." Finally after about five minutes, someone said, "Oh, Miss Smith, you don't *straighten* your hair." But they really didn't know until then.

Afterwards, some of the children decided that when they grew up they would have an Afro haircut. We took a vote. The boys didn't like my hair this way, but most of the girls did.

I think the Afro is aesthetically better, but also it's an obvious expression to anyone who sees me that I'm black, and that I'm not ashamed of being black, that it's part of my culture and I want to retain this part of my culture. A lot of people do it because it's the vogue now, but I like it for its cultural values . . . My students are black and I'm black, and because I'm in a black community I can perhaps get a little bit more accomplished than a teacher with whom they couldn't identify as readily.

So how do the white teachers manage?

I haven't found it to be the case this year that the students didn't get along with their teachers because the teacher was white. That's because all the teachers at Ocean Hill *want* to be here. There's no one here who doesn't want to be here, and they know it's a black community. Previously this school had teachers fresh out of college who had to get their tenure. After their two or three years they'd pack up their bags and leave. The teacher-turnover rate here must have been the highest in the city. It's typical of any black community. It's supposed to be an undesirable community. The children are supposed to be under-achievers, slow. The ideal is out in Flatbush.* I don't know if I'd be a good teacher in Flatbush. I don't know why, but I just have a feeling I wouldn't make it out there.

All the new teachers who came into this district [during the teachers' strike of 1968 and subsequently] were interviewed. They were asked why they wanted to come here, and whether they thought they were going to fit into the goals of this system, which was to get teachers involved with their students, not have *them* stand *here* and the students *there*, with that invisible wall between them. The teachers here are not the typical teachers. Have you seen

---

* Flatbush, two miles from P.S. 137, is a 99 percent white, middle-class Irish-Jewish enclave. Owner-inhabited dwellings stand on generous plots fronted by privet-bordered lawns. It has remained substantially unchanged since the late 1920s, despite real estate booms before and after both world wars. Since its founding by the Dutch in 1634 it has always managed to maintain some degree of isolation, though it has long been part of "middle Brooklyn." The King's arms remained on display in the town's inn for fifty years after the American Revolution.

the long hair, the beards, the sports jackets? You couldn't do that in Flatbush. The principal would call you in.

And the children aren't afraid of the teachers. They know them as people. They see them after three o'clock. They call them. The teachers take them for trips in their cars on weekends.

The kids here are getting a different kind of school experience than I had. I had an elementary school teacher who was very nice, but she was a little distant. I didn't know anything about her. The children in Ocean Hill–Brownsville learn that a teacher is the same as any other person. Like the first time that I told my students that I had a mother. "A *mother*? You have a mother?"

When I was in school, a teacher was not real to us in many respects. She came in, she produced information; at three o'clock she went her way and I went mine, and nine o'clock the next day is when I saw her again. I never called my teacher on the phone.

But here, we were learning about communications. The children were busy swapping phone numbers and somebody came up very timidly and said, "Miss Smith, can I have your phone number? If you give me your number, could I call you?" I said, "Of course." She was a little bit leery, but she called "just to say hello." After that a lot of the children called.

I have one little girl from last year who still calls me. We talk about everything, her little brother, her school, her new teacher, her piano lessons. I've never spoken to her for less than half an hour. She talks to me about things in her world, but she knows that I'm listening. She enjoys talking to me and I enjoy talking to her. Finally I have to say, "I have to go now. I'll call you back or you call me." They like for you to call them too.

Steven calls me, then says the next day, "Miss Smith, I called you and you weren't home. Where *were* you?" I said, "Steven, I was out. Maybe I went to the store or I had a date." "A date!" They've seen my boy friend. He has a sports car and they just love his car. "Miss Smith," they ask, "is that *man* coming to pick you up in that sports car today?" And one day last week Steven said, "Miss Smith, how come you're not married?" This took me completely unawares, so I said, "Steven, I'm waiting for you to grow up." He said, "Oh, Miss Smith, by the time I grow up, you're going to be too old."

Steven is really something. When I come in late he says, "Miss Smith, you overslept, didn't you?" And it's the truth, and I say, "Steven, you're right."

What made you choose teaching?

I never wanted to be a teacher. I grew up in Brooklyn. We lived in the Fort Greene housing project for about seventeen years. My father's an elevator operator in a city hospital, and my mother was a seamstress, a machine operator in a factory, until she became ill about five years ago.

The elementary school I went to was pretty [racially] balanced. I was in a special progress class for students that they felt had superior ability. When it came time for high school, all the black kids went to Eastern District High and the white kids to Erasmus Hall. I was supposed to go to Eastern District too, but my mother said, "She's taking Latin and they don't have it at Eastern." So I got into Erasmus and went on to Hunter College. There were very few blacks at Erasmus. And Hunter—well, most colleges are white. My school career has been predominantly Jewish, oddly enough.

My parents finally bought a home in east New York, but when I was twenty-one I decided to make my move into independence. That could really be a book in itself. There's a whole thing that black people have: a young girl just doesn't move out on her own if she's not getting married. My mother was very upset. It took about six months before she would even talk to me again. And occasionally now she says, "When are you coming home?"

After college, I planned to be a physical therapist, but I didn't want to go to school for another year right away, so I was working as a technician. The job was too routine, too stagnant. I was ready to leave it when I met a friend who was going to the Board of Ed. for a teaching exam. I said, "I didn't know you were majoring in education." And she said, "I didn't, but the Board of Ed. is giving a walk-in exam."* I didn't know if I'd be a good teacher, but I knew I didn't like being a technician, so I took the exam and passed it. I started teaching last year and I sort of fell in love with it . . . The money? Just about the same.

The first year was very exciting because it was new. It was a real challenge. I had a second grade—2–5 (2–1 was the brightest and 2–5 was the bottom). I *knew* that all of them needed that extra something. But this year's class is grouped heterogeneously and I find that difficult to work with. In this group—Lola, there's not anything she doesn't already know that I'm going to teach to the class. She's reading on Grade 6, her math is on Grade 4. I give them something and two seconds later Lola's finished and: "What can I do? Can I help?" So I use her as an aide, helping other students, but sometimes they resent that because she has a smart attitude like, "Don't you know *that?*"

I don't think Lola should be skipped, put with fourth-graders next year. She's just not ready for it emotionally.

---

* An emergency qualifying examination given to teacher candidates at the request of principals facing staff shortages, mostly in elementary schools. The tests, emphasizing language ability, were graded immediately or in a matter of days. Substitute-teacher certificates for a limited period were issued to those who passed and were subject to extension when the need warranted. The walk-in exam procedure was operative in New York City during the general teacher shortage of the mid-1960s and particularly during the UFT strikes of 1967–68.

She's hypersensitive about a lot of things, especially about her teeth. Seven years old and she's got sixteen cavities.

I had a conference with her mother, to tell her that Lola had to go to the clinic. And she said, "The reason that I haven't taken her is that I had to take another one whose teeth are just as bad as hers but who's older." The nurse who examines their teeth gave me two slips—only two out of all my children—saying that they could go to the clinic. I gave one to Lola, but her mother didn't take her that day, and to another student whose mother didn't take her either.

One day Lola was so upset. She had evidently teased someone who retorted by taunting her about her teeth. Children can be very malicious, they really can. She was very upset, wouldn't do any work. She just cried. I had to take her out and talk to her. But that one day didn't make a difference; I had to do this continually. I tried to boost her up and said, "Lola, maybe they're a little bit jealous," and that sort of pleased her. I think that's another reason why she does well in her work. She knows the nature of her handicap; so she figures, I can excel in something else—sort of compensation.

Who's the kid that's been on your mind the most this year?

Woody, because he has so many problems. Harold, he's hyperactive. He sits right here near me, so I can say, "Harold, you're not paying attention," or "Harold, stop doing this." He's mischievous, but Woody just disrupts the class constantly. One day he was acting up and I said, "Elwood, I have to write your mother a note."

He took the note and went home for lunch and he didn't come back. I wondered what happened, so I went to his house and asked him why he didn't come back. He said his mother left him with his younger siblings. He had to take care of them. So I said, "When you come to school Monday, bring the note signed." Monday came and Elwood didn't come to school. I went to his house again and his mother was there. She had kept him out of school. She said she had someplace to go and Elwood had to stay and take care of the baby, about nine, ten months old. Elwood is seven; there are three younger than himself. He's very poorly cared for, doesn't usually eat breakfast. He lives right down the block, but he gets here about nine thirty, ten, ten fifteen. Other days when he's not in school I see Elwood with a bag of laundry. He's going to the laundry and he's got his younger brother with him because he has to take care of him. He just has too many responsibilities for a seven-year-old child.

When he's in class he really acts up, but at three o'clock when I see him on the street, he just loves to talk to me. The problem is that I've got twenty-six children and I can't sit down and just talk to Elwood. I usually have a prep once a day, one period when I'm just supposed to prepare lessons. Usually I take a child with me on my prep. Nothing structured. Sometimes we'd just take a walk or go get a soda or talk. The days when I took Elwood with me he didn't act up. I think Elwood wonders, Does anyone really care, or is *no* one interested? He's not a dumb child but he just gives up. I say, like, "Elwood, copy what's on the board," or if I have up here "Class News" everyone knows what to do—write what day it is, and it's cloudy; that's class news. But Elwood has not been in school regularly enough or has not had enough encouragement to sit down and do any sort of work on his own. He has to have individual attention. If I could encourage Elwood at every step he'd be much better. He would have attention, so he wouldn't be acting up. Some children I'll force; I'll say, "You sit there and you're going to do the work." But Elwood, his mind isn't free to sit down.

Couldn't you get someone to help you with Elwood?

I do have an assistant, a paraprofessional. We are supposed to plan together and conduct the lesson somewhat together, but I haven't been able to reach that ideal. What usually happens is that I give the lesson, somebody needs help, and she'll go around. That's when she plays an important part. They know her and she spends a lot of time with them.

Elwood does turn to her sometimes, but usually, when she comes in in the morning, everybody wants her to sit next to them. It's sort of like, if she sits next to me, I know she's going to work with me today. But Elwood doesn't get here until ten, so someone has already claimed her.

If there were some consistency in Elwood's attendance, I would be able to get some improvement. There have been times when I've seen his mother and said, "I missed Elwood in school today. What happened?" She'd say, "Oh, he had a headache, so he stayed home," but he's outside playing. The next day or two she'd send him, and then he's gone again.

Most parents, practically any parent wants his child to do well in school. 'Cause if you do well in school, then they think you've got it made. Theoretically it's true. Harold's mother says, "Let me know when Harold acts up. If he does something today, let me know, let me know." She's going to correct him.

Which means she's going to whack him?

Probably. I don't believe in beating a child every time he does something wrong, so I don't want to put myself in the position of having to say, "Harold, I'm going to tell your mother." But when she sees his report card saying that his behavior has been unsatisfactory, she's going to say, "I told you to let me know." It's like a threat that the parents hang over their kids' heads: "If you act up, you're going to get it." And they do get it.

I was thinking about this yesterday when I read the children parts of a book about Harriet Tubman. They didn't know what slavery was. We had to talk about it. They said, "How were the slaves treated?" And I told them. Then it sort of came to me that our parents, their grandparents, were beaten. They knew that this beating did make them knuckle under. When they got a beating they knew they had to behave or things would be worse for them. The slave owners didn't sit down and talk to them. They just got a physical beating. Yesterday when I read to them that Harriet got a beating with a leather belt, the kids said, "Miss Smith, I get beatings like that." I think this is a carry-over from the days of slavery. I know when I was coming up, I got my beatings. Definitely. Black parents don't sit down and talk. They don't talk with their children. There's not that much talking, especially in the lower-income areas. They feel, Well, my parents did it to me and I didn't turn out all that bad. So they see the benefits it had, question mark.

One day at the beginning of the term, I gave an assignment to the class for homework and Steven said, "Miss Smith, I don't know what to do." And I said, "Steven, weren't you paying attention?" He started crying. He said, "If I don't know what to do, my mother's not going to be able to help me. Then I'll get a beating because I won't have my homework done."

For the first few days I would explain it again for Steven at three o'clock. Then one day I said, "Steven, I'm not going to explain it because I think you know it." He cried, but he came back the next day with the work done. They lack self-confidence, many of them—basically all of them—in one field or another.

Steven has shown a lot of development. He's still very immature but he has progressed. At the beginning of the term he just sat there and started crying, "I want my mommy. I want to go home." And I said, "Well, you're seven years old now. You've got to be a big boy and grow up and realize that when you're in school you have to do your schoolwork." I'm pleased now with Steven's relative maturity.

Another child who's improved tremendously is Mary. Because she'd had open-heart surgery, she'd been in this special class with a very small ratio of pupils, something like six or seven to a teacher. She was accustomed to getting the teacher's attention whenever she wanted to have it. She'd use her heart condition as an excuse. Like at the beginning of the term she'd say, "Miss Smith, tie my shoe."

"Don't you know how to tie your shoe?"

"No, my mother always ties it." So I went to her mother: "Would you please teach her." And she said, "Mary knows how to tie her shoe. She just wanted you to do it." [She smiled.] Mary's a little manipulator. But she doesn't do that as much now . . . Mary's mother makes a lot of her clothes. The first thing Mary does when she comes in is to say, "Miss Smith, my mother made my skirt." She's saying, My mother cares about how I look; she takes the time to make something for me.

Anything that their mothers do for them, they really enjoy. It lets them know their parents are interested in them. There's one little boy, Douglas, who's very, very quiet. Usually you're so busy taking care of the others that you sort of neglect the quiet ones. I just forget that Douglas is here. He doesn't get up, he doesn't have an outgoing personality, he just sits there. One day Douglas— the first time he ever approached me even to ask for a piece of paper or a pencil—said, "Miss Smith, look at the book my mother bought." My immediate reaction was just to say, "Oh, Douglas, that's nice." Then I thought, this is Douglas who doesn't give any problems. So I called him back and said, "Let me see. Oh, this is nice." It occurred to me that he was saying, I want you to notice me today, for a while, anyway. Since that day I've tried to pay attention. I send him down for the mail, things like that. I've spoken to his mother once or twice. I think she does take an interest in him. She made him a couple of dashikis.

Douglas is the only one that has never said anything to me that didn't have to do with school. Everyone else tells me about their dog or their brother, or "Do you know what my cat did last night?" And they like me to call their homes even though it's to tell their mothers something they have done wrong. They like that attention, they really do.

Some things they do for attention bother me. Everybody tells on everybody else. I can't get them out of that habit. If I'm out of the room, before I can get in again, it's "Miss Smith, you know what happened?" "Miss Smith, I saw him take this one's pencil . . ." It wasn't the same when I was in school. We didn't tattle on each other. But these kids are really rough on each other. I haven't been able to stop their tattling and I really am disappointed in myself.

Now that it's just about over, how does your second year as a teacher look to you?

I don't think I've done as much as I wanted to do this year. And there was one particular day when I said, "What am I doing? I'm not teaching them anything." We had been in assembly. I'm the assembly leader, so I have to stand up and lead songs and give out the commendation cards, etc. I ask the other teachers to watch my class. But a fight started and half of my class got up out of their seats while I was conducting the assembly and just rushed up front to tell me, "Miss Smith, this one's hitting that one!" It was really upsetting that they hadn't felt any kinship for one another, some sort of bond, or that they didn't have any concept of, well, this isn't the right time.

I was really disappointed and I started saying, "Inez, what have you done? You really haven't done *anything*." I was so upset that I had to go home for the rest of the day. I told Mrs. James [the principal] and she said, "Well, it happens occasionally. Go home and don't think about them." Luckily it was a Friday. On Monday my children said, "Miss Smith, what happened to you?" They were really concerned. I said I hadn't been feeling well. I didn't tell them the truth. I was disappointed in them but I think it was my fault, a shortcoming on my part that caused it. I let them *know* that they've disappointed me when I feel it's justified, but I don't think it was justified that time.

There's another thing. Teachers do bring their personal problems into the classroom. When that happens, I've really got to say to myself, "Inez, put this out of your mind," because on days when I don't, I yell. I yell a lot anyway. I really do, too much, and I realize it and try to stop it, but I can't. It's because I expect quite a bit, but I think they're realistic, my expectations. Last year they weren't, because I wasn't aware of what each child could accomplish, of what was within their grasp. This year I am aware, and I'm very disappointed when I know they can do something and they don't do it.

You know, I started teaching with no education courses. I'm taking some now for two reasons, to satisfy my requirements for a license and because I do want to start on my master's. Teachers seem to feel that on the whole the education courses they have had are worthless, a waste of time, no good. Professionals of education feel that if you haven't had any ed. courses you shouldn't be behind the desk. I don't feel that I've been handicapped in any way except perhaps in making up lessons plans, which I usually don't follow anyway. I know what I'm going to do.

You're supposed to put down your aim, your procedure, your motivation, the questions you're going to pose, and if you don't do it all that particular day, you're supposed to carry it over. I did it last year very faithfully. Any first-year teacher needs a lesson plan. You can't just go into a classroom and try to pull things out of the sky. You do have to have an idea of what you're going to teach and its significance to the child. But once you write it down, you don't have to look at it again. I did it this year very skimpily, but next year I'll have to do it again because I'm going to teach fifth grade.

I'm becoming a little smug with myself because I know I can teach second grade successfully, so I need a challenge. I think I can do a lot for our fifth-grade students. They don't have any women teachers here above the third-grade level. I think it's important for the children to see women in the upper grades, just as it's important for them to see men in the lower grades.

Teaching fifth grade is a little bit scary. The second-graders, they're pretty easy to handle because they're little and you can tell them, "You'd better not do that again." But it's going to call for a lot more on my part to work with twelve-year-olds. I don't know if I want to stay on the elementary level. Eventually I might want to go up to high school. I don't know about college. I enjoyed working with the lower grades because I'm really helping to shape their lives. It's a great responsibility, but I feel that if I can be open and flexible and teach them how to evaluate things I'll be doing a real service to my fifth-graders, too.

MARION MOULTRIE
Philadelphia

I used to call myself a traditional teacher, sticking to the old ways, but I've sort of changed my thinking. Not in the basic needs but in the way of reaching these needs, of meeting them. I believe in freedom and in creativity but I feel that the child needs the basics as well.

A few years ago, if you had a quiet class, and the children were writing and giving you back what you wanted them to give back, you were a good teacher. You had no trouble from the administrators. Children used to sit at desks and it was one of those rote things: memorize and repeat. Whereas now, it's more or less an active thing. The child is in on the planning, he's in on the carrying out of the activities, and on the evaluation of the activity.

Stoddart-Fleisher Junior High, in some Philadelphians' opinion, is just "run-of-the-mill." But in Room 100, Marion Moultrie, open of manner, warm of tone, teaches an "opportunity class" consisting of children whose disruptive tendencies their regular classroom teachers can neither suppress nor reform. She is black, buxom, matronly, thoughtful. Schoolteaching was not her first-choice profession. She has lived in Philadelphia for two decades.

When I finished college, I went right to the social workers school. Then I did social work for about three years. I came into teaching after I started raising a family. It gave me more time with my own children. I got out at two thirty and had my summers off. I like teaching and I even find that teaching is social work, to a degree. My background was case work rather than group work, so I sort of tend to work with individuals.

I've been teaching in Philadelphia for eleven years now. My first job was teaching special classes. One of them was the oldest group of delinquent girls in the city. They were called O.D. girls, orthogenic delinquent. I enjoyed that much more than I do teaching in regular classes now. The children accomplished a bit, but they were proud of their accomplishments and they worked hard. Some were a bit slow but some were able to do regular classwork. Working in small groups, you had from eighteen to twenty in a class. They probably knew why they were there and you didn't have the problem you tend to have in a regular class, discipline-wise. At least I didn't. Once you got over to the child that you were interested in his welfare, you'd really made a friend for life and I think it was generally worth it.

Eleven years ago is in some respects like a century ago. Has the development of the civil rights movement changed your feelings about teaching, and has it changed the kids that come into your classroom?

Well, it hasn't changed my feelings about teaching. I was raised in the South. My dad was a Baptist minister and he was a very proud person. He taught us even then that black was beautiful. So much so, that he didn't allow my sister and I to play with a white doll. He said he didn't want his girls . . . he hated the thought of his girls nursing white babies or cooking in white kitchens. There were seven of us and we all went to college. So every Christmas he would collect the dolls—you know, every auxiliary in the church would give the pastor's daughter dolls—he collected the dolls but he would always buy us a colored doll; and that was years ago.

My dad did not allow us to ride in the back of the bus. He drove us. In the movies, you'd have to sit in the balcony, so he didn't allow us to go to the movies. He would take us to a nearby larger town. All right, I knew there was such a thing as prejudice or whatnot but, as I said, we were sort of shielded from it. When I hit Philadelphia up North in my early twenties, I expected a different type of thing. The first week, I started to run into it. Yes.

But going to school in the South, the teachers were proud of being teachers and we were sort of taught that black was beautiful. So much so, that I sent my children back to my hometown in North Carolina to go to school one year, when they weren't getting what I thought they should get here. My sister teaches there and my father at that time was living.

I don't think that my feelings about the world have changed too much in these eleven years I've been teaching. I was considered a free thinker years and years ago. When my children started college, they got involved in the civil rights movement and I encouraged them. I didn't try to pull them back. My parents didn't pull me back. I had my moments about it though. They went to school in the South and they traveled with groups that went to Mississippi, and I went on some of them myself.

But the children have changed from what they were when I started teaching. In the communities they're getting quite a bit of what they call black history on their own. They're being taught in small groups and everybody's telling them how to do their own thing. They're being taught that black is beautiful and they're being taught black power. It affects what they think they should be getting in school. Even from seventh grade right on up, you can tell the difference in the children.

Do you think that's good or bad?

I—it has to be either good or bad, I guess. I think sometimes it's good and sometimes it's bad. Sometimes they're being taught by persons who may be well versed in black history, but not too well versed in other facts of life. They seem to neglect some of the other very important moral and "just living" issues of today. And the children, it's different to them and they really swallow it hook, line and sinker. They tend to build a resistance to what they're learning in school. It has forced education more or less to bring them something that's more relevant to their everyday living. So I guess *that's* good.

But then, I wonder sometimes, *How* good? My question is, Do the children really want to know only about their present-day lives—as they say, "Where it's at"? Do we stop there? Don't they want to lift their level? Their everyday living, to me, is not ideal, really. So give them something that is relevant, but also—motivate them. Give them something that will make them come up higher . . . In my particular class we're working on a unit dealing with urban studies. We're attempting to approach it from the child's point of view, from where he is now. Attempting to have them decide: Well, is this the type of environment you want all your life, and what can you do about it?

I think even teachers, to some extent, are being a bit confused. You have a lot of teachers, young teachers, who feel they're missionaries at this thing. They're quite sincere. They really want to give the children what they want, and what they think they should have that's relevant to their everyday living. So they teach English according to the way the children talk, what they hear on the street. They tend to let them begin sentences with small letters. They aren't learning the basic skills and the basic concepts.

To me, I feel that once they get those concepts and those skills, then maybe you can experiment with them where they are. But now, they aren't going to be prepared to go out and get a job. They aren't going to be prepared even to fill in application blanks for a job.

Well, which comes first, the skills or the freedom of self-expression?

I think the freedom comes first, but there should be certain standards for that as well. Basically all people want to do the right things and correctly. Nobody really wants to be different particularly. In being creative, it doesn't mean that you have to be different in certain basic things.

I really think you need new techniques and methods in order to motivate and I believe in experimenting too. But I think the teacher and the child should have mutual goals. I think every child wants to be able to get a good job when he gets out, wants to live in better living conditions. I think that's basic with them.

But the young feel that adults have failed them. Some of my son's friends say that the job they have to do, *we* should have done, and that we, I mean black parents, let them down. They realize that as black people we have just been left out, that we weren't important enough to even give us a space in history that we felt we deserved. It's that type of thing which has made up part of the present negative reaction.

I go along with this new freedom. I find I have changed and I'm learning as well as the children. But I find it's destroyed the basic faith that the young, both black and white, had in our country. It's turned down patriotism. That's been destroyed. And maybe some of the basic things that people need to hold on to, to live. It doesn't affect me because I have made my path already. But the thing that gives me strength, today the young people probably would not accept.

My children tell me, "Momma, you're using your religious background as a sort of panacea." But I tell them, "Everybody needs something. It doesn't have to be a religious background, but you need something to sort of hold on to and it keeps you going and it gives you strength."

IRENE HIGHSMITH
Philadelphia

We water down everything for the kids now. We make it easy for them to fail, by making things too simple. If you're going to teach a child and you want him to *learn* something, you don't *lay* it in his hand so he doesn't have to learn it but simply memorize it. If you teach him enough *about* it, then he should become *inquisitive* enough to do that extra—and find out more about it by himself. We spend— I do a lot of library work. "Go to the library," I say. "You can do anything with this topic you want to do. I'm not restricting you to one page, one paragraph or what. Go and get as much as *you* feel satisfied with."

The time is 3 PM. On Stoddart-Fleisher's third floor, Irene Highsmith has taught five general science classes, seventh and eighth grades. She takes a deep breath and seems, physically, to loosen up a little. Aside from that, the dreary, demanding late-November day has not visibly affected her; she's no novice—fifteen years in the Philadelphia system. And maybe ending the day with her "next-to-the-top" eighth-grade class helped. In the classroom just emptied by the bell, her presence and personality were a sudden reminder of Eugenia Clarke's comment that "some of the black women have been very loving but strong . . ." Each in her own way, of course.

They're a very good class. It's not a show we put on *with* them. It's just the natural way they *are* great. In eighth-grade science the first half of the year we spend on matter, the structure of matter, elements, compounds, mixtures. The second half we teach machines and energy—wheels and axles, springs and pulleys. Children still have to know these things. In fact, I had planned to make oxygen today, but the lab assistant was out Friday and she didn't get my equipment set up. We do far more with children now in junior high. As I tell my kids—I say, "I'm teaching you material that I never saw until I got to college."

We say they don't do well at all in high school. In fact, if they took advantage of what's being offered, many of them, they should do well.

Everybody is talking about "relevance" now—what's related to the child, to his environment and all this business. But I still like to think that a certain amount of academic material is necessary, relevant or not.

Kids in junior high have to take science courses. It's required. How do you cope with the kids who don't give a hoot?

You have many who don't and they'll tell you so in no uncertain terms. When I see a class for the first time I try to capture their interest as far as the area is concerned, which means starting some kind of a discussion. I might say, "This year we're going to study matter." Okay. Well, a kid said to me, "What do I need to learn that for?" Then: "Did you eat breakfast this morning?"

"Yes."

"What did you eat?"

"Toast, milk, cereal, an apple."

"Okay. Did you ever think where they came from? What they are composed of?"

Actually, his attitude was: "Who cares what they are made of? They taste all right and I eat them. Gotta eat *something*." But from that we got into a discussion because there were a few kids who picked up, in terms of the composition of matter . . . We went on from that to: "You're wearing clothes, so you're wearing fibers. What are your clothes made of?" This sort of thing.

I do believe there is such a thing as natural curiosity in

people, more so in children, but we tend to smother it sometimes. In the case of this kid, his curiosity had already been smothered, about some things. But in this group discussion it was turned on to some extent by the other kids, who disagreed with him, or who showed by what they said that they knew some things he didn't. And if it hadn't been for that relation, I could see that kid becoming a problem in the room; I think this is what made us make it as far as we did.

Have you always taught general science?

I started as a science substitute. Then I was moved after a year and a half to a math assignment in another school. I have a degree in biology and I studied physical science, too, at Livingston College in Salisbury, North Carolina. It's a small church-related school. When I was there we had only about five hundred enrollment. It's grown quite a bit. I would say we had good teachers. If you know anything about the South, most of the Negro teachers—we call them black now, we used to call them Negroes—to them, education was *the* thing, so they got as much as they could . . . Now, this was the problem: you had good teachers, but if the school was not accredited (and some of them were not), you had certain deficiencies when you graduated. When I came to Philadelphia they said I needed at least three more college credit hours of education courses. After I taught for two years they certified me without that, but I did have to take audio-visual aids and Pennsylvania history . . .

High school? That was in Reedsville, North Carolina, my home. Looking back, it was good at that time for what was considered good. But I can see many things we didn't have, and yet I can see many things we *had*. For example, everybody now is concerned about black history. I was taught black history in my black high school. This was a requirement. Now they talk about it, you know, as if it's something . . . away from everything else, but it was part of our curriculum. We took it—without any questions or without anything. We had textbooks and all. I don't know what has happened to them . . . We did detailed studies. We didn't just skim across the top like they're doing now. Last year, or the year before . . . at one of these Board of Education seminars where we have to look at television and then have a sounding discussion afterwards, one of the teachers stood up and said, "I never heard of black history. Nobody ever taught me any black history."

Is black history any use to you, as a science teacher?

Yes. Now, I say yes because you have a lot of children who now are becoming very, very conscious of blackness, or should we say, aware of black. And instead of saying you're going to talk about Joseph Priestley and oxygen, you could just as well talk about Benjamin Banneker and some of the things he did.

I've done this every year with my seventh-graders. They get a list of famous men and women of science. I think I gave them a total of thirty-four different scientists that they had to make reports on last year. Along with Thomas Edison, Alexander Graham Bell, Marie Curie, we used Banneker, George Washington Carver, Charles Drew. This is what I use for them to do in independent study. So they look up the lives of black scientists too. The Board of Education put out some sort of little . . . I don't know where it is offhand; that shows you how much I thought of it. It's sort of like an anthology—in other words, the total idea now seems to be not to separate people because of color but to include their contributions in the whole. Rather than make a big issue of this guy being a *black* man who did this, he's a *man* that did this.

But for the time being we have to catch up with all that's been kept away, just left out completely. So if we can sort of bring it together now, maybe in the next twenty years, I guess, when my son starts being this doctor or whatever it is he's planning on doing . . . He said to me one day, "Mommy, what would you say if I married a white girl?" I said, "You're ten years old now. By the time you're ready to marry"—which I hope he will be at least twenty-four, by the time he's old enough to be independent—"race won't be the problem." So who will care what color his wife is? . . . But, there'll be some other problem to take the place of that . . .

7

THE
COMMUNITY

Government and its institutions are accountable to power alone. The schools serving the poor will continue to shortchange their students until such time as the poor can obtain a meaningful voice in the public arena.

—Dr. Henry M. Levin, School of
Education, Stanford University

ALLAN STEINBERG
New York

I'm working with a group of human beings, as a kinder-garten teacher. So there's a question of what children need. What do they need to make them open, fully developed human beings, sensitive, aware individuals? And what do they need just to survive in the world the way it is now, and not necessarily to make them better people so they can take over the world and improve it. There's a hierarchy of needs here and I'm not the one who says what it is and orders it. The parents decide what they feel is important for their children to have.

Black people in this country, in my interpretation, are still in a colonial status. They're trying to get out of it. They feel their children have to be able to compete with others, in the groups that have already made it. So I'm not necessarily aiming for the ultimate in education. Right now, black parents are not asking, "Is it moral for my child to be an actor in cigarette or liquor commercials?" They're asking, "Why can't *my* child be in a cigarette commercial?"

Middle-class kids from Great Neck or wherever are saying, "I see society the way it is and I don't like it. I'm dropping out." A lot of young black militants are con-cerned with this, too, but the black parents are more con-cerned with giving their kids the ability to compete on an equal-or-better basis, for economic well-being. The answer is reading, arithmetic and language. I can understand that . . .

Traditionally, a man teaching in a pre-primary class-room is confessing to limited academic ability and possibly: "Hmm. Pretty faggotty job for a man." Nonsense, as anyone would know after watching Allan Steinberg at work. He's six-foot-one, thickly mustached, totally un-fop-pish, intellectually self-assured. Conceivably he rates a few extra masculinity points for being the only Jewish male in the personnel of P.S. 137's kindergarten, which has an enrollment of seventy-one children, ages under-five to six and a half. The personnel consists of two other staff teachers, nine paraprofessional assistants and a director, providing a complement of four adults for each of three classes, or an adult-child ratio of approximately one to five. The kindergarten was set up after community control became operative in the Ocean Hill-Brownsville District. Housed in a church building several long blocks from the main school and intensively committed to an experimental program, the place has somewhat the feel of a mini-school. In addition to his own group of twenty-two, Steinberg is responsible for the language and music programs; no extra points for that—it's part of the job.

Steinberg is twenty-three, married, and has a B.A. in music from Queens College, 1968. He's a teacher by chance as much as by choice: the historical chance of war in Vietnam and the personal choice against participating in it.

In kindergarten, the way it goes in most places, the teacher thinks it's important for a child to play with clay and paint because it develops the child's whole personality. Myself, I like working with art materials but my children don't get much chance to do that. This bothered me quite a bit in the beginning. I had to ask myself, "Is it valuable for everybody?" and I came up with "No, it isn't."

Here the parent can't cope with a child who comes home dirty all the time. He doesn't have changes of clothing. And he doesn't feel that the child is getting something essential. So the parent's view of the program is very negative. He doesn't send the child to school or discourages the child from going. So the teacher's view of the parent becomes very negative. He sees this parent as possibly resisting even the moral and spiritual development of the child. So the parents and teachers are opposing each other simply because they don't have a system where they have to confront each other and work something out—right? We're worlds apart, professionals and laymen. Nobody's talking to each other, and because nobody's talking, everybody hates each other.

In my school they're talking to each other. Now, that in itself causes problems. You may discover that you're not in agreement. But once you discover that, you're in a lot better position to work out something for the benefit of the child. A lot of professionals don't concede that the parent loves the child, that parents know what's right for the child. They feel, I know better than that guy, that woman. Well, if you know better than someone, how can you talk to him, except down your nose?

The parents in this district picked this program because it deals with skills.

Steinberg is talking about a program developed by psychologists Carl Bereiter and Siegfried Engelmann at the University of Illinois for implanting language and math skills in preschool and primary-grade children. Their methodology is embodied in two books,* detailed manuals of technique and lesson content for classroom use by teachers.

The Bereiter-Engelmann rationale is bluntly behavioral: "The reason for failure is irrelevant" and "the educator has somehow failed to use the hard-nose, product-oriented reasoning that characterizes the engineer."†

The parents at P.S. 137 chose the program for kindergarten through second grade from eight possibilities exam-

---

* Siegfried Engelmann, *Preventing Failure in the Primary Grades* (Chicago: Science Research Associates, 1969); Carl Bereiter and Siegfried Engelmann, *Teaching Disadvantaged Children in the Pre-School* (Englewood Cliffs, N.J.: Prentice Hall, 1966).
† *Preventing Failure in the Primary Grades*, p. 2.

ined in parents/school administration discussions. Its attractiveness to mothers and fathers sick of seeing their children short-changed by the school system is clearly suggested by such statements in the book as: "This is a catch-up program for the child who is seriously behind in basic arithmetic and reading skills." And: "The disadvantaged child can be viewed as a child who has had poor teachers."

In essence, the Bereiter-Engelmann program is a sophisticated system of teaching-and-learning by rote and by drill. As such, it has sharp critics among those who believe that "you can't teach children, you can only help them to learn" and that the purpose of education is not simply to equip children to "make it" economically, but to help them become human beings capable of shaping their own destinies and society's toward nobler ends than those now commonly sought. It contradicts the concept of education as "ecstasy."*

I worked my way into teaching sort of gradually. This is the end of my first year in a public school system where I have full responsibility. Last year I was an assistant teacher in the Sunnyside Progressive Nursery School, which had a Bank Street approach, a lot of free play and that sort of thing. I was still at college. And the year before, I was an assistant teacher at a city-run Day Care Center on the Lower East Side. That was not a good experience. I ran up against an awful lot of sadistic people who were doing perfectly horrible things under the name of their being good for the child.

I had a child, six years old. His father was a sailor, never home. His mother was never home either. The kid would come to school, half starving, and he threw fits,

---

* George B. Leonard, in *Education and Ecstasy* (New York: Dell, 1968), contends that education must become, characteristically, a profoundly joyful experience: "Not fun, not simply pleasure as in the equation of Bentham and Mill, not the libido pleasure of Freud, but ecstasy, *ananda*, the ultimate delight."

temper tantrums. He could take a chair and hurl it across to the other end of the room. I would talk to him, hold him and just try to comfort him, and it was as if I were to talk to my cat. He was absolutely wild, all rationality gone.

The directors and some of the teachers there didn't feel I was authoritarian enough and didn't set limits enough. This one day the child started throwing a fit and the director's solution was: "You tell him you're going to take him down to the office and you're going to sit that child right in front of the director." Okay, but this child didn't understand what I was saying to him; it was no threat to him. Besides, it didn't mean anything to *me*. It didn't prove anything if this child sat down and was good in the director's office for half an hour and then came back. What was learned by it? I wouldn't be solving the problem. I told her I wasn't going to do it, because I was afraid that if I tried to get that child down the stairs from my room to the office, he was going to crack his head on the stairs.

The Day Care Center was sharing a building with a settlement house and the people there used to look aghast at us. There was this guy I'd known, the friend of the director of a camp I'd worked at. I said, "I've got this problem and I don't know what to do with it."

He said one thing to me (it was the beginning of all the questioning I do): "Everything a human being does is a kind of language. It's saying something. It's an attempt to communicate. With every flick of the finger, every hostile action, every smile, every breath, this child is saying something to you. What is he signaling to you?" Up to that point the only thing I was concerned with was, What should I do to get the kid to stop? I wasn't even considering, Well, what does it mean? And that's absolutely essential to understand before you can try to stop it. So I look at that year as like a beginning.

The Sunnyside year was beautiful. I was the assistant, but the teacher and I handled it as sort of a team-teaching thing. Some days I would take responsibility, some days she would. That was my last and most meaningless year in college except for one great course, but I had something human and decent going in that nursery school. I looked forward to it every day.

I have a lot of respect for people at the Sunnyside school, although they absolutely detest everything this experiment stands for. A lot of people in early-childhood teaching are opposed to what we're doing—the behaviorist approach: a very structured curriculum based on the idea that three curriculum areas are the essential ones to stress, at the sacrifice of other things. They're more concerned with what they call the development of the whole child—spiritual values, they call them.

But these people are supportive of community control. When the strike was going on I ran into people from the Sunnyside school at a demonstration down at City Hall. They were very happy to hear that I was at Ocean Hill, but when I told them about working in the Bereiter-Engelmann program they were very disappointed.

What happened with you during the teachers' strike?

I went in from the very first day. I knew beforehand that I was going to go in. It was hard, because I believe in unions. I was a union member the year before and I know where we'd be without unions. There was a picket line in front of the Annex for a few days and then there were police barricades. I used to feel a little jumpy walking past the police because they had antagonistic looks. They were all white; not a single black cop in front of the school. You know, they have a union, too, and a lot of people simply saw this as union busting. A lot of people still do. Matter of fact, I'm still getting the union newspaper and it still talks about the people who favor community control as being basically anti-union. That's a gross misjudgment of the issues. A whole bunch of people I was friendly with, who I thought were progressive, were on the side of the union in this. They felt it was just a bunch of irresponsible black racists who were "causing all the trouble."

I didn't feel personally uncomfortable about "black racism." Frankly I feel less uncomfortable with black racism at this point than I do with the Jewish teachers who were on the line outside the school. One teacher who says to a pupil, a white kid, "When you go home, ask your mother how come she's a nigger lover." This happened in Queens because some white parents refused to support an anti-integration school boycott. There were millions of these incidents. Of course, there's prejudice on both sides, but that was not the issue.

In the course of the year, have you noticed any anti-Semitism among your kids?

No, I haven't. I don't think the kids know I'm Jewish. I really wouldn't be surprised to hear "Jew" sometime, but I don't feel I'd really be that shocked by it. Because it's just a word, you know. Lenny Bruce once did something very appropriate about words. He went out on the stage and said "Nigger-nigger-nigger, kike-kike-kike" until it became a *sound*. Which is exactly what it is when these kids use it: a sound, not an expression of hate that they understand. They don't know what it means. If a kid came out and told me that I was a bastard or something, then I'd know he was mad at me. And that would be upsetting maybe. But if he used the word "Jew," you know, why should I worry about that?

But to get back to my Sunnyside friends, there's a difference in philosophy. I can't give you their point of view. I used to hold it, but I can't give it to you anymore. Did you ever read *Walden II* by B. F. Skinner? Well, this is a program devised by people that have certain things in common with B. F. Skinner. The Sunnyside school I would put as being closer to A. S. Neil in *Summerhill*. They start off with a philosophical assumption about the nature of man, that man in his genes is naturally good and that certain things done by society blocks this out. So that if you give a child love—and A. S. Neil goes to the point of praising the bad things a child does so he'll do more of it and work it out—he will naturally mature into a sensitive human being. You don't infringe upon the child with your values and things. I think the Ocean Hill–Brownsville position, if you take it to its logical conclusion, is that when man comes out of the womb, he's not necessarily bad or good. He learns to behave by the way he reacts to his environment.

I'm somewhere in the middle . . . If I go against the grain of my students' social experience, well, maybe I'm making better people of them, maybe I'm killing them.

I can give you very concrete examples of this. I accepted some kinds of values as being universal, intercultural. In my neighborhood where I grew up, which was a Jewish ghetto, the universal approach to children was, Don't hit. Come and tell me about it and I'll go bawl out somebody or other's mother. I find here, that if I were to take that approach, I'd be undercutting parents. In this district, it's not necessarily all that unacceptable—if a kid hits you, you hit him back so that the kid will learn that he can't get away with physical violence. Many parents in this area say things that encourage their kids to strike back when they're struck. This struck me as very strange. My values are a product of my learning as a child, so this runs against my grain.

Why do you care if you do undercut the parents?

Why do I care? Well, these children live with their parents. I'm here for how long—ten months. I asked one of the children today if he could remember what his pre-kindergarten teacher's name was and he couldn't remember. But you know, he knows what's going on in his family. He spends how-many-hours-a-day in my class and then he's home with his family or with his friends. I play a small part in his life, really. And if I influence him in such a way that he doesn't know how to react outside of school, well, in a sense I'm messing him up.

What's your own feeling about the rightness or wrongness of a kid hitting back?

What I would teach *my* kids? If I were to hit a child to punish him for something he was doing, I'd be showing him that it's perfectly acceptable to act out any feelings. So, if I get angry, fine, I smack the first person I walk into as he comes down the street. I don't want that. I believe that it's a good thing for people to be able to sit down and express their feelings in another way. That's what I would want my own children to learn, and maybe that's what I want these children to learn too, but it doesn't necessarily mean I'm going to teach them that.

You see, you're getting an idea of a teacher who hasn't made up his mind about what's right for the kids in the class he's teaching. I know what I believe in personally, but the problem is that what you believe isn't necessarily the only "right" answer. It's right for me, but maybe not right for the child, not right according to his parents, perhaps. Therefore I'm hesitant to shove it down his throat because he's going to live out the rest of his life with something that may not be right for him.

If I teach a child that it's not right when a kid pushes him a little, that he should let the kid know, by giving him a good belt, that he can't mess around with him, then I'm also subjecting him to the inability of his own group to understand this kind of seeming passivity. It's foreign to them, so they're going to put this child down. He may be doing it because I said it's right, but then they'll slug him around. I'm not there twenty-four hours a day; I don't know what happens to him.

These children use different language than the children at Sunnyside school. They settle their arguments differently. Another thing, my children at the Sunnyside school, when something was wrong or they were unhappy, they had very little difficulty in expressing it through crying. Here at Ocean Hill–Brownsville I have a few children I have not seen cry at all. And I have many instances of children who'll stand up proudly and put their shoulders back and say, "I don't cry."

This is another thing that works against my grain, personally. It's probably because crying is considered a sign of weakness. I've heard children call other children babies when they cry. I've heard their parents say, like when a child says to them, "I don't cry" when the doctor gives her a needle, the parents say, "Of course not, you're a big girl now." The implication is obvious—big girls don't cry.

If a child came to me and was hurt and was crying, I would be sympathetic rather than say, "Stop crying." The child is crying because this is a way he knows of expressing himself. I don't want to cut off individual expression. When something like this comes up, I don't hit it too hard, because I don't want to absolutely subvert everything a child believes in. But when a child is making fun of another child *because* he's crying, I say, "Sure, he's crying because he's hurt," and then I will ignore the teasing thing completely. I don't want to give any attention to it. But I feel sympathy toward a child who's hurt and I'll naturally go over to him and try to make him feel better. I make no bones about it in front of all the children.

I'm afraid to make a moral issue of either the crying or the teasing. I have strong convictions about it, but I have *other* strong convictions too. That I'm not the only person in their lives. Their parents tell them, "You're not supposed to cry," because they know from their own personal experiences better than I do. I've never had to scrape for a living. I've always been well off. I've never been in a situation where dog eats dog. I've always been able to make choices. The parents know what it's like to have people take advantage of you, to climb up without worrying about what happens to you. For a lot of people here, that's the way it is.

I make moral judgments, but it's very often hard to say what is right and what is wrong. I argue pretty vociferously with some parents about these things. I say what I feel, but I don't try to get the last word. In the end it's their life. I may know more in the field of teaching and reading than the parents, but I don't necessarily know more about children. I've never had children. Okay! I have respect for the parents. They love their kids and how can parents who love their kids not want the best for them?

How do you deal with hitting in the classroom?

When I see one child continually picking on another, deliberately trying to get the kid, I'm going—to a certain extent—look the other way when the child who's fooling around gets what's coming to him. Certainly I'm not going to lean very hard on the kid who hits back. I really can't bring myself down to say, "You can't do this. It's not allowed in my classroom." I might say, "I think it would be better if next time . . ." Sort of ease it.

If the persecution continues, do you intervene?

Well, yeah. One child at the beginning of the term, when he would stand on line, would pinch, kick or scratch the child in front of him. I used to believe: This kid's hostile; Freud says this kid's hostile, that makes this kid hostile.

Then someone suggested to me that it might be nothing more than: "This boy has not yet learned proper ways of approaching other people." This was a professor of behavior modification out at the university at Stonybrook; we have funds for him to come and observe. I had gone to him and said, "Could you watch this child in the classroom?" He asked me a couple of questions about what I thought the problem was. He must have been very clever because he asked questions that led me into thinking what this child's home life was about. He didn't give me the answer—which was good on his part. I found it myself. The boy—his name is Narciso, Puerto Rican—his family has a grocery store. After school he's in the store all the time. His older sister gets jobs to do. She's old enough to tackle things, so that makes her feel pretty good. Narciso, on the other hand, is too young. His parents don't let him help with the store, but they're not playing with him or talking to him because they're serving the customers. You see, he's ignored. So Narciso learned a long time ago that when he knocked a box over, his father yelled at him, and that was better than nothing.

I was floundering around before I talked to this professor. Some of the things Narciso did made me angry because I felt it wasn't out of ignorance but like a deliberate thing. And of course it *was* deliberate, to get my attention—not to get me mad, but to get my attention. After that I ignored his pinching or just took his hands down without calling attention to it. And when there weren't any bad things going on between him and another child I've simply walked over to him and said, "Narciso, go ask so-and-so if you can play with him." Even rehearsed with him getting him to say the words. He'd say, "Can I play with you" in a whisper that Jimmy couldn't hear. So I practiced with him saying it loud, and it worked. It was simple. Now he's doing very well. He's happy, enthusiastic as he wasn't in the beginning, and I feel very close to him.

I had a chance to sit down and tell him how much I liked something he did. You should see the way his face just lit up. It's amazing. He was so happy, and seeing him so happy I just sit up and say, "Hm hm. It's going to work." That makes me feel good, and the better I feel the nicer I treat him and everybody else, and the less cold, the less turned off I feel. It's like a spiral. For him too. The more I concentrate on his good things, the more good things there are about him, really. I don't know whether I accept behaviorism for everything. It may not work for every child and sometimes it may get kind of rigid—it begins to sound like rats in a maze. But with Narciso it worked and that's something.

While he was making you angry, how did you cope with your anger?

I didn't express it in an open way, but I think that it must have come across. I wasn't as affable with him as I was with the other children. I was probably a little bit guarded, because I didn't know what was going to happen. Generally I didn't raise my voice to him because I knew that wasn't going to do either of us any good. There are children in the class who I do raise my voice to and I don't feel the least bit anxious about it because they don't take it badly. When you've got a relationship with another person and you know that so-and-so doesn't hate your guts, then if he criticizes a simple specific thing that you do, he's not going to walk out on you, he's not going to get mad because of one little thing.

Narciso has made great strides this year. He's been learning how to talk to me and to other children. He's come a long way in academic work, which is what the program is about—so that's a lot. Engelmann talks about interviews with a kindergarten teacher in a traditional setup and she says, "Well, yes, these children have come a long way." And he asks, "What have they learned?" and the teacher can't say anything. Well, I can say, he's learned this and he's learned that. He's satisfied the academic requirements. He's made progress. I think he's made some strides in what I call spiritual values too, and there was some question whether this was going to be subordinated so that he could learn to read. I don't think it has been.

Spiritual values—what does that mean?

Concretely, it's important for children to learn how to have a good time with other children. I've seen children who, when given the freedom to choose what they want to do, will always sit off in a corner with some material that is neither messy nor involves them with anybody else. Look at what that child is lacking. I think it's a very important part of being a human being to have friends. Narciso has friends now. Children go to him and ask him to play with them, where formerly they shied away from him.

The academic requirements aren't very explicit. There's a curriculum, but it's ungraded. Wherever a child stops this year, he'll go on next. We're not giving them marks—good, mediocre, unsatisfactory—or anything like that. The program has a progression of skills. One thing depends on your ability to do another. It's a logical process, so, as the kid moves along in the system, he hasn't simply accumulated meaningless bundles of facts.

Not only does he know that two and two equals four. I'm not even interested in that. What we're interested in is, if you were to write down two plus two equals *what*, he'd have some *system* for finding out the answer. If you can't count, you can't do anything in math.

My wife and I were talking about our mathematical backgrounds. We had to add, okay, nine plus three equals twelve. You put down the two and you carry the one. What does that mean, carry the one? It has absolutely nothing to do with the true values involved, but that's the way we learned to do it. We were learning a trick to get us through, and that's all. I remember when I got into algebra and I was all messed up because I didn't realize that seven plus three equals X was really addition, in a different form.

We're giving children a basis for understanding what computations they're doing, rather than just having them go through the motions and be able to perform them. They're substantially beyond most kindergarten kids in arithmetic.

Why are you working with small kids, instead of teaching music?

I'm not doing music because of what Queens College did to me in music. That's a long, long story. Besides, to be a music teacher in New York, you teach the clarinet, the violin, the cello, and again, skills. Well, this year has taught me there are some skills that are okay to teach, but not in music. Why should you aim absolutely at skills in music when there's absolutely nothing out there in the real world that's saying, "If you don't learn these skills, you're going to die." No reason.

I don't think the kids in junior high and high school are getting anything good out of the school bands. They don't have very much fun with it. My kids are having fun learning skills. But I have time for music, too. My kids look forward to that.

It happens in Steinberg's room almost every day, entirely informally. Sitting, standing, moving around the room, he plays his guitar competently, casually, he and the children singing together. He makes no effort at instruction; music in this room is just something to do and to dig.

We sit down there and we start singing and I really feel they're having a good time. They sing very well for kindergarten children, carry a tune pretty well, enunciation no bad. Their rhythm is fine. A lot of the songs we do are rhyming songs. Like I do a song: "The ants go marching one by one" and the kids have to make up something that rhymes with "one." It's to the tune of "Glory, Glory, Hallelujah." It's fun. Like:

> "The ants go marching one by one
> The little one stops to suck his thumb.
> The ants go marching two by two
> The little one stops to tie his shoe (or to say 'Boo')"

The one that I really get a kick of is:

> "The ants go marching five by five
> The little one stops to say 'Oh jive.' "

We can't make up new rhymes for that anymore, there has to be "Oh jive." It's *got* to be. I think it's great. And, of course,

> "The ants go marching three by three
> The little one stopped to take a pee."

Usually they come up with that, so I'll sing it. I won't snicker about it, although I have a couple of kids who will snicker. Recently there was a discussion about a man who is fat, had a big belly. So somebody said, "There's a baby in him." I said no, only women have babies inside of them. I just gave them the information that was appropriate and I left it at that. Most of these kids didn't know that men don't have babies. Like in the boys' bathroom, there's a standing urinal against the wall: one day one of the female teachers came in and a couple of children asked if she was going to use it; I told them, "No, she can't use it because she doesn't have a penis." I didn't use the word "penis" because they don't understand it. I said "wee wee" because that was the word I'd heard them use. I didn't get any snickers or anything. They seemed to accept it as if it weren't important, because of the way I said it.

How has it been to work here with the paraprofessionals; they're older than you, not as well equipped aca-

demically, culturally quite different? Mrs. Trench, for instance?

Mrs. Trench? Oh, I think she's great. Good paraprofessionals can be enormously helpful. Not all the parents working here are as warm as Mrs. Trench. A couple of them are rather rigid; not necessarily frightening to the children or anything, but not as ebullient as she is.

I had watched Mrs. Trench sitting with a dozen children, leading a Bereiter-Engelmann sing-song, hand-clapping numbers drill: "Zero plus one is one" (clap-clap); zero plus two is two (clap-clap). There was a joyousness in the exercise that seemed, just then, to neutralize the threat of robotism in any such teaching method. Mrs. Trench transformed the exercise into something benign and productive by her unfeigned enthusiasm, her resonant contralto voice, her large smiling deep-brown face, the comforting quality of her presence. She was having fun, and the wholeness of her participation in this arithmetical chant told the kids it was okay for them to enjoy what they were doing, and they did. In solo drills, she gently pulled at the hem of a little girl's dress when the child hesitated in counting past three to seven. Two other children ran quickly and correctly through similar exercises, standing next to Mrs. Trench's chair. She hugged them, not as "positive reinforcement," but out of sheer impulsive pleasure.

The paraprofessionals are parents, community people. They're an important part of this program . . . I realized from the beginning that it was not easy for me to delegate responsibility. I had a tendency to take on jobs that I should be giving to the paraprofessionals. It was difficult not to tell them the way things were to be done. It's a hang-up you get over. Of course, I have certain responsibilities, even by law, that these parents don't have. I have to fill out forms that they're not supposed to fill out. I have ultimate responsibility for setting routines. I get paid more. But the paraprofessionals have opinions to offer. And I don't have to come and ask them how a child is doing in reading or in math. They come to me. We don't have to schedule meetings. We just sit down and discuss these things. It's a continuing process.

We have a very fast-paced schedule. There's a lot of things we're trying to get done, a lot of curriculum to cover and a lot of experience areas we're trying to get the kids into, to say nothing of getting them to the bathroom and back again. And it goes only from nine to one. So we sit down, like when something's not working, and they'll say, "Why don't you do *this* instead?" Or people offer to take something from me so that I can be free to work with a child. Things like that. It didn't start off that way, but we were able to make changes, very fast, just off the cuff, all the time. Where would I be without them?

If some of them seemed stand-offish to you, I can't blame them. I was hit by something Mrs. Lofton [director of the kindergarten] told me the other day—how many visitors we've had, 360-some. And each and every one of them, in spite of instructions that were given, sat down right in the middle of a lesson and started asking questions of the kids and arguing with them and with me, right there, over the program. One week I had twelve visitors in my room. Another day I had nine. Mrs. Lofton had told them: Three in a room, don't talk to the teacher. These are supposed to be reasonable adults and they came in and they were disruptive. *They* could have used some behavioral reinforcement as far as I was concerned. A couple of times I said as nicely as I could for them to please leave my room, and I got funny looks. Most of the visitors are, like, principals of schools, or teachers. And one day I just said, "Get out!" Mrs. Lofton was nice enough to keep them away from my room for a while after that, because when I saw them looking through the little peephole in my door, it turned me off and then my kids started turning off, too. I got over that. I learned how to ask people to leave.

We're going crazy with paperwork now. Our program is being tested by an objective group from Stanford University. They've tested the children, with little pieces of standardized tests. And now that they've finished testing, we, the three teachers here, are supposed to evaluate every single test. We're going out of our minds . . .

Okay: end of your first year as a full-responsibility teacher. What do you feel?

When I came here I was already in favor of community control in principle and this program was what the parents had picked. That was reason enough to give it a try. But I began with the feeling, Well, I don't know how this is going to work out. Then, being the only male teacher and the only white in the Annex, that was a strange setup at first. People talked about chitlins and I didn't know what chitlins were. I'm the only man, and when they talked about their stockings I started to feel uncomfortable. You know, I don't care about women's stockings and I can't stand to talk about the bargains that some lady, any lady, got anywhere. So in that sense it was a little uncomfortable for me. But being able to sit down with them and talk about things, I began to feel like a part of what was going on.

People here didn't know anything about me and I didn't know anything about them. We would have to ask questions of each other, like, white people asking black people, "Do you get sunburned?" I have the feeling they know more about me than I know about them. They've seen *my* customs on TV. As employees, many of the black parents have been in white homes and business places much more than I've ever been in theirs. But what did I know about them when I got here? I've learned a lot this year . . .

One day I was feeling a little bit down. Someone was bad, it was hot, and my throat was killing me. Then Mrs. Lofton came in and said, "Man, what would we ever have done without you?" That's a positive statement, you know? I feel rather valued.

GEORGE ANDREAS
Washington, D.C.

In essence, with these kids, I'll put it succinctly: they gotta move, they have to move physically, they gotta use their hands. They've got to have space, a variety of materials to work with, their own time limitations within reason, *no* force at all and they gotta have a lot of love and warmth. That is what every ghetto or in my estimation every city operation needs. Let's look at it realistically. They're still having thousands of dropouts, right? So, ergo, the system, the so-called educational processes aren't working, period.

The Morgan Community School Annex is obscurely located on the northwest side of Washington, D.C. Even the black cabdriver has to think about how to get there. From Scott Circle, it's a northwesterly zigzag run of twenty-some blocks. Meandering, we cross the intersection of 14th and U Streets where the days of fiery civil insurrection erupted following the news of Martin Luther King's assassination. We make it to the school door. Exterior: eroding red brick, busted sidewalks; circa God-knows-when. Interior: paint-sick woodwork, old plumbing, old wiring, old everything. But within the spaces of this infirm, afflicted structure something new is happening. The school trying to become a part of its neighborhood, educationally.

The bleakness of George Andreas' large classroom is brightly contradicted by the use of wall and blackboard space. Almost every square foot has something tacked, taped, written or drawn on it, each for a good working reason. The corners are cluttered with cardboard cartons, improvised storage units for materials and children's paperwork. It's three o'clock and the kids are gone, yet the room gives off a sense of activity. There has been struggle here, the not-always-happy struggle, of teaching and learning.

Meet Andreas in some quick stranger-to-stranger encounter and he could be anything—cop, an airline pilot or a coal miner (which he was in his teens). He is powerful, square-built, well larded; his manner is positive, with just a touch of studious courtesy in it. Talking, he doesn't sound like a teacher but more like a guy who's been around and knows how to handle himself . . .

This boy who just left us [there had been an interruption], he came to us in September, eight years old, couldn't read. Didn't really know the alphabet. Now he carries his weight minimally. We're proud—he is too—that now he *wants* to come to school. He *likes* it and he's accomplishing something. Probably we can build on that without any problems. You see, these kids, they come in very suspicious of adults . . .

Another interruption. Nora, nine, standing in the doorway, says something about a parade. Andreas fends her off with no sweetness in his words but plenty of light in his manner: "Do you mind? I'm having a consultation and I'll see you tomorrow, okay? Go on, Nora, go ahead. I'll see you tomorrow."

What kind of a parade? It's for the elections we're having on Sunday. This is the only locally elected school board in the city.

Community-controlled?

Not completely. It's a joint operation. The board here chooses people, they go downtown, and downtown passes judgment on them. They're hired by joint consent of the local board and the Board of Ed.

Why did you apply for a job at Morgan?

When I taught out at John Burroughs in Northeast (Washington), of my own inventory, I found out that teachers have no recourse to making effective curricula, effective decisions of any kind and any type of grievances they had—they had no one to go to. I tried to explain to the supervisors and the principal that practically the whole school was below grade in reading level.

It was rampant throughout the other schools. Dr. Hansen* hid this stuff under the rug. It took a school board vote, before he resigned, to get the true records, and he had a crash reading program but it wasn't worth a darn. There are thousands of these kids who need individual attention, and this curriculum hasn't changed since the year one.

I stuck it out at John Burroughs for a year and a half. Then I got injured in my classroom. I was out for about eight months and [subsequently] I went down to the slum of Anacostia where I spent six months.

What was this school injury?

Well, the chairs were flying through the air and I wrestled with a kid. I fell to the floor and my disk popped out. You see, I had a lot of sixth-grade kids that the other teachers couldn't handle. They would end up in my room because, one, I was male, and I let them do their own thing. I didn't force anything on them, and they became quiescent and cooperative except when they'd come in with

* Carl Francis Hansen, Superintendent of Schools, 1958–67; Assistant Superintendent, 1947–58.

their hostilities. There could be a glance or a touch and they'd be off. That was one of these incidents.

Finally I ended up here about three years ago. I heard about the changes that were to take place, so I wanted to be where I could be instrumental in shaping a curriculum that would be challenging, entertaining and commensurate with kids' abilities here.

And this is one way they broke the ice—with a community school. Here we can conjure up our own programs without worrying about the old biddies coming in and taking notes and going downtown, or down here, and telling the principal that his or her teaching is not sticking to the book, it's not effective. And how can they do it after twenty minutes of sitting in a room? They don't even know the kids.

When they had the Strayer Report* about fifteen years ago, they made recommendations. They came back from Chicago ten years later [with another report],† and not one recommendation was implemented because they have the old biddies with the buns in the back who wouldn't change anything. They still operate on the old country-school system.

Andreas mentioned "the old biddies" several times during our conversation. Clearly they were his private symbol for school-system bureaucracy and its old-hat pedagogic agents in the classroom.

You work with kids in the seven-to-nine age group and you don't have a graded structure. A kid doesn't say, I'm in the first grade or the third grade; he says I'm in Mr. Andreas' team. And if he or she makes enough progress

* A survey of the District of Columbia public schools by George D. Strayer, professor of education administration, University of Washington (state), conducted for the House and Senate Subcommittees on District of Columbia Appropriations in 1949.
† A survey of Chicago public schools directed in 1963–64 by Robert J. Havighurst, professor of education and human development at the University of Chicago.

after a few months, they can go to another team, or work through both teams, with a team project, or their own project. They can study with anybody. We emphasize reading and arithmetic. In between we sandwich whatever little thing they want to do, drawing, or cutting, in artistic work, sculpting.

They came in, in September, non- and minimal readers. A lot of kids here didn't know beginning sounds and they would go up and trace this against words of their own. They didn't know the alphabet. They couldn't write. Now they read, they know their basic math and they don't have the hostilities they had before.

We operate on a person-to-person basis. They get their papers, we sit down, and the accent is on the positive. No matter how poor or pathetic-looking it is, it's good, because they're producing. Is it good to do it that way? . . . In the beginning it is. But after that you start saying, "Well, don't you think you could have done this a little better, or be a little more neat and could you correct this," and so on. That comes in the second or third month. Later the kid begins to see for himself. He'll say, Oh, I did this over here or over there. I could have done it a little more neat, I think I made some mistakes, here, and there. And you say, "What do you feel like doing about it?" He says, Oh, I'll go back to my seat and work on it and let so-and-so work with me. If they like the kid and they work with him, I say, "Go right ahead." If it's reading, fine; math, fine; or if it's just plain that they like to sit down and draw a lot of pictures and they help each other, criticize. And they'll sit there for an hour. Or they'll go up in that corner there. The most aggressive one will put words on the board and they'll have their own little reading program, where they're not worried about any chastisement. Or they'll take that little thing over there [Andreas indicates another blackboard area]. On the top they'll play tick-tack-toe, then they'll digress into basic math. [They do this by making use of numerals already chalked in an adjacent space.]

We have four teachers and two interns for a hundred and three kids. I'm a teacher and the coordinator for the four rooms. It's one of the best ratios in the city but here's the irony—you need more because so many kids need individual attention. We'd like to do more with them, they'd like to do more with us. But we don't have the personnel or the space. There are those of us who will go and sit on the rug and do our work.

The first board [he indicates it] is what we call the early-bird work. The kids will come in and sit down, and then after they've had their milk and cereals we'll say, "What would you like to do first? Do you want to have words and color reading* or do you want to do your board work over there?" They'll say, "Well, we'll start with the board work and we'll do the other things later."

In September we had quite a few kids who couldn't do anything. Now everybody can read, alphabetize, add, subtract. They'll just automatically sit down and work and— try to stop them. Once they get a lock on that and I say, "Well, let's go and do some reading," a lot of them, they'll scream, tear the papers, and throw the pencils down—"I want to finish my work. I want to be left alone!"

Then there are those who don't feel like doing anything because of problems at home. There might be lack of food, or paranoia . . . They'll sit down and they'll start drawing pictures, come up and do this, or they'll go back and do that. But this [freedom to choose their own activities or passivities] is after they have learned their alphabet and how to read minimally.

---

* A visual coding method for indicating the sound contributed by a single letter or letter combination to the correct sound of a whole word. Thus green may represent the correct vowel sound in *fair* and *fare*; red, the correct vowel sound in *boat*, *note* (or *both*). The applications of this method have a far wider range of complexity and refinement than indicated here.

Don't you ever wonder whether you're patronizing these kids, being merely compassionate, because you don't expect very much of them?

No, no, not I! I used to do that. But I'm like a sergeant at times. I don't become sycophantic or saccharine about their work, not most of the time. They'll come up here and I'll say, "Look. Now isn't that sloppy?" I'll let them have it and it shakes them up. I mean, there's a balance. After I've gained their confidence I can be very straightforward with them and they won't feel hurt.

How do you gain their confidence?

By listening to them in the morning, sharing my coffee, a pat on the head, giving them spending money, telling them how nice they look—all affirmatives in the beginning.

Do they also feel that you respect them?

Yes. They know that. Because they tell me, "Last year so-and-so used to beat me and wouldn't listen to me and I wouldn't do any work for them." And they'll write notes to me—"I love you Mr. Andreas" and "I like working with you." And they'll go home and tell their parents.

The ones I'm proud of are those that came in with a really negative attitude and wouldn't do anything. To me, they're my smartest kids now, because they work. A boy by the name of Julian, last September and October, he used to run out the door, fight, scream, throw things. Now [June] he's almost completely tranquil, does his work very happily, has a sense of humor.

What made the difference was that I didn't force him. I asked him, "What would you like to do?" He said, "Well, I don't want to sit here. I want to go to the library and go through books." I said, "Go right ahead. What are you going to do when you get tired?" He said he'd come back again. I said, "Are you going to do some work for yourself?" He said, "Yes."

There would be days when I wouldn't see him in my room. I'd take a sneak in the library and there he'd be, from nine o'clock in the morning, eat his lunch and go back again. Eventually Julian started working on his alphabet and on forming basic words. Then he began to say, I feel like reading, and he'd sit down with the group, which he'd never done. Well, he got it from both sides. I would check with Mrs. Parham because her forte is language arts. We'd find out where he was and what he could do. Then I'd talk with her and she'd make some recommendations and I'd sit down and work with him—"How do you form your A's, your B's? Can you make a word out if it? Can you sound it out?" I'd sit with him for twenty minutes, half an hour.

There are some others, kids named Welch, Roberts, Kemble. They had emotional problems last year. They—I don't go into their histories. That prejudices the case already. You see, I don't do that. I take them as they are, talk with them, observe them quite a bit during the first few weeks, take 'em in to Mrs. Parham to see who reads where and who can write. They had no comprehension of the alphabet. Now they're quite capable.

In fact, Wendell wouldn't do a thing till one day he got up and got his crew and he conjured up his own play. Wendell Roberts, the kid who had a gross inferiority complex, wouldn't read, wouldn't write! He did his own play. And here's a kid who wouldn't move out of his seat for three months, just about. How come?

Because he found out he wasn't going to be put down verbally or physically. You see, they know me. They can make a thousand mistakes. I don't care, as long—and they'll join in the chorus—"as long as you *try* and you *do*." Wendell would not make his move till he was sure he was not going to be made a fool of, not going to be humiliated by his peers and he was not going to be hit at.

His play was about a circus. We read a story in a book and he said, "Do you mind if I make a play out of it?" I said, "Sure, go ahead. How are you going to go about it?" Wendell said "So-and-so's going to be the bear, Eric's going to be the clown and I am going to be the ringmaster." Even though he couldn't read the word "ringmaster" when he saw it. He got eight or ten kids together. They got papers and crayon, made their own costumes. They went over there [indicating a corner of the room] and practiced for about an hour while I was over here teaching reading. Others were working quietly doing their math. Wendell's group didn't disturb anybody, even though they made a lot of noise, imitations of animals, et cetera. They went down and put it on for other classes. They came back completely enthused. Wendell's teacher from last year told me he wouldn't do anything.

Were you pleased?

Pleased? It was a moment of discovery. It happens. There was one kid, Wade, who sat for several months. I couldn't get him to read with me very much or do the stuff on the board. He had no confidence. Wouldn't commit himself. So I let him trace letters and fill in missing words under pictures in his workbook. One day he went back there [to his reading group]; I saw him sit down and I was curious. I circled around and he didn't know I was in back of him. Well, he took a book, second-grade level, and read up a storm. My eyes almost bugged out. He got confidence. It was all there, internal, and this day he just decided he was going to commit himself. He was reading to his buddy and his buddy looked around. He couldn't believe it either. I let him go till he was finished. Then I said, "You know, you sort of shook me up." He says, "Why?" I said, "Well, I didn't know you could read so well." He was all smiles. He said, "I just felt like doing it."

About the question of language, the language of the "subculture." Do you have much trouble with that?

I don't fight it. I did have trouble understanding for a while. Then my hearing became attuned to the syntax, the inflections, all the idioms. There's no problem now.

What are your discipline problems here?

Well, discipline—if you say you want them to sit down for an extended period and they don't want to do it, and they don't want to do what you have on the board, and then they start reacting violently, they are a discipline problem. It can last for a minute or for weeks, if you want to call that a discipline problem. It's a matter of definition. I wouldn't call it that. I would give him, her, them, a choice of what they want to do. Teachers can create a lot of discipline problems. I mean one kid will rear up and hit another one in the face and you can say, like the old-timers, "Go at it, settle it outside, in the hall," or, "Why did you do this or that?" . . . forget it. Find out, after they settle down—"What would you like to do? Do you want to work with me, help me go through some papers?" . . . Find their interest and let them have choices.

Are you telling me that teachers often make *discipline problems through inflexibility and narrow concepts of classroom behavior?*

A human being, a member of *Homo sapiens*, has to sit *here* at nine fifteen and sit in *this* block, then *that* block and so on, and do all this according to a time period—that's a bunch of you-know-what. Kids are the most volatile, curious, grasping beings you can meet. And the problems of education today are to find and devise new methodologies, new curricula, materials and so on, to open new vistas to these kids.

Suppose you give all this new stuff to the "biddies with the buns in the back"? What's that going to accomplish?

That depends on City Hall. They have to be *told*: "This is what we're going to do. If you don't have any objections, fine. If you do, tell us why. How can we change your thinking, or what would you like to do?" Like the kids, you give *them* a choice, too . . . *Can* teachers change? Teachers *must* change!

What makes you think City Hall is going to do anything about it?

Well, that's my point. Several weeks ago the whole administrative staff from downtown spent Friday and Saturday and Sunday, two hundred people, to discuss, implement, to be decisive and everything about getting these policies effected from the Passow Report.* They brought Professor Passow and his staff from Columbia and they did a $250,000 report. They were here about one year. They hit every level, vertically, horizontally, teachers, parents and so on. And now they're trying to make that effective. This is—again—how do you get City Hall to move?

It's not all a question of innovation, either. There are those who need the regular traditional methodology, materials, and programs, and there are many on the other side of the picture that have to get away from this boxed-in, lockstep learning—from the idea that you come in at nine and sit down and do this and that, close the books at nine thirty, go out until ten, and so on. They have to have different materials. And they need people that care.

I like manipulative materials like they use in the Montessori schools—variety is important, so they can be comfortable in choosing and working. We're in the Bank Street readers now, though we still have to suffer along with some Dick and Jane until next year. Downtown was sandbagging us. We didn't get materials for a lo-o-ng time.

* An exhaustive study of the Washington, D.C., school system commissioned by Dr. Hansen, directed by A. Harry Passow, professor of education, Teachers College, Columbia University, and completed in 1967.

They were misdirected, mis-routed. We had to go buy our own. That's improved some. Because they tried to take the school away from us last year and it didn't work out. They, I mean downtown.

You care about these kids. What do you feel about their parents?

I don't know a lot of them, but those I hear from through the kids or through the neighborhood grapevine, I feel sorry for, yet I don't. Because these people gave up a long time ago and they give vent to their frustrations on the kid. Maybe they don't want the kid in the first place. Then they got economic problems. The husband left, or the wife left and they're stuck with the millstone, not a human being or a child. Maybe society has been in their eyes [a pause] *mean* to them and they've given up. All of these things enter into the picture.

Maybe a lot of them gave up because they didn't have a teacher like you. Was that their fault?

No.

Do you visit your pupils' homes?

I'm so tied up with teaching and administrative things. I meet parents at our little social functions and as I go walking up the street. I talk to them on the porches and so on. My interns see a lot of them. Bill goes out frequently. So does Mrs. Parham. She lives in the area. Herbert and Mrs. Hatfield are out quite a bit. They keep a check on why kids aren't in school, whether they need shoes. All these things come into play. If it rains, quite a few of these kids won't be here.

You have to do preventive shoe providing? What are your resources?

We do quite a bit. Community people, business people chip in. Some foundations give us a little money.

We dig it out of our own pockets. I've spent two hundred dollars this term, maybe more, because I paid for a couple of trips. I don't care. The thing is it is helping *kids*, not *a* kid. It's helping them get confidence in themselves and the desire to come to school. They're producing. They're seeing for the first time in their lives that they have some worth. That they can learn.

Most of the trips are local, but a crew from the upper school went to New York this morning and they'll be there overnight. And, uh, this is between you and me, but I dished out of my own pocket especially for this one kid. He used to be a real hostile, aggressive, malicious person at the beginning of school in September. He had the maniacal look. He'd sneak in here and beat the kids' heads against the wall—till he got to like me. He'd come up here, do my boards. I'd give him a quarter, buy him some ice cream, let him have some money to buy clothes. He quit beating kids. He's clean now. He doesn't have the maniacal look anymore. I sponsored most of the money for his trip to New York.

You made that sound so easy. He changed, for you, just like that?

It wasn't easy. It's just that I've learned not to make issues out of nothing. Or rather, I've learned to spot the real issues. I've learned to be very flexible. I've been in trying circumstances before. I've learned to "tune it out." I love to walk, or go into the library, or go down to the park and jog. Plus, I don't have to worry about that biddy coming here with that black book—the Spanish inquisitor.

This is tough. This is not an easy profession, teaching in the ghetto. Because you're a mother, father, saint; you're everything. If I make one gross mishap in the way of not paying attention to a certain kid at a certain time, or yelling too loudly, I can see the change take place in that kid. He or she won't work because I hurt their feelings.

Do you feel guilty about it?

Yes. I apologize to them. And that's rare, for an adult to apologize to them, especially a teacher. But too many apologies will ruin the whole thing. We have to be perceptive.

What's your idea of a good teacher? Did you ever run across a definition that pleases you?

No. I've been trying to make a good definition for myself. It's tough. The fact that I got—that these kids were nonreaders with emotional problems, which have somehow subsided or disappeared, and that these kids find themselves coming to school happy and that they can read, and that they have choices that make them happy and that make them work, I would say that is a good teacher, someone who has the respect of the kids, the love, and the kid is producing at the same time. That, to me, is a good teacher. The kid does it for himself, for you, or in spite of you, or in spite of himself. I'm rambling but . . . these are the thoughts that come to mind.

Andreas grew up "in the coal mines" near Wilkesbarre, Pa. His parents were immigrants from Czechoslovakia, poor, illiterate.

They just came over and went into the mines. That was their life. Period. My father started when he was nine. He put in approximately fifty-six years. He died when he was eighty-two. A lot of what he did and said rubbed off on me. He said that everybody has a sense of dignity, not in the same words; that you should have a lot of compassion for your fellow-man and not be afraid of pain; to work and not give up easily if trials come; to live with yourself. I couldn't have lived with myself in ——, where I began teaching.

There were no black miners in the smaller towns. The only Afro-Americans he encountered were on opposing teams when he played high school football. He "picked coal, worked in a grocery store for practically nothing, on a beer truck, and in an attorney's office as his clerk." He always wanted to go to college. His family didn't have the money.

Nothing. I cried in my senior year. I saw my friends take off. Their parents had money because they were teachers or politicians. There were seven of us. Naturally it was rough during the depression but it didn't affect my learning. I used to read and still do, avidly. I had several football scholarships offered to me, but the war broke out . . . I would have gone anyway. I would have worked in the cafeteria or something. Instead, I spent three years in the infantry. I was scheduled for D-Day, but I was kept behind and put in for the Battle of the Bulge. The first day, I wondered about mankind when I saw the bodies piled up on the tier—Catholics, Jews, Protestants. My friends. In just one day—they were gone. That's when I forgot about labels. Every human being has a dignity that should be respected.

After the war he attended George Washington University under the G.I. Bill, then worked for the federal government for four years in a job he described simply as "intelligence research" but "it wasn't intelligent and it wasn't research. Sterile atmosphere." He studied for a year at Johns Hopkins, then taught in the wealthy suburban areas.

I didn't like it. I was the only male teacher in the school. They gave me all the problems. Plus the parents . . . If I didn't give the kids the grades they expected, they'd go up there [to the school authorities] and complain. You have no recourse, either. In the middle of the year of lot of teachers left. Down here, they have what they call the community board. And that's where it's hashed out. The pay was quite a bit better in the suburbs but I'm single. That's why I could make the choices I did. If I were married, it would be a different story probably. I'd sell bits of my soul. Don't rock the boat and be comfortable and so on. Education has more sheep in it than the whole continent of Australia.

If a lot of people had been honest with themselves about how ineffective the schools are, you wouldn't have the problems you have today. But the teachers lie, the principals lie, and the administrators go along with them. Nobody rock the boat. Intellectual hypocrites. Take physical confrontations, like Stokely Carmichael went down and sat on Hansen's desk. And he said [to Hansen], "Instead of going up to Congress with your hat in your hand and asking for a million and a half, go and tell them the truth. About the books that are lousy, about the books that you don't have and should have, about the materials you don't ask for, and the counselors you need." He went on and on and on. Hansen didn't do it.

You're telling me that a little hell-raising is needed?

Definitely. It's like a Damoclean sword. It can work for or against you. It depends on whom you're doing it with and with what you're doing it. I believe in confrontations. Sitting on a desk and yelling and screaming, I don't mind that. But when it comes to destroying property and assaulting people, no. Isn't it terrible to see your fellow-man disfigured and beaten upon?

Your tone is very matter-of-fact. In all you've said there's been the underlying suggestion that "anybody can do it if he really wants to." Yet much of the academic literature makes it seem that to move even one kid from apathy to action depends on mysteries of some kind.

No. The mystery is internal. But you have to give the externals to bring it out.

Maybe there is a mystery—the mystery of the good teacher, and the lousy one. Because no matter how much we learn—

Why go to a teacher? Why don't you go to the kids? Ask the kids.

We left the building together. I told him I was going down to Scott Circle in a cab and offered to give him a lift. He said "No, thanks." Well, then, how would he get home?

"Walk," he replied. "I only live a couple of blocks away."

JERRY LONG
New York

Jerry Long's classroom. The slogan WORDS ARE POWER *runs across one wall in cut-out letters two feet high. Closer to eye level, on another wall: "These Men Use Words Powerfully: Malcolm X, Richard Wright, Langston Hughes . . . Get With It. Read!" The stuff that impresses visitors but . . . I asked Jerry, "What's it for?"*

The message to the children is that language can be as useful as any skill they have now for coping with the oppressive world they live in. Their values are power-oriented because of their personal experiences on the block, because of what they hear from parents participating in power struggles with the Establishment, so called, and what they see in the movies and television. They use the power of words daily, whether they know it or not. They can put somebody down, they can "jive" with them, use mean, insulting words, either self-ridiculing or directed at others. They know the words "nigger," "faggot," "honky" are powerful words. I want them to understand the relation between the possession or pursuit of power and the mastery of language—which is something kind of new to them; that to grasp the language helps to seize the time.

Jerry Long. Short, white, twenty-eight; on second glance, sturdily built. Round-featured under a flat swirl of longish black hair. Closely bristled, clean-shaven face. Dark shirt, corduroy jacket, nondescript slacks. Manner: warm, undefensive. Speech and movement: lively. Hip but non-hippie. Grew up in a Michigan farm community of eight hundred. A General Electric plant moved in when he was thirteen. The population zoomed to fifteen hundred.

At the University of Michigan he abandoned graduate anthropology: "I found the graduate work, for me, would be trivial. Identification of pottery styles, hundreds upon hundreds." He used his second undergraduate major, English, to become a teacher. His first teaching job was in a private school—English, Grades 8 through 12, for three years.

My first impulse may have been to avoid military service. I couldn't stand authoritarian kinds of life. But more, I was dissatisfied with my earlier jobs, first at a newspaper, later at the Department of Welfare. They were rigid and in a bureaucratic way impersonal. Even casework was primarily a matter of filing forms and waiting for approval. I wanted something where I could feel as if I were affecting someone's life. I'd always felt that teaching was for people who didn't have anything else to do. Now I was beginning to realize its potential for achieving what was becoming increasingly important to me—the integration of my personal interest in literature and politics with my work.

In the ideal situation, where you can work with a small number of children and significantly affect their style of life, and give them basic skills they're going to need, I respect the vocation very highly. It's a marvelous place to dedicate yourself. However, that ideal situation doesn't exist. It means that now you are functioning as a recorder and quasi-baby-sitter for an educational bureaucracy that is too big to cope with its problems.

How did you get to 201 [Arthur A. Schomburg Intermediate School]?

Because of the low pay and very poor working conditions, I organized for the UFT [United Federation of Teachers] at the private school where I was teaching. I was forced out of my job but I remained very active in supporting UFT causes. In roughly the same period I took advantage of the Board of Education's ITTP, In-Service Teaching Training Program ("Instant" is the pet term). I met three or four people in the course . . . One was a friend of the acting principal . . . so I came to 201 in September 1967, interested politically more than educationally. That was the year the union was striking for its new contract. I was very interested in the union. I wanted to join the picket line or anything else to do with the strike.

We had three days of orientation before school opened. I knew nothing of the peripheral issues. They bordered on the sense of alienation that East Harlem felt from liberal politics in New York and particularly what the UFT was doing.

The third day they introduced us to the governing board and I first heard of Mr. [David] Spencer and Mrs. [Babette] Edwards.* In the course of all of that talk was revealed this horrible situation between the UFT and local

* Members of the governing board of the Arthur A. Schomburg (I.S. 201) Complex and activists for community control of public schools.

communities. It was really a deadly, a hateful relationship. I suddenly had to rethink everything in terms of where my biggest obligation was, whether it was to the children—a concept that's bandied around during a strike—to the UFT, to the governing board or to the principal, to my friends or to whomever, myself. So it was a very tense week. As it turned out, about eighteen of us out of the one hundred and ten on the faculty decided to break the picket and come into school.

Some people had come to 201 because of the political glamor—black people fighting for community control. Others had come because it was a place you could get a job. But whatever the original motivation, the decision we eighteen made, to cross the picket line, was agonizing, and we had to make it at the literal last moment.

I arrived very early on the first day of school because I had big qualms about crossing a picket line. The first person I met inside was a reporter from the *Washington Post* at seven o'clock in the morning and he wanted an interview. That was the first strike [September 1967]; 201 was prominent in the headlines then. The chapter chairman was accusing the local community of doing all sorts of things that they simply weren't doing: people had been beaten up on a picket line, the school was teaching racism, they were harassing white teachers—charges that were trumped up, politically motivated. The strike was settled on contractual issues, for salary alone. So we finally got ready to open the school. By the end of the first semester, I think we had two assistant principals out of five, no principal. Miss Banfield [then the acting principal] had gotten ill and resigned. We had two guidance people out of five and we were short about twenty teachers. That's 20 percent of the staff. That can mean as many as twenty classes uncovered and there are twenty-five kids in the class, so you figure out . . . The first year we turned over about sixty teachers. Most of them were white. We didn't have supervision. It was a horrible first semester. Then they sent the district superintendent over and put him in charge of the school. He was only there a few days . . . I walked into the office and he was sitting at his desk reading *The New York Times*. We had no books for the eighth grade and I asked him if he could get hold of some SRA [Science Research Associates] reading materials. He said, "Well, I'll ask around." He was very curt and unfriendly. He did attempt to get us some supplies we had been begging for from the Board of Education. He hired a bunch of teachers. Six or eight were introduced, I remember, the beginning of the second semester in the teachers' cafeteria. That same day we had a LeRoi Jones assembly* scheduled. Those teachers, I never saw them again. They all rushed out in utter fear. We lost about twenty as a result of that assembly.

So there we were, functioning without a principal, having to do all this extra work, and the political pressures from the outside community, dealing with the union, were as strong as they had ever been. And then the next year Ocean Hill came along . . . So the cycle sort of began again the following year, the cycle of pressure and tension.

You're halfway through your third year now. On the whole, what's it been like to teach in this school?

Sometimes I feel a little fraudulent because I find myself conducting lessons in much the same way they were given to me. It's been a struggle with myself to overcome that because I feel other approaches are necessary. They need to know how to write, to read, to count, and right

* A student assembly scheduled as part of a regular school day, it included presentation of a pantomime created by Imamu Baraka (Leroi Jones) and his Spirit House Movers and Players. The play was ideologically black nationalist/separatist. It contained intense expressions of black resentment against white domination which some whites in the audience found psychically disturbing. The school's records, however, show only one resignation immediately following the "Leroi Jones assembly."

now this is the aim of the community. But the point is, how to get it across. So the method really becomes very important. What has it meant to teach in this school? Well, it meant a lot personally in how I will work in with black children. I never knew any poor black children before I came to 201. I've learned a great deal about their style, their humor, their use of playfulness, their really clever use of language.

MMMmm, what has it meant to teach at 201?

I was in a quandary to know, the first year I was there. We debated it, whether or not this community really wanted white teachers. I don't think they had decided that themselves but now I think they have. I think they're convinced they want the best teachers they can find regardless of color. As it turns out, black people having grown up in Harlem are best equipped to cope with the children, though I know black teachers at the school who aren't doing so well at communicating the skills. However, in the first few months at 201, when I was struggling, dealing with adolescents who brought to school a hostility, I could have said, "Maybe they're right. Maybe the *only* teachers who can teach here are those that grew up in the community and know how to say the right words and wield the right kind of authority."

So the first thing I had to decide for myself was, I had something to contribute. The next thing I felt was, What do I have to contribute in terms of what this community is doing politically? I was very acutely aware of their pride and their complete resistance to having outside influences dictate their needs. For example, someone from my own racial and economic background coming in with good ideas that had worked in other situations and trying to impose them politically when the occasion called for it.

I found that this community's struggle for control is one where I and other white teachers must participate as sort of technicians. This is also true for black teachers who are not politically motivated. We have very specific skills, in the subjects we teach. Our support for the broad political concept *is* needed. But in terms of what we *do*, it is our presence in the school, our hard work and our seriousness that are needed. Our skills as a teacher, but not our political ideas, political techniques, organizational methods or anything else. The community has those skills themselves.

I think a lot of whites might ask themselves, Why do they want to get involved with black people? Because oppressed people are symbolic of a place to make change in a corrupt society. I suppose that's why I went there. For one thing, I didn't want to be, in the image of my friends and myself—in quotes—a public school teacher. To me that was not a flattering, a fulfilling image. So I said, Well, I'll be a teacher in a hot political school that is radical, and that's a generic term, because my so-called radical ideas didn't necessarily coincide. But I was going in as a technician, on the terms of the black community. They were operating an institution that *they* were controlling, that *they* were making political decisions . . . where they were saying, "Look, we'll run our own show. Help us if you can, but in the way *we* think you can be helpful. " Originally I didn't know my role. I didn't know what they wanted me to do or what I wanted to do myself.

We'd lost all of these teachers and each time we lost them there was a heated discussion. Particularly among whites as to whether it was worth staying or not because we felt—they felt, I didn't feel it—that we were being badgered and insulted, challenged to defend our right to be there, etc., etc.

Was it right, for example, when LeRoi Jones brought in a bunch of kids from his street theater project in Harlem, for our famous assembly, to yell, "Honky! Honky! Get the white teacher!" and literally point at teachers in the audience? Was it right for the chairman of the governing board to stand up and say, "I can't protect your safety if you support the UFT when you come into this community"? These were terribly urgent questions for most people —including the governing boards. But for me the real question became: Was I ready to go into not only a black school and a Harlem school and a decayed city institution of education, but was I really interested in community control, and in what that glossed-over term meant in a really oppressed community? Was I really committed to the principle that the community must decide the answers to those questions? The school I teach in has the lowest economic level in the whole city.

So I realized that when I went there I had made a contract, so to speak, with the community. Not as some people would see it, to keep my mouth shut and do whatever was asked of me, but a kind of a contract to a principle that I really believed in—that people in a local community, regardless of how poor or so-called unskilled or so-called uneducated they were, could really decide what was important for them and particularly for the children.

I had to ask myself, Do you really believe that if the parents of this community had full power to decide what's best for their children that they're going to opt for what the outside community called "racist" lessons, only revolutionary classes? My first commitment was that parents of this community could decide what was best for their children. What they might decide might not be necessarily in detail what I would decide, but, you see, the political reality is more important than our disagreement. That was the overriding concern when we started getting bitched at, or when things got really sort of nitty-gritty with the rest of the teachers. I decided early that the way to answer the question of crisis was my sincerity in contributing the skills I had in teaching, usable by the community. Could that contribute to a bigger political cause? I didn't know. All I could say was that, Damn!—it would be nice if I could contribute something . . .

And the surprising thing—not surprising, really—I found that . . . Jesus, the things the people seeking community control were after were the same things parents had been after in my little farming community in Michigan: Can my kid pass the standardized test to get into a given college?

Is that all you want to give the kids?

Well, no. But I have to decide what I want to accomplish in terms of opening up new worlds and helping the kids see themselves and me and other people in a different light. It becomes very, very subtle whether or not I use the children for my own satisfaction that I have been fashionably "innovative" or whether I have really fulfilled the desires of the community. As any teacher, going into any school, I can *invent* the needs of my children, no matter how hip or relevant I am. And then you can peddle it as innovation. But I'd better look at my hypothesis of where the kids' needs come from. Too many teachers starting out have held too many romantic notions of the ghetto child. They hypothesize that the need of the ghetto child is to be liberated from himself, or needs to answer some preconceived notion of criticizing the system. All of these things used by teachers are valid: criticism of the system, creative approaches to the child's use of language in writing and poetry. I use them, but the deeper question is, you know, What are the immediate needs?

The immediate needs of the children are to cope with a white racist society in a school system where all sorts of slick devices such as "qualifying examinations and interviews" and other elimination procedures are used to hold the status quo in so-called specialized high schools. Our principals have had to literally bang on desk tops to get 201 students in. One of these so-called specialized high schools sits in the middle of Harlem. But it's got only a minority of local kids. For example, one of our really talented eighth-graders, whose work has since been exhibited at the Museum of Natural History, with a fantastic portfolio, was left out because his reading score was a few months too low. The kids I'm teaching need the skills that other people have failed to teach them.

I saw something on your blackboard that said "Sense and Soul. Private" and something else that said "Personal Writing." What did all that mean?

It's a personal folder for each child, a diary, and I appoint someone in the class to be in charge of the folders. Periodically I ask them to write until they fill a page. Now I mean that very elementarily. I mean "to write," to use their pencil on a piece of paper. Obviously, the first thing they ask is, "What do I write?" and I tell them, "Anything you like. The only thing is, you must fill a page. I will look from a distance that you have filled the page but I will not read it. Neither will anyone else, unless you say so." Say they can write a paragraph. That's not enough. They can go to any book, preferably one that they like, and copy out of the book.

I want them to feel that whatever they want to write can be written. If they want to use profanity, or to say something about me, their parents, the school, the community or anybody, that they can be entirely free, without fear of correction or censorship. You see, we're dealing with a great deal of shattered self-images. Every time they put a pencil on paper it's red-marked "wrong." They fail, fail, fail, fail.

If they'd like me to read what they have written, they put an X on it. I will read it just to tell them about their sentences, their spelling, their commas, mechanical things. If they put a Y on it I will tell them, Yes the ideas are good or bad or weak, or I agree or don't agree. Or they can put both and I will comment on both. And if they want, they can get a grade on it. Originally nobody wants me to read anything. Then eventually I get more and more students who want an audience for what they have to write. I never suggest any topics; that's the important point.

So, sheer physical familiarity with writing, that's number one. Number two, also for self-expression. I want them to feel that they have to write, and if they have nothing to write for themselves, they have to copy. Eventually they're going to see that, well, if I'm only writing for myself, why copy out of a book? I must have something to say to myself. But they have to believe that you really don't want to read it, that they're really doing it for themselves. A lot of students, for weeks, will do nothing but copy, but one time something has pricked them, made them angry or happy, and they'll write and write.

When I give a sentence-completion assignment, a rexographed worksheet, I usually get 95 percent homeworks handed in—"Fill in the blanks . . . blah-blah-blah"—If I ask them to write a composition or a list of "Things That You've Thought About" there's a tremendous resistance. I'm trying to break down this resistance, in an innovative way, to accomplish a very traditional goal. Black children leaving 201 must be able to succeed in high school, and my job is to provide them with language skills.

Now! There are other skills they will need. That's why I have things on the board like "Words Are Power." You see, I want the children to have a certain self-esteem, a confidence. When they get in a classroom where they are a [color] minority I want them to feel adequately prepared to deal with a fast-talking teacher or glib classmates in the classroom. Now! They know what is injustice: they can sense it, they can feel it intuitively, and from the experience of their growing up in New York City. What they need is the ability to take the feeling and verbalize it. Put it in writing. To deal with someone who's trying to talk them out of it or is rationalizing stupidly. The same kind of skills,

I imagine, that people like Stokely [Carmichael] and [David] Spencer and [James] Baldwin and Rap [H. Rap Brown] had to learn outside of school. If I can say, "Look, nobody's going to listen to you unless you make yourself clear, unless you can say what you mean . . ." Now, I'm not saying, "Unless you can be polite, unless you play games," but I'm saying simply, "Unless you know the right words to say what you re-ee-eally mean." Now, how can I implement that? I can rely on what's already available, like literature, poetry and working with other teachers who know what they're doing, in terms of social studies.

In a black school, the language arts can't survive without the social studies. For example: look, if you have to write an essay on "My Most Difficult Experience," why not make it the experience of racism. Last year I collaborated on a six-week series of lessons with a social studies teacher. His emphasis is heavily on contemporary black studies. He tried to take the facts of African history and relate it to life in Harlem. I gave them lessons in composition, grammar, vocabulary, spelling; how to communicate what they had learned in writing, poetry, essays, speaking. We had debates, individual talks, class discussions.

What kind of literature do you rely on?

Richard Wright is particularly easy to use because there are lots of incidents that deal with his adolescent years . . . I remember one of the kids saying, "Do all black people today have to go through what he did?" I was all prepared to answer that with: "No, they don't, and the reason they don't is because they've learned to use words." You know, to fit right into my little pattern. But one of the kids beat me to it by saying in effect, "Yes, they do. A lot of times the things they deal with are a lot nicer, a lot more polite, but they mean the same thing. The same old shit." So I've had a lot of success in using literature. Right.

Langston Hughes. Very easy to teach. The Simple* stories. With some of my classes that are better readers and read a lot more on their own I've used Ralph Ellison. Selections from *The Invisible Man.* Just to get the kids interested I use Paul Laurence Dunbar and James Weldon Johnson, 'cause they know usually "Lift Every Voice." I've had a lot of success with *The Autobiography of Malcolm X,* selections from it.

Isn't Ralph Ellison over the heads of eighth-grade pupils?

Right. But I take certain selections, paragraphs. I did a lot of things with the concept of *The Invisible Man,* though. At first they thought it meant somebody from a science fiction movie. Eventually I got them to think Well, no, it doesn't only mean that. Look how Ellison uses the idea . . . One girl wrote a beautiful and extremely articulate short story called "Invisible Me" that picked up on the Ellison theme of racism, but it was also a very pertinent story of being young and female. I like to use the lyrics of popular songs, too, on occasion. "Sitting on the Dock of the Bay" written and sung by Otis Redding. It talks about loneliness and isolation. You know, you can really have a big trip on that. It's lots of fun with the kids. You can do a lot of basic-skills lessons on these things.

What I'm trying to do is—see, they are forced to compartmentalize their life quite a bit—there's the real world of when they talk to their friends and get scolded by their mothers and have to go to the store, have to tend the little brothers and sisters, get to go to the movies, go to a

---

* Jesse B. Semple, nicknamed Simple, was created by Langston Hughes in 1943. The first and scores of subsequent Hughes-Semple dialogues appeared in the writer's weekly column in the *Chicago Defender.* In book form, beginning with *Simple Speaks His Mind* (Simon and Schuster, 1950) and a number of later collections, Simple holds a permanent place in general American as well as distinctively black American literature.

social party. And then there's the forced world, where they have to behave as they're told to behave in school, in home, in church, on the playground and the basketball court.

Now, I want them to see that they can carry over the coping skills they use in what they consider their real world into the so-called unreal world of the classroom. Not that I'm co-opting them—though I am—not that I'm conning them—though I am. It's a sort of legitimate con because I'm saying, "Look, get to know your verbal thing well, and then, when the time is right, pop it on somebody. *Pop* your dissatisfaction with the racist world. *Pop* your dissatisfaction with lack of opportunity and your boredom, but do it in a way that it's going to be effective. Be able to challenge the teacher without calling the teacher a name. You may get results."

What happens when a kid says or shows he's bored with what's going on in your classroom?

I might say, "If you're bored, you may sit in the back of the room and read on your own." Or, I would try to keep tuning him in to something the other kids were saying. Adults forget that they very rarely start off interested in a topic, that what interests them is what's being said as the topic develops. Even in college classes you sit there and the professor says, "Tonight we're going to discuss community control," and everybody goes, "Yyghhh," until somebody says something that tunes them in.

What they don't do on their own, in the halls or elsewhere, at this age, is to discuss. They inform and report but they don't discuss, so they have to get turned on; they have to be introduced to the joys of discussion, which is an evolutionary thing; you fall into enjoying it once you've done it a while.

On good days I'm lucky, to have everybody involved. And sometimes I have to bore them for the sake of my own information, to use in the future. I'm constantly teaching myself. What is it that turns kids on?

ALAN KELLOCK
Brooklyn

The first week of school one girl said, "You are the Afro-American history teacher? You don't look like you know anything about Afro-American history." There was this immediate antagonism over the fact that they were coming to an Afro-American history class for the first time only to find a white face at the front of the room. This was expressed quite openly and I was prepared for it.

I always took the offensive, in a friendly way, and said, "Do you say that because I'm white?" They got kind of uncomfortable and they'd say, "No, you just don't look like the type."

In appearance Alan Kellock is cool, upper-middle-class WASP; medium-long but disciplined hair; assertive though unexaggerated beard and mustache; shirt, suit and necktie worn with casual Ivy League effect. He's in his mid-twenties.

To disarm them I usually found a way of communicating that I had lived in Africa for some time, without being ostentatious and saying, "Here are my credentials, so accept me." I'd maybe pull out my slides from Ghana—I have very beautiful slides—which they all got interested in and they'd fire questions at me, very interesting questions about my relationships with Africans, about the wild animals, all sorts of things. As I was able to field these questions, it began to break down some of the hostility. Usually by the third class session, that kind of antagonism had disappeared. I never encountered it after the first week in any class I taught, because they got to know me as an individual and that I knew my field very well.

Allan Kellock walked into his classroom at I.S. 271, Ocean Hill–Brownsville, the day most of New York's sixty thousand teachers and supervisors began the longest, bitterest school strike in the city's history—September 9 to November 17, 1968. The bedrock issue was a redistribution of political and administrative power which would enable community populations to control the schools in their districts.

In the year preceding, the Board of Education had made tenuous but irrevocable gestures toward meeting the demand of black communities for control of their schools. Three demonstration districts were constituted: Ocean Hill-Brownsville in Brooklyn, the I.S. 201 complex in Harlem, and Three Bridges, largely Puerto Rican, on the Lower East Side. These were conceived by the board as pilot models, not of community control but of "decentralization," based on locally elected governing boards. To the three communities involved this was not an experiment, to be "scrubbed" on the basis of anyone's evaluation save their own. Having touched power, they grasped it, and undertook at once to use it, extend it and to make it permanent in the interest of the kind of education they hoped to develop for their children

It is doubtful that the Board of Education, from the very beginning, had any deep intention of allowing the undertaking to succeed. It is certain that the leadership and the membership majority of the United Federation of Teachers felt threatened by the prospect of having to deal with community-controlled school boards of even limited authority. Win or lose a few points, they felt much more secure and comfortable with the centralized bureaucracy of the Board of Education, which, in turn, felt more comfortable with the union bureaucracy. Moreover, the UFT already had a $10 million stake in the making of educational policy. A clause in its 1967 labor contract gave it the unprecedented power to direct the expenditure of that *amount on developing education programs, primarily the More Effective Schools program. In essence, it was a strike to keep substantial power out of the hands of community (especially black and Puerto Rican) populations.*

Not everybody stayed out. Thousands of UFT members taught school throughout or during some portion of the strike. For the schools of the three demonstration districts hundreds of new teachers had to be hired. Kellock was one of them.

The conditions for teaching during the strike were idyllic. I think we accomplished more during the strike than any time since. One of the reasons being that the atmosphere created a kind of solidarity between the staff and the student body, and between the staff and the community.

I had always planned to teach at college level. When I was at Antioch in the early sixties they had a program to encourage everyone to spend a year abroad. Most people take off for Italy, France or Germany. I wasn't so keen on going with the mob. An opportunity came up to go to the University of Ghana, so I spent my junior year there. I guess one of the reasons is that I was involved with the civil rights movement. I went through the transition from N.A.A.C.P. to CORE to SNCC in the days when whites did those sorts of things, and the appeal of going to Africa was directly related to that. You know, a curiosity about the origins of black people, and so forth.

I grew up in a Long Island suburb. My father's a publishing executive, also an Antioch graduate; my mother too. Very insulated from black people. Only when I got to Antioch and worked on things like voter registration in Dayton did that really change. I never went South. After I got back from Africa I kind of dropped out of the movement. I was conscious of the African nationalist patterns and I began to project them onto the situation in the

United States. I just felt that it wasn't particularly my struggle. I didn't articulate it this way because at the time I didn't realize what was making me uneasy. By about '66 people like Stokeley Carmichael began to provide the intellectual justification for what I was feeling.

In Ghana and at the American University in Egypt I got very much interested in the African Studies boom that was just taking off then. When I finished at Antioch, I went to the University of Wisconsin. I got my masters' and I'm finishing my doctorate now in African history. About a year ago I felt I was stagnating in graduate school. I'd been in one university or another for eight straight years and I just got a little fed up. I wanted to get out of it for a while.

I'd been reading about the introduction of African studies in the public schools and I knew that there were damn few people around who were really knowledgeable about Africa. Those few were being grabbed up by the universities. And I was kind of intrigued by what I suspected was going to be a political struggle in school systems in urban areas. It began to appear that it was going to get explosive in the next couple of years.

I chose New York mainly because I wanted to be back here. I really wanted to teach black history in a white school, but as I made the rounds I became aware of the fact that administrators were giving lip service to teaching black history. They really weren't moving on it, or if they were, they were anxious to emasculate the contents. So in desperation I came over here to McCoy's* office last July. I was very hesitant. I didn't feel there was much of a role for me in this school, but they were anxious to have me. I wasn't so uptight about teaching black kids per se. I felt I could do that, but I was uptight about teaching black history in a black school, more for reasons of community rela-

* Rhody McCoy, then Unit Administrator of the Ocean Hill-Brownsville Demonstration District.

tionships than for the kids, though I wasn't sure how they'd react to me teaching that subject.

I should explain the structure of the Afro-American history program. Sixth grade is Africa, about up to the slave trade. Seventh grade does the slave trade and Afro-American history up to about the Booker T. Washington–Du Bois split.* The eighth grade is supposed to concentrate entirely on the twentieth century, relating back to the nationalist movements in Africa in a comparative sense and zeroing in especially on Malcolm X. I concentrated more on Africa.

One of the things I did the first week was to go around the room and have everybody give me the image that came into his mind when somebody mentioned Africa. Some of the kids came into classes with ideas about Africa that made the Klan look liberal. We put them on the blackboard—the myths and lies. Like Africans wear no clothes. They're all savages, cannibals. They live in trees and whatnot. Pretty much a straight Tarzan image that they'd gotten from TV. We kept lists in each class, and after a couple of months I'd drag out the list and say, "Look at what you told me in September." They were very shocked that they could have said those sorts of things.

As the year went on, they actually went to the other extreme and began to look for things that were very nationalistic in interpretation of Africa and the past. I tried to minimize exaggeration but I didn't discourage it. I felt, for instance, that to say ancient Carthage was an all-black empire—which was what some of my colleagues were teaching—was going too far. I would gently try to work in a slightly more balanced point of view, but I was never very insistent on pure objectivity. I didn't see that it was essen-

* Definitely enunciated in the essay "Of Mr. Booker T. Washington and Other Things," in W.E.B. Du Bois' *The Souls of Black Folk*. Originally published in 1903 by A. C. McClurg but now available under several imprints.

tial at this point. When we tell the truth about George Washington and Abraham Lincoln, then I'll worry about an accurate interpretation of Kankan Musa* or somebody like that.

Another thing I tried to get across to my classes early on was that because I was white I obviously couldn't express to them pride in Africa the way some of the black teachers could. But I could at least show them that I admired Africa a great deal and through my admiration they could get pride. At first I tended to overestimate the handicap I was working under. Little things like pronouns—saying "they" instead of "you" or "we"—can make a difference in your presentation. On the other hand, black history for kids that are twelve, thirteen years old is a process of such basic debunking of standard stereotypes that anybody who knows the field and has the right sympathies can get across what has to be gotten across. With older kids, particularly at the college level, you're going to get into problems that make the arguments for black teachers in black studies more compelling. When you have a seminar, like at Antioch, and you're dealing with black men's hang-ups about white women, you can't have a white man running the seminar. You're just not going to get anywhere. But with kids twelve and thirteen you're not going to deal with those kinds of problems.

I found more difficulty dealing with black history in America because there were cultural mechanisms that the kids were bringing into class—defensive mechanisms about slavery and whatnot—which were not true for Africa. They could easily say "they" for Africa, but they could no longer do that when it came to Afro-Americans. Kids would go along with the glory of ancient Mali or Ghana and identify

* Mansa (Sultan) Kankan Musa ruled the empire of Mali in the medieval Sudan from 1307 to 1332. By the measures of size and wealth, it was one of the greatest states in the world of its time.

with that. Then they'd feel the dehumanization of the Middle Passage* across the Atlantic. But very often when we'd get to some of the iniquitous parts of slavery, they'd suddenly shift, as if they were talking about somebody else. The main mechanism was a feigned lapse of memory. There's a great deal of knowledge about slavery and about the last two hundred years communicated in their families, which they bring in with them. But there's some sort of process suppressing it. Perhaps it's an unwillingness to talk about it too openly with a white teacher.

When we got to the slave revolts, they were very turned on by Nat Turner and the others, but I also found some surprising questions. Some kids questioned why it was, if there were so many courageous people during slavery, they weren't freed sooner; and when they were freed, while it wasn't the magic wand of Abe Lincoln, it was not entirely due to forces coming out of the black community. They had a little difficulty following some of the nationalist interpretations of that period which they had heard outside of the classroom.

There's a shortage of books on Africa, so I did a lot of my own stuff. I have kind of a prejudice against textbooks because it's so easy to slip into just rote learning. So, for instance, I typed up a couple of pages with a hypothetical situation of how the slave trade began in a certain kingdom in West Africa. The basic concept here was that African kings got involved in the slave trade against their will, that it was sort of like the junkie syndrome—I used that analogy—that forces beyond your control compel you to continue to escalate. But I wrote this in such a way that the kids had to figure out this concept. It wasn't stated. I

*Slave-trading ships sailed a three-legged course: outward bound, for West-Coast Africa, to barter manufactured goods for captive Africans; a Middle Passage from Africa to the West Indies, to sell the slaves and buy sugar, cocoa, coffee, etc.; a homeward passage, to sell the West Indies produce; and to start all over again, having turned a handsome profit on each leg of the voyage.

suppose that's the problem-solving technique with the inquiry method.

I got some of my ideas from Malcolm Cowley's book on the slave trade* and also from Basil Davidson's *Black Mother*,† which was useful in showing the way African rulers were caught up in this vicious circle. Often you had the paradox of a chief being very opposed to the slave trade but having to engage in it for survival. I handled the difference between slavery in Africa and in the United States by saying that it was inappropriate to call the African situation slavery. We defined slavery in terms of the American experience because that's what everyone really means when they say "slavery." But I pointed out that we needed other words and concepts to explain the African situation. We called it serfdom or something like that. Incidentally, a lot of students thought Africa was just a continent full of slaves before the Europeans got there and that's why they went there—because they heard there were all these slaves that they could just pick up and carry over here.

We were short on materials much of the year, but now we've probably got the best Afro-American history department in the city, equipment-wise. There are, I guess, about a dozen new book titles on Afro-American history in stock now, but there's almost a nonexistence of suitable materials which try to integrate Afro-American history and the mainstream of American history. Not so much that one should integrate these for melting-pot ideological reasons, but that much of Afro-American history only makes sense in terms of a larger context.

I'm not sure that this is an important point at this age level; we are mainly concerned with overcompensating and

* Daniel P. Mannix and Malcolm Cowley, *Black Cargoes: A History of the Atlantic Slave Trade* (New York: Viking, 1962).
† Basil Davidson, *Black Mother: The Years of the African Slave Trade* (Boston: Little, Brown, 1961).

anybody who says differently is lying. But we're going to approach a time pretty quickly when this concentration on Afro-American history is going to produce a whole new series of questions. In terms of how we're going to interpret, let's say, the Civil War or Abraham Lincoln. Clearly he was a kind of racist, even though he was privately antislavery, and he was anything but benevolent in his Emancipation Proclamation. These new Afro-American studies are bound to have an impact on the glorification of "white" American history.

This is supposed to be an experimental school district. How experimental has it been?

The grade school is doing innovative things with reading programs and whatnot. But here there's no pretense of innovation, though there's lip service paid to it. I don't want to speak for the black militants—they should answer for themselves—but I have the feeling they define innovation in terms of survival in the liberation struggle, in very political terms. My observation of their classroom approach in many cases is that they're very traditional, authoritarian teachers. Which is a conflict we have in this school because many of the white teachers are anti-Establishment, New Left-oriented. They're very anti-authoritarian and they project this in the classroom. I was guilty of this at first but I changed because I don't think it's appropriate. I'm not really much impressed with innovative approaches to urban black schools, at least the "do-your-own-thing" type.

I'm not basically an educator so I'm not schooled in these sorts of ideas. My own approach is that in addition to the need for new content, which is so obvious in my field, I just try to come up with ways to disseminate a lot of new information, but ways that will help the kids learn how to think. That's basically the approach I stuck to all year. I used the device of myth versus truth, and why these myths developed, as my main theme. This was perfect because I had so much unlearning to do. I mean, I had to divest the kids of so many of their own false ideas and derogatory self-images.

You know, when the kids fought each other it was always accompanied by fierce anti-Black epithets. I broke up the fights but I never disciplined the kids for fighting. Instead I always made a lesson of it, tried to show how, historically, the white man has put his foot on the neck of the black man by divide-and-conquer. And that this was true in Africa, America and in Ocean Hill–Brownsville with the school crisis. This business of stopping the fight, sitting them down and showing them how through their lack of understanding of their own history they're perpetuating their enslavement—I never had such a hushed audience as when I was going through that little act. It was one of the few times that I've really felt we were in some kind of soul session. The girls would say, "Tell it, brother!"

A lot of these kids, though definitely a minority of them, have been strongly influenced by black nationalism. They throw around a lot of rhetoric, although they don't always have a very good understanding of it. One time a kid rapped for ten minutes about Malcolm X and Marcus Garvey. It was kind of fuzzy. Five minutes later, he got into a quarrel with one of his friends and he said, "You god-damn black bastard" and punched him. So I immediately grabbed him and pulled him up front.

"Do you see this fool?" I said. "He stands there for ten minutes telling us that black is beautiful but the minute he gets angry, what does he say?" They all said, "Yeah, how about that," and went into a discussion of why, when he was angry, he was saying that black was ugly, and when he was cool and collected, he was saying black was beautiful. It didn't really get to a group-therapy thing in the sense that this was true of almost all of them, but they got the point. They realized that it's one thing to express this rhetoric and another to really feel it.

The kid was very embarrassed. He was quite defensive about it at first. He tried to explain it in terms of the negative features of the person he attacked, but the kids were great in pushing him back to look at himself.

One of the most satisfying things this year: I took one day each week for current black events. We got into some fascinating stuff. We had debates, films. Guests came in to talk—anything related to current black developments. One day we had a debate about whether black men should serve in the U.S. Army or should be exempt. A lot of the kids had never thought it out before. Much of their thinking was done out loud in class, which was good because there were no set positions and they were all able to exchange ideas. At the beginning, most were—well, I guess they'd never really thought about any alternative. They felt it was their duty, like everyone else's. Finally they arrived at a position that was almost unanimous: that they should not be subjected to the draft and fight in Vietnam. The only kids that ended up staunchly for black participation in the Army and fighting in Vietnam were very devout religious kids who tended to invoke God as an answer to the rational and militant arguments.

Just after this, the Fort Jackson case broke, down in South Carolina. Three black GIs, Andrew Pulley, Albert Madison and Lawrence Hart, were put in the stockade for petty offenses; it was harassment. I gave a lecture-type presentation of what happened, and the kids, on their initiative, wrote sixty or seventy letters to the three GIs. I stressed that if they wanted to write letters they were to work into them their ideas from the debate . . .

One of the letters, to Lawrence Hart, in excerpted form: "they say our school is the baddest thing around but our school is together . . . our school was alright untill the union teachers came back. We have a new major subject Afro-American-History, and today we studied about the G.I.'s in Fort Jackson. And I feel that you are doing what you think is right . . . And whenever you get out I wish you would visit my school. Yours truly, R.W./P.S. Let Whitey fight his own gotdamn war."

They also sent about forty letters to the base commander. Their letters were released by GIs United Against the War and were published in *The Young Socialist*.

Did the kids or you ever hear from the men who got the letters?

Oh, did we! The men claimed that it was the best thing that had happened to them. They just wept, that kids this age would write and show that kind of political consciousness. Joe Miles, who started GIs United, came here in April and spoke to the kids in the assembly. Then two or three weeks ago Andrew Pulley, right after he got out of the stockade, came all the way up here. He was just practically in tears thanking the kids for this moral support. So it became quite a project for the five classes that I had. It was written up in the *Times* even. The kids had a great time with that; it became a weekly thing to summarize the latest developments at Fort Jackson. When nine more soldiers got busted *they* came in and told *me* about it. They had the *Times* clippings on it. They had apparently alerted relatives who read the *Times* to watch for stuff about Fort Jackson. And if there was any TV news they made notes of it. I thought this was very healthy.

Do any of your students do any independent reading, history, biography, so forth?

I didn't stress reading all that much. It wasn't something which I prodded them to do but I've had many kids doing a lot of it. Running down to the library and getting books on Harriet Tubman, and all the standard biographies, and a few other things besides. Evidently things came up that they wanted to know more about, particularly individuals.

Usually there are three, four, five youngsters in every class that I develop a relationship with. I'm pretty close with Matthew. He's a kid who thinks, asks questions. In my sixth-grade class particularly, there are so many like him, so many dynamic individuals, that I've developed a tendency to deal with them intensively and kind of ignore some of the girls who are on the periphery. I went too much in one direction and I've been aware of it for a while now, but you can't carry thirty kids. If you can carry twenty-five, you're doing a hell of a good job.

My eighth-grade homeroom class, that I had all year long, we did a lot of things together outside of school. They were over at the house for dinner and parties and stuff like that. I took them on trips to places like Coney Island. We didn't make any pretense of educational objectives, just went to have fun. In fact, some of the kids have my phone number and call me at home when they're in my neighborhood. I'll probably see quite a few of them this summer.

The parents, the majority of them, were very traditional, had conventional expectations and attitudes about education. I never met a parent who was not interested in what was going on here and what his kid was involved in, contrary to what one hears from union spokesmen. In the fall [1968], when I first came in, we had a lot of meetings at night which were well attended by parents. Whenever the subject of the new teachers* was brought up we had standing ovations. It was quite moving but very undeserved. So there was a reservoir of good will to tap that probably wasn't there normally. I can remember incidents of people coming up to me and other teachers on the street during the strike and thanking us for coming in to teach their children.

But on the question: Do the parents have much feel-

* Replacements for UFT members who went on strike.

ing about having all black teachers in the school? On the surface I would say I don't see much evidence for that. But I suspect that deep down great numbers of the parents really would like to see all black teachers in their schools, though they won't admit it to the whites here.

I don't recall ever having discussions with parents where I felt that we were really communicating without façades and formalities . . . I can tell that they're keeping quite a bit in reserve and they're treating me out of respect for my position, rather than my personality, or my individuality.

Most of the contact with parents was initiated by me. I used it as an arm of classroom control, particularly for my own official [homeroom] class. The official teacher is a kind of disciplinary intermediary between the kids and the administration. If one of my kids is causing a lot of problems in other classes, I go to the parent.

Have you had any pressing discipline problems?

In my sixth-grade class I've had some restlessness for the last two or three weeks, but on the whole, as long as you keep the class really interested, keep their minds occupied, the rewards are handsome. They give a lot of trouble to some teachers simply because they bore them to death. But I've had some fairly serious incidents. Like a kid with a gun. I was standing in front of the room and he was waving a pistol at me . . .

In February I had picked up a class that was a combination of all the most disruptive kids with the worst reading scores in the eighth grade. We called it the super-hostiles. I had them for Afro-American history, but the first three or four weeks I accomplished absolutely nothing with them. During that time I had the gun incident, got stabbed in the leg with a hatpin, and from the word go, I got verbal abuse like I never heard. I remember one time a girl was in there with a transistor radio. I asked her several times to turn it off and I finally had to grab one of the paraprofessionals and he got her to turn it off. As soon as he left, she turned it back on and called me "You dirty white Jew." I was so taken aback that my response was "You're only two-thirds correct. I'm not Jewish but a lot of people think I am." The response wasn't effective for some reason, but this was a turning point.

The gun incident was earlier, the first week I had this class. I think he had the gun as a conversation piece. It was the beginning of the period. As I got ready to start the class, I noticed there was a lot of noise and kids were clustered around him. There were notches on the gun and they were discussing it, who killed who and that sort of thing. He was sitting at the first desk and he had the gun between his legs and he was waving it at me with this grin on his face. I know I telegraphed fear initially, I was so shocked. I couldn't maintain my cool and I just reacted. It was, you know, five seconds too much hesitation before I collected myself and walked over to him. Then I said very calmly and unauthoritatively, "Please put the gun away." I didn't say "Give it to me" or anything. I just walked away because I wanted to give him the chance to do something without badgering him. But he knew he had me and he was playing with me. He kept the gun out, so I went over a second time and I talked a little bit more about how he was disrupting the class and he didn't really need it in class— something very innocent like that. Then he put it in his desk. But I was very aware of it, there in that desk, and I wasn't about to provoke anyone. I didn't know the class and I just had no confidence how they would line up, so I was most anxious to bury the whole incident until I had built up a few more credits with that group.

As soon as the class was over I went down to the dean's office. I said, "Hey, there's a kid in my class, first period, with a pistol. He was waving it at me and I thought you'd like to know about it. He's in such and such a room now."

And he said, "Well, didn't you take it away from him?" I said, "No, I didn't," and he said, "Why not? What the hell's the matter with you?" He was enjoying a sadistic moment and I just got pissed. I walked out. From then on I handled discipline problems myself. I've never gone to a dean again, and I've never referred a kid to anyone else.

Then the next week there was a kid, a Puerto Rican named Rolando, sitting in the back of the room. Rolando is one of those kids that I guess every urban school has. He's completely a man on his own. He walks in and out of the building, does whatever he wants and no one bothers him. I quickly realized this and kind of treated him differently, but he used to come in and play cards in the back of the classroom. This was a challenge that I couldn't ignore because of course you need other people to play cards, and that would compete with what I was trying to do.

So I went back and said, "Please put the cards away." This kid was fearless. He'd say anything to anybody. He looked up and said, "You want me to deal you in?" He kept on playing and got even more disruptive. So I was just cruising around his desk formulating my strategy. He had a hatpin in his hand and he jabbed me right in the calf as I went by. It was near the end of the period, so I decided I was going to deal with him by himself. I wasn't going to bother in front of the class because he was too good at manipulating opinions. So I said, "I'm going to see you when the bell rings."

The bell rang shortly after that and the class piled out. Sure enough, he sat there. He wasn't going to be intimidated. So I said, "Let's go somewhere where we can talk." I took him down to one of the faculty rooms. I said, "I know why you stabbed me."

"Why?"

"You didn't do it to hurt me. You just wanted to get my attention."

He said, "Of course I didn't want to hurt you. Otherwise I would have stabbed you in the eye."

We stayed there for an hour, talking. I asked him what he wanted to do. He's fourteen now, and he's illiterate, really illiterate. I said, "What do you want to do when you get out of school?"

"You mean when I'm sixteen?"

"Yeah, when you're sixteen."

"I'm going to get married so then I can leave my wife and collect the welfare checks."

He had plans, what he was going to do with the money. He was going to save a little and then he was going to go into business with his brother, in electronics. He had it all worked out. And he appreciated that hour that I spent time just talking to him. He asked for a cigarette and I let him smoke in there.

From that point on he never gave me any trouble because I guess he decided I was interested in him. When he came to class, he tried to develop an interest in Africa, in where things were. He was fascinated about geography. At the end of the marking period we had an exam. This class [the "super-hostiles"] was quite serious about the exam, even though they didn't give a shit about the work. They were mark-conscious, which surprised me. Rolando, above all, was concerned about the exam.

I gave him his copy and he came up very sheepishly and said, "I can't read it."

I said, "What do you mean, you can't read it?" I had tried to give the easiest exam I could to give them some incentive. I said, "Read this sentence." He could get "the" and "and" and that was about it. It was just incredible. I've never seen a kid like that in eighth grade, any grade.

He said, "Read the question for me." So I read him the first question; it was multiple choice. He immediately answered correctly. "You know," he said, "if you can read me all the questions, I'll answer them and then you can mark me."

I said, "No, I can't do that." I was thinking very conventionally. I had twenty-nine other kids waiting for me.

"Please," he said. "I've got to do this. I've got to see how good I can do."

I sent him down to the library and had the librarian give him the test orally. He got the highest mark in the class—ninety-six or ninety-seven. He only missed one thing. He's very bright but he just can't relate to the printed word. What do you do with a kid like this? There's no structure I know of anywhere in the city that can save this kid.

I think I could teach him to read if I had an hour alone with him every day for a few months. He's receptive to just about anything I try to do. I've helped him break down his resistance to learning. He's brooding over the fact that here he goes into the ninth grade and he can't read—how's he going to learn anything now? He's begun to see already his own tragic waste—which is unusual at that age.

For a while he was coming to school just to come to my course—just never went to any other classes. I was kind of gratified in the ego sense, but I was also torn professionally because I should have gotten him to stay for everyone else. But the "super-hostiles" just happened to have very weak teachers, which was another reason that it was difficult to deal with them. Here was a class deliberately composed of malfunctioning kids, misfits, and they were given twenty-two- and twenty-three-year-old teachers—all white—who really don't know what they're about themselves. The kids got extremely cynical about school because of this.

After I lost this class because of a scheduling change, Rolando would come to see me once in a while, but he just stopped attending school. I saw him yesterday. He stopped by to find out if he graduated. He didn't even come to graduation. He stopped in yesterday only to pick up an award, for being a monitor, which, you know, gives the big kids a chance to work out their aggression on the little ones.

But to get back to the class. After about a month had passed and I hadn't blown my cool in the sense that I didn't shout and scream and stomp, I was beginning to make some kind of a dent. I was getting a nucleus of eight to ten involved, and there were about twenty-five altogether. Anyway, one day I came in and a group was sitting here, some of them at my desk. They were involved in a very heated argument about whether there was a God or not, and how do you explain creation and that sort of thing. So I thought, Great, I can co-opt this and make a lesson out of it, which is something I did a lot of this year. I intervened just enough to get them to talk one at a time. It worked for about two minutes. The feelings were so intense that pretty soon they were all shouting at each other again.

The object of attack was a kid who'd been going to some of the Muslims' religious-education, political-education classes. He was arguing against the diehard, very emotional Christians—not too effectively because he was so much on the defensive that he was shouting and antagonizing people. So I sat here and the kids were all waiting to see what I was going to do. I took a real deep breath and said, "Explain the difference between a black man and a nigger." The kid jumped out of his seat—I'm here and he's right there. He's about five ten and he's all set to go. My immediate reaction was that I was ready for him. I wasn't scared because I can take care of myself.

But the fascinating thing was that the guy who pulled the gun on me, and Rolando and a third kid, big and tough and expert in karate—the three of them immediately swarmed up and intervened. They took this kid and pushed him back a step or two. The kid who had pulled the gun on me said to him, "You don't understand what he means. By getting angry you're only showing your disrespect for yourself," which is one use of the term "nigger" among blacks.

It was all I could do to contain my elation with this kind of a thought coming from this kid who I thought was going to gun me down a week or two before. They tried to explain to him what they thought I was thinking. They could see what I meant. But the Muslim kid, to save face, continued to be belligerent. So when they finished I said, "Now, look, do you still think I called you a nigger? Okay, let's go settle it outside." So I asked the class to stay until we came back and we walked up and down the hall. I explained to him that I didn't say he was a nigger, but that I did mean that he had been acting like one at that moment. And that given his Muslim associations I would have expected him to act with more dignity; but in spite of that, he was acting more like a nigger than anyone in the class at that moment.

All of a sudden, it dawned on him what I was talking about. He looked up at me and said, "Oh, yeah. I see. Thanks a lot, Mr. Kellock." And from that time on for the rest of the year that kid—he'd ask me questions, we'd come in here, in the classroom, and talk. It was beautiful.

I was so amazed that those three kids came to my defense. The karate guy told me later that he didn't think I was going to be any different from some of the other white teachers whom they constantly harassed, but then he thought he'd give me a second chance because I'd had the guts to say "nigger" in front of them all.

This is the end of the school year. What about next year?

I'm leaving Friday. I've felt like I had quite a bit of success. Even though I'm white I think a lot of kids benefited from learning black history from me. I've been asked back, but I have a unique opportunity to work in white communities where I can have a broader impact. This spring I did a fifteen-week in-service-training teachers' course in Garden City [New York] on black history and culture. It progressed from a purely academic interest in black people on the part of the teachers to the problems today and finally to the problems of "us," "we" and "I," in terms of racial hang-ups. I was so encouraged that we could make that much progress in fifteen weeks that I decided I ought to do as much of that as I can next year.

This summer I'm teaching at Columbia at a summer institute of Afro-American history. We're bringing in forty-five teachers and thirty administrators for four weeks of intensive lectures and seminars. I'll be handling African history and methodological problems of teaching it. Next year I'm going to teach at St. John's University because it's only five hours a week on campus, two or three lectures and a seminar. That gives me more time to devote to in-service courses.

I sent out a hundred letters proposing in-service courses to schools in the metropolitan area, telling of my teaching experience here and my background in African history. I got back fifty to sixty responses. A lot of superintendents asked me to teach in their school system, but I got quite a number of letters from high-income predominantly white communities on Long Island—and from schools in New Jersey and Westchester—expressing interest in setting up in-service courses. What I hope to do is teach an in-service course a day.

My approach is to explain to the administrators that we're going to study black history and culture as a way of understanding white racism. Particularly the white racism of each individual in the course. I don't say this in advance to the teachers themselves because I don't want to encourage all sorts of defense mechanisms any earlier than necessary.

By next June I hope to have worked with about a thousand teachers, which is, you know, a small dent, but it's more than I'm doing here.

8

THE
LONG-DISTANCE
RUNNERS

There must be a complete overhaul of those false educational values based on a frantic race for grades, with super-specialized, speed-up training for a dehumanized elite, and a dead end for the vast majority of our children . . . We teachers can play a small but significant part. Above all, we must ourselves believe in this, and teach our children of all races and colors to respect each other, to live together, learn together, play together, and thereby enrich each other's lives . . . But this world of tomorrow demands first of all that there be a world of tomorrow.

—Rose Russell

BELLE SCHECKNER
Bronx

Belle Scheckner's fourth-grade class is the oldest-established permanent project of its kind at P.S. 53 in the Morrisania section of the Bronx. She's a teacher who needs freedom to teach. She's had it longer than most; she just never waited for a benign administration to "free" her. She has kept it because big-city schools have been increasingly under pressure to show and tell that such freedom exists within their walls. Her long-exercised humanistic bent has strong, positive benefits for her classes. In the rest of the school, the force of her example is inevitably limited by bureaucratic formalism and an average rate of teacher indifference. Yet her energy and zest remain undiminished after twenty-four classroom years, seventeen of them in her present school, including eight as the school's UFT shop chairwoman.

"Listen, if we love, we get energy." The statement has to be true. I've been watching it happen all day. Now I'm listening to her own critique of her day's work as we drive through heavy late-afternoon traffic to her mid-Manhattan apartment.

For her husband, Charles, it's been an equally strenuous teaching day at Benjamin Franklin High School, but he's interested . . .

As I said in the car, I don't believe in teaching reading as such. Reading is a sort of last step. First, people have to have ideas, have to be able to articulate them in their head. Then when they see the written word, they'll be able to have some relationship to it.

In my experience, most of the children who haven't been able to read were looking at English words as though they were part of a foreign language. They had, at best,

389

only a very limited popular vocabulary. So I had to begin by trying to introduce concepts, ideas that you find in universal literature, in current events, which were completely outside of their thinking process. I teach fourth grade, but—Charles, what would you say about the high school grades?

CHARLES SCHECKNER: At what age the children should begin reading, and what the techniques may be to introduce them to reading, is an open question. They *have* to learn to read because our society requires it, but beyond that our kids deserve to know what the world is really like. They need the bank of ideas. They need to satisfy their natural curiosity. Reading brings our kids so many facets that are satisfying in themselves: the pleasure of reading; the fact that the world is not Lenox Avenue, the world is not a shabby street. Without this knowledge of reading the kids cannot translate what may be very fertile ideas of their own. Nor can they discuss the very things that concern them, poverty, aspirations, social change, etc.

You said technique is an open question. Doesn't the choice of technique have some importance in teaching kids to read?

BELLE SCHECKNER: Teachers and educators are much too concerned with techniques and gimmicks. When they come to their conferences, they evaluate a technique, find it doesn't work and introduce a new one. People are given grants because they've discovered new techniques instead of discussing the essence, the content, of what they're presenting to people to read. In our classes I'm concerned with people who don't have the experience of the language as we present it to them in school and in the literature. When they're confronted with learning as drudgery, learning how to read, either with phonics or word drills, they become more disturbed with it each day and completely, in many instances, reject the *idea* of reading.

So what do you do? And how do you do it?

I think you saw from our experience today, we do a great deal of discussion in which there is a reading experience. We've received letters from children in England or Ireland. I read the letter and gave each one a copy, and then they felt they wanted to read it for themselves. People who weren't able to read, having this personal thing in their hands, a letter from other children, it made them feel they were *almost* able to read it. The next step: I would say, "What will you answer them?" And the class would say, "Oh, we'll tell them about things in New York City, the schools, the games we play, things we enjoy doing." For them to write this letter, I had to rexograph a list of words, and they could draw on this list to help them say what they wanted to. Another time they wanted to write letters to Mrs. Martin Luther King. Well, *this* was a reading experience. They read their letters out loud. Our class newspaper is a reading experience, too. I'm talking about kids who've reached the age of ten, who had great difficulty with reading. They find it very distressing. They've been *told* they can't read. So the idea is to build up experiences as a basis—an interest which will outweigh their distress and their lack of self-confidence . . .

CHARLES SCHECKNER: There is something fundamentally wrong, even primitive, that a child born in the United States comes to high school, his *ninth* year, and cannot read three sentences. What good is talking about a free society when children who are the most deprived, who most need an education—

He's hacking at the surface of the table with the broad edge of his palm in angry, rhythmic accompaniment. I interrupt: "Wait. Your karate chop is making my microphone bounce . . ."

Karate chop? Oh . . . These students know they cannot read and all sorts of defensive attitudes, emotional disturbances, feelings of inferiority come up. The child realizes he's a failure. He's a *failure!* There's no mystery involved. If our society *wants* to cure this problem they can do it. It requires concentration. It also requires a dispersion of our facilities, human and material. It will not be done if you simply draft an English teacher and say, "Here you have a reading class. Go and teach them reading." Under our present education system, this cannot be done. We can live together in school only if the teacher himself is so understanding of the human problem, as well as the educational problem, that he learns how to make children feel that coming to school is worthwhile.

BELLE SCHECKNER: There's such hypocrisy about the whole idea of reading . . . People are put into cages based upon their reading levels, and the children know what's happening to them. It all is related to the question of what is the purpose of education in the elementary schools, or the high schools? There never is a consistent approach to what *should* be, what *is* the philosophy of education. Why do we have the children going to school? What do we want to teach these children? I think this is basic, before we can do anything else.

What do you want to teach them?

Two things: one is, to know who they are, what factors in this society are making them what they are, and what they can do about changing these factors; two, they can make for a much better life than they're having at the present time, that the whole heritage of world culture can become theirs, that they can make it serve their needs.

CHARLES SCHECKNER: It's no good saying, as many do, that reading is a middle-class prerogative, in the sense that one doesn't have to read because the audio-visual media, television, the movie screen, have preeminence. I don't believe that for a moment. You ask our children, "Why did

Frederick Douglass learn to read, even though being caught at it meant a flogging?" . . .

I think Belle is correct. The purpose of education is to *change*, to change one's life for the better. And who deserves the change more than those who want it the most? I think ghetto children are perfectly capable of understanding that reading means something beyond X more dollars in their pockets. I am saying that we want to learn to read not just as a verbal rose in our lapels but simply to make progress for the human race. And who can say no? . . . We are confronted more and more by the children in the ghettos, the *millions* of them, who need reading to fortify and develop the inspiration and aspiration toward change.

How do you judge whether your kids are progressing?

BELLE SCHECKNER: Well, I'm glad you're not my supervisor, because if you mean achievement levels and so forth, above or below grade, I don't know and I don't care. I try to evaluate their growth as human beings, how much the concepts we discuss, the books we read, the social situations we've experienced in the classroom—how these have really seeped into their lives, not only in school but outside, too. What do I do when I see a child isn't progressing? One thing I *don't* often do is call the parents in. In the main, the kids with the greatest problems are those whose parents have great problems. Not that such parents are indifferent, but they're already fighting on too many fronts, so to speak. Just the same, I do meet every one of their mothers. It's important for me to know what kind of people they are and I like them to get to know me. I go to people's homes. Some people don't want me to visit them, so I don't. If they do, I visit. I've attended social gatherings arranged in the neighborhood so that parents and I could get to know each other. That takes some preparation.

Let's face it. Life is difficult for many of the children's

families. John (that's not his name) is a very difficult child in terms of his relationship to other children. I was eager to know his mother, and as soon as I met her I began to realize something of his problem. She came to school drunk. Her husband is a complete invalid. So, this little boy needs a great deal of attention. I try to spend free time with him, or lunch hours . . . There are thirty-five individuals in this particular class. Many of the parents are faced with severe problems of overcrowded housing and unemployment.

I should add that in class I work with one group at a time, in math for example, because they're on different levels. But before we divide up in these groups, we discuss, and they really understand that people have developed at different rates, based on their experience, other factors. We have discussions on psychology in class from time to time, because I think the secrets of psychology shouldn't remain a secret of the ed. courses; that the children ought to understand them because they're the ones who are living with each other. They're very relieved to find that other children have problems similar to their own, and that together they can be more understanding of each other.

So many situations occur during the day that become lessons. We had a whole big thing early today on a young person who came from another class and interrupted wildly. So we discussed how people are disconcerted and what happens to a group and its members in such a situation—you know, group dynamics. And, you know, we have about two hundred and fifty words in our vocabulary list that come from real-life situations in our classroom and from the children's personal experiences.

Learning in Belle Scheckner's room is not an entirely unconfined, constantly fished-in stream of collective consciousness. She structures her day as a compromise between

*Board of Education curriculum dicta and her own profes-
sional ideas of what life in a classroom ought to be.*

I present the program in the morning. I never say,
"What do you want to do first today?" But I do feel it's
important to explain my reasoning to them. There are
certain basic subjects we're supposed to cover: math, reading, science, language arts. So there's a block of work that I
present to them, but we try to relate all the subjects to each
other. Part of it is creative writing. At the beginning of the
year I did suggest some things they could write about
because it was a new experience to them. To encourage
them I rexograph their material for them to take home and
to present to other classes, too. And something they seem
to enjoy very much at this point is a multivolume encyclopedia we have in the room. Each child chooses a volume.
Maybe the M's look good to a particular child on a given
day. But we've talked about so many things in class that
most of the children can usually find some name or subject
or idea that will attract them. I don't think anybody who
opens an encyclopedia, if he doesn't feel pressed to come
up with an answer to something right away, can keep from
browsing in it page after page.

Now, if it's a group thing, they will get up and suggest
we should have dancing, or we should listen to some
records that somebody likes.

Dancing is big in Room 409.

A good teacher is interested in art, in music, in literature, in people, in politics, in life . . . I paint . . . I
never studied dancing but I've always danced, all my life.
I've taught them. I make these steps up, you know, ballet
style, folk style. At the beginning of the term they were
ashamed to get up. It takes a lot of freedom to do this kind
of thing; the boys would laugh . . . But now many of

them get up and dance. We usually end with rock-'n'-roll; the kids bring their own records.

The ballet records—there's a lot of Tchaikovsky—are Mrs. Scheckner's.

Very often I take my boots off and dance with the kids barefoot; I'm more comfortable that way. They couldn't care less. Never even stop to look at me. When some of my friends come in, teachers who feel as I do, and dance along with them, the kids don't say, "Oh-my-God, a teacher dancing!" Well. I'm a human being . . . they accept me as such. They're not awed by me, the way kids used to be awed by teachers.

What do you do about teaching math in your class?

I try to show them how mathematics is in every phase of their life. One of the first equations we study is Life equals Time. You just can't say that without understanding it and seeing its application, with very little help, in many simple forms. Like birthdays, for example. Space can be measured, too. It has to be. They sit in class and they have to allocate space. Several children sharing a table is a use of space, and the spacing of words in speaking. I try to let them grasp space as a concept and that in a very important way math is a means of understanding the relationship between time and space. I tell them they'll understand more and more about that as they continue to live, but that we can begin by an awareness of the uses of time and space.

But getting them interested in equations as a concept is a more interesting and meaningful way for them to learn arithmetic. Instead of just saying, "Two and two are four," we've done a good deal of arithmetic algebraically. Quite a number of my kids have brought in algebra books they borrowed from older brothers and sisters going to junior high, or from the library. It's not only the clarity with which you present it but the teacher's own excitement in presenting it. Teachers have to be aware constantly that they are competing with television, that the kids come to us after seeing maybe five or six hours of it at home at night. We cannot operate as of old, you know . . .

They do very well in mathematics. Not only simple arithmetical operations. They get tables, graphs, from newspapers. We've looked at bar graphs showing how many schools are integrated in different parts of the country. I'm as much concerned about teaching them concepts as I am about arithmetical operations. But I bring in ads from the local supermarkets for ham, beans, soap, and they do—what-do-you-call-them—mathematical skills (adding, subtracting) from those ads, and they love it that way. A lot of the kids go to the store for their parents, so the whole thing is real.

From the grab bag of ideas she keeps wide open in her classroom, Belle Scheckner helps her kids pull out and examine social realities as well as mathematical truths: urban problems, elementary Afro-American history, civil rights, the war in Vietnam. Mrs. Scheckner's class thinks of Martin Luther King not only as a man who wanted to see his people "free at last!" but who was "very much aroused against the war in Vietnam and against poverty . . ."

Others have questioned the deep concern in my classroom with current events, say the war in Vietnam. How relevant is the Asian situation to nine-year-olds?

Last term, Dexter's father, who was about to go into the Army, came to school to say goodbye to him and to Dexter's brother who'd been in my class the year before. (The father wasn't living with the family and wasn't allowed to visit their home.) While he was in the States, he came back when he could to see the boys. Then he was sent to Vietnam. And there was this dramatic coincidence . . .

The children had told me they wanted to debate whether the war should continue and this day they were selecting sides. Oh, so many of them wanted to be on the side to have the war end. But someone *has* to be on the other side to have a debate, and I said, "Even if you don't feel it, if you just pretend—in order to have a debate."

So just then, Dexter's father walks in, and he's limping. He'd been shipped home with a leg wound. The children remembered him. They noticed the limp, too. I explained to him and to another soldier he'd brought with him what the children were preparing to do. He said: "Oh, a debate. Let me hear it."

That's when one of the children said, "There isn't going to be any debate." I wanted to know why. This nine-year-old said, "Oh, no. We can't debate *that* because we want Dexter's father home."

What did Dexter's father say?

No words. He's not a very verbal man. He answered with his eyes. I saw the tears . . . Oh, dear . . .

CHARLES SCHECKNER
Harlem

Benjamin Franklin, Harlem's only academic high school, is crowded far beyond capacity by 4,400 students, 55 percent Puerto Rican, 45 percent black. It has been totally "non-white" for most of the quarter of a century since the end of World War II. Unlike many ghetto schools across the country, it has been relatively tranquil. The potential for sidewalk conflict between the student/community forces and the school/police authorities has never been entirely absent and the predictable tensions have been there, a quiescent malaise, but flexibility has prevailed on both sides in hassles over major issues.

During the teachers' strike of 1968, half of Franklin's faculty remained on the job. Two years later, some teachers gave active support, most displayed a careful neutrality, in a student/community campaign which won the appointment of Melvin Taylor, a Black, ex-GI, thirty-nine-year-old science teacher, as acting principal. The campaign reached its peak in a week-long student boycott and a sit-in of parents joined by a sprinkling of teachers who had earlier walked with their students on the picket line. Remembering the bitter antagonisms of 1968, most of the teachers chose not to enter the building that week.*

Charles Scheckner was a supporter of the Taylor-for-principal campaign. He has been teaching English at Ben Franklin for eleven years. He's fifty-eight, a native New Yorker. At sixteen, he dropped out of high school straight into the Great Depression. For years he hunted, found, lost unskilled jobs in light industry, then donned the white collar in New York City's newly formed Department of Public Welfare . . .

Belle was working there, too. We met at a time when the turbulence of that period was generating a lot of fresh ideas. We were both interested in a young trade union [of

---

* Taylor thus became one of the only three black principals in the city's sixty-three academic high schools. His appointment was bitterly opposed by the Central Council of Supervisory Associations, the most powerful organization of professional groups in the school system. And Albert Shanker, president of the United Federation of Teachers, commented that Taylor's appointment "has created open season on the city's schools. Any group of people who can shut schools through violence or the threat of violence will now be able to name their choice to a $25,000–30,000-a-year job." Nevertheless, the neutrality of the teachers at Franklin might not have been possible without the tacit acquiescence of the union's top leadership.

municipal employees] that was just beginning. I heard her speak . . .

I went back to high school, nights, after I married Belle. I spent my summers studying. And then I was caught up in World War II; everything was important. Those were years when my own education, as an American, as a member of the Depression generation, was somehow enriched by adversity. Being unemployed, not having a dollar in my pocket, discovering that there was something called fascism and Hitler and World War II—this was my education. I learned in the streets, by trying to find a job, by identifying myself with oppressed people, by trying to understand what fascism meant, by working in factories, by organizing people into trade unions, by having some vision of a better life. And all of that serves as my equipment as a teacher. So if I'm able to relate to kids—black kids, foreign kids, Oriental kids—or relate to teachers who were much more sheltered or protected, or fortunate because they went to regular colleges during the day and had campus life, it's because of these decades.

If that's so, what can teachers educated since then use as the human bond between them and the kids in a school like this?

The only way they can learn, unless they grew up with similar kids, or in a family which had some suitable world outlook, is to learn by doing and experiencing. I don't want to seem melodramatic, but they have to learn in the fires of life, by themselves. The problems of our time have caught up with everybody: the big city; the question of sharing the wealth; the question of the needs of the black people; Puerto Rican people, others who make up our school population. The teachers must learn, and are learning, how to grapple with these real problems.

How are they going to learn if, unlike you, they grew up affluent, comfortable and, in effect, alienated?

If we assume that learning means you take the correct, essential step to meet and solve the problem, then this is very tough and this has all kinds of mingled results. For many teachers there won't be any learning as I understand it, in terms of solving current problems satisfactorily. But they will take sides nevertheless. They will do so in the sense that they consider the teaching situation a threat, because so many students challenge, question and rebel. They will take sides in terms of something called law-and-order—regimentation. They will have to relearn American history, especially the history of black Americans.

I hope you've been talking to a lot of the new teachers. They might have a lot to tell you. This is the generation that's closely affected by the war, by the need for change; a generation more in sympathy with the oppressed and black people, with the ghetto situation. I believe that there is a large number of young teachers who, in grappling with the problems of life today, will sympathize socially and politically with our kids, who will assert their ideas in their union, in their church, or in any political organization which spells out the task which must be done. This is a *citizen* problem.

You're fifty-eight. What about the generation preceding, the "silent generation" who were the young citizens of the McCarthy period? A lot of them are teaching school now. Can any of them learn to do what you hope today's young teachers will?

In my own personal experience I've seen very few who made qualitative changes in the sense that they outlive old prejudices, old modes of thinking. All you can say is that given strong, new direction and administration many of them will come along on the basis of necessity. This is their job; they want to satisfy the powers that be. But if you are thinking that they have suddenly discovered a vision that represents a qualitative step forward in terms of democratic change, the next step forward that will elevate the neglected masses of American people, I think this is too much to expect at this time.

In our society people are driven by economic necessity, various fears, self-interest, strong-man control. Here and there on the basis of personal friendships they may be inspired by somebody they think is brilliant. I think the question is answered generally by the large currents of movement in the country.

Does that mean the white teachers of the "silent generation" must be largely written off in this connection?

Today we are involved in severe struggles everywhere in the urban community. Teachers who cling to old concepts of authority and privilege resent change and they'll resist "re-tooling" their social thinking. Other teachers of this generation will adapt slowly but will recognize that they cannot avoid history, the upsurge of the black people and other minorities who are demanding sweeping changes in the educational structure, among other things. Maybe changing times will bring about a greater unity of the two generations as circumstances force them to participate more in the struggles affecting our society—peace, civil liberties, anti-poverty, et cetera.

Many male teachers are here because of the war, the draft situation. They bring in the rebelliousness of the campus. This clash has been real. We experienced it during the teachers' strike. We experience it every day in terms of physical appearance: long hair, beards, dress, ideas. The man and woman over forty or in the fifties may be getting accustomed to it now. But at the beginning, it was dealt with in a very hostile way: these youngsters were "freaks." These were the nonconformists. They don't have regular lesson plans, they don't want to wear a tie. You see . . . ?

What happened here during the strike?

It was a time for very intensive self-examination. Half of the staff, about a hundred teachers, came in, but not everybody for the same reasons. We didn't ask anyone why. Some may have wanted the money. The silent assumption was that we all thought the strike was wrong, morally, for reasons we'd gone into. I personally thought the strike was racist and that it was also an attempt by the union, by all means, to thwart any sort of control by the community of its own schools. And many of us thought the union was deliberately lying about dismissed teachers. No teachers were dismissed.

Also the union did a pretty good job of furthering polarization by getting police, for the first time friendly to the strikers, and very, very hostile to so-called "scabs" like ourselves.

Some teachers felt we should at all costs avoid confrontations that would lead to bitterness or collision with their colleagues outside on strike. This was explained at faculty meetings inside—that we were not looking for incidents. Some things *were* said on both sides. There were harsh words passed, mainly between students and teachers. Here and there anger flared for a moment, but we tried to cool tempers. This was a waking of students, too. *They* were taking sides. They saw a Black issue and they thought that the teachers outside were racist. On a few occasions the teachers outside called us scabs as we went in, but they regarded many of us as people with fine records as union members and as outstanding teachers, so there was agonizing on that score.

Are teachers really bound by lesson plans, textbooks? A lot of teachers say they're not.

Most of the teachers are bound by them. I am also considerably bound by this, though I have learned to be flexible. We are bound by the administration. Controls are very tight in that respect. There is a departmental chairman, who's given a syllabus, who checks on his teachers. He distributes textbooks. He *tells* them what the course content should be.

And by the way, should a teacher use the classroom for something called "indoctrination"—I'm not so sure what that means today—he would be challenged and he would be treading on very thin ice. It could mean anything. But, you see, if it means that the student is encouraged to rebel and to take the road of open defiance, then there would be a reaction. See, it's one thing to consider both sides of a controversial question, but if a teacher suggests or poses "Organize, strike, defy!"—this is indoctrination.

Well, what happens if a kid asks you what you think about the war in Vietnam, and you give him a pro forma answer, a "schoolteacher" answer, and he persists, "I want to know your personal opinion"?

I would be honest with the kid. I'd say, "You're asking me a personal question. I will give you my *personal* answer. I want you to clearly understand, since you are a young adult, that I am not a free agent. I am a civil servant and bound down by rules and regulations. But you asked me a fair question and I think I can answer in all candor." And I proceed to give my personal answer. And I have done it. I would qualify it by saying that "If I have offended you in any way, please remember that you asked me for my personal opinion. I feel very strongly about this. This is my opinion." And I give it! But a student will seldom ask a teacher for a personal opinion unless an atmosphere of complete trust and confidence has been set up in the classroom. Generally speaking, if a student has very little respect or regard for a teacher, he will not care to ask for the teacher's personal opinion. But if he does look up to that teacher as some sort of guide or as a person who has some moral authority that he, the student, wants to rest on, then I think the teacher has been paid a compliment.

No obstacles to the free flow of opinion seem to exist in Charles Scheckner's one-semester comparative literature course for twelfth-graders on their way out—to college, or just plain out. This session, the second, is attended by eighteen students whose interest Scheckner hopes to arouse today in "the psalm as poetry." He is still only a partly known entity to them, but it's clear from the atmosphere and from their bearing that each, whatever the individual motivation, has entered the drab, cramped room with some degree of willingness to be interested. He begins by reminding them that the day before, they had discussed Genesis and the Fall of Man. For two or three minutes he asks questions and gets competent answers from a wide scattering of seat locations: What is a psalm? Under what conditions were psalms used? We've been talking about the Old and the New Testaments—what does the word "testament" mean? To this last question, the responses are hesitant, incomplete.

SCHECKNER: . . . This is a promise, an agreement by Jaweh, God, Jehovah, promising Man the protection of God if Man is faithful to him. (Remember we must avoid the question of religion.) He promises him life everlasting if you are faithful to God. All right, students? Now all I want you to do today . . ."

He introduces three English forms of the 23rd Psalm: the King James version, the John Wycliffe translation and the Anchor Bible treatment. The differences between the three, read aloud in the course of the session, are forcibly apparent even on first acquaintance. Reading Wycliffe, he makes the point in passing that "This is a very good example of Middle English. It belongs to a period when the language is undergoing some changes. Our language is not a pure language. It's been fed by many sources . . ." For fifteen or twenty minutes there is discussion of general style, words, imagery, symbolism, the elusiveness of mean-

ings in poetry. Deliberately or otherwise he tries to instill the kinds of information college-bound students need for feedback purposes: "John Wycliffe was born, maybe, in 1334 but we do know he died in 1384 . . ." But the real pull for him and his students is toward interpretation.

SCHECKNER: What was the mood of the psalmist?

VARIOUS STUDENTS: Dedicated. Loving. Trustful. Devotion. Dependence. Comfort.

EULA [Softly]: Paranoid.

Scheckner hasn't heard her. Her neighbor speaks up: "She's saying 'paranoid.' "

SCHECKNER: Paranoid? [Gently] Why, Eula?

She tries to explain, but Scheckner remains puzzled by her choice of the word. It interests him because he is apparently sure that she has not chosen the word impulsively or mindlessly.

SCHECKNER: Are you saying, if I read you right, that a person who has a complete sense of dependency might be paranoid?

EULA: No. That's not it.

Scheckner is reluctant to let the matter go. He would like to get her to identify and give form to the thought that led her to say "paranoid."

SCHECKNER: All right. But that's a strong word. Could you really justify this word if you had to write an essay?

EULA: Yeah.

SCHECKNER [Still interested but baffled]: Okay. I'd enjoy reading it. I haven't thought about it myself but, you know, it's your song. The psalmist wrote it for you. You have the right to react that way. [He addresses the class] Did you ever feel yourself in a complete state of trust, or dependency, or faith that might justify this mood—wait, I'm not making myself clear. Is it *good* to have this kind of faith in anything?

CLASS: Yes. No. It all depends . . .

SCHECKNER: All right. Let me paraphrase the psalmist: "I know that people are gonna beat me on the head, call me names, even meet me with violence, and though they do, I know I'm right! I'm gonna win! And the cause that I believe in will triumph!" DeSousa, is there anything wrong with faith? I'm not talking about religion, but faith!

DESOUSA: I personally think it's essential, for a person to live. You have to *have* something to carry you along, something to fight for, something to give your life a purpose.

GLENN: I think you should have faith because you can't always go whole-heartedly for yourself. If you're going to latch on to something for yourself, you attempt to do something, and you fail at it, it would put you down altogether. You wouldn't have anything to stand for. Then you would really like to have something above you that would help you try to pull back up there.

A STUDENT: I don't understand why he says, "Thou preparest a table before me in the presence of mine enemies."

VIOLA: I think I can answer that. The psalmist says that in the sense that He—"I'm providing you with the energy to fight back against 'mine enemies.' I'm aware that you are there." So, I can keep my faith even though "mine enemies" are at me.

OLIVIA: I thought of it more as a table where I could sit down with my enemies.

SCHECKNER: In that case, you do have quite a lot of faith.

HERNANDO: [In a heavy Spanish accent] Like, what Olivia says contradicts what religion is saying in this psalm: "Please give me strength to fight" and she is actually saying this is a round-table negotiation to talk with them. Right? So isn't the attitude kind of contradictory here?

OLIVIA: Well, maybe it's a question of what kind of

fighting you need. Whom are you fighting? I didn't say either kind. It *could* be negotiation. It could be physical, also, like it was with David and Goliath. But you can also talk, negotiate, compromise.

Time is running out. Scheckner is obliged to divert their interest from the 23rd Psalm to a briefing on future assignments. These range from The Iliad *to* Don Quixote. *In the minutes before the end-of-the-period bell, another issue comes up, concerning the Fall of Man.*

REBECCA: I was thinking how selfish God was about the Tree of Life and punishing Adam and Eve.

SCHECKNER: You don't think He should have had an angel there with a fiery sword guarding the Tree of Life?

REBECCA: I don't think He had to. Because if they were innocent already, why tempt them?

SCHECKNER: [In a mock-melodramatic tone]: How dare we sit in judgment!

REBECCA [Laughs]: Why not? What kind of a mean God—?

SCHECKNER: Heresy! Heresy! Heresy!

REBECCA: I also think he was selfish because of the fact that He needed something to point on, to always check himself by keeping people on earth; by saying "Well, so-and-so can have *these*. These *other* people are *my* problems. I'll take *them* . . ." And Satan, by having some of them, he could say, "These are my problems. I'll take *them* . . ." You know? We're just the games that They play.

There's a moment of brooding silence in the room . . .

SCHECKNER: [Sounding a litte subdued]: Shakespeare also said that the gods play games with us—

REBECCA: Then why should we believe in them?

SCHECKNER: But that's not the question. Class, as we read—as we read literature, I think it's good for you, and for me, to get up and say, "Listen! No one is going to play games with me! I want to be the master of my own destiny! How about that? Let's keep it in mind for future discussion. Thanks [as the bell rings] very much.

ZAPHRIRAH BAUMAN
Harlem

You become a hack unless there is some deeper personal purpose in your teaching. Even to those who go in with certain ideals, bucking the system becomes such a chore that they either succumb or quit. This is my twenty-third year in the same school. It's the only school I've ever been in.

Zaphrirah Bauman is in her early fifties. The Hebraic sonority of her first name was long ago sacrificed for brevity. Everybody calls her Zippy, and she is. Her school, P.S. 186, grades pre-K through 5, is on 145th Street in West Harlem. Both of her children went there. She describes it as "seventy years old, a five-story building with few facilities, a makeshift lunchroom that can serve ninety children when we have to feed nine hundred, a gym that's just an empty loft, no outdoor play space." For eighteen years she taught Grades 3, 4 and 6, but mostly Grade 5. Then she became the school's music specialist, one of a cluster of teachers who take over classes during other teachers' "free" or preparation periods. Before and briefly after her marriage she taught music in a private music school and at home.

I had to give up piano teaching. My children were young. By 1945 my older son started kindergarten. We lived in the area of the school and I began to attend PTA meetings. The teacher shortage was acute. At every meeting the principal appealed to the parents to recommend anyone who had a college degree. I raised my hand at one meeting and he asked, "Yes, Mrs. Bauman? Whom do you know?" I said, "Me." And he just jumped. He had me come right into his office. So I thought I would stay with it just until my children were older, but I was hooked. It soon changed into a job that I felt really concerned about.

First, I was concerned about learning how to teach; I did not feel well prepared. It soon became evident that I also had to know more about the children I was teaching, more about the community in which we lived. My children were *attending* this school and I didn't know much about my black neighbors.

I also had to find out for myself that your classroom atmosphere and the ability to carry on a sustained teaching program depends on the framework you set, from day number one. You have to develop guidelines that the children understand, so that they know what they may and may not do, so that they know the reasons why, so that day-to-day routines don't become a source of waste of time and disorder. You have to establish your expectations from the children; to set *their* sights on what you hope they will achieve with you. Some aspects of this teaching skill any teacher can learn through intuition and experience if she realizes the importance of it.

But—more than that. It's the feeling children get about the teacher's attitude toward them as individuals, as people, as a social group, that carries over in your manner, in the way you attack subject matter, in the way you speak to them—about anything.

Children will test any new teacher. The added element here is that more often than not the teacher is white and the children are black. They *know*, they know very quickly, how a teacher feels about them. They talk with each other about one or another teacher and how she regards them. And you can't help but notice that when some of your colleagues talk about "those little animals" or "those little savages," that the children know *that*, too. Sometimes it's said within children's hearing.

When you faced a new class the first school day in September, what did you do? What did you tell them?

I introduced myself. The children introduced *them*selves. We had to get to know each other so we could work together. Then I tried to give them a very general but challenging overview of what new growth we could expect. I have no set speeches. I look around at the children and I just go. I have to get the feel of the children, too, to be able to do this. You dramatize the exciting things. We're going to learn the whole history of how our country began. "We're going to work with numbers that are this long across. Can you read this number now—and I write something on the board. No, they can't, but we'll learn how. We're going to do our own research. We're going to work in committees, write stories and poetry." You don't dwell on it too long but you try to arouse their interest. Once over lightly in a very broad palette of what they can expect to do and—"If we work well together we'll also have time to take trips, visit people, invite guests." Anything that sounds challenging.

Some of those kids sitting there must be saying to themselves that they don't give a damn.

Yes. But children do naturally want to move ahead. If defeat has set in, then that's your challenge. For a good many of the years that I taught fifth grade I was assigned to classes that were far behind in skill subjects. If I got the clue from them that they'd given up on reading, then I had to find ways to make reading offer new excitement. I also found that I could get clues from the children as to what interested them and use that as a jumping-off place for greater achievement in skill areas. In a number of cases it worked with science.

I had one child in particular . . . a terrible behavior problem. He's in college now and still comes back to see me regularly. His interest in reading was aroused through science. I started bringing rock and shell collections my own kids had at home, and he started building an exhibit for the science fair; I said, "If you want to know more, you have to read, you have to do your report, and so forth," and the kid jumped. He also needed glasses desperately and nobody had ever taken the trouble. The glasses plus the motive were enough. . . .

But in a more general way I've found that teaching about black history and the black struggle for liberation, the civil rights struggles, is effective motivation. At first I had to bring it up because the children didn't. I kept bringing it up, and their first reaction generally was, What does *she* know about it; what is she trying to prove? But almost invariably it not only sparked the children but became an absorbing pursuit within the class on whatever level and in whatever direction it led. This became my most valuable and most successful technique. This isn't so unusual now because it's so much in the fore of everything that's going on. But when you go back several years, the children came to school without any consciousness of any of this and it started to grow in the class. In the fifth grade it was particularly easy because we were studying the history of America from the time of discovery and as far as we could go, and it became very easy to integrate it with the regular curriculum.

It also became a source of interest to them because it was not in the textbook. If I happened to discuss Columbus or Balboa and brought in that there were black explorers there with them, you know, the reaction was one of surprise and interest. "Well, then, let's find out. Who were they? How did they get there? How did they get involved? What did they contribute?" And this became part of the continuing study that we did. It also came in with current events related to the struggles of the black people during the sixties.

One illuminating incident. At the time that Martin Luther King organized the bus boycott in Montgomery, my fourth-grade class and I were discussing the reaction of the whites in Montgomery. One little boy, Clinton, who was always very actively involved, didn't participate. At the very end he raised his hand and said, "Mrs. Bauman, if you were living down South instead of up here, would you still be saying the same things you're saying now?" *Fourth grade!* And I said, "Well, Clinton, you know me well enough now. What do you think?" He said, "I'll have to think about that." Three or four days later he came up to my desk and said, "I've been thinking about what you said and I think if you lived down South you'd still say the same thing." It was a great compliment and I've never forgotten it. And I think that in its own way it's symptomatic of how children can begin to feel towards a white teacher and towards themselves.

There was another fifth-grade child who, after I introduced the class to the Langston Hughes–Milton Meltzer *Pictorial History** saved his allowance. Bought a copy. It *never* left his hand. He carried it with him wherever he went. This was the one and only time that I really had a group of what might be considered IGC's (Intellectually Gifted Children), though we didn't have that designation in our school.

What did this book represent in his life? Did it change his achievement levels?

* Langston Hughes and Milton Meltzer, A *Pictorial History of the Negro in America* (New York: Crown Publishers, 1956).

It changed his direction, his self-image, his outlook toward life and learning. He was doing well in arithmetic and in spelling and in reading, but he wasn't *alive* towards school as he eventually became. He began to study and to do reports and to look for other sources. He became *involved*.

I think, generally, so much of the teaching that goes on is mechanical, rote teaching even in social studies, or science; where the teacher's always *telling* the kids, doesn't make them think through. "Why is this so?" or "What do you think the outcome is?" "Now check and see if this is, indeed, the outcome." And if you figured it out, "Great!" And if you didn't figure it out—"Why?" Children are not being taught to *think*. They're often treated as little robots, you know, and they're spoon-fed facts, or the mechanics of doing things, without any real understanding. When you see a group of children sitting there and their eyes are dull and they're tuning you out, you have to be able to put that gleam in their eyes, and when you see that gleam, that's your gratification. Then you know you're getting through.

You have to watch the luster level in the kids' eyes all the time?

Absolutely. And if I found that I was losing them, I had to change direction. I've often found myself veering off from what I had planned if a child raised an unexpected question. I'd pursue that tack because that's what the kid wanted to know. On the other hand, you become alert enough to know when the question is just a diversionary tactic. You have to be on your toes.

How did black history get into the curriculum at your school?

Years and years I had to battle the principal [not her present one]. First he didn't agree there *was* a field of knowledge called black history. Then the argument became: "Why black history any more than Italian or German or any other kind?"

I said, "America is the history of black and Italian and Jewish and all. But in this school there has to be an emphasis on black because these children are black and have to have some pride in their own heritage. But, also, because whatever mention there is of blacks in the books we give them is distorted, falsified, without foundation in fact and the kids get a prejudiced picture. They get a white middle-class picture." And I showed him the textbook.

Then his argument became: "Well, show me in the Board of Ed. publications where it says that this should be part of the curriculum." And, of course, it didn't say specifically, but I had to look for obscure references such as "pride in the American heritage" and that kind of thing. After about twelve or fifteen years, when it became a broader hue and cry than just my voice in P.S. 186, that was when he allowed me to form a faculty committee to prepare materials. Of course, he never did very much to see that it was carried out in any classrooms. We ran off reams of material. We discussed it at staff conferences. Then it went into desk drawers and stayed there. I was the only white teacher who volunteered for our black history curriculum committee and when we got together, very few of the black teachers had any semblance of background in the field; but that was nine years ago. I certainly agree that black teachers should be teaching this and related subjects but there have not yet been enough of them who are prepared to do it. After all, most black schoolteachers are products of the very school system in which we are teaching.

We've had three principals since that particular one. Most principals no longer offer resistance, but neither do they do anything much to implement it. And since the vast majority of teachers are totally uninformed in this area, little really goes on. The Board of Education did hand everybody a pamphlet on black history, which was prepared by a white Jewish high school principal. It was distributed, never discussed, never studied, never implemented. The revised social studies bulletins introduced three or four names of black Americans and that was it. So that there are very few classrooms in which any black history is being taught.*

In one of my classes there was a little White Russian emigrée girl. That year every child had to do some project with his parents—artificial as far as I was concerned, but it was a directive from the district superintendent. So I assigned a project in black history, and this little girl came back to tell me her mother said she was not interested. I was a bit taken aback but I had a brainstorm. I said, "Did you ever hear of Pushkin?"† I knew this child studied Russian after school. "Ask your mother if she would help you find out more about Pushkin."

She came back with the most beautiful report, recited a few of his children's poems in Russian, translated them. And her report included the fact that Pushkin was black; and *she was part of the class*. She made a special contribution. When I told the school librarian about this incident, she said, "Who's Pushkin?"

These are intuitive flashes that many teachers, alas, cannot use because their own backgrounds are so meager in literature, art, music, science, or what have you. They just don't have it. It never ceases to shock me that so many teachers never go to a theater or to a concert or to a museum.

* Subsequently, Mrs. Bauman reports, "This has changed some. Principals now realize that it's good policy to be able to point to the inclusion of black studies in their schools. So, where possible, a cluster teacher [see p. 409] is assigned to this area."

The effect of such an arrangement can very well be to relegate black studies to the fringe of elementary and junior high school curricula along with music, art, "home ec." and "phys. ed."

† Alexander Pushkin (1799–1837), Russian poet and dramatist. He was a descendant of Ibrahim Hannibal, an African, who was a general in the armies of Peter the Great.

Are you telling me that the kids in ghetto schools suffer from culturally deprived teachers?

Unhappily, yes. This is also true in white middle-class schools. But so many white middle-class kids come from culturally rich homes that the damage isn't as great.

What makes culturally deprived teachers?

The same society that makes culturally deprived schools and colleges. Teaching stopped being a prestigious profession because since the 1940s so many people with college degrees have been needed in so many fields offering much higher salaries. In general our growing technology and the change in the whole structure of employment has drawn the most capable people away from teaching. Until recently the vast majority of new teachers, black and white, came in totally unprepared to teach minority-group children. They've had no previous personal experience in poor neighborhoods, and had done no reading on their own. There now seems to be the beginning of a reverse trend.

I never saw so many teachers, men and women, who read nothing but the *Daily News*. They have no interest in what's going on in the world except in terms of their own well-being. Couldn't care less. And it manifests itself in ways that affect the children directly. For example, there's a teacher who worked in my school during the 1968 strikes. No principle entered into this at all. The level of her thinking was, "I want to buy a house, I want the money." It had nothing to do with *any* of the issues that were involved She's not the only one. Several of us who were very much involved were boasting all through the strike that except for three teachers our entire staff was in. We didn't find out until after the strike that a good many of them were there not because of their support for community control or because of their opposition to Shanker's policies.* They

* Albert Shanker, president of the United Federation of Teachers; arch opponent of black and Puerto Rican demands for decision-

wanted the money or they were people who wouldn't strike no matter what the issues were. Some of them didn't strike the year before, when the rest of us were out. At union meetings, staff meetings, these people never participate, never speak up. You never get their thinking. Then, when they have to take a stand, that's when you begin to find out. Some of them happen to be fairly good teachers. Some not. Many have skills and experience but it's technical. It's not that they have soul. This they do not have. It's missing. There's been a little change recently. The colleges now are at least paying lip service to preparing teachers for urban teaching, but I have so far seen few concrete results where I am.

The teacher's own personality is a very big factor. In elementary schools a good part of your time is spent teaching children to live in a group situation—to respect the rights of other children, not to disrupt, because others want to learn; or when you sock somebody it may be fun for you but not for the other kid. If one teacher says, "Johnny, sit down because you're disturbing Mary," and another teacher says, "*I told you to sit down!*" it makes a difference. There are a *million* ways of telling Johnny to sit down. Every little thing that happens is an item in the conditioning of the children's attitude toward the teacher, toward each other and to the group. If you love the subject and you hate the teacher, that's not good.

How does it happen that you've stayed in the same school for twenty-three years?

I stayed in my school because I felt I had an important role there, that I could try to achieve something in terms of relationships with the children, the community, my colleagues, and so on. I also wasn't going to be part of the general flight from the ghettos, if I had any choice. I

---

making power in the curricular and administrative conduct of the public schools in ghetto communities.

think, too, that my association with the Teachers Union—not to be confused with the United Federation of Teachers—gave me a perspective, an outlook, that helped me learn and grow as a teacher.

The Teachers Union was formed in 1916. Between 1935 and 1964, it led successful campaigns for improved salaries and working conditions. The example of its victories, and of its ability to absorb defeats, slowly made it possible for the inert majority of teachers to cross the gentility barrier to unabashed, effective trade-union organization. The Teachers Union never permitted its pursuit of teachers' well-being to come into conflict, however, with the education needs of the pupils, for whose intellectual development they held themselves solemnly answerable.

It was a tenet of the Teachers Union that whatever is educationally and humanly bad for school children is professionally and morally bad for teachers. Accordingly, it did decades-long battle against the concept that children in deprived or disadvantaged environments are, by definition, unteachable. It proposed alternatives to the steadily developing caste system of education based on socioeconomic status which was becoming more and more a matter of racial oppression. In Harlem and in Bedford-Stuyvesant, in the mid-1930s,, the union made common cause with black and Puerto Rican parent/community groups to campaign for new school buildings, reduced class sizes, enriched curricula, the hiring of black teachers.

Through the joint work of its Harlem and Educational Policies committees, the union became a persistent advocate and a practical resource for the study of black history and culture. It published bibliographies, prepared and distributed classroom materials and conducted courses to study means (sometimes devious ones, to avoid administrative displeasure) of using these materials in the curriculum. For twelve years, 1952–63, New York Teachers News, the union's official newspaper, produced an annual Negro History Week supplement. Single copies or classroom-size batches were mailed free of charge, on request, to teachers, principals, librarians and community groups in New York City and in many other parts of the country. It also conducted a year-after-year campaign against racial bias and factual distortion in history and English literature textbooks. A high point in these efforts was the union's 1950 publication Bias and Prejudice in Textbooks in Use in the New York City Schools, citing chapter and verse from a fairly long list of books surveyed by the union's Harlem Committee.

None of its principles, policies or practices had ever endeared the Teachers Union to the New York public school and governmental establishments. During the 1930s and well into the postwar forties this controversial radical-led organization was something to be endured by the authorities because it could not, then, be cured. The cure came certainly and brutally to hand in the late 1940s and in the 1950s—the Cold War time of McCarthyism, loyalty oaths, legislative investigations of "subversives," and conversion of the AFL-CIO into an obedient Labor Front for the advancement of official U.S. policy at home and abroad.

Dismissal or ousting-by-pressure of several hundred Teachers Union activists, official banning of the union from school buildings, and the mood of political fear which pervaded the entire system steadily eroded the union's base of popular support. The teacher shortage in the 1950s and 1960s was acute, and working teachers, tired of being near the bottom in the economic heap, had overcome their distaste for straight-out unionism. Thus the United Federation of Teachers, formed in 1960, quickly won election as the teachers' bargaining agent. The school administration resigned itself to living with the lesser evil of AFL-CIO "labor statesmanship."

The Teachers Union made a graceful and spirited exit.

Several days before disbanding, it published its last issue of New York Teacher News. Its members formally resolved to join the UFT, as individuals. Thenceforward they would "loyally and actively participate in the formulation and support of policies, programs and actions best suited to create a school system second to none . . ."

Many former Teachers Union members, however, refused to join in the 1968 UFT strikes. They were not alone. In all, several thousand teachers remained in their classrooms in Black and Puerto Rican communities.

Those teachers who opposed Shanker's policies, who supported the struggle of the Black and Puerto Rican communities to have a say in the running of their own schools, got together. A meeting was called the evening before the strike. Over three hundred teachers responded. "We organized as the Ad Hoc Committee of Teachers for Community Control. [Zippy Bauman was chosen as Chairman.] We formulated a program for keeping the schools open and for helping teachers understand the true issues involved."

After the strike, many of the active dissidents were ousted from their positions as UFT functionaries. The Ad Hoc Committee reconstituted itself as the Teachers Action Committee for advocacy of three major concepts: "democratic unionism, quality education and community control." Following the 1971 convention of the American Federation of Teachers, the dissidents changed their name to Teachers Action Caucus to identify themselves explicitly as a formal opposition group. It now participates as such in union affairs and enters its own slates in union elections. High on its list of priorities is "a closer, more active alliance with the Black Caucus of the UFT, along with building TAC as an organization of Black and white school staff."

This is my fifth year as a music specialist. Every forty-five minutes I have a different group of children coming into my room. The job can be just baby-sitting or you can make it an educationally worthwhile experience. I don't just teach them songs about birds in the spring. A lot of material I choose for both singing and listening will grow out of the black experience or I will try to relate it to something that is happening in the school or in the world or someplace. I draw connections from everything I teach to other relevant experiences in the children's lives.

She itemized at random: a song from Liberia; another from Cental America; "Just Whistle a Bit," by Paul Laurence Dunbar and John W. Work; "Ballad for Americans" by Earl Robinson; spirituals which black slaves used as freedom songs; Spanish, Puerto Rican and Yiddish songs.

Where do I get this kind of material and how do I get enough of it? I have to hunt for these things. They're all too rare and far between. I search. I'm constantly searching. By now I've built up a pretty fair repertoire, but—I'm still searching.

PAUL BECKER
Brooklyn

My father said, "Why do you want to be a schoolteacher? *Marry* a schoolteacher. *You* go out and take some accounting courses; be an accountant."

I really had the same attitude as my parents, that teaching is a good job for a woman. But when I started to student-teach, I met some wonderful people, like the man who made me into a teacher, at Alexander Hamilton [Vocational High School]. His name is—well, never mind. That was a very tough school, a difficult situation. But those kids—they loved him! I saw lessons I won't see again if I live to be a hundred. Through him I was introduced to the Teachers Union, and these were marvelous people, and I said this is where I have to be.

They were people who just didn't accept a bad school system. They said, "We're in it and we have to fight to make it better." They really loved the kids and I could see the dedication that existed—the kind of dedication that you don't have, unfortunately, in New York today. You see, in New York City—I guess it's the same all over—the people who came into the system in the last ten or fifteen years had absolutely no idea of the job they were doing. They're only concerned with bread-and-butter issues, with "I got an extra program." I know people who, from the day they walked into the classroom, all they thought about was taking promotion exams to become chairmen and principals. When it comes to real concern for the kids and for the learning process, it's "Ah, I'm not concerned with that." That's their attitude.

Is your old mentor still teaching?

Oh no, no. After I did my student teaching I was drafted. I was overseas in '53 when I read his name in the Paris edition of the *Herald Tribune*. They had fired him. He was one of those teachers who were dismissed during the McCarthy period. A beautiful teacher, magnificent, an artist in the classroom.

The McCarthy years scared away those people who would be the most questioning, the most adventurous, the people who wouldn't take just the established answers for things, the people who were the experimenters. The people who were left in the system didn't ask too many questions, didn't challenge too much. You see, school teaching is a good job, especially if all you want to be is a civil servant. Many teachers are just like Post Office employees except that they're handling children instead of mail. There's a whole slew of civil servants rather than teachers in the schools. And I think the McCarthy era was a major factor.

These teachers belong to the silent generation, but the kids today are not silent. There's a complete noncommunication. They want to beat the kids on the head: "Call the cops in." The cops! This is the approach. Of course, some of the kids do crazy things. They're kids. Their protests sometimes take on political forms and sometimes vandalism. But these teachers—educators should *understand* what protest is, and there's a complete lack of understanding.

Paul Becker is youthfully forty, soberly attired, neatly bearded, a well-favored man of slightly less than medium height. His dark Eurasian-looking eyes, gentle, engaging, suggest that he feels as well as knows; his quick, frequent smile and free flow of cogent speech confirm the impression. Becker has been on the staff of George W. Wingate High School for fifteen years. During the last three, his time has been divided between two functions: classroom teacher of black history, and dean of students.

Wingate draws its enrollment largely from the Black community of Brooklyn's Bedford-Stuyvesant area, "Bed-Stuy" for short. In the late 1960s and through the turn of the decade, Wingate was one of the nation's truly uptight schools. The perennial antagonisms between the teaching and administrative staffs and the black students reach critical intensity now and then, producing spasms of disorder, vandalism, personal violence. Some of the white teachers, their racial fears heightened by the institution's atmosphere (which they intensified), regarded a trip from their classrooms to the teachers' john as an exercise in counterguerrilla reconnaissance. A few, but Becker in particular, walk through Wingate's halls of anger serene, unthreatening and unthreatened.

The school system is going to be in chaos for about five years. There was a big split in the schools on account of the [1968] strike. I was on the executive committee of my school UFT chapter before that. Then the UFT began to go crazy on me. I didn't go along with them. As a result I was completely on the outs with the teachers who struck.

After the strike the kids had a feeling of disdain toward the teachers. Absolute resentment. This was not true of other strikes. The kids admired the teachers then. They walked with us on the picket line; we were fighting the Establishment. But here they had the feeling that the strike was directed against them.

Since then most teachers find the black kids very hostile. I'll see a kid in the hallway, he doesn't know me. I'll tell him something—he's out in the hall after the late bell has rung and I'll tell him to go to class. If he doesn't know me, I'll get a little expression of hostility. More now than there used to be. But most of the time the word has gotten around. The kids know me.

There's a way you talk to kids, you know. You walk into the boys' lavatory and it's full of smoke. The kids are standing there smoking. They did that when I went to school, so it's nothing new. My first puff on a cigarette I took in the boys' bathroom in Lafayette High when I was fifteen, sixteen. So you walk in and you could say, as some teachers do, "Hey, you, what are you doing here?" and take them to the dean. Or you can say, "Come on. Let's go, gentlemen. It's time to go to class." All right. They'll throw their butts away. Who cares about the cigarettes? We know they smoke.

After the strike this whole place was in an uproar for a few weeks. You know, there were outbreaks in the school. Teachers were getting up at faculty meetings, asking the principal to provide them with walkie-talkies on the third floor because they didn't feel safe. Only a few of us said, "Wait a minute. We're educators. Let's deal with this problem as educators, as teachers. We're dealing with children."

But no. "Call the cops! Walkie-talkies! We want police around!" They had about forty or fifty cops here. I walked in one day and the teachers, a whole bunch of them, were sitting around playing poker. I said, "If you don't break up this gambling, I'm going to call the police." They just looked up. They didn't think it was funny.

Wingate, in 1971 at any rate, attained greater tranquility than it knew during the 1960s. The increase in black and in Spanish-speaking student enrollment to 95 percent of the total, prompted a teacher exodus, mostly "old guard" types, amounting to about one-third of the staff. Their replacements are young, less defensive, more at ease than were their predecessors in the school's "all-black" atmosphere.

Bread and butter is part of teaching, but also there's the knowledge that when you walk out you've done a day's work, you've done a good job. You can see it in the faces of the kids, the kids you've helped and the kids who look to you. In the hallway, the kids'll come to you with various problems. They want to stand around and just *schmoos** a little: "What do you think about such-and-such a college?" I say, "Well, what do you think of it?" Of course they don't want to ask what I think. They want to tell me what they think, so I say go ahead and tell me. They bat it around. They love to argue.

One hopeful thing: The teachers who are coming in now—not all, you get a mix—but I detect a new breed of teachers coming in now. Teachers who were not raised during the McCarthy period, who are adventurous, who

* The Yiddish equivalent of "rap"; "chatting" is for goyim.

experiment, who care for kids. I have a kid [a teacher] in my school. I *call* him a kid; you know—anybody under thirty. He came into the school system just to avoid the draft. Now that he's in it, he loves it. He asked for five general courses last time. Most teachers avoid general classes like the plague. They're the slow kids.

See, there are three courses in the high school: the academic course, which prepares kids for college; the commercial course, which prepares them for business; and the general course, which prepares them for nothing—the kids graduate and they really have very little, they get no real skills, just an attendance certificate.

Most of the kids who get out of the general course, they'll shop around a little bit. Some of them will try to get into night school to take up something. But they're not prepared for any kind of college or real technical training. They've taken watered-down math, watered-down history, watered-down English. Most of their reading scores are very low. And most of them are black and Puerto Rican kids.

Most people don't realize this in New York City. The parents have been assuming that having their kids graduate from high school is something very good. I saw some figures a few months ago. Now, how many Puerto Rican people are there in New York City? About a quarter of a million people roughly. Only something like three hundred Puerto Rican students in the entire city graduated with academic diplomas. I think I'm even being generous there. Most of the Puerto Rican kids graduate with general diplomas. Practically all the black kids graduate with general diplomas. Then they go out on the job market and they're useless. They haven't taken any language. In math, they've taken something called Record Keeping, which teaches them to add some figures together. It's no good, no use. If a kid works behind the counter in a retail store for three weeks he'll learn as much as school offered him in two years. No algebra, no geometry.

So this teacher who came in, he wanted to teach five courses in general math because he said, "I want to do something with these kids. I want to work with them." Now, this is unheard of. He was looked upon in his department as some kind of a nut.

He just came into the school system this year. He makes a lot of mistakes, naturally, but he's a very sincere young man. He's one of the new breed that I really feel good about. They're young people who have a social conscience. They're not interested in getting ahead in the school system. They look at the kids and say, "I've got to help them. I've got to do something for them." What they see is a possibility that these kids have the capability of changing their own lives, and they want to help. These young teachers are like the kids who went down to Mississippi* or the kids who are demonstrating against the war.

They have a very healthy attitude. Now, you must understand, teaching is not just a good attitude. You have to have a skill, too. If you have a wholesome attitude toward those kids, it still will take you several years to become a good teacher. You need technique as well as heart.

But one of the problems in the school system has been that they've only concentrated on technique and not on heart. You know, a person can be an excellent technician and have disdain for the kids and he's no good. It's like being an artist. A good craftsman without real heart is nothing! A guy with heart who doesn't know how to put it down on paper or canvas isn't much of an artist either. But a kid like this who comes in with enthusiasm, a love for the

* In the early 1960s, particularly in 1962 during "the COFO summer," an intensive nonviolent campaign to break through the barriers against black voter registration in Mississippi. COFO is the acronym for Council of Federated Organizations, which comprised the Student Non-Violent Coordinating Committee, Congress of Racial Equality, Southern Christian Leadership Conference and National Association for the Advancement of Colored People.

kids *and* the technique can be a big help. Each year you get better. Within three, four years he's going to be an excellent teacher. I only hope that he has the heart to stay.

Now, the first class I ever had was at Alexander Hamilton in 1951. I was young, twenty-one years old, from a middle-class, quite conservative background. My first reaction—I was frightened. Not only black kids, but working-class kids frightened me. The language was different. They didn't hesitate to use a curse word that I was brought up to think was terrible. You-don't-say-this-in-school kind of thing.

I didn't understand the kids at first. It was almost a shame that they would assign an inexperienced young teacher to a situation so difficult. I don't think we realize ourselves the inner feeling of racism that most white people have. We like to think of ourselves as unprejudiced, but you know, we grow up apart from black people. There's a feeling that somehow they're going to attack you, they're going to mug you. I remember I told a kid to sit down and he sneered at me and I felt threatened.

This feeling of being frightened pervades most teachers today in a ghetto situation. It's either a fear or sometimes it takes the opposite form, where a teacher is tough and he's going to show these kids who's boss.

One thing I found very early in my teaching career: the supervisory staff in the New York City school system by and large was no help at all. I got no help from my chairman, no help from the principal. They told me, "Go into the classroom and just keep them quiet." You know, if you keep them quiet you're a good teacher. "Tell them stories," someone told me. "They like stories." . . . Tell them stories!

My chairman was in the middle of a license exam for principal. He was at the Board of Ed. every other day. That's all that concerned him, see? He gave me no help at all.——* was the assistant chairman of the department. He was an English teacher, but in the vocational high schools English and social studies departments are combined. My license area was social studies, so he came in on my classes during his free time. And he invited me into his classes. Not only did he criticize my lessons but he gave me something above just the normal technical details. The first time I remember talking with him, he spoke about what it is in these kids' lives that is meaningful. How much you can draw upon, even with your own different background.

I remember him using a boxing story about a boxer; it was a story about *pride and dignity!* I observed his class when he was teaching this particular story, and he had every kid talking about his own experiences—about what happened to him when he took a girl to a dance or his teacher stopped him in the hallway. Then—got back to the story to show how the author was talking about the same thing.

I began to realize what the heck teaching was for, really. I mean when I'm teaching them about the Greeks and the Romans, what is it to them in terms of their own lives? What is there about history that's meaningful in the lives of these kids?

After my first term I began to feel more secure in the classroom. Feeling more secure, you want to reach out. You don't have to fear. You know how to get a class started, how to ask that question so you get the best kind of response. You know the homework and what the lesson is like. But it's more than getting the kids interested because *you're* interested. You want to get them interested because there's material to be interested *in*. It's knowing enough about the subject so you can bring to them the things that you know. And the kids do become interested and all of a sudden—you have a relationship.

My second term I was beginning to master the teach-

* Becker's blacklisted mentor.

ing skills—no thanks to the Board of Education, but to a fellow teacher. You must understand, those were very terrible days, in '51, '52. The administration was so scared—and in the middle of *this* I was learning how to be a teacher.

I was a substitute, and then after my term in the Army I was appointed to Wingate High School. The school is in Crown Heights, Brooklyn. It was about 20 percent black when I started, but the parents in Bedford-Stuyvesant fought like the devil to get their kids into Wingate. The only high schools in Bedford-Stuyvesant were about fifty or a hundred years old—who *knows* how old? But Wingate was a new school and it offered a nice new program. Gradually more and more black kids came.

For about nine years I was a homeroom teacher. Then they asked me if I would do part-time guidance. Although I was not a guidance counselor by training, I had very good rapport with most of the kids. So I did teaching in the morning and in the afternoon, guidance work with the kids. I advise them on their programs, write out recommendations for them to colleges and jobs and things like that.

I teach American history and economics and latterly an Afro-American history course. Three or four years ago social studies department chairmen were dead set against it. Some of them called it "apartheid." Suddenly my chairman came to me and asked me to develop a course. They had no curriculum, naturally. I drew one up, selected the books, assembled the materials, aids and so on. Now, we know that this is done to cool things off a bit.

So little is known about this field that when *Eye Witness*, by William Katz, came out, my chairman asked me to look at it. I did, and I said, "It's an excellent book. I like the documentary approach." He said he didn't like its treatment of Reconstruction. I said, "Well, why do you want to have a black history course? You know the whole purpose is to correct the distorted image that has been portrayed."

He's a little worried about the course. He wants to make sure the right things are taught. And what are the right things in many cases? For one, he says to me, "Our purpose is to make sure that the kids don't break out." Now, of course I'm not going to encourage kids to break out. I said, "My purpose is teaching the truth, not just calming things down. If your purpose is to calm things down, it'll have the opposite effect because the kids know when they're being conned."

For example, a member of my department said to me a couple of years ago when I taught a lesson on slavery, not in Afro-American history but in regular American history, that I portrayed slavery as too evil. He said this would make the kids resentful and make them hate whites.

I said, "This is the silliest thing I ever heard. First of all, it's a white teacher standing there, teaching the course. Second, many of them hate whites anyway. Third, the unit I teach on this deals with the whites in the abolitionist movement *cooperating* with the blacks," and so on.

That's the problem in New York. So many of the people who are saying we need black history now are not sincere. They could take it away any time. Social studies is supposed to teach kids how to think, how to analyze a problem, how to debate a problem and let them come to their own conclusions, instead of being an apology for the status quo. But in my department, out of about twenty social studies teachers, there are maybe three who teach like this.

Some of the others have been openly racist. I had an episode about four years ago. I walked into the department conference and they were having a good time, all in fun, you know, laughing at a vicious anti-Black joke that was written out on the blackboard. I came in and sat down. I waited for someone to say something because I wanted to see if anybody else would. But they were all having a good time. They didn't think it would offend anyone. When the man who was acting chairman at that time came in, he laughed too. He was going to start the conference.

"Wait a second," I said. "Are we going to have *that* on the blackboard?" And I launched into a tirade. "If that isn't erased I'm going to take a picture of it and send it in to the N.A.A.C.P. to show them what goes on in this department."

Nobody else protested. One man—you know, there are always people in the middle—said, "It's nothing to get excited about." I yelled at him. I never got so mad. At the next department conference I brought up an item: "Look, I want this department to behave as if a black person were a member of it. It's time we understood that we don't behave a certain way because all of us happen to be white." And that has made me a kind of an outcast in the department.

There are no black teachers?

There are no black teachers in the social studies department. There are no black teachers in any major department in my school. That's one of the problems in New York, where, on the high school level, most of the black teachers are in minor subject areas—music, home nursing, home economics—but not in the major departments like English and social studies. New York has the smallest number of black teachers in any urban area.

Some young black teachers are coming in now. From what I've seen, they have more of a feeling of wanting to do something for the black kids. Some have an ultranationalist approach. But it's a mixture. Some are purely opportunistic; they want to get ahead. But all of them were virtually united on one thing, and that was the UFT strike.

They opposed it up and down the line, ultranationalistic or ultraconservative. Most of them saw it as an attack against black people.

Would you say the black teachers coming in are as well equipped as the new white teachers?

Yes. But that's not saying they're exceedingly *well* equipped because many white teachers are not, either. You know, the people who entered during the depression, some of them had to pass the world's most stringent exams. But today we have instant exams. You know, walk in, and walk out with a license.

When you first started teaching did you say to black kids when they recited, "That's very good," even though you didn't think it was up to the standard?

Yeh. But I found myself doing it with most kids. You learn a certain technique. Every kid has pride in himself. A kid'll get up and recite in class or give an answer, and even if the answer is wrong you very often say, "Well, that's good, a good point, but I was thinking of something different." And you just write it on the board and the kids forget about it.

I found that many black kids who were verbally intelligent—the kids would articulate beautifully—if you gave them a verbal test, they would do very well. If you gave them a written test, they wouldn't do so well. They hadn't gotten skills in writing in elementary school, so I had to make allowances that way. But the kids really want to learn. They don't want to feel as if you're leaning over for them. They would resent this.

So many people feel that they have to teach one way to one group of kids and one way to another group. It doesn't work that way. If a teacher is presenting good relevant material, and he is really involved in it and he likes the kids, he's going to *get* the attention of kids, white or black.

I don't have all integrated classes because of the tracking system and the general diplomas. We have honors classes, too, and these are, by and large, all-white. But if I had a class of all white kids, I'd think it was very important to those kids to also understand what black people have done in our history. You see, if a teacher teaches broadly, he knows that the discovery of the New World encompassed many more things than just a few Europeans coming here. First of all, there were black people who came with Columbus. But more than that, along with the development of the New World comes the development of the slave trade with all its evils and difficulties. I'll take pains to show them that world history is not just European history, that Africa played a major role and that its civilization is relevant. Well, now, there are black kids in the class, they begin to feel themselves and the white kids as part of a whole. And when we study the Civil War, we discuss the role of slavery, the war itself, and black people and their role. I always did this in American history. Now there's a big rush to "get the Negro in." So what they do is they throw a few Negroes into the curriculum. They'll have a picture of Crispus Attucks. All right, that's important, but history isn't a catalog of "Event A" or "Event B." You have to recognize the interchange between peoples, between civilizations.

I teach the Constitution today. Now you can just get up there and talk about it, list things on the board. But what's meaningful about the Constitution in these kids' lives? The most meaningful thing is, Is it lived up to? Is the Fourth Amendment that protects them against search and seizure lived up to? Are civil liberties lived up to? It means saying to the kids, "Does a police officer have the right to knock on the door and demand to come in and search the house?" It's teaching kids about their constitutional rights. Where to get a lawyer if you're in trouble, what the courts are like. Most kids have an idea that a police officer has a right to ask them any questions he wants and they have to answer.

I ask a kid, for example, "What is the meaning of democracy? What does the word mean?" "Well, it means there's an American flag in the room," the kid says. "That's democracy." Thet have no conception of what the word means, or what civil rights are. You take the Fourteenth Amendment. You can do a marvelous study just on that alone. Very few people know that Congress is obligated to cut down the representation for states which deny people the right to vote. Well, I read that to them and we got involved. We talked about the importance of implementing provisions of the Constitution. Now, this stuff is really fascinating. History is rich, rich in its relevance to people's lives—to the kids' lives.

These are mostly seventeen-year-old kids. We had some discussion a few months ago when we studied, as a unit on the Constitution, "Does the President have the right to order draftees to go to fight in Vietnam?" Now, you can teach the Constitution as saying this is the power of the President: A . . . B . . . C . . . D . . . He's commander in chief, he's this, he's that. Or you can teach in terms of how does it affect these kids who are sitting in front of me. Is it relevant to them? Well, of course it is. The kid's going to be drafted. Does the President have the right to order him to go to Vietnam even though it's not a war that's declared by Congress? The kids were really ripping. They were really hot about this thing. The black kids are particularly interested because they want to know how it is that *they're* going out there to fight.

That's the topic of conversation these days among the kids. In my economics class we got into a side issue for a few minutes, on the student rebellions, and so on. One of the white kids says, "What do these students want? They can't take just everybody in college. They have to have a high average and so on."

So one of the black kids said, "Look! It's easy for you cats, because you come from good schools and we don't. You see, it's a matter of life and death. We don't go to college. We go to Vietnam." So it's as simple as that. This made the lesson, you see. There's wonderful things going on below the surface with the kids these days. Of course, some of the things get off on a tangent, and they're the ones that capture the headlines, but the kids are thinking. They're very articulate, very concerned with the world, and your teaching has to reflect this.

There's never really been a good evaluation of *how* kids learn, particularly in the ghetto situation; of how the curriculum meets their needs. That's a phrase I hate to use because it's used all the time—"meeting the needs of the students." They have these curriculum bulletins that come out month after month. And there are still teachers who put them aside and throw them away and in the end nothing changes. *"Plus ça change, plus c'est la même chose,"* you know? And the teachers go on and on doing the same thing year after year and the kids fall farther and farther behind.

You find people who go on teaching over and over again a rigid curriculum, same homework assignments, same lesson plans. It's not all their fault either, you know. Many are afraid to experiment. Their supervisor will want smoothness, no trouble.

I had hell to pay just to get some transparencies for an overhead projector for my Afro-American course. You know, you always see pictures of George Washington, Thomas Jefferson, but how do they know what Frederick Douglass looked like? I took the Langston Hughes–Milton Meltzer book, *Pictorial History of the Negro in America*, and cut it up. I wanted to make slides of this. We have all the equipment in school. I asked my chairman, "Give me about a dozen slides. Here are the pages." He ordered the book for me but he said, "You have to order the material for making the transparencies from the Board of Education. We won't get it till next September." So I said, "What the hell do I do till next September?" You *know* what I do? I've been passing around the loose pages so the kids can see them. But it would be wonderful if I could flash them up on the screen. You can *teach* that way. And not only that, I can direct the whole class's attention to it at once. So I have to wait till next September.

It's rigid, it's rigid. There's a bureaucracy that's involved here. Administratively, the superintendent and principal don't want to change it. And the teacher doesn't want to either, because it's too much trouble. They don't want to buck the administration.

If the kids were really learning, you could get away with a rigid curriculum. Black people don't want to throw the curriculum out. They want their kids to learn how to read. They want their kids to learn foreign languages. If it takes French to get into college, they want to learn French.

But the problem with rigidity is, it's not only in the curriculum, it's in the whole approach. Here's a story:

About three, four years ago I was sharing a room with a teacher. He was an old-timer. He'd be in retirement a year or two and he'd been doing the same thing year after year after year. I came into his class as he was picking his stuff up and I saw the homework assignment that he had on the board. He'd given it to a monitor to copy and he hadn't even looked at it.

I said, "Joe, this is your homework assignment?"

He looks at the board and says, "Oh, I made a mistake. Gee, I haven't changed my lesson plan."

The homework assignment was: "Give the arguments for and against the admission of Alaska and Hawaii to the Union."

Now, that was a standard social studies lesson until 1959, when Hawaii became a state, a year after Alaska, but he's still using the same yellowed lesson plans five years later. And the monitor copies it on the blackboard and the kids copy it into their notebooks . . . "for and against the admission of Alaska and Hawaii to the Union."

The administration doesn't even bother to check on what the teacher is doing. My chairman wouldn't know if I didn't give a test all term. I'm on maximum.* I'm an old-timer. So he comes in once a year and he says that things are "good-good" but the window wasn't opened wide enough or some such nonsense.

They work with new teachers a little more, but there's no formal check on all of the things that a teacher does. The chairman doesn't ask, "How many tests do you give?" or "Hey, how about not giving a test for a while?" I tried something a couple of months ago, a "take-home" test. I didn't even ask my chairman because he's liable to say no. I give them the questions ahead of time, give them a week to look up the material and to bring back a really well-written response. I'll give them six questions to look up at home and then I'll test them on three of them. They don't know which three it's going to be, but if they did a good job on those six they don't have to worry about passing the test.

Some people'll say, "What the hell good is that? They're taking it home and looking it up." But what's the purpose of a test except to review and know things. I don't want to spring anything on them, catch them on anything.

One of the problems, because you feel a certain way about kids, you realize very early in the game that your job doesn't end in the classroom. You have to fight. You have to join with others to try to change things. So you begin to find that you're split in forty different directions in order to make the system better. Last night, for example, I spoke at a meeting at Brandeis High School. They're trying to organize a group of people who are opposed to the present drift of policy [in the United Federation of Teachers]. Particularly the split between those who should be allies—

* Highest salary level for his category.

the black community and the union of teachers. What more natural allies could there be to fight against the board, the bureaucracy, instead of the teachers being allied *with* the bureaucracy?

We're running an opposition slate in the union now. We have hopes. That's part of the whole thing too—your empathy, your full commitment. And the kids know it. They don't know about my outside activities. I never tell them. But they know I'm committed.

Becker's reticence is a matter of classroom propriety; actually his role as a UFT activist has been common and public knowledge about which he has no qualms. He succeeded Zaphrirah Bauman to, and subsequently retired from, the chairmanship of the Teachers Action Committee. He has run twice for the UFT presidency on the TAC slate against Albert Shanker, not winning office but using the elections to warn his fellow teachers that the fence between the school grounds and the inner-city street is no longer real.

PHILIP STERLING grew up in Cleveland, Ohio, and worked there as a reporter for the *Cleveland Press* before moving on to newspapers in Nebraska and New York. For many years he was on the Press Information staff of CBS Radio and Television. He is co-author of several biographies of significant black Americans and of Puerto Rican national leaders; editor of an anthology of Negro humor, and author of a biography of Rachel Carson. He shares working space with his wife, who is also a writer, at home in Greenwich, Connecticut.

VINTAGE WORKS OF SCIENCE
AND PSYCHOLOGY

VINTAGE FICTION, POETRY, AND PLAYS

VINTAGE CRITICISM,
LITERATURE, MUSIC, AND ART

VINTAGE POLITICAL SCIENCE
AND SOCIAL CRITICISM

VINTAGE HISTORY—AMERICAN

VINTAGE BIOGRAPHY AND AUTOBIOGRAPHY